BASEBALL
AND THE
AMERICAN DREAM

BASEBALL
AND THE
AMERICAN DREAM

Race, Class, Gender
and the National Pastime

Edited by
ROBERT ELIAS

M.E. Sharpe
Armonk, New York
London, England

Library of Congress Cataloging-in-Publication Data

Baseball and the American dream : race, class, gender, and the national pastime / Robert
Elias, editor.
   p. cm.
  Includes bibliographical references and index.
  ISBN 0-7656-0763-8 (alk. paper)
   1. Baseball—Social aspects—United States. I. Elias, Robert, 1950–

GV867.64.B37 2001   00-066140
306.4′83—dc21   CIP

Printed in the United States of America

The paper used in this publication meets the minimum requirements of
American National Standard for Information Sciences
Permanence of Paper for Printed Library Materials,
ANSI Z 39.48-1984.

BM (c)   10   9   8   7   6   5   4   3   2   1

To my children: Madeleine, Jack, and André.
May the national pastime give you as much pleasure as it's given me,
and may all your dreams be fulfilled.

TABLE OF CONTENTS

PREFACE

Love America and hate baseball? Hate America and love baseball?
Neither is possible, except in the abstract.

—John Krich

To develop this book, I've taken a strange road. For more than two decades, I've been teaching and doing research about the underbelly of America: on war, crime, racism, sexism, poverty, violence, repression, victimization, imperialism, corporate tyranny, and government corruption, and on related and similarly "uplifting" themes. I've given America a hard time, and in some ways it has returned the favor. For the uninitiated, in contrast to these weighty themes, taking on the subject of baseball might seem a bit frivolous, or at least irrelevant. So how did I happen to focus on the national pastime?

It turns out that I have a history with baseball about which I was not, until recently, fully aware. In his book, *Baseball and the Cold War*, Howard Senzel describes the experience of first embracing and then abandoning baseball:

> In the process of forming my . . . moral attitudes, baseball got closed out [and was] . . . taken over by another drama—politics. Racism, Imperialism, Anticapitalism, Revolution, Drugs, and Rock and Roll Music replaced baseball as the arena where I could define myself as an insider. . . . Without sentiment . . . I turned my back on baseball. Invigorated by that great American energy of progress and self-development, I was moving on to more important things. Baseball was dying inside of me, but . . . I saw it only as an awakening out of childhood and into the wonderful world of serious things.

I had an intense baseball childhood but, as Senzel describes, I left it behind for more "serious things." Indeed, sports—including baseball—seemed, after a certain point, not merely irrelevant, but positively counterproductive. In retrospect, despite my "puppy love" for the sport, I guess I eventually viewed baseball as an "opiate for the masses" that would only obscure people's true condition in American society.

Under those circumstances, then, why would I allow baseball back into my life? Senzel describes the rediscovery of baseball and how the game, rather than being frivolous, has a serious and personal meaning:

> [T]here is a part of me that has been in turmoil . . . and which still asks me, "Why baseball? Why not Greek tragedies and symphonies? [or] economics, history and philosophy? And if it must be so esoteric, why not something closer to a master plot?" . . . And now, finally, I can answer that question, because baseball is now a part of me that I can see. [A]nd it runs deeper than other culture. Not traditional philosophy and . . . history, because in my identity . . . [b]aseball is so deeply rooted that it is not subject to will. Baseball is the strongest, least vulnerable, and most confident piece of myself that I am in touch with: . . . the metaphor of baseball . . .

And so, as I went about trying to put into perspective years of frustration about the American system, I stumbled back into baseball—or it stumbled back into me. This probably began a bit more than a decade ago when I joined a Baseball for Peace tour of Sandinista Nicaragua. In the face of interventionist and counter-revolutionary Reagan administration policies, we spent a few weeks in Nicaragua—under difficult conditions—playing baseball, repairing war-torn baseball fields, donating baseball and construction equipment, and generally trying to use baseball to build goodwill between the American and Nicaraguan peoples. For this eye-opening insight into baseball's impressive influence, I'm indebted to Baseball for Peace director, Jay Feldman. But it was not until far more recently that baseball's ramifications finally hit home for me.

After years in the sobering process of "tearing down" what seemed to me the injustices of American society, I became more interested in how to "build up" the best in our culture. In particular, I wanted to understand what good there was, if any, in the American dream. Aside from all the pomp and circumstance, what really was that dream, how did it begin, what does it mean today, and how could it be constituted more positively for the future? When I groped around for a productive tool for completing this task, suddenly there again was baseball. I began to sense what some baseball scholars have long known: the national pastime is not merely a diversion, but rather a long-standing reflection of the strengths and weaknesses of American life. But in line with Senzel's insights, baseball presented itself to me, I suspect, for far more personal reasons: it was a hidden part of my identity (as I now sheepishly admit to some of my friends) and could now serve as my refuge from the ravages of America's strife and conflicts. Baseball has returned as a metaphor for me. It serves not as a hiding place (however tempting it might be to have one), but rather as a buffer against the continuing problems in the American system.

But more than that, rather than being an "opiate," I now see that baseball need not obscure social conditions but instead can serve as a revealing mirror of American life—a reflection we can use constructively rather than destructively. Baseball offers a common denominator that cuts across conflicting political ideologies. Baseball provides and also illustrates some of the best that America has to offer. It also features some of the more disturbing characteristics of U.S. society. Baseball is an enigma, but in the end, despite the contradictions, it serves far more as an inspiration than anything else.

The French philosopher Albert Camus once wrote, "The true patriot is one who gives his highest loyalty not to his country as it is, but rather to what it can and ought to be." That's the perspective I now apply to baseball and also to our broader society and the American dream. When America and the national pastime fail to live up to their ideals, having a critical perspective seems like the only truly patriotic response. As James Baldwin once suggested, "Precisely at the point when you begin to develop a conscience, you must find yourself in conflict with your society. It is your responsibility to change society if you think of yourself as an educated person." And so, we should pose (and this book specifically asks) some critical questions: What should baseball and America be? When and why do they fall short? What can be done?

The essays that follow provide no definitive answers to these questions. Readers can draw their own conclusions. The authors in this collection offer a variety of perspectives on baseball and the American dream, from rousing endorsements to sharp critiques, and many views that fall somewhere in between. More important than drawing any fast and fixed conclusions is the need to stimulate new interest in baseball's importance to our society, however one assesses the sport or the state of American culture at the moment.

The contributions to this book began with the Davies Seminar and Forum that I conducted in the Fall of 1998 at the University of San Francisco. The Davies Program sponsors courses and public presentations on the theme of "exploring American values." The Davies Committee selected my proposal, "The National Pastime and the American Dream: Baseball as Cultural Mirror." Students were selected to be Davies Scholars for the course, and a series of distinguished academics and other experts were invited to be Davies Fellows. Most of the essays included in this book are their papers and public lectures.

These essays are organized as follows: In the Prologue, Laura Ward solves a mystery that returns us to some of baseball's earliest days and most basic values. In the Introduction, I provide an overview of baseball's relationship to the American dream. Thereafter, the book contains three sections, each of which reflects a major barometer of the American promise; they examine, in turn, issues of race, class, and gender.

The first section, "Dreams of Diversity," examines the experiences of African Americans, Latino Americans, Asian Americans, and Italian Americans in baseball. The section begins with writer Roger Kahn's memories of Jackie Robinson's ordeal in breaking the color barrier, followed by sociologist Peter Dreier's essay on Robinson's contemporary relevance. San Francisco Giants manager Dusty Baker describes his professional experience in the post-Robinson era.

Historian Samuel Regalado uses the Horatio Alger myth to examine the role of Latinos and Latin Americans in baseball. Hall of Famer Orlando Cepeda adds a personal note when he describes the challenges he faced as a Puerto Rican in American baseball. The poet Andrei Codrescu follows this with his tale about New York Yankees pitcher Orlando Hernandez's flight from Cuba to the American "Shangri-La."

The early baseball experiences of Asian Americans and other ethnics during the first half of the twentieth century are described by historian Joel Franks, and filmmaker Kerry Yo Nakagawa traces the history of Japanese American baseball and the quest to recognize its contributions. John Pinelli shares his memories of growing up as the grandson of the prominent ballplayer and umpire, Babe Pinelli, whose life epitomized the Italian American experience. "Dreams of Diversity" ends with sociologist William Edwards examining the "common [baseball] dream" across races and ethnicities.

Part II, "Material Dreams," examines the role of class and economics in baseball, beginning with historian Paul Zingg's description of Hall of Famer Harry Hooper's rise from poverty to stardom with the Boston Red Sox. Using the case of Shoeless Joe Jackson to illustrate her point, literary critic Suzanne Griffith Prestien shows how myths and nostalgia may contribute to misleading impressions of the American dream. The state of baseball in the mid-twentieth century is discussed by historian Jules Tygiel, using the "shot heard 'round the world" as his point of departure. Sports physiologist George McGlynn takes a critical look at his own experience in baseball's minor leagues in the 1950s.

The novels *Man on Spikes*, *Shoeless Joe*, and *The Tortilla Curtain* are used by attorney Randy Torrijos to examine America's often conflicting material values both inside and outside baseball. How independent minor leagues provide an alternative to the majors and a "field of dreams" for their workers is discussed by mathematician Thomas Stillman, who also describes his experiences as official scorer in the Western League. Sports sociologist Jeremy Howell follows this with an assessment of baseball's contemporary economics, and Hall of Fame sportswriter Leonard Koppett concludes the section by examining the changing American baseball dream.

"Gendered Dreams," the book's final section, considers the role of women in baseball, beginning with an essay novelist Darryl Brock and I wrote on women's involvement in the early days of baseball. Sociologist Gai Ingham Berlage provides a broader history of women's hidden participation in baseball, particularly as ballplayers. And the myths and realities portrayed in *A League of Their Own*, a film about the professional women's baseball teams of the 1940s and 1950s, are examined by former All-American Girls Professional Baseball League player Lois Youngen. Sociologist Anne Roschelle takes a critical look at gender relations in contemporary baseball, describing women's continuing problems on the sidelines. Journalist Joan Ryan concludes the section and the book with her memories of being a baseball fan as a young girl, and the baseball relationship she had with her father.

Many have contributed, directly and indirectly, to the completion of this book. I want to thank them all, and—contrary to tradition—also blame them for any shortcomings the reader might discover herein. In particular, I'm grateful to my students, the Davies Scholars, and especially to Laura Ward, who also served admirably as my research assistant. I appreciate the support provided by the late Louise Davies and by Gerardo Marin and the Davies Forum Committee, and the additional financial assistance granted by Alan Ziajka and the Creating Community Committee, and by Robert Waters and the Multicultural Action Program, all at the University of San Francisco.

Of course, I'm very appreciative of the presentations and the essays provided by the many contributors to this book—the Davies Fellows. They have taught me a great deal, and I feel honored to have hosted them. Among the academics involved, I've been especially inspired by the scholarship of Paul Zingg and Jules Tygiel. I'm also particularly gratified to have had Dusty Baker, Orlando Cepeda, and the late Bill Rigney participate in the project.

Several people helped me immeasurably in the day-to-day logistics of running the Davies Forum that led to this book: My thanks to Marie Baillargeon, Marlon Villa, Dave Pangaro, Mike Armstrong, and especially to Sharon Li, the Davies administrative assistant who put up with my endless requests. Thanks to George Parker for his help with the book's illustrations. I appreciate the support given by Rosalynn Tonai, Gary Otake, and the National Japanese American Historical Society in San Francisco. And I want to thank M.E. Sharpe editors Peter Coveney and Peter Labella, for believing in my project, and also editorial assistant, Esther Clark, and project editor, Susan Rescigno, for their assistance.

Various faculty colleagues of mine at the University of San Francisco gave me valuable encouragement and moral support during the Forum and the writing of this book: My appreciation goes to Pamela Balls-Organista, Michael Lehmann, Brian Weiner, Thomas Stillman, Michael Stanfield, Elliot Neaman, Ange-Marie Hancock, Michael Robertson, and Alan Heineman, in particular.

Finally, I'd most like to thank my immediate family: my children, André, Madeleine, and Jack for indulging my endless baseball references, and my wife and colleague, Jennifer Turpin, for tolerating what she describes (with obvious exaggeration) as the nonstop, "sensurround [baseball] sound" that has characterized our household over the past couple of years.

Douglas Tilden's *Ball Thrower*, Golden Gate Park, San Francisco (photo by Laura Ward).

PROLOGUE
The Missing *Ball Thrower*

Laura Ward

THE *BALL THROWER* WAS CREATED BY SCULPTOR DOUGLAS TILDEN AS A SYMBOL OF national pride. The sculpture (see opposite page), which depicts an old-time ballplayer apparently winding up to pitch, was originally named *The National Game*. Tilden submitted it in 1889 to an International Exposition held in Paris that commemorated the centenary of the French Revolution. Thinking he would fare better by submitting his *Ball Thrower* to the American, rather than the French, section of the Exposition, Tilden was astonished when the Americans rejected his entry. Undeterred, he then submitted the *Ball Thrower* to the even more challenging and prestigious Salon des Artistes Français. Membership in the Salon would be the highest honor, opening the doors to fame, publicity, and public commissions. Ironically, he was accepted by the French, and by recognizing the unique *Ball Thrower*, the French judges initiated Tilden's public career in the United States. He went on to become one of California's leading artists.

At a time when most sculpture depicted rugged Western pioneers or political and military heroes, Tilden instead chose to focus on American sports. He sought "inspiration for the development of a national patriotic art with a 'truly American Spirit.'" According to biographer, Mildred Albronda, Tilden's "creative impulses" reflected "the material American culture, especially of the far Western region of the United States. Tilden felt that he had reached 'a point of contact' with the American people because he was 'attuned to the passionate liking of youth for athletics.'" The *Ball Thrower* was intended as an enduring monument to the importance of sports, and particularly baseball, in American culture.

On July 8, 1891, the *Ball Thrower* was unveiled in San Francisco's Golden Gate Park. It had been purchased and donated to the park by William E. Brown, a local railroad magnate. According to the *San Francisco Bulletin*, the sculpture was "so prized by the art connoisseurs that replicas have been ordered by Tiffany's of New York." The *Ball Thrower* was dedicated only two decades after Golden Gate Park was established in 1870. The park began as a thousand acres of sand dunes and brush west of Divisadero Street, and by the time the sculpture was erected it had been transformed into a real people's park, filled with monuments to civic virtues.

The *Ball Thrower*'s dedication paid homage to an exciting time—it was the childhood of America's passion for baseball. The 1880s and 1890s were an age of amateur baseball mania; there was a team in every town. Likewise, professional baseball had surged out of Cincinnati in 1869, and was transported all the way out West to California via the transcontinental railroad. The major leagues had existed since 1871, and by 1891—when the *Ball Thrower* was dedicated—the National League had just beaten back the challenge of the Player's League to establish itself for good as the "senior circuit."

Baseball has come a long way since then, and one hundred years later, at the height of the 1998 baseball season and the climax of that year's exciting home run race, I decided to pay a visit to the old *Ball Thrower*. I hoped my pilgrimage would help me better understand baseball's current role in American society. Part of the media hype that surrounded Mark McGwire's and Sammy Sosa's home-run race was the claim that "Baseball is back!" But I was skeptical. By studying the *Ball Thrower* I might answer a few of my questions about this claim: From where did baseball return? Was there really something better about baseball this season? What did baseball being "back" mean to Americans (other than another opportunity to buy a home-run race video or a commemorative hat)?

According to my Golden Gate Park map, the *Ball Thrower*, monument 35, was located somewhere between monuments 34 and 36, the Chinese Pavilion and General Halleck's statue, respectively. The *Ball Thrower* looks across the Main Drive toward the Conservatory of Flowers and the President Garfield monument. Further along the drive are the museums, polo grounds, horse stables, and even a few captive buffalo. I wondered about the *Ball Thrower*'s position on my map. How was it that baseball fit between Harry W. Halleck, Abraham Lincoln's Civil War Chief of Staff, and James Garfield, the assassinated American president? They say that Lincoln played the game in his coattails. But Garfield had no apparent connection to the sport, even though his successor, Chester A. Arthur, received both the Cleveland Forest Citys and the New York Gothams at the White House, and had been inspired enough to announce, "Good ballplayers make good citizens."

I followed my park map and found General Henry Halleck staring over the drive at his monumental compatriot President Garfield—but I could not find the *Ball Thrower*. All that remained was the pedestal where the *Ball Thrower* once stood. As the late summer tourists took portraits by the conservatory, and then strolled casually under Main Drive to listen to vagrant musicians, I wondered what thought, if any, drifted through their minds when they finally encountered the vacant pedestal?

Park visitors most likely greeted the absence of the *Ball Thrower*'s antiquated symbolism with little distress. But his absence raised new questions for me: Perhaps the missing *Ball Thrower* was a reminder of a time when proud Americans could identify with each other through the common language of a sport that was unique around the world? Maybe the monument represented not only Tilden's ideals, but also the American dream? Did its absence symbolize the loss of that dream, its values, and that era? Why was the baseball player gone while Halleck, the war hero, and Garfield, the slain president, survived? Baseball has often been associated in the past with individualism, justice, integrity, democracy, and hard work; could the *Ball Thrower* have meant that much to Tilden as a representation of American values?

A century ago, the situation was much different. As a sport, baseball had much less competition than it has today. And playing baseball was widely linked with athleticism, manliness, and youthful vigor. These days, we usually do not view baseball as the most athletic of sports, even if it embodies some of the sporting world's most difficult skills. The newspapers of the time suggested that the *Ball Thrower* bore a close resemblance to Tilden himself. It should not be surprising that Tilden would want to create a baseball figure, an icon of Americanism, with which he could also be identified.

I decided to climb atop the pedestal in the warm breeze where the statue once towered, and began to get a feeling for our new national pride—one that the old *Ball Thrower* could never represent. If this baseball statue were erected today, instead of a century ago, what symbol of American values would it depict? In light of the memorable 1998 baseball season, the monument might look like Mark McGwire, but the *Ball Thrower*, his unmarked uniform lying rigidly against his bronze chest, was too anonymous. He never would have appeared on the side of a Wheaties box. He provides no opportunities for consumer accessorizing. Indeed, far from the *Ball Thrower*'s generic pose, all of our new symbols of national pride have a consumer identity. The *Ball Thrower* cannot compete with the Levi's logo, the Nike swoosh, and corporate rock music. Abroad, the American is the Marlboro Man, not the *Ball Thrower*. A brand name and a corporate image now represent American values.

I stepped off of the pedestal and watched as park patrons strolled by in their New Balance sneakers, listening to their portable Sony disk players. They did not even glance toward the missing statue, and I realized that the ways American values are identified and communicated have changed since the 1890s. Our expressions of national self-esteem no longer generate public sculpture. Instead, we get commercials. Advertisers determine our values just like they determine our fashions, our cars, and our music—and they even tell us where we can buy them. Few unifying experiences in American life since World War II have not been created by television and mass marketing, and so it may be that a relic like the *Ball Thrower* no longer represents American pride. In the 1890s everyone could relate to baseball players, but by the 1990s Americans seemed to care more about the relationship between personal image and brand names. Americans no longer find their symbols in metal monoliths but rather only in corporate icons.

Whatever explained the statue's absence, for me it nevertheless was a metaphor for a change in America and in what baseball means for Americans. Baseball no longer seems to represent a unifying set of values or a common experience, and thus it vanished from the Golden Gate Park as a symbol of national self-esteem. Like the *Ball Thrower*, baseball still appears on our national map, but its role as an American symbol has quietly eroded, and been replaced by new consumer identities.

In the spring of 1999, I returned to Golden Gate Park and so had the *Ball Thrower*. The statue had been cleaned and the marble base had been replaced. Yet another set of questions arose: Did this signify that baseball was back after all? Did it mean that baseball had "cleaned up its act" and could now resume its prominence in American life? Did the sport merely need a new foundation upon which it could build a new future?

My search for the missing monument made me realize that baseball cannot mean to modern Americans exactly what it meant in the late 1800s. Nevertheless, I was glad the *Ball Thrower* had returned. The graceful competitor had been updated for the 1990s, and bears no new corporate logo as the price of being restored to his original condition. The statue's inscription remains the same: "Dedicated by a friend of the sculptor as a tribute to his energy, industry and ability." At the very least, the *Ball Thrower*'s return suggests that baseball is here to stay. As our national sport and pastime, baseball may still represent the best of American culture.

INTRODUCTION

American Dreams

Author's Irish-American grandfather, Edward Foran, in a Bronx, New York, sandlot, circa 1920 (photographer unknown).

A FIT FOR A FRACTURED SOCIETY

Baseball and the American Promise

Robert Elias

> *The country is as American as baseball.*
> —Reggie Jackson

> *For those who can see the field of dreams, they should not retreat to their paradise, making it an idol, but forsake paradise and live among the people, sharing the good news.*
> —Kevin Brooks

> *America is a very materialistic culture where everyone works very hard to accumulate as much as he can and to notice who has accumulated how much, lest he himself fall behind. And in the strife of this endless backbreaking accumulation, there is a little haven called baseball.*
> —Howard Senzel

HISTORIAN PETER BJARKMAN HAS WRITTEN THAT BASEBALL "IS A GAME WHICH SURELY does not mean half of the things we take it to mean. [But] [t]hen again, it probably means so much more." So true. And for that reason, we can proclaim, unflinchingly, that baseball reflects some of the nation's noblest aspirations. There's perhaps no better way to see them than to examine baseball's relationship to our quintessential national quest: the pursuit of the American dream.

As John Thorn has argued, "The national pastime became the great repository of national ideals, the symbol of all that was good in American life: fair play (sportsmanship); the rule of law (objective arbitration of disputes); equal opportunity (each side has its innings); the brotherhood of man (bleacher harmony); and more."[1] Indeed, there is much "more": to both the American dream and to baseball's role in it. But what is that dream?

A Dream of Greatness

For all our historical preoccupation with the American dream, rarely have we examined very closely its true meaning and implications. A sizeable literature invokes the concept of the American dream but few studies critically assess it. Most of the writing blindly celebrates the dream while rarely exploring its values. With few exceptions, even critical assessments focus almost entirely on concerns about America not living up to the dream rather than on whether it should be pursued in the first place.

We rarely consider the uniqueness, if not strangeness, of even having a concept of the American dream. Could we imagine, for example, other successful societies (since surely we use the term "dream" to imply success) having such a phenomenon, much less being obsessed (as we are) with it? Is there such a thing as the Swiss dream or the Dutch dream or the Japanese dream? Besides "the American way," is there also the Swedish way or the Australian way? And when citizens of other countries violate national norms, are they engaging in un-French or un-German activities, as they would be engaging in un-American activities if they did so in the United States? Not likely.

And why does our national obsession manifest itself as a dream? Why not focus instead on the American "condition," as a reflection of the reality of our society? Or is avoiding reality the whole idea? Is the American dream a daydream, designed to divert us? A dream, of course, can be real and also good—that's the American dream we're all asked to believe. But a dream can also be unreal—"it was only a dream." And a dream can represent something other than what it seems: in some cases it might provide us useful insights, but in others it can disguise our deepest and darkest secrets. Even worse, a dream can be a nightmare, revealing horrors for those for whom the dream is an illusion, and even for some of those who have apparently achieved the dream but then wonder about the price.

Given these different possibilities, isn't it odd how automatically we associate the American dream with all that is good and pure? Surely it's a testimony to how deeply ingrained we are with the concept, and to how supremely confident we are in the American way. The American dream, therefore, represents only our highest aspirations and achievements. And why not? After all, isn't America number one? Perhaps. But if so, then maybe we owe it to ourselves to probe more deeply what the best of America actually represents. We might find that the values that embody what's "best" are more obscured than illuminated by the American dream. But let's begin with what the dream is supposed to be.

What are the values and objectives of the American dream, and to what extent are they fulfilled? First, we should recognize how the American dream has evolved over time. While many of the fundamentals have remained the same, the American dream of the nineteenth century differed from that of the twenti-eth century, and some changes occur even from one generation to another. Second, the American dream might not mean exactly the same thing to all people, even though it's often represented as our universal, common bond. The American dream for the white middle class, for example, might differ from the dream held by African Americans from any class. Thus, we should avoid overgeneralizations. Even so, enough of the American dream remains common over time, and across race, class, gender, and other differences.

What are the common ingredients? The American dream views the United States as the land of opportunity where sufficient dedication and hard work guarantees individual mobility and success, for natives and newcomers alike. Our land is a "melting pot" where people of all races readily commingle, and live and work together as a united citizenry. The dream promises wealth and riches for all who energetically seek them, regardless of one's class, gender, religion, and ethnicity. The path to success relies on vigorous competition in the free-market system where political freedoms protect individual choice, initiative, and participation, and ensure fairness, justice, and equality.

The Horatio Alger work ethic relies not merely on sweat but also on ingenuity. Those who effectively apply themselves can make their fortunes; everyone else will at least be middle class. The individual pursuit of material gains will enrich not only individuals but also the broader society. And beyond individualism, the dream offers God, family, and the nation. The American dream makes the country special: it nourishes the American people, it seduces foreigners to our shores, and it spreads the American way far beyond our own borders.

A Dream Deferred?

Support for the American dream has been widespread.[2] But some of the praise is revealing. One advocate, for example, claimed, "This American system of ours . . . call it Americanism, call it capitalism, call it what you like, gives to each and every one of us a great opportunity if we only seize it with both hands and make the most of it." Unfortunately, those are the words of the famous American gangster, Al Capone. What does that tell us?

But assuming we endorse the driving values of the American dream, to what extent has the dream actually been fulfilled? While rags-to-riches tales abound, the reality of the American dream presents a far more sobering picture. Whether measured historically or by contemporary standards, critiques of the American system have proliferated. Concerns have been raised about the increasing gap between the rich and the poor, and the persistence of our class society. The middle classes—always exaggerated in size—have been shrinking, with most people losing ground in wealth and income. Unemployment persists, and most new employment tends to be low-wage, dead-end, if not seasonal, jobs. Hard work often leads to meager gains. More people are in debt—often for products they don't need—than ever before, lured by easy credit and seductive advertising. Real economic opportunity seems more and more restricted to the few. Hunger, malnutrition, and homelessness affect tens of millions of Americans. Quality health care and education are not widely available to most people. Working class families struggle to survive. More and more children grow up with the ravages of poverty.[3]

Racial and gender discrimination, and other inequalities, persist, and inter-group conflicts abound. Immigrants now more typically encounter America as a nightmare rather than as a dream. Industry and agribusiness, in the pursuit of profits, progress, and unrestrained growth, have ravaged our land and fouled our living environment. Crime and violence threaten our daily lives, and state re-pression—masked as "law and order"—steadily escalates. Democracy seems re-served for the few not the many. Having real choices has become an illusion in both the political and economic arenas. Political freedom, meaningful participa-tion, and procedural fairness have deteriorated, and justice is only a faint hope for many people.[4]

Arguably, for these and other reasons, the United States has not actually ful-filled the promise of the American dream. And if some people have realized some of the goals of that dream, then it nevertheless sometimes seems like it's more in spite of the American system than because of it. If we look closely then, and transcend the mythology of the American dream, we can see it not as an inevitable reality but rather as a dialectic of U.S. society: the dream and its contradiction (see Torrijos in this volume).

Reconsidering the American Dream

But we must analyze the American dream in more than material terms. Even if the United States faithfully serves as a genuine land of opportunity, some won-der nevertheless about the values it asks us to live by. Even for those who have apparently "succeeded," there's a nagging sense of the "poverty" in the affluence they attain. The symptoms are many: Cutthroat competition undermines hu-man cooperation. The free market cripples civil society. No tactic in the quest to "get ahead" seems too vile or violent. Business ethics become increasingly an oxymoron. Winning at all costs creates a society of losers and also-rans. Keeping afloat in our hypercompetitive society gets harder and harder, as stress, burnout, and the quest for success increasingly take their toll on rich and poor alike.[5]

Materialism and commercialism put a price tag on everything, as people and human relationships become commodities. Culture and intellectual develop-ment increasingly give way to profits and aggression. Our jobs have less and less meaning and satisfaction, as mere toil increasingly replaces any sense of craft. Technology, rather than promoting liberation, makes us work harder and longer. Our increasingly throwaway society pollutes our atmosphere, as we mindlessly manipulate and dominate our natural habitat.[6]

Likewise, excessive individualism sacrifices genuine community, promoting lost identity and a spiritual malaise. Exaggerated private lives undercut public spaces and morals. Obsessive liberty cancels norms of personal responsibility. Lip-service democracy gives way to persistent American elitism and hierarchy. Rigid religious doctrines sacrifice true human spirituality. Free-market mantras serve more as an opiate than liberation. The American "culture" of art, film, and music is increasingly corrupted, often reduced to selling the American dream for corporate sponsors. Ceaseless mobility tears apart our families, our relationships, and our communities. Our lives are progressively more alienated and lonely, starved for meaning and human connections. Men still subordinate women, and male hierarchies continue to reign. Unrestrained capitalism impedes real democracy and economic well-being, yet we keep imposing it both at home, and—through our interventionist policies—abroad as well.[7]

Perhaps these views paint too stark a picture of the American condition. Maybe more progress has been made than we've acknowledged. Even so, the doubts and shortcomings are real enough for concern. We're warranted in cross-examining the American dream. Surely all these objections cannot be easily dispelled. And they leave us with an America in question. They should make us wonder not merely whether the material promises of the American dream have gone largely unfulfilled, but also whether we should be pursuing that materialism to begin with. Do we instead need a "new American dream?"[8]

Baseball as Cultural Mirror

To more specifically examine the performance of the American dream, both in theory and practice, we could choose from many mirrors of U.S. society. Certainly a variety of institutions might be viewed as revealing reflections of how we're doing, and of where we've been, where we're headed, and where we should—perhaps—be going instead. We might examine, for example, American education or American work or American families. Or, we might look, more generally, at American culture and its indicators of the state of American society.

Our mirror here, however, will be American sports, themselves arguably important ingredients in the broader U.S. culture.[9] James Robertson has described their significance:

> The games of modern Americans are rituals, . . . significant dramas which [they] believe are an important part of the realities of their lives. . . . They

matter. . . . In the beginning . . . [t]he ideas . . . celebrated by the rituals were clear to all: the existence in . . . every place in America, of democratic, classless equality in communities . . . of hard-working, independent individuals.

The rituals *really* created communities. . . . The belief that they [still] do so continues to be an available American myth. . . . The games and their teams . . . provide opportunities for communication among townspeople . . . [and they] have ritualized several of the essential qualities of industrial life and . . . generated terminology ("teamwork") and an imagery which dominate American perceptions of that life. . . . The teams . . . and . . . the logic of the rituals of [their] games . . . have long been . . . major elements in the integration of society.[10]

Charles Springwood takes this even further since for him sports provide the "symbolic expression of the values and beliefs of the broader society, thus strengthening the structure of the economic, political and cultural hegemony of dominant groups."[11]

But one particular American sport arguably surpasses all others in reflecting U.S. society: the national pastime—baseball. Roger Angell has suggested, "Baseball seems to have been invented solely for the purpose of explaining all other things in life." Well, perhaps not everything. But uniquely among U.S. sports, observers have long associated baseball with the essential features of the American national character. Baseball provides a revealing metaphor for American society and values.

Roger Kahn has cautioned us about overdoing the metaphor. He's argued, "No existential proclamation, or any tortured neo-Freudianism, or any outburst of popular sociology, not even—or least of all—my own, explains baseball's lock on the American heart. You learn to let some mysteries alone, and when you do, you find they sing themselves."[12] And Jules Tygiel and Harold Seymour have rightly warned us against the false nostalgia of assuming that baseball's appeal in America stems from its inherent attributes.[13] Instead, those who developed the game in the post–Civil War era grafted onto baseball the values of modern, urban America, which the game has merely perpetuated ever since. According to John Thorn, "Baseball had become more than the mere reflection of our rising industrial and political power and its propensity for bluster and hokum: the national game was beginning to supply emblems for democracy, industry, and community that would change America and the world."

Even with these caveats about baseball's appeal, the game has nevertheless long contained values that comprise the basic ingredients of Americanism and the American dream. About baseball, for example, Walt Whitman said, "Well—it's our game; that's the chief fact in connection with it: America's game. It has the snap, go, and fling of the new American atmosphere; it belongs as much to our institutions, fits into them as significantly as our Constitution's laws; is just as important in the sum total of our historic life." More recently, former Yale University president and former major league baseball commissioner, Bart Giamatti, claimed that baseball "is the last pure place where Americans can dream. This is the last great arena . . . where everybody can learn the lessons of life."[14]

Similarly, Roger Kahn has called baseball "the game of unbroken dreams, where we can watch our hopes renew themselves each spring, and dissolve (or prove) themselves each fall, to be followed by an identical cycle the next year . . . the cyclical pattern . . . never ends, the dream never breaks, across decades, lifetimes and generations."[15] And George Grella has described it this way:

> [B]aseball, not football, will always be our National Pastime, the Great American Game. Occupying a unique place in our national heritage, this most American of sports speaks as few other human activities can to our country's sense of itself. . . . The game is as instructive, as beautiful, and as profound as the most significant aspects of American culture. It should be compared not only with other sports, but with our other indigenous arts—our painting, music, dance and literature. . . . In its theory and practice baseball embodies some of the central preoccupations of that cultural fantasy we like to think of as the American Dream.[16]

But if baseball has been associated with the American dream, then what, more precisely, is the relationship? Does baseball merely illustrate the American dream, and provide us lessons for how to achieve it? Is baseball itself a route to the American dream, held out for all but satisfied by only the select few who have the requisite skills and determination? Or does baseball reflect various, if not serious, problems with the American dream, either in its accessibility or desirability? Does baseball serve as an opiate to distract us from the realities of the American dream? Does the game, instead, challenge the American dream and its driving values? Or does baseball perhaps serve as a refuge from the endless strife and accumulation the American dream perpetuates?

Maybe baseball is no single one of these things. Certainly the game has represented different experiences for different groups and individuals at different times and places. Baseball has a long established tradition that extends back nearly to the earliest years of the American republic. During that history, it has uniquely mirrored the trends in the culture at large. For many observers, baseball has—over the years—represented both the successes and failures of the American way. Arguably, Americans should care about baseball because it has been, and remains, a barometer for the health of American society.

A Field of Dreams?

More specifically, with what ingredients of the American dream has baseball been associated? How has the game reflected the best in American culture? To begin with, baseball has been credited with promoting democracy and good government, and has been connected to political institutions from the White House to the Supreme Court. Francis Trevelyan Miller claimed, "Baseball is democracy in action: in it all men are 'free and equal,' regardless of race, nationality or creed. Every man is given the rightful opportunity to rise to the top on his own merits. . . . It is the fullest expression of freedom of speech, freedom of press, and freedom of assembly in our national life."[17] Baseball has been linked to the development of both community and individualism. While baseball helped us, after the Civil War, to solidify ourselves into a nation[18] (see also Brock and Elias in this volume), "an accompanying industrial upheaval," according to David Voigt,

> destroyed the people's sense of community as a fixed place, and moved Americans to embrace collective symbols like the Flag, the Constitution, the Declaration of Independence, along with popular heroes to substitute a feeling of national community identity. . . . Having abandoned royal and aristocratic heroes, Americans took to glorifying the self-made man of the Industrial Revolution. The new pattern deified the myth of the ordinary man rising to the top, an image that reflected a deeply felt hope that the American people really do rule.[19]

Baseball has been viewed as a fertile ground for that "self-made man." The game helps develop skills for individual success, especially the work ethic and other values for the business world. Business leaders have praised baseball as a model of competition. In the early twentieth century, *American Magazine* editorialized, "Baseball has given our public a fine lesson in commercial morals. . . . Some day all business will be organized and conducted by baseball standards."[20] More recently, baseball has been called one of "the last outposts in our high capitalist society of individual meritocracy," and when ballplayers cash in on their talents, it's considered a part of "the American way."[21]

In his study of baseball in the Progressive era, Stephen Riess claims, "The national pastime was portrayed in such a way that it supplied some of the symbols, myths and legends society needed to bind its members together." Richard Crepeau has written that baseball "most typified American institutions and teachings in the 1920s and 1930s," including the values of democracy, opportunity, and fair play. As David Voigt has suggested, "Players found baseball to be a promising road to individual recognition. Perhaps as much as any institution, American baseball kept alive Horatio Alger's myth that a hungry, rural-raised,

poor boy could win middle-class respectability through persistence, courage and
hard work." And for those on the sidelines, baseball nevertheless served an important role in developing individual identities. The fan's affiliation with his or
her team has often exceeded in vigor his or her attachment to church, trade,
political party—all but family and country, and even those have sometimes
emerged all wrapped up in baseball.[22]

Baseball, according to Voigt, has also been considered "a primary vehicle of
assimilation for immigrants into American society, and as a stepping stone for
groups such as Irish-Americans, German-Americans, and Italian-Americans—
each of which entered the professional ranks of the sport in waves between the
1870s and the 1930s. . . . The brilliant success stories of [various] . . . hyphenated
Americans kept the myth of the American melting pot alive in baseball."

Likewise, leaders of immigrant groups advised their peoples to learn the national game if they wanted to become Americans, and foreign language newspapers devoted space to educating their readers about the American game. Harold
Seymour has observed, "The argot of baseball supplied a common means of communication and strengthened the bond which the game helped to establish
among those sorely in need of it—the mass of urban dwellers and immigrants
living in the anonymity and impersonal vortex of large industrial cities. . . .
With the loss of the traditional ties known in rural society, baseball gave to
many the feeling of belonging."[23]

Baseball has helped acculturate players. Stanton Green, for example, observes
that, "In the chronicle of immigrants to this country, baseball has been very
much a mirror of the rise and assimilation of ethnic groups, from early Irish to
the most recent arrivals, the Japanese. The transition from Jackie Robinson to
Hideo Nomo is a fairly interesting reminder of this country's immigration pattern. Now Latin American and Asian ball players are the new immigrants."[24]
(See also Codrescu in this volume.) But the game has also helped assimilate the
fans. One of our well-known immigrants, Romanian émigré Andrei Codrescu, has
written, "With citizenship and a baseball signed by all my friends . . . I started to
understand large tracts of American writing that had been closed to me. . . . The
whole late fifties, the early sixties art movements that established America as the
leader in painting—abstract expressionism, pop art and the rest, were all secretly and not so secretly cornball attempts at a vision of America in a state of
baseball."[25]

Baseball has been used to demonstrate the racial and ethnic mobility that
occurs in an egalitarian, opportunity society, both for immigrants and natives
alike. Buster Olney has observed:

> More than a half-century after Jackie Robinson broke baseball's color barrier,
> America celebrates his legacy, which is reflected in today's game. [Sammy]

Sosa and pitcher Pedro Martinez are from the Dominican Republic, shortstop Omar Vizquel from Venezuela. Colorado's Larry Walker is Canadian. [Derek] Jeter's father is African-American and his mother is Irish. The Dodgers' Chan Ho Park is from Korea, Hideo Nomo is Japanese. [Mark] McGwire and . . . Tony Gwynn are both Californians. The lines, once hard and impenetrable, are all blurred. . . . When Orlando Hernandez, the defector from Cuba, signed with the Yankees, catcher Joe Girardi noted the variety of the New York pitching staff: Kansas City Irishman David Cone, Andy Pettitte of French descent, the Panamanian-born Ramiro Mendoza, Hideki Irabu of Japan. And David Wells, Girardi mused, he's from Jupiter.[26]

In addition, baseball has been viewed as scientific and well-constructed—a reflection of American ingenuity and a symbol of American progress and modernity. As Michael Novak has put it, "Baseball . . . is a cerebral game, designed as geometrically as the city of Washington itself, born out of the Enlightenment and the philosophies so beloved of Jefferson, Madison and Hamilton. It is to games what the *Federalist Papers*, are to books: orderly, reasoned, judiciously balanced, incorporating a larger plan of rationality."[27]

Baseball has been used to demonstrate the benefits of play, team spirit, and sportsmanship. Playing the game has been regarded as a preventative against things such as crime, violence, delinquency, and even the stresses of modern life. Baseball, it is said, promotes positive values such as honesty, fair play, wholesomeness, and other aspects of the American way. It has been associated with healthfulness, and especially with manliness. Baseball has been widely represented in our language and literature. It exudes beauty and grace, and carries an aesthetic appeal for many observers, who have described baseball as "poetry in motion," "a work of art," and "a form of music." The game has been linked to patriotism and nationalism, and has been thought to promote American prestige both at home and abroad. Baseball has often been associated with the armed services, and with enhancing America's mission around the world. For these and other reasons, baseball has been what Harold Seymour has called a "badge of Americanism."

Dreaming of Heroes

Among those who have worn that "badge" most prominently have been the heroes of baseball. The sport has been unique not only in generating memorable heroes within baseball itself but also genuine American heroes that have far transcended the game. Those heroes have been caught up in the values and mythology of the American dream, and also illustrate some the dream's subtle changes over the years. One of baseball's earliest heroes, for example, was Christy Mathewson, a baseball superstar, a confidant of U.S. presidents, and one of the most famous Americans of the early twentieth century. The transition from Mathewson to Babe Ruth, as the new hero of the 1920s, suggests a transformation in the American character if not in the American dream. Baseball changed from the skillful, scientific "inside game" to the brawny, long-ball "power game." Baseball "smarts" gave way to baseball "instincts." And in their personal lives, puritanical heroes gave way to the risqué heroes of the roaring twenties.

As George Grella has suggested:

> No legend in or out of baseball compares with the real life and exploits of Babe Ruth. . . . His deeds and life are an American epic. . . . More than any individual, Ruth saved baseball and America's faith in itself by introducing a new heroic age in our national game. . . . With the properly obscure origins of the mythic hero, Ruth came out of a background of poverty and trouble with the law, was introduced to baseball at . . . reform school, and rose to be . . . an immortal legend while still an active ballplayer.

According to Richard Ben Cramer, "Ruth found a match between his enormous appetites and the national agenda. America had made the world safe for democracy. We were rich. We were strong. In the '20s we were ready to play, with truly American force. While the market soared, we knew God loved America, and sent us the Babe to prove it."[28]

But if Babe Ruth got people excited about being an American in his era, then our next major hero, Joe DiMaggio, did more to remind us of America's past glories. As Cramer has put it, "He [DiMaggio] was, at every turn, our idea of the American hero—one man we could look at, who made us feel good. For it was always about how we *felt* . . . with Joe. That's how it worked. No wonder we strove, for six decades—the nation, its presidents, its citizens, almost everyone—to give Joe the hero's life. It was always about us. And, of course, that he knew."[29] Few of us think of DiMaggio as merely a (great) baseball player; he represented something far more important for America.

The list of heroes continues, right up through the present day. Vilified at first for challenging American apartheid, Jackie Robinson nevertheless succeeded, and became another American hero, far beyond baseball's boundaries. Robinson was a pioneer in the civil rights movement and he symbolizes an important component of the American dream: the quest for racial equality—even if we remain today far short of achieving that objective (see Dreier, Kahn, and Edwards in this volume). More recently, it was not the home-run race of 1998 but rather a different kind of heroics that began to resuscitate baseball and its role as an American ideal: Another hero, Cal Ripken, broke Lou Gehrig's record for consecutive games played. We admired him in 1997 for continuing his streak, and admired him again in 1998 when he voluntarily ended it for "the good of the team." Ripken, like Gehrig before him, tapped into another powerful ingredient of the American dream: the work ethic. Remarkably, these men became famous in America because they worked hard; they had admirable work habits, they never complained, and never missed a day.[30]

And, of course, in 1998 Mark McGwire and Sammy Sosa also became household names in America, even among many people who cared little about baseball until their heroics. Among other things, McGwire and Sosa played into formidable American values of individualism and power. Fans, both new and old, even began rooting against their home teams if it meant a chance for McGwire or Sosa to challenge or break the home-run record. While this seemed to sacrifice local community in favor of individual pursuits, the home-run race nevertheless promoted a broader sense of national community, with some interesting consequences. For example, while it did not last forever, in the early going several fans returned valuable home run balls, shunning the money in favor of history and community.

As Richard Ben Cramer has suggested, people were in awe of the power Sosa and McGwire generated with each mighty shot. Arguably, the home run reflects the American psyche. Its rise in importance in baseball, via Babe Ruth, paralleled America's rise—for better or worse—as a world power after World War I. We've been addicted to that power ever since. Likewise, we've been uniquely motivated, as a people, to conquer space. We long for new frontiers: the wild West, foreign nations, the seas, outer space, cyberspace. Mastering frontiers has long been our quest, and a chance to prove ourselves. The conquerors count among our heroes. But while frontiers keep disappearing, there's always the ballpark, where we're impressed by nothing moreso than watching a home run instantly vanquish the field's vast green space. Couple this with McGwire's repeated references to the American dream, and with Sosa's calls for a new Dominican American dream (which also conveniently implies U.S. racial harmony and our immigrant-friendly shores), and one is left with profound (if not misleading) messages about American greatness.

Second Thoughts on the Baseball Dream

Of course, baseball's long association with the American dream might also have a downside. It might mask some uncomfortable realities about both the national pastime and the American promise. And yet the contradictions make the relationship all that much more intriguing. For example, even as strong a baseball advocate as Harold Seymour has written:

> What began as a children's game was gradually taken over by adults who
> regimented it and endowed it with their own ideology, derived from the ben-

efits they thought . . . [the] sport possessed for health and character and even patriotism. . . . [B]aseball may be seen as a huge but unplanned campaign to impose . . . values that would make the growth of capitalism easier by using an opiate to distract citizens from imperfect working, learning and living conditions. This perception provides an antidote to the . . . view of baseball as . . . expressing some deep, natural affinity between the game and the values of this country's people.[31]

More specifically, questions have been raised, for example, about continuing race problems in baseball. According to David Voigt:

In both baseball and the broader society, ideals and realities have routinely clashed along economic class lines, but the gap has been even more evident along racial and ethnic lines. The opportunities for some groups have been few rather than many, and for some races, virtually all access has been choked off for long periods . . . certainly, for African-Americans and Native Americans, and often . . . for Asian-Americans and Latino-Americans. . . . As some of the barriers to . . . the American dream have fallen in more contemporary times, we nevertheless often find, both inside and outside baseball, that progress . . . still [falls] well short of our American ideals.[32]

While the stories of African American, Asian American and Latino American baseball players are often inspiring (see Baker and Cepeda in this volume), their paths to success often seem more in spite of the American dream than because of it (see Regalado and Nakagawa in this volume)—not the least of which are the continuing barriers to racial equality.[33]

Some also worry about the lingering obstacles to women's participation in baseball. The writer Susan Berkson has written, "Ken Burns [in his *Baseball* book and documentary] calls baseball a metaphor for democracy. But he's wrong. Instead, it is a metaphor for sexism. The great theme is that it's a boys game; women have been shut out again and again."[34] Although women have been much more involved in the sport throughout our history than we commonly understand (see Berlage and Youngen in this volume), this discrimination against women remains largely true (see Roschelle in this volume).

While the prejudices remain, some signs of hope might be on the horizon. A Northern League player, Ila Borders, has been quite successful as a woman pitcher in the men's minor leagues. Former major league baseball commissioner, Fay Vincent, has said, "If women were able to play competently, the big leagues will hire them to play. I think the day will come when there are no barriers against women playing with men. . . . It has to start at the lowest levels."[35]

But thus far, while some women have been passionate baseball fans and sometime players, the game has rarely been their profession. Claims that women cannot compete or that they lack baseball skills mask the deeper realities of discrimination: the biases that block girls from getting the same kind of training and experience that's widely available for boys, and the prejudices that continue to impede those few women who excel in the sport despite the disadvantages of their youth. And the barriers extend to baseball roles other than playing the sport. Former umpire Pam Postema, who was driven out of baseball not very many years ago, summed it up colorfully in the title of her book: *You've Got to Have Balls to Make It in This League.* Thus, we still have to wonder whether baseball can be a part of the American dream for women.[36]

Even short of race, gender, or other barriers, there are other, formidable deterrents to playing professional baseball (see McGlynn in this volume). Some players who make it to the majors—even some superstars—eventually wonder about baseball's relationship to the American dream. At the peak of his illustrious career, for example, the Brooklyn Dodger great, Duke Snider, claimed the dream was killing him:

> It's like anything else. From the outside it looks great, and when you're a kid dreaming, it looks like a helluva dream. Then you grow up, you're in the major leagues and all of a sudden baseball isn't so great—and sometimes it can be a nightmare. . . . When I was a boy . . . I used to dream about playing in a World Series. . . . Last autumn when I played in my fourth World Series, . . . the dream had changed. While we were beating the Yankees, I was dreaming about being a farmer . . . [and] the day when baseball will allow me to settle down to raising avocados in the California sunshine.[37]

Despite pulling down one of baseball's highest salaries, Snider questioned the supposed glories of even the most successful ballplayers. He lamented baseball's link with the American dream, claiming, "When you seek the dream you expect it will make you better or different, but you end up being the same person and that's disappointing." While we might fault them for being ungrateful for their now impressive salaries, some more contemporary major leaguers apparently feel some of the dream's same emptiness that Snider experienced in the 1950s. Or alternatively, they realized their major league dreams too early to "cash in," and now—in their declining years—remain shut out from baseball's riches.

In addition, economic inequalities often prevail in baseball on several different levels, between minor leaguers and major leaguers, between players and owners, between big market owners and small market owners, and so forth. As John Thorn has suggested:

The lie of baseball is that it's a level playing field. That there's equality. That all the inequalities in American life check their hat at the door. That they don't go into the stadium. That once you're there, there's a sort of bleacher democracy, that the banker can sit in the bleachers and converse with the working man next to him. This is a falsehood. You have class and race issues that mirror the struggle of American life, playing themselves out on the ballfields.

The economic problems generated in baseball by the American dream might go even further. Gai Berlage worries about the corporate values that are routinely ingrained into children by competitive sports such as baseball.[38] Others warn us about the increasing control of the game by media corporations whose interests have nothing to do with baseball's welfare (see Howell in this volume). In addition, Peter Carino, in his review of *Ballpark: Camden Yards and the Building of an American Dream*, tells us that the book's author, Peter Richmond,

> demonstrates his awareness of what a grand ballpark can mean to a city and the game. At the same time, [the book] does not shrink from the more unsavory elements marking the culture this dream represents: the machinations of power brokers, the sweetheart subsidies granted by politicians to the private sector, and the class structures that belie the nation's claim to democracy.[39]

According to Tom Goldstein, baseball is being run "by network executives, marketing consultants, and PR 'wizards.'" Thus, the "long-term *quality* of the game no longer matters; it's merely the short-term *perception* of how baseball is doing that's important." Goldstein argues, "Baseball is America's newly found 'cheap' natural resource. Our communities have become strip mines, and the fans are the precious commodity to be plundered."[40]

The labor-management conflict in baseball in the early 1990s also took a significant toll. As Leonard Koppett has suggested, baseball's

> inviolable connection to the past would be broken, and the separation of baseball business from business on the field would no longer be possible in [anyone's] consciousness. . . . [E]specially [for] those not involved in the business . . . the cancellation of the 1994 World Series was a breaking point. Popularity and prosperity returned quickly once play was resumed, but the nature of the baseball experience was altered forever. . . . Personalities and games became inextricably linked with dollars, [which] became a factor in understanding outcomes and one's reaction to the . . . games played.[41]

Likewise, Stephen Lehman has lamented the alarming and growing economic disparities in major league baseball. He resents the perpetuation, if not promotion, of those gaps by appeals to the American dream. Such appeals can be found, for example, in former Los Angeles Dodgers' manager Davey Johnson's recent reaction to concerns that rich teams (like his) are cornering the best baseball talent with high-priced contracts. "Parity is not the American way," according to Johnson. "The American way is to dominate somebody else."

While domination might, indeed, be the American way, Lehman nevertheless suggests these contradictions:

> Parity isn't the issue. . . . The Bill of Rights, the Civil War, women's suffrage, the various civil rights movements of this century—none were about parity. When Lincoln invoked at Gettysburg 'the proposition that all men are created equal,' he wasn't talking about parity. Lincoln knew full well . . . that some people are born smarter, healthier, more resilient, better able to strike a three-inch leather sphere traveling ninety-five miles-per-hour with a three-foot wooden club than other people. . . . What Lincoln and Jefferson and Adams and Martin Luther King, Jr. were talking about is equal opportunity, equal protection under the law: that is, the level playing field.
>
> [Davey] Johnson could point to the U.S. government's genocidal domination of North America's native peoples, to any number of [U.S.] imperialist military excursions . . . during the past two hundred years, and to the monopolistic economic steamroller of American mega-corporations . . . to bolster his view of the American Way. But none of those behaviors are inherently American . . . [or] the logical extension of this country's great experiment in popular democracy. They're more like the natural tendencies of monarchies or fascist states than democratic ones (and . . . more like football than baseball).[42]

Presumably, then, we have more than one American dream. If so, which one do we want to live by? Many observers have now compared baseball and football in America,[43] but is Lehman's implication correct: that we can and must choose between a football American dream and a baseball American dream?

Lehman believes we're losing the baseball dream; owners have extorted cities and taxpayers for new ballparks, thus diverting scarce public resources, and yet their ability to field competitive teams remains just as unlikely as before. As Lehman argues, "In at least half the major league cities in America and Canada, there will be no hope and . . . no faith . . . [but rather] only the certainty of being dominated by the wealthy and powerful. And that is not a model for healthy competition. It is not the American (or Canadian) Way."

The Lure of Nostalgia

As we search for the genuine "American way," it's tempting to invoke the past. If only we could return to the "good old days," our problems would be solved (see Ryan in this volume). Baseball helps us connect to our glorious past. As one of our oldest and most unchanging institutions, it oozes nostalgia. Baseball—and increasingly, baseball literature (see Prestien in this volume)—take us back to a simpler time when things seemed less fleeting and confusing. As songwriter Paul Simon asked, "Where have you gone, Joe DiMaggio? A nation turns its lonely eyes to you." And, as George Grella has argued:

> Along with its happy connections with . . . the divine in America, baseball provides us . . . a . . . reminder of our rapidly disappearing past. . . . [B]aseball recollects an earlier and calmer time, forming an organic and unbroken continuum back to those days when men played the game on the Elysian Fields. . . . [B]aseball responds to . . . the deepest yearnings of the American soul. . . . Suggesting a pastoral vision of peace and harmony, it feeds both our memories and our dreams, our sense of the past and our awareness of the future.

But, as John Thorn reminds us, "If America survives anywhere as more than a memory, it is in baseball, that strangely pastoral game in no matter what setting. . . . As hindsight improves upon foresight, memory improves upon reality."

In our alienated culture, we long for community. We rally around things that can unite us and make us feel good about ourselves and our society. The danger, however, comes when nostalgia is used to sanitize the past and divert us from present realities. Is baseball once again the "national pastime," or is it merely the "national past tense," nostalgically describing an idealized, bygone era that perhaps never really occurred?[44]

As Ron Briley observed a few years ago, "In [Mickey] Mantle's final days, many of his admirers . . . , dominated by white males, recalled lost youth and yearned for [the good old days:] an America free from crime, decaying morals, culture wars, economic insecurity, and social conflict." But this was "mere wishful thinking for Americans uncomfortable with changing perceptions of race, gender and class." It was a longing for "the way we never were."[45]

Has nostalgia been unfairly attacked? Harvey Kaye worries that critics "fail to distinguish between nostalgia as memories . . . and a sincere missing of or longing for times past, and the commercial and corporate exploitation of nostalgia." He wonders whether "the recollections people have, the sense of loss and the desire for the restoration of a past time's pastime express their legitimate feelings . . . that something is missing." Alternatively, Stanley Cohen claims the game's immersion in nostalgia occurs because baseball is the only sport "that understands time and treats it with respect." "The history of other sports," says Cohen, "seems to begin anew with each generation, but baseball . . . gets passed on like an inheritance."[46]

Is baseball nostalgia simply natural or has it been generated to serve some social function? Each year, thousands of Americans make a pilgrimage to Cooperstown, New York (site of the Baseball Hall of Fame) and Dyersville, Iowa (site of the *Field of Dreams* filming). In his study of those sites, Charles Springwood found that a nostalgia for a lost America motivated far more visitors than a quest for baseball history. Springwood believes this kind of nostalgia has "help[ed] to stimulate a neo-conservative discourse . . . packaged in doctrines of urban-rural tension, family values, race, gender and nationalism."[47] Reflecting on this phenomenon, Bill Brown reminds us that the 1980s was an "era when remembering became . . . a newly commercialized endeavor (the boom in the business of collectibles, the boom of the video-cam industry). . . ." As our historical consciousness continues to deteriorate and as our memories atrophy, "the more the cultural industries thrive . . . [and the more that] baseball [becomes] newly visible as an object of longing." Springwood's "geography of baseball nostalgia," demonstrates the role baseball plays in helping "to legitimate a longing for the past . . . [and perhaps even a] nostalgia for longing itself—the longing to long, the feeling that feeling as such will enable us to feel some alternative to the numbness of the everyday."[48]

In the past, sports have been thought to eliminate waste, promote the work ethic, impose social order, stimulate democratic participation, and produce healthy bodies. But as Springwood demonstrates, "sport [now] serves instead as a mode for generating history." It helps produce what Michael Kammen has called "heritage by consumption," "whereby the memory business serves emotional, business and political interests."[49]

According to Springwood, "Visitors [to Cooperstown and Dyersville] experience . . . a kind of personal purification wherein they . . . make contact with the simple life, the work ethic, childhood, fatherhood, marriage, the importance of family and home, the meaning of the father-son bond." In other words, they connect with many of the potentially lost values of the American dream. As Bill Brown argues, while fan allegiance to contemporary baseball, as played on the field, waxes and wanes, "a flurry of baseball books, movies and television specials . . . compensate . . . by recalling the great game that baseball once was. . . . [By] the mediation of baseball—via radio, film, television, newspapers, magazines, baseball cards, cereal boxes, underwear ads— . . . the sport seems to preserve its mesmerizing power rather than being rendered obsolete by new pleasures or new technological regimes." In the case of Dyersville, the field lives on beyond the *Field of Dreams*, the film that created it. In a world where life has increasingly become a movie, the field is real to visitors to the extent that it remains true to the film.[50] And thereby, it keeps alive a part of the American dream.

But for whose interests? William Fischer has complained about the proliferation of baseball films and literature:

[I]t seemed as if the game of baseball . . . was now being sold as proof—or a barometer—of the conservative revolution . . . improperly used as a symbol of moral purity, as romantic bedrock in [the] . . . modern days of evil. . . . In the book [*The Natural*], Roy Hobbs strikes out . . . and is left in ignominious defeat, a human being swallowed by his own human faults and weaknesses. And yet [this] . . . was transformed [by the movie] into a "feel-good" story about a "can-do" America.[51]

According to Fischer, the Reagan administration of the 1980s pushed the themes of "Bringing America Back" and "Family Values," while watching the middle classes shrink and corporate values flourish: "While celebrating the romanticism of the Cowboy alone on the trail with his horse and the moonlight, a society emerged that is less human, and more alienating and artificial." To compensate for this decline, we were given baseball. As Fischer wonders:

> What could better reaffirm our long-held values than a game rooted in purity and romance? What better way to smooth the rough edges of a mechanistic society than a game which glorifies individual triumph in a team setting? What better way to expand our increasingly limited world vision than by loving a game which is a soulmate of the imagination?

The conservatives, Fischer claims, "use baseball as an icon of romantic, preindustrial purity, substituting the fantasy of rustic life for the reality of the suffering that actually existed. The same 'captains of industry' have . . . presented this pastoral metaphor . . . as an escape from the chaos into which their industrial society has evolved."

Baseball's Deep Resonance

But perhaps baseball can play a more positive social role. While the national pastime has sometimes been manipulated for social-control objectives—such as to sanitize the American dream—this may not be its inevitable function. Indeed, we've seen baseball serve other, countervailing, even progressive, purposes.

Observers such as David Voigt have suggested the limits of baseball's influence on American culture:

> Baseball reflects a society whose people are groping for a new social and cultural equilibrium. . . . Some demand that our society not only mouth platitudes such as equality and justice for all, but also practice them. While baseball as a social institution is more in the baggage train than in the vanguard of such causes, its study offers reflections of such vital movements.

Likewise, Robert Heilman has warned us against "falling into some schmaltzy *Field of Dreams* heartwarming hyperbole" about baseball. His examination of the small-town amateur baseball [that keeps the sport alive in America] was, according to Heilman, "better than any dream: It was a field of reality, with all the unexpected beauty and the grittiness of every day life."[52]

Heilman argues that baseball needs no justification: "Ennobling it with lofty claims of social benefit is really a disservice." Baseball can, however, serve as an "indicator species" for the society; its rise and fall is a measure of the community's overall health. "When baseball dies out in a community," according to Heilman, "it means there is no community there anymore, just a place with a name, some fixed boundaries and a rootless, fragmented population."

Similarly, Leonard Koppett has argued that we should not fool ourselves into believing that baseball will regain the glories of its nineteenth century roots and mid-twentieth century successes. While the game has not changed very much, "baseball, the business, will have to adapt to being only one entertainment among many," and "[t]he feelings, associations, mental constructs, and treasured lore we took for granted" will not necessarily survive. According to Koppett, "What really matters is what happens on the field when they play the games. All the rest . . . is . . . something that has no tangible existence but only the significance our minds attach to it."

We must take these reservations about baseball's role seriously. And yet baseball might have within it the possibility of being a more creative social force than we think, well beyond merely being the "games" or merely "reflections," "indicators," and "baggage trains" of contemporary society. The complexities of the twentieth century have left many people confused about their society and world. They often view life as chaotic, out of control, lacking in any meaningful shape. They long for an antidote to contemporary social trends.

According to some observers, the increasing role of sports in American society provides not merely a diversion but also a unifying force. As Leverett Smith has suggested: "In the late nineteenth century [sports] were considered either irrelevant if not immoral or as a manifestation of the dominant spirit of the nation. By the second half of the twentieth century they are being considered as a kind of repository for values thought to have been lost in the confusion of the modern world."[53] And if in the modern world baseball provided a semblance of community in large, increasingly alienated urban centers, then in the postmodern world perhaps the game can help us make sense of an emerging, fast-paced information age.

We should likewise consider baseball's continuing importance for many Americans on a profoundly personal level. For example, William Fischer reminds us, in W.P. Kinsella's words, how baseball is a "'metaphorical poultice' for those wounded by our contemporary society," and how the game "provides the medium for those enlightened enough to dream." Similarly, Harvey Kaye

has described how baseball was fundamental to developing his progressive political consciousness. [54]

Certainly we must take a critical approach to the national pastime. It's tempting to be overly sentimental, yet we should not underestimate the power of
baseball's appeal: We want baseball to be good, we want it to be pure, we want
to be able to keep loving it. For some of us, it's our refuge, our salvation. Some
people feel as intensely about baseball as they feel about their nation—they're
baseball patriots.

While we can debate whether baseball remains the "national pastime," the
sport nevertheless retains a strong hold on the society; it remains deeply engrained
in the American character. According to George Grella:

> The game reveals to us an unending drama, both comic and tragic, of thwarted
> hope and vain ambition, of glorious fulfillment and sublime achievement, of
> the necessary contests between cities, regions and generations; it combines
> this drama with a fabulous narrative of a thousand extraordinary tales. Learn-
> ing to accept both victory and defeat, the random hand of fate, the endless
> possibility of reparation and improvement, we are daily instructed in the con-
> duct of our lives. Like the greatest works of art, the game suggests to man his
> godlike potential: it reveals to him . . . the transcendent capabilities within his
> life, his spark of divinity. The game, expanding space and dissolving time,
> allows us to sense that old American yearning for pure, unbounded possibility,
> that marvel of infinity and eternity.

Similarly, Joseph Sobran claims, "Our deepest norms of order can still be seen in
operation on the diamond when they've been adulterated everywhere else. Baseball is our Utopia—not in assuring us of the victories we dream of, but in guar-
anteeing ideal conditions even in defeat."[55]

Baseball's resonance repeatedly manifests itself. Celebrated author, Don
DeLillo, has recently written a blockbuster novel, *Underworld*, in which he offers
a stunning, and at times overwhelming, document of the Cold War and American culture. Based on the premise that "global events may alter how we live,
even in the smallest ways," the novel weaves together interlaced stories to create
a fragile web of connected experience that encompasses the messy history of
America's last five decades. Through Korea, Cuba, and Vietnam, through oil
embargoes, student demonstrations, and the arms race, DeLillo writes a history
and black comedy of the psychic fallout from the nuclear terror foisted on us by
the superpowers. The novel climaxes in the near future, when capitalism, the
Internet, and a new, hushed but largely unexamined faith in the future have
replaced the Cold War's blend of dread and euphoria. With this book, DeLillo
invites us to ask: What is my place in American history? How have I shaped it
and how has it shaped me?[56]

What could possibly hold such a complex and profound plot and history together? Nothing, other than the "Shot Heard 'Round the World." *Underworld's* prologue is set during the final, legendary game of the 1951 playoffs between the New York Giants and the Brooklyn Dodgers (see Tygiel in this volume). The game's glorious and shocking outcome—the home run hit by the Giants' Bobby Thomson off the Dodgers' Ralph Branca—generates the narrative for the book's 800 pages. The "shot" shades into the simultaneous grim news that the Soviet Union has just tested an atomic bomb. And the scramble for the home run ball, and its mysterious passing from hand to hand in subsequent years, takes the reader deep into modern Cold War memory and into the soul of American culture—from Bronx tenements to grand ballrooms, from McCarthyism to B-52 bombing raids over Vietnam.

In baseball's evolution, we see key American issues being played out: politics and nationalism, labor-management conflicts, class and economic inequalities, religion and spirituality, expansion and foreign affairs, race, ethnic and gender relations, and much more. It reflects a host of age-old American tensions: between workers and owners, scandal and reform, urban and rural, the individual and the community, and so forth. In many ways, baseball is a kind of barometer for the society. It's no coincidence, as Frank Deford has suggested, that the last two words of the national anthem are "play ball." Thus, baseball holds tremendous possibilities; it still strongly reverberates in America. If it also has its shortcomings, then fixing them can enrich and even rescue American society. As former major leaguer Bill Lee once said, "Baseball is the belly-button of our society. Straighten out baseball, and you straighten out the rest of the world."

Constructively analyzing baseball can help us better understand the game and ourselves. The object is not to tear down but rather to unveil and then build up. For example, baseball has been racist, yet—through Jackie Robinson and Branch Rickey—it also led the way for greater integration not only of American sports but also American society. For the first time, an American sports institution—baseball—took the lead in reshaping U.S. culture.[57] Likewise, baseball has been sexist, yet it was by far the first sport to allow women to play professionally, and to allow girls to play in the little leagues.

Baseball has been classist, in the economic sense, and yet—through Curt Flood and Marvin Miller—it also pioneered the end to wage slavery not only in baseball but in all professional sports, and it might yet serve as a model for America's broader labor movement. Consider Flood's explanation for challenging the reserve clause:

> I guess you really have to understand who that person, who that Curt Flood was. I'm a child of the sixties. I'm a man of the sixties. During that . . . time

this country was coming apart at the seams. We were in Southeast Asia. . . . Good men were dying for America and for the Constitution. In the southern part of the United States we were marching for civil rights and Dr. King had been assassinated, and we lost the Kennedys. And to think that merely because I was a professional baseball player, I could ignore what was going on outside the walls of Busch Stadium [was] truly hypocrisy and now I found that all of those rights that these great Americans were dying for, I didn't have in my own profession.

This suggests a sport that's deeply intertwined with its times (see Koppett in this volume). Baseball has played a transformative role in the past; it can do so again in the future.[58]

Restoring Baseball's American Dream

How can we unleash the potential in baseball for progress while also harnessing its more manipulative or less constructive forces? For example, if Jackie Robinson opened baseball to people of color, and if Curt Flood returned some control of the game to the players, how and who can return the game, now, to the fans? Cal Ripken, Sammy Sosa, and Mark McGwire might have begun the process. Nevertheless, in our spectator culture, where most of us watch our games and our society passively on the sidelines, how can fans and citizens be brought more into the center of the action?[59] As Andre Mayer has argued:

We need to get Americans involved again, paying attention, understanding what's going on. They don't have to be on the field, but they should be in the park, not just watching on TV. I mean this literally, because baseball has more than metaphoric meaning to American life. It is the backbone of our national culture, of our common mental discipline. What René Descartes is to France, Abner Doubleday is to America. Baseball inculcates the habits of mind essential to our survival as a free people.[60]

Arguably, the present and future of our national pastime and of America are intertwined. America seems poorer without baseball on center stage. Can baseball regain its influence and importance in U.S. society? Why has baseball begun to recover? Is it because it has helped distract us from crises and tawdriness, away from presidential scandals, economic failures, and unfulfilled promises? Are we desperate for more wholesome personalities? Do McGwire and Sosa seem like decent people we can embrace as heroes in good conscience? For example, Joan Ryan has written about

the uncommon joy of watching a man rise so magnificently to the occasion. In a year [1998] when our most powerful men have been diminished by their

lack of courage and class, McGwire played his role as if scripted by Steven
Spielberg. . . . Watching McGwire made me suddenly understand why Clinton's
behavior has been more destructive than I've acknowledged. McGwire's dignity and humility lifted everyone around him. . . . The strength of McGwire's
character got people to deliver the best in themselves.[61]

Is baseball recovering because it's a redemptive force, helping us restore faith in
our society? The "good old days" might not have been better, but perhaps baseball can give us hope for renewal?

If baseball is coming back, and if it is to once again make a positive contribu-
tion to U.S. culture, then it must abandon its self-congratulations for what have
been isolated and individual (rather than systematic and institutional) accomplishments (the Sosa-McGwire home run race), however impressive. Also, as
Peter Gammons has suggested:

Unfortunately, most of the [recent] anniversary celebrations [of Jackie Robinson
breaking the color barrier] have dwelled on the past. Baseball can assume its
place as the sport of the American dream, but it will not happen by looking
back. If indeed baseball is on the brink of a renaissance, then what it needs is
creative vision.[62]

It's not clear whether "creative vision" will emerge from baseball's ruling
establishment. But a new direction for baseball can nevertheless also come from
baseball players and their union, and from baseball fans and their communities.
Baseball could provide initiatives to help reform not only the national pastime
but also American society. It could lead the way on worker's rights and in revi-
talizing the labor movement. It could promote genuine racial equality and improve race relations. It could push for serious enforcement of antitrust laws and
provide new models of public or cooperative ownership for teams and other
corporations. It could concern itself with its consumers—the fans—as humans
and not merely as commodities. It could promote new breakthroughs in women's
access to the game and to sports and American institutions. It could be a progressive influence in America to push back the greed and conservatism of the
1980s and 1990s. It might even be a force for curbing aggression and promoting conflict resolution in U.S. foreign policy—such as the "baseball for peace"
tours to Central America in the 1980s and the recent Cuba-Baltimore Orioles
exhibition series.[63]

At its best, perhaps baseball is better than American society. As Reggie Jackson once suggested: "The country is as American as baseball." Baseball has within
it the capacity to help make the American dream one that's more worth attaining, and to make it one that's far more accessible to far more people than the
conventional American dream. There are disturbing signs that America is a

culture in decline. The increasing attempts to impose the American way abroad seem correlated with an increasing tendency for Americans to question their society at home. Can baseball provide us some salvation? Perhaps society ought to be looking up to the best in baseball. As journalist Bill Vaughan once wrote, "What it adds up to is that it is not baseball's responsibility to fit itself into our frantic society. It is, rather, society's responsibility to make itself worthy of baseball. That's why I can never understand why anybody leaves the game early to beat the traffic. The purpose of baseball is to keep you from caring if you beat the traffic."[64]

How can the national pastime help fulfill the American promise? John Thorn has put it this way:

> Fundamentally, baseball is what America is not, but has longed or imagined itself to be. It is the missing piece of the puzzle, the part that makes us whole . . . a fit for a fractured society. While America is about breaking apart, baseball is about connecting. America, independent and separate, is a lonely nation in which culture, class, ideology and creed fail to unite us; but baseball is the tie that binds. . . . Yet more than anything else, baseball is about hope and renewal . . . gloriously pulsing with the mystery of the seasons and of life itself. This great game opens a portal onto our past, both real and imagined . . . it . . . holds up a mirror, showing us as we are. And sometimes baseball even serves as a beacon, revealing a path through the wilderness.[65]

For those of us pursuing a new and better American dream, it's a path we should all be gladly taking.

Notes

1. John Thorn, "Our Game," in *Total Baseball*, eds. John Thorn, Pete Palmer, Michael Gershman, and David Pietrusza (New York: Viking/Penguin, 1997), 6.

2. Robert J. Samuelson, *The Good Life and Its Discontents* (New York: Times Books, 1995); David Stephen Cohen, *America* (New Brunswick, NJ: Rutgers University Press, 1990); James Crimmins, *The American Promise* (San Francisco: KQED Books, 1995); Geoffrey Perrett, *A Dream of Greatness* (New York: Coward, McCann & Geoghegan, 1979); Esmond Wright, *The American Dream* (Cambridge, MA: Blackwell, 1996).

3. Nancy Folbre, *The New Field Guide to the U.S. Economy* (New York: New Press, 1995); Holly Sklar, Chuck Collins, and Betsy Leondar-Wright, *Shifting Fortunes* (Boston: United for A Fair Economy, 1999); Richard H. Ropers, *Persistent Poverty* (New York: Plenum Press, 1991); Studs Terkel, *The Great Divide* (New York: Pantheon Books, 1988); Donald L. Barlett and James B. Steele. *America: What Went Wrong?* (Kansas City, MO: Andrews and McMeel, 1992); David Beers, *Blue Sky Dream* (New York: Doubleday, 1996); Benjamin DeMott, *The Imperial Middle* (New York: William Morrow, 1990); Katherine S. Newman, *Declining Fortunes* (New York: Basic Books, 1993); Katherine S. Newman, *Falling from Grace* (New York: Free Press, 1988); John E. Schwarz and Thomas J. Volgy,

The Forgotten Americans (New York: W.W. Norton, 1992); Wallace D. Peterson, *Silent Depression* (New York: W.W. Norton, 1995); Mike Davis, *Prisoners of the American Dream* (New York: Verso, 1986); Ben Hamper, *Rivethead* (New York: Warner, 1991); Burke Hedges, *Who Stole the American Dream?* (Tampa, FL: INTI Press, 1992); John E. Schwarz, *Illusions of Opportunity* (New York: W.W. Norton, 1997); Holly Sklar, *Chaos or Community?* (Boston: South End Press, 1995); Jonathan Kozol, *Rachel and Her Children* (New York: Crown, 1988); Nancy K. Frank and Michael J. Lynch, *Crimes Against Health and Safety* (New York: Harrow & Heston, 1992); Jonathan Kozol, *Illiterate America* (Garden City, NY: Anchor Press, 1985); Jonathan Kozol, *Savage Inequalities* (New York: Crown, 1991); Lillian B. Rubin, *Families on the Fault Line* (New York: Harper Collins, 1994); James P. Comer, *Maggie's American Dream* (New York: New American Library, 1988); Jonathan Kozol, *Amazing Grace* (New York: Crown, 1995).

    4. Jennifer L. Hochschild, *Facing Up to the American Dream* (Princeton, NJ: Princeton University Press, 1995); Ruth Horowitz, *Honor and the American Dream* (New Brunswick, NJ: Rutgers University Press, 1986); Berman E. Johnson, *The Dream Deferred* (Dubuque, IA: Kendall/Hunt, 1996); Sut Jally and Justin Lewis, *Enlightened Racism* (Boulder, CO: Westview Press, 1992); Ted Ownby, *American Dreams in Mississippi* (Chapel Hill: University of North Carolina Press, 1999); Jay MacLeod, *Ain't No Makin' It* (Boulder, CO: Westview Press, 1987). Jerry Mander, *In the Absence of the Sacred* (San Francisco: Sierra Club Books, 1991); Douglas S. Massey and Nancy A. Denton, *American Apartheid* (Cambridge, MA: Harvard University Press, 1993); Ruth Sidel, *Women and Children Last* (New York: Penguin, 1986); Ruth Sidel, *On Her Own* (New York: Viking/Penguin, 1990); Elizabeth Szockyj and James G. Fox, *Corporate Victimization of Women* (Boston: Northeastern University Press, 1996); Phillip Anastos and Chris French, *Illegal* (New York: Rizzoli, 1991); Alejandro Grattan-Dominguez, *The Dark Side of the Dream* (Houston, TX: Arte Publico Press, 1995); Eugene Nelson, *Pablo Cruz and the American Dream* (Salt Lake City, UT: Peregrine Smith, 1975); Robert Suro, *Remembering the American Dream* (New York: Twentieth Century Fund Press, 1994); Robert Winter, *Land of Opportunity* (Monrovia, CA: River Rock Press, 1994); Andrew Rees, *The Pocket Green Book* (London: Zed Books, 1991); Roy Morrison, *Ecological Democracy* (Boston: South End Press, 1995); Dan Butterworth, *Waiting for Rain* (Chapel Hill, NC: Algonquin Books, 1992); Barbara H. Chasin, *Inequality and Violence in the United States* (Atlantic Highlands, NJ: Humanities Press, 1997); William M. Adler, *Land of Opportunity* (New York: Atlantic Monthly Press, 1995); Patrick Du Phuoc Long with Laura Richard, *The Dream Shattered* (Boston: Northeastern University Press, 1996); Steven F. Messner and Richard Rosenfeld, *Crime and the American Dream* (Belmont, CA: Wadsworth, 1994); Tony Bouza, *The Decline and Fall of the American Empire* (New York: Plenum Press, 1996); Jeffrey Reiman, *The Rich Get Richer and the Poor Get Prison* (Boston: Allyn & Bacon, 1998); Gregg Barak, ed., *Crimes by the Capitalist State* (Albany: State University of New York Press, 1991); Noam Chomsky, *The Common Good* (Monroe, ME: Odonian/Common Courage, 1998); Carol Nackenoff, *The Fictional Republic* (New York: Oxford University Press, 1994); Mona Harrington, *The Dream of Deliverance in American Politics* (New York: Alfred Knopf, 1986); Michael Lind, *Up from Conservatism* (New York: Simon & Schuster, 1996); Michael Parenti, *Democracy for the Few* (New York: St. Martin's Press, 1995); Andrew Bard Schmookler, *The Illusion of Choice* (Albany: State University of New York Press, 1993); Gerry Spence, *With Justice for None* (New York: Penguin, 1989); Gerry Spence, *From Freedom to Slavery* (New York: St. Martin's Press, 1995); Hunter S. Thompson, *Songs of the Doomed* (New York: Summit Books, 1990); Charles A. Reich, *Opposing the System* (New York: Crown, 1995); David Edwards, *Burning All Seasons* (Boston: South End Press, 1996).

5. Paul L. Wachtel, *The Poverty of Affluence* (Philadelphia: New Society, 1989); James Oliver Robertson, *American Myth, American Reality* (New York: Hill & Wang, 1980); Erich Fromm, *To Have or To Be?* (New York: Bantam Books, 1976); Michael Lerner, *Surplus Powerlessness* (Oakland, CA: Institute for Labor & Mental Health, 1986); Richard Weiss, *The American Myth of Success* (Urbana: University of Illinois Press, 1988); Blaine Taylor, *The Success Ethic and the Shattered American Dream* (Washington, DC: Acropolis Books, 1976); Michael Lee Cohen, *The Twenty-Something American Dream* (New York: Plume/Penguin Group, 1993); Studs Terkel, *American Dreams* (New York: Ballantine Books, 1980); Alfie Kohn, *No Contest* (Boston: Houghton Mifflin, 1986); Frances Fox Piven and Richard Cloward, *The Breakdown of the American Social Compact* (New York: New Press, 1997); Jerome H. Skolnick and Elliott Currie, *Crisis in American Institutions* (Boston: Little, Brown, 1982); Charles Derber, *Money, Murder and the American Dream* (Boston: Faber & Faber, 1992); Robert H. Frank and Philip J. Cook, *The Winner-Take-All Society* (New York: Penguin Books, 1995); Douglas LaBier, *Modern Madness* (Reading, MA: Addison-Wesley, 1986); Gerald Loren Fishkin, *American Dream, American Burnout* (New York: Loren, 1994).

6. Arlie Russell Hochschild, *The Managed Heart* (Berkeley: University of California Press, 1983); Nicholas Mills, ed., *Culture in an Age of Money* (Chicago: Ivan R. Dee, 1990); Richard Sennett, *The Corrosion of Character* (New York: Norton, 1998); Celeste MacLeod, *Horatio Alger, Farewell* (New York: Seaview Books, 1980); Juliet B. Schor, *The Overworked American* (New York: Basic Books, 1991); William Irwin Thompson, *The American Replacement of Nature* (New York: Doubleday, 1991); Ferenc Mate, *A Reasonable Life* (New York: Albatross, 1993).

7. Robert N. Bellah, Richard Madsen, William Sullivan, Ann Swidler, and Stephen Tipton, *Habits of the Heart* (New York: Harper & Row, 1985); Jeffrey Louis Decker, *Made in America* (Minneapolis: University of Minnesota Press, 1997); Christopher Lasch, *The Culture of Narcissism* (New York: W.W. Norton, 1979); Christopher Lasch, *The Minimal Self* (New York: W.W. Norton, 1984); Philip Slater, *A Dream Deferred* (Boston: Beacon Press, 1991); James David Hudnet-Beumler, *Looking for God in the Suburbs* (New Brunswick, NJ: Rutgers University Press, 1994); Jim Wallis, *The Soul of Politics* (New York: New Press, 1994); Wiley Lee Umphlett, *Mythmakers of the American Dream* (Lewisburg, PA: Bucknell University Press, 1983); Gerald Jones, *Honey, I'm Home!* (New York: Grove Press, 1992); Murray B. Levin, *Talk Radio and the American Dream* (Lexington, MA: D.C. Heath, 1987); Margaret M. Mayer, *The American Dream* (Santa Barbara: University of California Press, 1994); Richard M. Merelman, *Making Something of Ourselves* (Berkeley: University of California Press, 1984); Daniel J. Boorstin, *The Image* (Kingsport, TN: Kingsport Press, 1961); Philip Slater, *The Pursuit of Loneliness* (Boston: Beacon Press, 1970); Joan Hoff, *Law, Gender and Injustice* (New York: New York University Press, 1991); Russell Mokhiber and Robert Weissman, *Corporate Predators* (Monroe, ME: Common Courage Press, 1999); Douglas F. Dowd, *The Twisted Dream* (Cambridge, MA: Winthrop, 1977); Michael Hudson, ed., *Merchants of Misery* (Monroe, ME: Common Courage Press, 1996); Labor Institute, *Corporate Power and the American Dream* (New York: Author, 1996); Michael Moore, *Downsize This!* (New York: Random House, 1996); Greg Ruggiero and Stuart Sahulka, eds., *The New American Crisis* (New York: New Press, 1995); Kevin Danaher, *Corporations Are Gonna Get Your Mama* (Monroe, ME: Common Courage, 1996); William Greider, *One World, Ready or Not* (New York: Simon & Schuster, 1997); Benjamin R. Barber, *Jihad vs. McWorld* (New York: Ballantine, 1996); Tom Engelhardt, *The End of Victory Culture* (New York: Basic Books, 1995); Wayne Ellwood, "Inside the Disney Dream Machine," *The New Internationalist*, no. 308 (December 1998): 20–37; Paul Farhi and

Megan Rosenfeld, "Exporting America," *Washington Post,* National Weekly Edition (November 30, 1998), 6–7; George Ritzer, *The McDonaldization of Society* (Thousand Oaks, CA: Pine Forge Press, 1993).

8. Betsy Taylor, *Enough* (Tacoma Park, MD: Center for A New American Dream, 1998); Tom Hayden, *The American Future* (Boston: South End Press, 1981); Frances Moore Lappe, *Rediscovering America's Values* (New York: Ballantine Books, 1989); Alice M. Rivlin, *Reviving the American Dream* (Washington, DC: Brookings Institution, 1992); Ernest G. Bormann, *The Force of Fantasy* (Carbondale, IL: Southern Illinois University Press, 1985); Richard C. Cornuelle, *Reclaiming the American Dream* (New Brunswick, NJ: Transaction, 1993); Dolores Hayden, *Redesigning the American Dream* (New York: W.W. Norton, 1984).

9. Wiley Lee Umphlett, ed., *American Sport Culture* (Lewisburg, PA: Bucknell University Press, 1990); John Lucas, "Sport—Mirror and Molder of American Society," in *Sport and the Humanities*, ed. William J. Morgan (Knoxville, TN: Bureau of Educational Research and Service, 1979).

10. Robertson, "The Rituals of Community" in *American Myth, American Reality*, 250–257.

11. Charles Fruehling Springwood, *Cooperstown to Dyersville* (Boulder, CO: Westview Press, 1996).

12. Roger Kahn, "Still A Grand Old Game," in *The Complete Armchair Book of Baseball*, ed. John Thorn (New York: Galahad, 1997), 87.

13. Jules Tygiel, "The National Game," *Nine: A Journal of Baseball History and Social Policy* 7, no. 2 (Spring 1999): 2–13; Harold Seymour, "Baseball: Badge of Americanism," in *Cooperstown Symposium on Baseball and the American Culture*, ed. Alvin L. Hall (Westport, CT: Meckler, 1990), 1–22.

14. Bart Giamatti, *Take Time for Paradise* (New York: Summit, 1989).

15. Kahn's views as described in William J. Fischer, "The Conservative Curveball," *Minneapolis Review of Baseball* 9, no. 4 (1990): 34–36.

16. George Grella, "Baseball and the American Dream," *Massachusetts Review* 16 (Summer 1975), 550–567.

17. Frances Trevelyan Miller, "Introduction," in Connie Mack, *My 66 Years in Baseball* (New York: Winston, 1950).

18. Peter Levine, *A.G. Spalding and the Rise of Baseball* (New York: Oxford University Press, 1985).

19. David Quentin Voigt, *America Through Baseball* (Chicago: Nelson Hall, 1976).

20. Quote from *American Magazine* (1913), as cited in Thorn, "Our Game," 6.

21. Philip Green, as quoted in Jamie Kitman, "Way Out in Left-Center Field," *In These Times* (April 1–7, 1987), 12–13; Pete Williams, "Face Facts: Cashing in the American Way," *USA Today Baseball Weekly* (December 3–9, 1997), 5.

22. Stephen Riess, *Touching Base* (Westport, CT: Greenwood, 1980); Richard C. Crepeau, *Baseball* (Orlando: University Presses of Florida, 1980); Voigt, *America Through Baseball*.

23. Seymour, "Baseball: Badge of Americanism," 27.

24. Stanton Green, as quoted in Edward A. Gargan, "Field for Philosophizing and Other Dreams," *New York Times* (June 27, 1998), B9.

25. Andrei Codrescu, "A Kind of Love," *The Muse Is Always Half Dressed in New Orleans* (New York : St. Martin's Press, 1993), 141.

26. Buster Olney, "Baseball: Ten Reasons Why It's America's Pastime Again," *Athlon Sports: Baseball* (1999), 19.

27. Michael Novak, *The Joy of Sports* (Lanham, MD: Madison Books, 1994).

28. Richard Ben Cramer, "The America That Ruth Built," *Newsweek* (June 24, 1998),

28; see also Daniel Walden, "Where Have All Our Heroes Gone?" *USA Today* (January 1986), 20–25.

29. Richard Ben Cramer, "The DiMaggio Nobody Knew," *Newsweek* (March 22, 1999), 53.

30. Carol J. Pierman, "Cal Ripken and the Condition of Freedom: Theme and Variation on the American Work Ethic," *Nine: A Journal of Baseball History and Social Policy* 7, no. 1 (Fall 1998): 118–129. While our admiration for Ripken and Gehrig has been real enough, it has not been entirely without ambivalence. We have also regarded with some suspicion certain achievements, both inside and outside of baseball, that have perhaps resulted more from longevity than skill. Recent Hall of Fame inductee, Don Sutton, for example, has been criticized for having more stamina than greatness. A similar view has been taken toward Pete Rose, although reservations about him as a hero also obviously reflect his other problems.

31. Seymour, "Baseball: Badge of Americanism," 28.

32. Voigt, *America Through Baseball*, 97.

33. Angel Rodriquez, "Foul Play: Despite the Growing Number of Latino Players, Baseball Lacks Latino Managers and Executives," *Hispanic* (April 1999), 33–36; Editors, "What's Behind the Shrinking Number of African-American Players?" *Ebony* 47 (June 1992), 112–116; Terry Jones, "Racial Practices in Baseball Management," *The Black Scholar* 18 (May/June 1987): 16–24; Frank Robinson and Berry Stainback, "Fighting the Baseball Blackout," *Sport* 79 (July 1988): 66–69; Peter Richmond, "Joe Morgan's Cool Anger," *Gentleman's Quarterly* (October 1988), 105–111; Gerald Early, "Performance and Reality: Race, Sports and the Modern World," *The Nation* (August 10/17, 1998), 11–20.

34. Susan Berkson, as quoted in Elinor Nauen, ed., *Diamonds Are a Girl's Best Friend* (Boston: Faber, 1994).

35. Fay Vincent in Kate Rounds, "Where Is Our Field of Dreams?" *Ms.* (September/October 1991), 44–45.

36. Pam Postema with Gene Wojciechowski, *You've Got to Have Balls to Make It in This League* (New York: Simon & Schuster, 1992); Ruth Coniff, "The Joy of Women's Sports," *The Nation* (August 10/17, 1998), 26–30; Colette Dowling, *The Frailty Myth* (New York: Random House, 2000).

37. Duke Snider with Roger Kahn, "I Play Baseball for Money—Not Fun," *Collier's* (May 25, 1956), 44–46.

38. Gai Ingham Berlage, "Are Children's Competitive Team Sports Teaching Corporate Values?" in *Fractured Focus: Sport As A Reflection of Society*, ed. Richard E. Lapchick (Lexington, MA: Lexington Books, 1986).

39. Peter Carino, "American Dream, American Reality," *Elysian Fields Quarterly* 13, no. 2 (Summer 1994): 74–76.

40. Tom Goldstein, "The New Politics of Baseball," *Elysian Fields Quarterly* 15, no. 4 (1998): 2–4.

41. Leonard Koppett, *Koppett's Concise History of Major League Baseball* (Philadelphia: Temple University Press, 1998), 446–447.

42. Stephen Lehman, "Intimations of Apocalypse," *Elysian Fields Quarterly* 18, no. 4 (Winter 1999): 2–5.

43. Lorraine Kee, "Lions and Christians," *The Nation* (August 10/17, 1998), 37–38; Damon Rice, *Seasons Past* (New York : Praeger, 1976); Thomas Boswell, *Heart of the Order* (New York: Penguin, 1989); Wilfred Sheed, *Baseball and Lesser Sports* (New York: Harper Collins, 1991); Leonard Koppett, *The New Thinking Fan's Guide to Baseball* (New York:

Fireside, 1991); Murray Ross, "Football Red and Baseball Green," *Chicago Review* 22, no. 2 (1971): 30–40; George Carlin, *Brain Droppings* (New York: Hyperion, 1997).

44. Dawidoff, Nicholas, "Field of Kitsch: Is Nostalgia Wrecking Baseball?" *The New Republic* (August 17–24, 1992), 22–24.

45. Mickey Mantle with Phil Pepe, *My Favorite Summer, 1956* (New York: Doubleday, 1991); Stephanie Coontz, *The Way We Never Were* (New York: Basic Books, 1992); Ron Briley, "America, Baseball and Historical Memory in 1956: The Way We Never Were" (unpublished paper).

46. Harvey Kaye, "From Bases to Superstructures: The Great Transformation of Baseball," in Harvey Kaye, *Why Do Ruling Classes Fear History?* (New York: St. Martin's Press, 1997), 87; Stanley Cohen, *The Man in the Crowd* (New York: Random House, 1981).

47. Springwood, *Cooperstown to Dyersville*, 89.

48. Bill Brown, book review of Springwood, *Cooperstown to Dyersville* in *Journal of Sport History* 24, no. 3 (Fall 1997): 438–443.

49. Michael Kammen, *Mystic Chords of Memory* (New York: Alfred Knopf, 1991). See also Mike Wallace, *Mickey Mouse History, and Other Essays on American Memory* (Philadelphia: Temple University Press, 1996); Elizabeth Long, *The American Dream and the Popular Novel* (Boston: Routledge & Kegan Paul, 1985); W.M. Verhoeven, ed., *Rewriting the Dream* (Amsterdam: Rodopi, 1992).

50. Neal Gabler, *Life the Movie* (New York: Alfred Knopf, 1998).

51. Fischer, "The Conservative Curveball," 36.

52. Robert Heilman, "Field of Reality," *Elysian Fields Quarterly*, 13, no. 2 (Summer 1994): 16–20.

53. Leverett T. Smith, Jr., *The American Dream and the National Game* (Bowling Green, OH: Bowling Green University Popular Press, 1975), 1–6.

54. Harvey Kaye, "All That Is Solid Melts into Air . . . or Baseball and Capitalism, the View from Left Field," *Elysian Fields Quarterly* 12, no. 1 (1993): 26–28.

55. Joseph Sobran, "The Republic of Baseball," *National Review* 42 (June 11, 1990): 36–39.

56. Dom DeLillo, *Underground* (New York: Charles Scribner, 1997).

57. William Marshall, *Baseball's Pivotal Era, 1945–1951* (Lexington: University Press of Kentucky, 1999).

58. Curt Flood with Richard Carter, *The Way It Is* (New York: Trident Press, 1970); Ron Briley, "The Times Were A-Changin': Baseball As A Symbol of American Values in Transition, 1963–1964," *Baseball Research Journal*, 18 (1994): 54–60.

59. Mike Lupica, *Mad As Hell* (New York: G.P. Putnam's, 1996); Tom Goldstein and Stephen Lehman, "Fighting Back: Baseball Fans of America in Revolt," *Elysian Fields Quarterly* 15, no. 2 (1998): 7–11; Ralph Nader, "Sports Reform Project: Fight to Advance the Nation's Sports (FANS)" (unpublished paper, 1998); Don Weiskopf, "Baseball Play in America: Restoring Baseball's Greatness" (unpublished paper); Sidney Zion, "What About the Fans? Fuhgeddaboudit," *The Nation* (August 10/17, 1998), 31–35.

60. Andre Mayer, "Pirates of Pennants," *Boston Observer* 7 (Spring 1986): 24–25.

61. Joan Ryan, "Setting A Shining Example," *San Francisco Chronicle* (September 18, 1998), F1.

62. Peter Gammons, "Foreign Markets Represent Baseball's Future," *Baseball America* (February 2–15, 1998), 6.

63. Peter Dreier, "Pitchers and Pickets," *Boston Sunday Globe* (September 4, 1994); Peter Dreier and Kelly Candaele, "Players Must Act Like A Labor Union," *Los Angeles Times* (May 19, 1996); Mark Rosentraub, *Major League Losers* (New York: Basic Books,

1997); Joanna Cagan and Neil deMause, *Field of Schemes* (Monroe, ME: Common Courage Press, 1998); Andrew Zimbalist, *Baseball and Billions* (New York: Basic Books, 1993); Gai Berlage, *Women in Baseball* (Westport, CT: Praeger, 1994); Kevin Brooks, "A Socialist Slider," *Minneapolis Review of Baseball* 11, no. 2 (1991): 39–41; David Driver, *Defending the Left* (Chicago: Noble Press, 1992); Gerry Spence, *Give Me Liberty!* (New York: St. Martin's Press, 1998); Robert Elias, "Baseball and Social Change," *Minneapolis Review of Baseball* 8, no.1 (1988): 24–27; Jay Feldman, "The Hidden Ball Trick, Nicaragua and Me," *The National Pastime* 6, no.1 (Winter 1987): 2–5.

64. Bill Vaughan, from his *Kansas City Star* column, as quoted in *The Sporting News* (August 15, 1970), 17.

65. John Thorn, "Why Baseball?" in *Baseball*, eds. Geoffrey C. Ward and Ken Burns (New York: Alfred Knopf, 1994), 58.

PART I

Dreams of Diversity:
Race, Ethnicity,
and Baseball

1

THE GREATEST SEASON
From Jackie Robinson to Sammy Sosa

Roger Kahn

As the years pass, I have to increasingly wonder whether anyone, besides myself, was alive—living, eating, breathing, smoking cigarettes—in the year 1947. In fact, has anyone besides myself ever even heard of 1947?

We all know the observation from Shakespeare's magical play, *The Tempest*, the line also inscribed on our National Archives Building in Washington: "What is past is prologue." This says beautifully and succinctly that only when we know the past can we understand the present; only when we know the past can we contend with the future.

America, 1947. Harry Truman is president. He's busy calling the Republican 80th Congress the worst Congress in history. The Cold War blows an icy wind. America alone possesses nuclear weapons. The Russians didn't get the bomb until 1949, but that doesn't protect the country from hysteria. People everywhere believe that under just about every bed in the United States lurks at least one deadly communist spy. No fewer than ten Hollywood screenwriters are sentenced to prison for refusing to tell Congressional witch hunters whether or not they have been members of the Communist party. We see people jailed not for acts—these people threw no bombs—but for ideas, for thoughts. We see in an America so gloriously triumphant in World War II—the "good war" and the war for freedom—the emergence of thought police. Fighting communism with the methods of fascism makes for unsettling times.

Joe Louis is heavyweight champion of the world. Sportswriters call him the "Brown Bomber" and the "Dark Destroyer." Racial labels are the order of the day. On Broadway, you can see the new Tennessee Williams play, *A Streetcar Named Desire*, starring an overpowering young actor named Marlon Brando. The movie that wins the Academy Award is called *Gentleman's Agreement*. It is a sober examination of upper class anti-Semitism. On television . . . well, in 1947, not one American in fifty owns a television set. Those who do get to look at tiny round screens that erupt into blizzards of white static whenever an airplane flies overhead.

The world of 1947 was profoundly different from the world we would know in 1998. But not in every single way. In 1947, the best team in baseball, the team that won the World Series, was—we can pretty much say this all together now—the New York Yankees. Only two African Americans played in that World Series. One was a forgotten pitcher named Dan Bankhead, who appeared as a pinch runner for the Brooklyn Dodgers. The other was Jack Roosevelt Robinson. He had a pretty good series, not a great one. Seven hits in the seven games, two stolen bases, a batting average of .259. But that is not and was not the point.

With precious little help from the press, the umpires, and the other ball players, Jackie Robinson integrated major league baseball in 1947. The big leagues had been off limits to blacks, a white man's club since the year 1884 when the brothers Moses Fleetwood Walker and Weldey Wilberforce Walker played for Toledo in what was then the second major league, the American Association. The policy of segregation that began in 1885 was unofficial and absolute. No documents attest to baseball's apartheid. There was simply an understanding among every major league club owner and every minor league club owner for more than sixty years that no blacks could play in so-called organized baseball.

Surely this shaped the nature of American life. If blacks were kept out of the national pastime, and told to go away and play in their own league, didn't it follow naturally that blacks could be prevented from attending outstanding schools and colleges, forbidden to move into attractive neighborhoods, barred from admission to pleasant country clubs and even, through various forms of intimidation, denied the right to vote? It surely did. America in 1947 was a society stained with brutal bigotry.

In 1997, the fiftieth anniversary of Robinson's entry into the major leagues, organized baseball produced a celebration and retired Robinson's number, 42, for all time. Very nice as far as it went, but baseball's publicists and promoters carefully excluded from their celebration the way things really were for Jackie Robinson as a rookie.

Branch Rickey, a complex white man with roots in southern Ohio, brought Robinson to the Dodgers. Pee Wee Reese, shortstop and captain with roots in segregated Kentucky, befriended him. But not many applauded Rickey's breakthrough move. The commissioner of baseball, A.B. "Happy" Chandler of Kentucky, refused comment. In some cases—this is one—a "no comment" speaks volumes. Jimmy Powers, sports editor of the *New York Daily News*, the tabloid that then had the largest circulation of any newspaper in America, wrote: "Robinson will not make the grade. He is a thousand to one shot." The *Sporting News*, which called itself baseball's bible, said Robinson was too old and couldn't hit. A prominent baseball executive said, "We can now expect the Branch Rickey Temple to be built in Harlem."

Rickey insisted that Robinson spend a season in the minor leagues and assigned him in 1946 to play second base for Montreal in the International League. That March, during an exhibition game against Indianapolis in Daytona Beach, Florida, Robinson slid home with a first-inning run. A local policeman bolted onto the field, drew his gun and said, "Get off the field right now, or I'm putting you in jail." During a regular season game someone on the Syracuse Chiefs sent a black cat on the field from the dugout. "Hey, Robinson," he shouted, "here is one of your relatives." For the record, Robinson did leave the field in Daytona Beach. In Syracuse, after the innocent cat had been caught, he hit a double. For that year in Montreal he stole forty bases and the fellow who couldn't hit won the International League batting championship.

At the end of that 1946 season, Robinson told me, as he was leaving the old Montreal ballpark, a crowd of fans swarmed about behind him. Robinson began to run. The fans ran after him. Then Jack began to cry. "I was crying," he said, "because here was a big crowd running after a black man—not to lynch him, but to get his autograph."

The next year, when Rickey promoted Robinson to Brooklyn, he thought the other players would welcome Jack. Here was a winning ball player. Here was a man who meant pennants and World Series shares. In an era when most ball players earned eight or ten thousand dollars a year, here was a man who meant "cash." It surprised Rickey when a half dozen Dodgers prepared a petition that said in effect, "If you're bringing up the colored guy, you'll have to trade us."

The petition was prepared by Dixie Walker, a native of Villa Rica, Georgia, who lived in Birmingham. Many years later, Walker expressed his deep sorrow for the petition, claiming that it was the dumbest thing he'd ever done and that it was motivated less by racism than by a fear of losing business back home in his off-season hardware company. But in 1947 Walker was a recent National League batting champion and team leader, and he got several other Dodgers to sign. Hugh Casey, baseball's best relief pitcher and an Atlanta native, supported the petition, as did Bobby Bragan, a third-string catcher from Birmingham. But if "Confederates" began the petition, "Union" forces did not lack for representation. Harry "Cookie" Lavagetto from Oakland, Carl Furillo from Reading, Pennsylvania, and Eddie Stanky from Philadelphia, also signed.

Harold "Pee Wee" Reese, from Louisville, underwent a crisis. He had grown up in a segregated community, and when he was young his father even showed him the local "hanging tree" for "when a nigger gets out of line." But as a Christian, Reese wondered how he could deny Robinson the right to inherit a small portion of the earth. He could not and he would not. Citing his financial insecurity and the petition's possible backlash, he refused to sign, thus implicitly challenging the team's racists. More recently, Reese said, "People tell me that I helped Jackie. But knowing my background and the progress I've made, I have to say he helped me as much as I helped him."

Word of the petition reached Leo Durocher while the Dodgers were on a spring training tour in Panama's Canal Zone. He was about to embark on what was probably the finest hour of his life. At one o'clock in the morning, Durocher—in his pajamas—assembled the players in an army mess kitchen. He told them what they could do with their petition:

> I'm the manager and I'm paid to win and I'd play an elephant if he could win for me and this fellow Robinson is no elephant. You can't throw him out on the bases and you can't get him out at the plate. This fellow is a great player. He's gonna win pennants. He's gonna put money in your pockets and mine. And here's something else. He's only the first, boys, only the first! There's many more colored ballplayers coming right behind him and they're hungry, boys. They're scratching and diving. Unless you wake up, these colored ballplayers are gonna run you right out of the park. . . . Fuck your petition. . . . Go back to bed.

If there was a single moment when the success of Robinson and what some called "the Noble Experiment" became assured, it came on a day when the Dodgers were taking infield practice in old Crosley Field in Cincinnati. Robinson played first base for Brooklyn in 1947 and Cincinnati, on the Ohio River, regarded itself as a border town. Fans began to jeer Robinson's every move. The Cincinnati players picked it up. They shouted at him, "Hey, Jungle Bunny. Hey, Snowflake."

Suddenly, Pee Wee Reese, the young Dodger captain, raised a hand and called time. The infield drill stopped. Reese walked over from shortstop to first base and put an arm lightly on Robinson's shoulders. There they stood white man and black man, number one and number forty-two. Reese said not a word but simply stared into the Cincinnati dugout. I do not believe we have known a finer moment in American sports.

During the recent and very exciting 1998 baseball season, numbers of television broadcasters asked me to make appearances as a guest on their shows. Everyone wanted to raise the same point. Wasn't the season of 1998, with Sammy Sosa and Mark McGwire, with David Wells and the new mellow-fellow George M. Steinbrenner, wasn't this the greatest season in the history of baseball?

The answer is no, not by a long shot. The greatest season was 1947. The greatest period? The ten years of Jackie Robinson. I'm not talking about home runs or perfect games or winning streaks. I am talking about something more important: the quality of American life.

Once Jackie Robinson made it, at a terrible personal cost, we all began to look at the nature of society. I remember being introduced at Ebbets Field to a charming California politician who was then unemployed. We watched a few innings together. Robinson, with his daring base running and his quick bat and his uncompromising color, the ebony arms extending beyond the Dodger sleeves of white, dominated. This politician was fascinated. A few years later he became Chief Justice of the United States. His name was Earl Warren and he would be the architect of integrated education with his decision in *Brown v. Board of Education of Topeka*. I believe Earl Warren's resolve for fairness in education took firm hold that night he watched Robinson in Ebbets Field.

"My demand," Robinson said to me once, "was modest enough." He was simply asking to make a living at the level to which his gifts entitled him. But see what flowed from that: a general recognition that all Americans should have equal economic rights. As other black athletes came forward—Roy Campanella, Satchel Paige, and the matchless Willie Mays—we began to recognize that black athletes and indeed that black citizens were a national asset.

We began to look at blacks not as a breed apart. We began to recognize that American apartheid was just plain wrong. I would say that if there was no Jackie Robinson there would have been no Martin Luther King, Jr., at least not as we remember him. Has anything else in American sports ever approached the impact of the season of 1947?

What accounts for Jackie Robinson's accomplishment? In white America you still hear a variety of cliches about African Americans: "Sure blacks can run and jump and slide and dunk, but can they think? Hey, that's the white man's game. Let Willie chase 'em in the outfield. Let Jim Brown run for daylight. Let Michael slamma-jamma. Fine for natural athletes like those guys. But for thinking, we gotta have whites. White pitchers and white quarterbacks and white coaches. Know what I mean?"

As one of those accused of having only "natural" ability, Willie Mays had some answers. When talking about athletic performance, he said:

> So much is mental. I believe if you can't think, you can't play [on a good level]. Baseball or any sport. . . . Some people who watched Jim Brown play football said, "Man he's big and fast and strong. He's gotta be good." But they don't realize that when Brown was running with the ball, he was always thinking. Cut back. Fake. Whatever. He was always thinking ahead, two or three moves ahead of the tacklers. Muhammad Ali. Sure he was big and quick. But he was such a good boxing thinker, he could figure the round he'd win in before the fight. Then he made his moves and it would come out like he predicted. He was another athlete who was great because he would think. Julius Erving in basketball. Dr. J. had all the moves. He had a great body to play basketball, but he had the moves because he knew how to think.

And when asked to choose the smartest baseball player he ever saw, Mays answers very quickly: "Jackie Robinson."

I rejoice with Sammy Sosa at his annual stipend of $10,625,000. I commend Mark McGwire on his tidy $9,500,000. Except for the San Diego pratfall in the Series, we had a glorious 1998 season.

But I know, too, that baseball's success and America's success were helped immeasurably by Jackie Robinson, who died, with very little money in 1972. He was a splendid friend, not at all sad. Before his death, I was visiting the Robinsons in North Stamford, Connecticut, and Mrs. Robinson, Rachel, whom we call Rae, said, "No single reporter, not one, has ever asked me this. If Jack had a hard day at the ballpark, if the bigots were yelling at him, did he take it out on family when he got home? He didn't," she said. "The only way I could tell was that he'd take a bucket of golf balls and his driver and start hitting them off the back lawn into the lake."

Then Jack looked at me and his eyes were twinkling. "The golf balls," he said, "were white."

2

JACKIE ROBINSON'S LEGACY
Baseball, Race, and Politics

Peter Dreier

NINETEEN NINETY-SEVEN MARKED THE FIFTIETH ANNIVERSARY OF JACKIE ROBINSON'S courageous triumph over baseball's apartheid system. When Robinson took the field for the Brooklyn Dodgers on April 15, 1947, he was the first black player in modern major league baseball.

The nation commemorated the Robinson milestone in a variety of ways. Major League Baseball honored Robinson by sewing patches on all players' uniforms. Major League Baseball also retired Robinson's number—42—for all teams.[1] President Clinton appeared with Rachel Robinson at a Mets-Dodgers game at Shea Stadium to venerate her late husband. There was also a proliferation of books, plays, symposia, television movies, museum exhibits, and academic conferences about Robinson.[2] Robinson's hometown of Pasadena, California—which virtually ignored him during his own lifetime—finally got around to dedicating the Rose Bowl Parade in his honor.[3]

Robinson's own life, as well as his legacy, reflects the nation's political and ideological struggle over race relations. Robinson is more than a baseball icon. He is a symbol of America's ongoing ambivalence about race. Even the celebration of Robinson's role in integrating baseball was fraught with irony. In the midst of the fiftieth anniversary hoopla, our collective memory of this great American hero, and of this critical episode of our country's history, became entangled in current ideological wars over race and politics. The Robinson celebration paralleled an ongoing question in America's race relations: how much progress has there been—in baseball as well as in the larger society?

Thanks to Richard Rothstein, Jim Whitney and Bill Domhoff for their comments on an earlier draft of this essay. This essay is dedicated to the memory of Bennett Harrison, whose friendship, as well as whose passion for baseball, racial equality, and economic justice, are sorely missed.

The Basic Story

Many consider Robinson, who lived from 1919 to 1972, as America's greatest all-around athlete. He was a four-sport star athlete at UCLA, played professional football, and then played briefly in baseball's Negro Leagues. He spent his major league career (1947 to 1956) with the Brooklyn Dodgers, was chosen Rookie of the Year in 1947 and Most Valuable Player in 1949. An outstanding base runner, with a .311 lifetime batting average, he led the Dodgers to six pennants and was elected to the Hall of Fame in 1962.[4]

The grandson of a slave and the son of a sharecropper, Robinson was fourteen months old in 1920 when his mother moved her five children from Cairo, Georgia, to Pasadena, a wealthy and well-planned conservative Los Angeles suburb of about 50,000 people. A 1939 Columbia University study ranked Pasadena the nation's most livable city. But during Robinson's youth, black residents, who represented a tiny proportion of the population, were treated like second-class citizens. Blacks were only allowed to swim in the municipal pool on Tuesdays (the day the water was changed) and could only use the YMCA one day a week. In its movie theaters, blacks were limited to the segregated balcony. Robinson's mother Mallie worked as a domestic. The family lived in poverty in an all-white neighborhood, where Jackie faced constant racial slurs and taunts.

When his older brother Mack returned from the 1936 Olympics in Berlin with a silver medal in track, only three people turned up to greet him at the train station. There was no hero's welcome—no ticker-tape parade, no key to the city. In fact, the only job the college-educated Mack could find was as a street sweeper and ditch digger.[5]

Ironically, Robinson's Pasadena background played a role in Dodgers general manager Branch Rickey's decision to select him out of the Negro Leagues to break the sport's color barrier—as much for his personal characteristics as for his baseball skills. He knew that if the Robinson "experiment" failed, the cause of baseball integration would be set back for many years thereafter. He could have chosen other Negro League players with greater talent or name recognition, but he wanted someone who could be what today we call a "role model." Robinson was articulate and well educated. Although born in the segregated Deep South, he lived among whites in his Pasadena neighborhood, at school, and in college, and he played on integrated sports teams. His circle of friends during his adolescence was a multiracial group called the "Pepper Street Gang."

Rickey knew that Robinson had a hot temper and strong political views. As an Army officer in World War II, Robinson was court-martialed (although later acquitted) for resisting bus segregation at Ft. Hood, Texas.[6] Rickey calculated that Robinson could handle the emotional pressure while helping the Dodgers on the field. Robinson promised Rickey he wouldn't respond to the inevitable verbal barbs and even physical abuse. Rickey could not count on the other team owners or most major league players (many of whom came from Southern or small town backgrounds) to support his plan. But the Robinson experiment succeeded—on the field and at the box office. Within a few years, the Dodgers hired other black players (including Don Newcombe, Roy Campanella, Joe Black, and Jim Gilliam) who helped turn the 1950s Dodgers into one of the greatest teams in baseball history.

After Robinson had established himself as a superstar, Rickey gave him the green light to unleash his temper. On the field, he fought constantly with umpires and opposing players. Off the field, he was outspoken—in speeches, interviews, and his regular newspaper column—against racial injustice. He viewed his sports celebrity as a platform from which to challenge American racism. During his playing career, he was constantly criticized for being so frank about race relations in baseball and in society. Many sportswriters and most other players—including some of his fellow black players, content simply to be playing in the majors—considered Robinson too angry and vocal.

Robinson's political views reflected the tensions of Cold War liberalism. In 1949, Rickey orchestrated Robinson's appearance before the House Committee on Un-American Activities so that he could publicly criticize Paul Robeson— the multitalented singer, actor, and left-wing political activist—who had stirred controversy by stating in a Paris speech that American blacks would not fight in a war with Russia. As expected, Robinson challenged Robeson's views. But he also seized the opportunity, a decade before the heyday of civil rights activism, to make an impassioned demand for social justice and racial integration. "I'm not fooled because I've had a chance open to very few Negro Americans," Robinson said. The press focused on Robinson's criticism of Robeson and virtually ignored his denunciation of American racism.

Shortly before his death, from the effects of diabetes and heart disease, Robinson said he regretted his remarks about Robeson. "I have grown wiser and closer to the painful truth about America's destructiveness," he acknowledged. "And I do have an increased respect for Paul Robeson, who . . . sacrificed himself, his career, and the wealth and comfort he once enjoyed because, I believe, he was sincerely trying to help his people." Indeed, his [Robinson's] increasingly pessimistic views reflected the evolution of the nation's race-relations climate.

When Robinson retired from baseball, no team offered him a position as a coach, manager, or executive. He became an executive with the Chock Full O' Nuts restaurant chain and became an advocate for integrating corporate America. He lent his name and prestige to several business ventures, including a construction company and a black-owned bank in Harlem. He got involved in these business activities primarily to help address the shortage of affordable housing and the persistent redlining against racial minorities by white-owned banks.

Both of these enterprises later fell on hard times and perhaps dimmed Robinson's confidence in black capitalism as a strategy for racial integration.

Nevertheless, Robinson's faith in free enterprise led him into several controversial political alliances. In 1960, he initially supported Senator Hubert Humphrey's campaign for president, but when John F. Kennedy won the Democratic Party nomination, Robinson shocked his black and liberal fans when he endorsed and campaigned for Richard Nixon. He also came to regret this support. He later worked as an aide to New York Governor Nelson Rockefeller, the last of the major liberal Republicans who supported activist government and civil rights.

Until his death, Robinson continued speaking out. He was a constant presence on picket lines and at rallies on behalf of civil rights. He was one of the NAACP's best fund-raisers, but resigned in 1967, criticizing the organization for its failure to involve "younger, more progressive voices." He pushed major league baseball to hire blacks as managers and executives and even refused an invitation to an Old Timers game, "until I see genuine interest in breaking the barriers that deny access to managerial and front office positions."

Within a few years after his death, however, Robinson was almost a forgotten man. While baseball aficionados continued to probe Robinson's life and legacy, he was no longer a well-known figure in popular culture. The name Jackie Robinson was once used as a metaphor for pioneers who broke social barriers, but by the 1980s his currency had begun to fade. In 1990, *Sport* magazine discovered that many major league ballplayers, including some African American superstars, knew little about Robinson except that he broke baseball's color line.[7]

This void can be explained, at least in part, by the mainstream media's virtual neglect of Robinson. During the 1980s, the *New York Times* published an average of seventeen articles a year that mentioned Robinson's name, peaking in 1987 with thirty-one references. The *Washington Post* ran an average of seven articles a year that mentioned Robinson, also peaking in 1987 with twenty-one.[8] The peak in 1987 was sparked by a controversy over racially insensitive remarks by Dodger executive (and Robinson's former teammate) Al Campanis on Ted Koppel's *Nightline* television show celebrating the fortieth anniversary of Robinson's breakthrough.[9]

From 1990 through 1996, the *New York Times* ran an average of nineteen articles with Robinson's name. As a result of the fiftieth anniversary celebration, interest dramatically peaked in 1997 with 175 references to Robinson, then fell back to eighteen in 1998. Robinson's name appeared an average of seven times a year in the *Washington Post* from 1990 through 1996, peaked at sixty-eight in 1997, then fell back to eleven in 1998.[10] In 1997, almost every major newspaper and magazine in the nation featured stories about Robinson, often using the anniversary as an occasion to examine the current state of race relations in baseball and American sports in general.

The Ideological Battle over Race and Politics

The dominant race-relations metaphors of Robinson's era—integration, the melting pot, and assimilation—were unambiguous. Progressives believed in a color-blind society. In the struggle for basic civil rights, it was easy to answer: which side are you on? In contrast, today's disputes over multiculturalism, affirmative action, racial preferences, and even (in the views of some black educators and playwright August Wilson) self-segregation make the political landscape more confusing, even for progressives.

Much of the celebration of Robinson's achievement—including the movies, the news articles, and the museum exhibits—was cast in a familiar ideological mold. These commemorations focused primarily on Robinson's accomplishments as an individual pioneer. The integration of baseball was framed as an individual's triumph over adversity, a lone trailblazer who broke baseball's color line on his athletic merits, with a helping hand from Dodger executive Branch Rickey. The most extreme version of this perspective appeared in the right-wing *National Review*, which used Robinson's success to argue against government policies like affirmative action. "Government had almost nothing to do with this triumph of the competitive market," wrote Steve Sailer. "Baseball owners finally realized that the more they cared about the color of people's money, the less they could afford to care about the color of their skin."[11]

But the true story of baseball's integration is not primarily the triumph of either individualism or enlightened capitalism. Rather, it is a political victory brought about by social protest, part and parcel of the larger struggle for civil rights and social justice. As historian Jules Tygiel explains in *Baseball's Great Experiment* (see note 4), beginning in the 1940s the Negro press, civil rights groups, the Communist Party, progressive whites, and radical politicians waged a sustained campaign to integrate baseball that involved demonstrations, boycotts, political maneuvering, and other forms of pressure that would gain greater currency the following decade.[12] This protest movement set the stage for Rickey's "experiment" and for Robinson's entrance into the major leagues. The dismantling of baseball's color line was a triumph of both a man and a movement.

Ironically, in the 1960s Robinson was often criticized by black nationalists, including Malcolm X and Stokely Carmichael, for being an Uncle Tom, a symbolic token. Today, some of their heirs view baseball's integration with ambivalence for its role in destroying the Negro Leagues. In his 1992 play, *Mr. Rickey Calls a Meeting*, playwright Ed Schmidt gave voice to this view.[13] It depicts a fictitious meeting called by Dodgers general manager Branch Rickey to enlist the support of boxer Joe Louis, dancer Bill "Bojangles" Robinson, and actor-activist Paul Robeson for his decision to promote Jackie Robinson to the Dodgers. In the play, Robeson (correctly) predicts that integration will lure black fans away from the Negro Leagues and threaten the livelihood of many black athletes. Robeson announces that the price for his support is for Rickey to arrange for an entire team of Negro League all-stars to be added to the majors.

The Transformation in Race Relations

In reality, most black Americans welcomed the integration of baseball, as much as they welcomed the end of separate drinking fountains. The demise of the Negro Leagues certainly destroyed the careers of many excellent black ballplayers who never made it to the majors. But this was a small price to pay to defeat Jim Crow. In today's cynical so-called post civil rights era, it is difficult to summon the excitement and fervor that greeted Robinson's achievement. It did more than change the way baseball is played and who plays it. His actions on and off the diamond helped pave the way for America to confront its racial hypocrisy. The dignity with which Robinson handled his encounters with racism among fellow players and fans, and in hotels, restaurants, trains, and other public places, drew public attention to the issue, stirred the consciences of many white Americans, and gave black Americans a tremendous boost of pride and self-confidence. Martin Luther King once told Dodgers pitcher Don Newcombe, "You'll never know what you and Jackie and Roy [Campanella] did to make it possible to do my job."

By hiring Robinson, the Dodgers earned the loyalty of millions of black Americans from across the country. But they also gained the allegiance of many white Americans—most fiercely American Jews, especially those in the immigrant and second-generation neighborhoods of America's big cities—who believed that integrating our national pastime was a critical steppingstone to tearing down many other obstacles to equal treatment.[14]

In fact, however, the integration of baseball proceeded very slowly after Robinson's entry into the big leagues. As late as 1953, only six of the then-sixteen major league teams had black players. It wasn't until 1959 that the last holdout, the Boston Red Sox, hired a black player. By 1997, black and Latino players were well represented on the field. Among major leaguers, 58 percent were white, 24 percent Latino, 17 percent black, and 1 percent Asian.[15] Despite the overall numerical overrepresentation of blacks and Latinos on major league teams, however, there is still some evidence that discrimination persists against African American players, and to a lesser extent, Hispanic players. A study in the late 1960s demonstrated convincingly that good black hitters were not excluded, but weak black hitters were excluded in favor of weak-hitting white players. In other words, teams were more likely to favor a white over a black player to be a benchwarmer or utility man.[16] A study in the early 1990s found that, in terms of both the positions they play (particularly pitcher and catcher) and the number and size of commercial endorsements they earn, blacks and Latinos continued to face discrimination in major league baseball.[17]

A major league team did not hire its first black manager—Frank Robinson, who led the Cleveland Indians—until 1975. By 1997, with twenty-eight major league teams, there were only four minority managers.[18] In the year when America was celebrating Jackie Robinson's achievement, there was only one black general manager in the major leagues—Bob Watson of the New York Yankees.[19] Overall, the proportion of blacks in front-office jobs reached 9 percent in 1989 and remained the same in 1997. When all racial minorities are included, the figures increase to 15 percent in 1989 and 18 percent in 1997; blacks represented 4 percent of all executives and department heads in 1990 and 6 percent in 1997. With all minorities included, the figure rose from 7 percent to 11 percent.

Robinson broke into baseball when America was a segregated nation. In 1946, when he was playing for the Dodgers's farm team in Montreal, at least six African Americans were lynched in the South. Restrictive covenants were still legal, barring blacks (and Jews) from buying homes in many neighborhoods (across the country, not just in the South). There were only a handful of blacks enrolled in the nation's predominantly white colleges and universities. There were only two blacks in Congress.[20] No major American city had a black mayor.

Robinson's triumph took place at a time of postwar economic expansion and optimism. After World War II, America held its breath, trying to decide what kind of society it wanted to be. As the Cold War escalated, many liberals feared that America's racial hypocrisy would be used by the Soviet Union to undermine the nation's credibility among political leaders around the world. During the war and its immediate aftermath, a few brave souls challenged what sociologist Gunnar Myrdal called the "American Dilemma"—the obvious conflict between its creed of equal opportunity and the reality of racial segregation. Labor leader A. Philip Randolph threatened to organize a march on Washington during the war if President Roosevelt didn't agree to begin desegregating the military and the defense industry. Thurgood Marshall and the NAACP began the long march through the courts that ultimately led to the U.S. Supreme Court, in *Brown v. Board of Education* in 1954, declaring school segregation unconstitutional. White southerners like Miles Horton of the Highlander Folk School, H.L. Mitchell of the Southern Tenant Farmers Union, Herman Nixon of the Southern Conference for Human Welfare, and a handful of others challenged Jim Crow. Former vice president Henry Wallace, running on the Progressive Party ticket for president in 1948 on a platform of abolishing segregation, forced the Democratic Party to put a moderate civil rights plank in its platform that year.[21]

In the postwar era, black Americans were moving into northern and southern cities and wanted a fair share of the nation's prosperity. But until the civil rights movement of the 1950s and 1960s, they did not gain basic political rights, much less their fair slice of the growing economic pie. With organized labor as an occasional ally, the civil rights crusade helped many black Americans move into the economic mainstream. Many blacks gained access to good-paying jobs—in factories, government, and professional sectors—that previously had been off-limits. In unionized firms, the wage gap between black and white workers narrowed significantly.[22]

Like baseball, American society—including our workplaces, political organizations and even friendships—is more racially integrated than it was in Jackie Robinson's day. But there is continuing debate about the magnitude and pace of racial progress, as reflected in a number of recent books.[23] Thanks to the civil rights revolution, America has witnessed the significant growth of the African American and Latino middle class and the dramatic decline of the overt daily terror imposed on black Americans, especially in the South. Racial minorities are now visible in positions of leadership and influence in almost every sphere of American life. There are impressive numbers of black and Latino political leaders, many of whom have garnered cross-racial support.

The number of people of color in Congress, as well as those at local and state levels of government, has grown significantly. A growing number of large, predominantly white cities have elected black and Latino mayors. Douglas Wilder of Virginia became the first black governor. Jesse Jackson ran for president. Ron Dellums became chair of the House Armed Services Committee and other blacks headed other key committees when the Democrats held the majority. Colin Powell led the Joint Chiefs of Staff. Colleges and the professions have opened up to blacks and Latinos. Thirty years ago there were hardly any people of color on Fortune 500 corporate boards, as television newscasters and daily newspaper editors, or as presidents and administrators of major colleges and hospitals. That is no longer the case. Although the glass ceiling persists, we have moved beyond symbolic tokenism.[24]

Despite this progress, race remains a divisive issue in America. The poverty rate among black and Latino Americans is three times that of white America. Almost half of black children live in poverty. Our residential areas remain racially segregated. About two-thirds of non-Hispanic blacks live in blocks that are 60 percent or more black. Among Hispanics, 40 percent live in blocks that are 60 percent or more Hispanic. At least two out of three white Americans live in essentially all-white neighborhoods. In most major American cities, more than 70 percent of the population (and more than 80 percent in many cities) would have to move to achieve full integration.[25] Moreover, poor blacks and (to a lesser extent) poor Hispanics, but not poor whites, tend to live in ghettos or barrios with high concentrations of the poor.[26] Even when black people move to the suburbs, they are likely to live in segregated areas—not because they prefer to do so, but because of persistent (though subtle) racial bias by banks and real estate brokers. As a result of residential segregation, our public schools are still segregated by race as well as income. Blacks and Latinos still feel the sting of discrimination in the workplace and by the police and the criminal justice system.

Robinson recognized the paradoxes of racial progress in America. "I cannot possibly believe," he wrote in his 1972 biography, *I Never Had It Made*, "that I have it made while so many black brothers and sisters are hungry, inadequately housed, insufficiently clothed, denied their dignity as they live in slums or barely exist on welfare."[27]

The Corporatization of Baseball and America

Besides the matter of race relations, baseball has changed dramatically in other ways since Robinson's day.[28] Then, baseball had little competition from basketball, football, and other sports for fan loyalty. Sportswriters rarely probed players' personal lives or potential scandals, allowing athletes to become All-American heroes—just as news reporters rarely looked into the private lives of politicians and business leaders.

In Robinson's day, most players' salaries were not much higher than those of average workers. Indeed, many players lived in the same working class and middle class neighborhoods as their fans.[29] Subject to the feudal reserve clause, players remained with the same teams for years, binding them to local fans. Robinson played before the emergence of the players' union. In his rookie year, he earned $5,000, the major league minimum. His salary never exceed $42,000—less than several white stars—even though he was undoubtedly the sport's biggest drawing card. His highest salary (in real terms) never approached the typical salary of a journeyman ballplayer today. During Robinson's last few seasons, in fact, the Dodgers sought to lower his salary. And at the end of 1956, the Dodgers traded Robinson to the rival New York Giants. This was prior to free agency, and Robinson was powerless to do anything about it. He had already planned to retire, however, so Dodger fans never had to deal with the affront of seeing Robinson in a Giants uniform.

Until the 1970s, most major league teams were owned by local businessmen. The teams were often dominated by the strong personality of owners who took a hands-on approach to their teams' affairs. They were similar in many ways to the famous newspaper publishers, who used their papers as a way to influence public affairs. Like the publishers, some baseball owners were tyrannical, while others were benevolent and public-spirited.

Today, baseball teams, like the nation's major newspapers, are no longer family businesses. They are owned by corporate conglomerates. The Dodgers, in fact, were the last family-owned team, until Peter O'Malley sold the franchise to

Australian media tycoon Rupert Murdoch in 1998.[30] For the corporate conglomerates that own today's baseball teams, professional sports is simply a business like any other subsidiary or product line.

The major corporate icons of postwar America—like U.S. Steel and Standard
Oil—have merged into giant, often unrecognizable conglomerates. Even some
of the names adorning contemporary baseball stadiums—such as 3Com Park
(formerly called Candlestick Park, the home of the San Francisco Giants, and
replaced by PacBell Park); Bank One Ballpark (the home of the Arizona Diamondbacks); Coors Field (the home of the Colorado Rockies); QualComm Stadium in San Diego; and Tropicana Field in Tampa Bay—reflect the corporatization
of baseball. These aren't even the corporations that own the teams, but instead
major businesses that pay millions to attach their names to baseball stadiums.[31]
At the start of the 1999 baseball season, teams were even floating around the
idea of putting corporate logos on players' uniforms.

Like the rest of American business (but protected since the 1920s by the
unique antitrust exemption), baseball owners have recently engaged in an orgy
of speculation. The sale price of the Baltimore Orioles, for example, went from
$12 million in 1979, to $70 million in 1989, to $173 million in 1994.

Under these changed circumstances, it is no wonder that baseball today is
beset by footloose teams threatening to move unless cities build tax-funded
megastadiums and by tense labor-management relations that have resulted in
player strikes.[32] Labor relations in major league baseball reflect the overall economic transformation of the nation. By Congress granting major league teams
an exemption from federal antitrust laws, players were virtually powerless.

The Major League Baseball Players Association (MLBPA), the players' union,
changed all that. It was not inevitable that the players would share in the team
owners' spiraling profits. But beginning in the 1970s, and accelerating in the
past decade, the union dramatically changed baseball's labor-management situation. The union solidarity of these rugged individualists leveled the playing
field between team owners and players. In 1970, the basic agreement gave the
players the right to bargain collectively, including the use of agents and binding
arbitration. With the support of the union, Curt Flood, an outstanding black
outfielder with the St. Louis Cardinals, initially challenged the reserve clause
(which kept ballplayers in bondage to their owners), after he was sold to the
Phillies following the 1969 season.[33] In 1972, the U.S. Supreme Court ruled
against Flood, despite acknowledging that the reserve clause was an "aberration" and an "anomaly," but it was finally overturned in 1976 after a challenge
by players Andy Messersmith and Dave McNally. Since then, players have had
the right to negotiate as free agents. Collective bargaining has forced owners to
submit to binding arbitration of salary disputes and share their profits with the
players. As a result, players' salaries, pensions, and other benefits have spiraled.

Major league players' average salaries have skyrocketed, from $36,500 in 1973, to $76,000 in 1977 (the first year after free agency), to $113,500 in 1979, to $597,000 in 1990, to $1.2 million in 1995. But average salaries can be misleading, however, skewed by the extraordinary high incomes of a few dozen superstars. A more realistic figure is the median income—$410,000 in 1995. That year, many ballplayers made closer to the minimum salary of $109,000 than the huge sums paid to future Hall of Famers. Of course, even by these standards, ballplayers' incomes have grown dramatically.[34] Even second- and third-tier players boast high annual salaries with incredible fringe benefits.

The economics of major league baseball today reflect what some economists call the "winner take all" society.[35] Even among highly paid ballplayers, there is a heavily skewed pyramid, with a handful of players earning extremely high salaries, while journeymen players earn much less—and then only for a few years at most. The difference between the average major league player and the average worker, however, is that the players have a strong union, while most American workers do not.[36]

While baseball players were enjoying the fruits of their union solidarity, most other Americans weren't so lucky. In the United States, unionized workers have higher wages, better pensions, longer vacations and maternity leaves, and better health insurance than their nonunion counterparts. Union strength, which reached a peak of 35 percent in the mid-1950s, allowed American workers to share in the postwar prosperity and join the middle class. Union pay scales even helped boost the wages of nonunion workers. Since the 1970s, however, overall union membership has steadily declined. It was down to 22 percent of the workforce in 1983 and fell to 16 percent by 1997—the lowest since the Great Depression. Omit government employees and unions represented only 11 percent of private sector workers that year. (In contrast, 37 percent of Canada's workforce was unionized).

In the past few decades, the gap between rich and poor has widened. Today, the top 1 percent of the population has a larger share of the nation's wealth than the bottom 90 percent. The richest 5 percent of the nation own 61.4 percent of total wealth and have 20.3 percent of total income. The most affluent 20 percent of Americans have 84.3 percent of all wealth and 46.8 percent of total income. Although a growing number of blacks have moved into the middle class, black homeownership rates and accumulation of wealth have lagged far behind, even when compared to whites with comparable incomes, educations, and occupations.[37]

Corporate America is making record profits. Corporate CEOs pay themselves large salaries and bonuses, while laying off workers, reducing the wages and benefits of those who hold onto their jobs, and busting unions. The theory that the nation's overall economic growth would somehow "trickle down" to the middle class and the poor never materialized. Since the 1970s, the majority of American workers (including many middle class white-collar and professional employees) have seen their incomes decline.[38] Real wages fell by 1.8 percent from 1973 to 1978, and by 9.6 percent from 1979 to 1993. A recent Census Bureau report revealed that almost one-fifth of the nation's full-time workers earn poverty-level wages. Even during President Clinton's second term, with the official unemployment rate below 5 percent, the purchasing power of the typical worker was still far below where it was twenty-five years earlier. And, the nation's poverty rate has not significantly dropped.

The vast majority of Americans of all races are on a slippery economic slope. As the middle class gets hollowed out by these widening disparities, the basic components of the American Dream—a steady job with decent pay and health benefits, homeownership, and having at least a week's paid vacation—are increasingly out of reach.

The erosion of America's labor movement is the chief reason for the declining wages and living standards of the majority of Americans as well as the nation's widening economic disparities. In the 1950s and 1960s, most American workers—or at least most white workers—believed they would work for one company their entire working lives. Union contracts and economic growth offered job security and the prospect of upward mobility (at least for their children). They could afford to buy a home and settle into a community. They, like their baseball heroes, would stay in one place.

Since the 1970s, however, the American economy has been transformed by a new set of rules and expectations. The global economy has hastened the development of footloose multinational corporations. Since the early 1970s, there has been a tremendous flight of previously high-wage (primarily manufacturing) industries from U.S. cities to locations with more "favorable" business conditions—low wages, weak or nonexistent unions, and lax environmental laws—found mainly in outlying suburbs, rural areas, and Third World countries.[39] All working people, including middle class professionals, now face these problems, although women, people of color, and immigrants are the most vulnerable to these pressures. Corporate mergers and downsizing have ridden roughshod over workers' lives.[40]

The Robinson Legacy

The political and economic upheavals of the past few decades—particularly the end of the Cold War and the hollowing out of the middle class—have led many Americans to look backwards for an alleged "Golden Age." There is considerable nostalgia for the 1950s, as if the 1960s ushered in an era of instability and insecurity. For certain, the earlier era was more "stable." Women and African

Americans "knew their place" and the Cold War provided Americans with a clear enemy that, while threatening, was more understandable than today's Third World terrorism and interethnic wars. The Reagan era played on this sense of yearning for a simpler time. The current backlash against the gains of the feminist and civil rights movements—reflected in the rise of the Christian Right and attacks on affirmative action—reveals how today's political leaders capitalize on people's economic and social insecurities by sentimentalizing the past.

Baseball has not been immune to these trends. The Robinson anniversary came at a time when Americans, disenchanted with the corporatization of baseball, were awash in baseball nostalgia. The baby boom generation is fascinated with the sport's history. Their aging baseball cards are now big business. Since the 1980s, films like *Field of Dreams, Bull Durham, Eight Men Out, A League of Their Own*, and *Cobb* have reflected their nostalgia for the sport. During the 1994 baseball strike, Ken Burns's PBS documentary about the game—which emphasized the sport's traditional racism and the importance of black players—kept millions of viewers in front of their TV sets for an entire week.

The growing interest in African American history has led to a renewed interest in the Negro Leagues, where Robinson played for only a year. Although the Negro Leagues came about as a response to Jim Crow, today they are celebrated as part of the black community's struggle for dignity and self-reliance within the segregated society. These leagues served as a training ground for a generation of players who, along with Robinson, changed baseball to a more aggressive, strategic style of play. Prior to the 1980s, there was only one serious book (Robert Peterson's, *Only the Ball Was White*) about the Negro Leagues.[41] Now there are several dozen. In 1972, following another wave of protest, the Baseball Hall of Fame finally began to induct great Negro League players who had been barred from major league baseball. Two decades ago, the popular film *The Bingo Long Traveling All-Stars and Motor Kings*, starring Richard Pryor, Billie Dee Williams, and James Earl Jones, captured the bittersweet triumphs and tragedies of the Negro Leagues. Thanks to the Robinson celebration, there have been several documentaries and television movies about the Negro Leagues. For example, the HBO film, *The Soul of the Game*, explored how Negro League greats Satchel Paige and Josh Gibson paved the way for Robinson's achievement. August Wilson's 1990 Pulitzer Prize–winning play, *Fences*, set in 1957, portrays the bitterness of a former Negro League player who didn't get the opportunity to play in the majors.

There is much we can learn from history, but not if we view it through rose-colored glasses. Little is to be gained from romanticizing the "good old days" of baseball's so-called Golden Age in the 1940s and 1950s. Back then, baseball, like America, was still a caste society. Robinson, like the activists in the civil rights movement, helped to remove many barriers to racial equality. But the progress we've made in race relations should not obscure the stalemate, if not the regression, we've made in overall economic equality.

Thanks to the civil rights movement, baseball as well as the rest of society reluctantly but steadily opened up positions in the highest-income sectors of the economy to African Americans and Latinos. A very small but highly visible number of blacks and Latinos now sit on the boards and serve as top executives of major corporations, just as a handful of blacks and Latinos now earn huge salaries playing (or serving in top management positions in) professional baseball and other sports. But these positions—for all races—represent an extremely small proportion of the nation's jobs, although their occupants own a disproportionate share of the nation's wealth.

True racial progress means more than bringing people of color into the nation's economic, political, and media power elite (the top 1 percent) or even into the professional middle class that comprises the top one-fifth of the population. Our goal should not simply be racial equality among the wealthy. It should be more wealth equality among all races. The essence of America's troubled race relations can be summarized by the following observation: corporate America has learned to live with affirmative action and laws against racial discrimination, but it steadfastly opposes policies to promote full employment, universal health care, and affordable housing for all.

There is still more to be done to assimilate people of color into the professional middle class and even into the upper class. But even if blacks, Latinos, and Asians composed their "fair share" of this top tier, it would not significantly challenge mainstream institutions or threaten the power and privilege of the corporate elite. However, full employment and decent wages, universal health coverage, and an adequate supply of affordable housing for all Americans challenge the foundation of the business elite's power and profits.

If there is one truth about race relations, it is that prejudice, bigotry, and discrimination decline when everyone has basic economic security. Economic justice is a precondition for racial justice. It is simplistic to argue that if you give people a decent and steady job, their hearts and minds will follow, but it is certainly true that full employment at decent wages makes interracial cooperation much more likely. In hard times, competition over a shrinking pie (or the crumbs from the economy's table) leads to resentment, bitterness, and racial tension. Studies show, for example, that the number of lynchings went up whenever the Southern cotton economy declined. More recently, economic hard times are correlated with increases in the murder rate, racial violence, and hate crimes. The past decade's rancor over affirmative action reflects this reality.

It isn't clear where Robinson would stand on contemporary political and social issues if he were alive today. But his willingness to speak out against exploitation and bigotry suggests that he would be dismayed by the failure of baseball's high-salaried ballplayers, whatever their race, to engage in today's political and social struggles.

In recent years, after decades of decline, the sleeping giant of American union-ism seems to be waking up, with a renewed strategy of organizing unorganized workers (especially minorities and immigrants), restoring the labor movement's political influence, and pushing for policies such as a high minimum wage and national health insurance. Indeed, many argue that today's revitalized labor movement is the new civil rights movement.

As a vice president of Chock Full o' Nuts, which had a majority of black employees, Robinson was often put in the awkward position of defending man-agement against the union, despite his friends' insistence that he was not anti-union, and in fact sought to be an advocate for the company's employees.[42] During his post-baseball career, when Robinson was most active in politics, labor unions were viewed as both allies and obstacles of the civil rights movement. A number of progressive unions, such as the United Auto Workers and the International Ladies Garment Workers Union, were key players in the struggle for racial jus-tice, but the mainstream of the AFL-CIO, and many individual unions, were often reluctant to admit black members or join the civil rights crusade. Even so, Martin Luther King recognized that unions and racial minorities share a com-mon agenda. He understood that appeals to racial pride, without a larger vision of economic justice that cuts across racial divisions, are a dead end. When he was murdered in 1968, King was in Memphis to lead a demonstration of predominantly black sanitation workers who were on strike.

One of Robinson's legacies should be to remind today's high-salaried base-ball players that they owe a great deal to their working-class fans. To ensure the allegiance of America's baseball fans and the general public, major leaguers and their union should be reaching out, lending their celebrity status to help other workers, not just through charity activities (such as promoting a local hospital or youth sports league), but by helping those who are organizing to improve their working and living conditions—just as the ballplayers have done.

For example, during the 1994 baseball strike, fans might have been shocked to see some St. Louis Cardinals or Chicago Cubs walking the picket lines with United Auto Workers members who were on strike against Caterpillar in nearby Peoria, Illinois. Ballplayers could show their support for the "justice for jani-tors" and "living wage" organizing campaigns in their cities. The MLBPA could help the hotel workers union's efforts by refusing to stay in nonunion hotels during road trips.

The union should also devote resources to help improve working conditions in other sectors of their own industry. It could set aside a small part of its large strike fund to help the ushers, ticket-takers, and other stadium employees who lose their incomes when players strike. The union could help organize their minor league colleagues, most of whom will never reach the majors. Their pay scales and working conditions are almost as miserable today as they were a generation or two ago. The MLBPA should support the workers at Russell Mills in Alexander City, Alabama, which makes most major league uniforms. It is "one of the most anti-union companies around," explained Billy Tindle, secretary-treasurer of the Alabama AFL-CIO.[43] And shouldn't the game's highly paid athletes speak out against the Wilson Company's exploitation of Haitian women who, in 1994, earned $1.07 for a ten hour day (ten cents an hour) stitching baseballs? The MLBPA has demanded that the owners "open the books" so the players can scrutinize the teams' financial conditions to show how they hide their profits with bookkeeping tricks. But the union could do more to undermine the owners' attempts to drive a wedge between the players and the nation's baseball fans by explaining that the teams don't need to raise ticket or concession prices to meet the MLBPA's terms.

One lesson of the baseball players' economic success is that the best route to upward mobility for American working people—not just miners and factory workers, but secretaries, nurses, computer programmers, sales clerks, farm workers, teachers, and others—is to join a union. We don't expect to see Albert Belle, Sammy Sosa, Randy Johnson, or Greg Maddux marching in Labor Day parades singing "Solidarity Forever." But let's recognize that these men—mostly from working class backgrounds—owe their economic gains not only to natural talent and hard work, but also to their loyalty to each other and their union.

Most ballplayers probably never heard of labor leaders like John L. Lewis, Walter Reuther, Sam Gompers, Mother Jones, and Eugene Debs, but they've learned that, as the song goes, "the union makes us strong." Until more Americans learn that lesson, our nation's living standards will continue to erode.[44] Today, the public is angry with both spoiled million-dollar players and greedy owners, just as they are fed up with elected officials and corporate tycoons, as suggested by public opinion polls revealing a dramatic decline in confidence in government and business institutions. Jackie Robinson's crusade helped move the country closer to its ideals. His legacy is also to remind us of the unfinished agenda of the civil rights revolution—a more equal society for all.

Notes

1. A few players who selected number 42 as a tribute to Robinson, including Mo Vaughn, balked at giving up the number, arguing that Robinson would be remembered better by others wearing his number than by taking it out of circulation. To compromise, then-acting commissioner Bud Selig agreed to allow active players wearing number 42 to keep it for the rest of their careers.

2. Spike Lee intended to make a feature-length bio-pic about Robinson, starring Denzel Washington, but could not raise the funding.

3. In fact, the Rose Bowl Parade in Robinson's honor took place on January 1, 1998. The 1997 parade only featured a float in Robinson's honor, which was sponsored by a Los Angeles–based Jewish organization (the Museum of Tolerance), and not any organization based in Pasadena itself.

4. Major sources regarding Robinson include the following: Joseph Dorinson and Joram Warmund, eds., *Jackie Robinson: Race, Sports, and the American Dream* (Armonk, NY: M.E. Sharpe, Inc., 1998); David Falkner, *Great Time Coming: The Life of Jackie Robinson From Baseball to Birmingham* (New York: Simon & Schuster, 1995); Harvey Frommer, *Rickey & Robinson: The Men Who Broke Baseball's Color Barrier* (New York: Macmillan, 1982); Larry Moffi and Jonathan Kronstadt, *Crossing the Line: Black Major Leaguers, 1947–1959* (Iowa City: University of Iowa Press, 1994); Carl E. Prince, *Brooklyn's Dodgers: The Bums, the Borough, and the Best of Baseball* (New York: Oxford University Press, 1996); Arnold Rampersad, *Jackie Robinson: A Biography* (New York: Alfred A. Knopf, 1997); Rachel Robinson, *Jackie Robinson: An Intimate Portrait* (New York: Harry N. Abrams, 1996); Sharon Robinson, *Stealing Home: An Intimate Family Portrait by the Daughter of Jackie Robinson* (New York: HarperCollins Publishers, 1996); Jules Tygiel, ed., *The Jackie Robinson Reader* (New York: Dutton, 1997); and Jules Tygiel, *Baseball's Great Experiment: Jackie Robinson and His Legacy* (New York: Oxford University Press, 1997, expanded edition [Original edition published in 1983]). I have benefited, in particular, from conversations and correspondence with Jules Tygiel.

5. The day after President Bill Clinton joined Rachel Robinson at Shea Stadium during an April 15 Mets-Dodgers game to celebrate the fiftieth anniversary, the *New York Times* ran a long story and two photos on the front page. In contrast, the daily paper in Robinson's hometown, the *Pasadena Star-News*, relegated the story to its sports page and ran an article from the Associated Press wire service.

The *Star-News's* treatment reflects the troubled relationship between the city and its most famous resident. "If my mother and brother and sister weren't living in Pasadena," Jackie Robinson said after his playing days were over, "I would never go back. I've always felt like an intruder there—even in school. People in Pasadena were less understanding in some ways than southerners and they were more openly hostile."

In his lifetime, Jackie was never asked to serve as Grand Marshal of Pasadena's annual Tournament of Roses parade and Rose Bowl game. Pasadena's northwest neighborhood, now the heart of the city's black community, has a community center, park, and post office named after Robinson, but there is no street or school named after the city's most famous resident and, more important, Pasadena's public school system does not incorporate Robinson's life into its curriculum. There is a small plaque on the sidewalk on Pepper Street, identifying where Robinson lived as a young boy. But there is no Jackie Robinson museum where young people can learn about Robinson's upbringing, athletic exploits, or his odyssey as a sports pioneer and civil rights activist. In contrast, Baltimore turned Babe Ruth's boyhood home into a museum. The recent national hoopla over Robinson embarrassed Pasadena into erecting a statue of Jackie and Mack Robinson in front of City Hall. For many of Robinson's friends and family, however, the city's efforts are too late to redress its past mistreatment.

6. In 1944, eleven years before Rosa Parks sparked the Montgomery bus boycott, Robinson (a lieutenant in the Army) was court martialed for insisting that Fort Hood, Texas, adhere to Army orders to desegregate buses.

7. William Ladson, "Jackie Robinson Remembered," *Sport* 43, no. 1 (January 1990): 38–40.

8. Yearly newspaper references to Robinson are taken from the Nexus-Lexis database.

9. On April 6, 1987, Koppel invited Campanis, along with sportswriter Roger Kahn (author of *The Boys of Summer*) to discuss Robinson's career and his legacy to celebrate the fortieth anniversary of Robinson's breakthrough. Campanis had been Robinson's closest friend when they were teammates on the Dodgers's minor league club in Montreal. Asked about the lack of a significant number of blacks in baseball's management level, Campanis said that "they may not have some of the necessities to be, let's say, a field manager or, perhaps, a general manager." He also said, "Why are black people not good swimmers? Because they don't have the buoyancy." These remarks cost Campanis his job as the Dodgers's vice president of player personnel. They also sparked a short-lived controversy over the shortage of African Americans in baseball's management echelons.

10. Other major daily newspapers followed a similar pattern. For example, the *Philadelphia Inquirer* ran no stories mentioning Robinson from 1990 through 1993, two in 1994, three in both 1995 and 1996, twenty-one in 1997, and seven in 1998. *USA Today* averaged eight Robinson citations from 1990 through 1997, increased to seventy-seven in 1997, and fell back to eleven in 1998. The *Miami Herald* ran no stories with Robinson's name in 1990 and 1991, one in 1992, none in 1993 and 1994, two in both 1995 and 1996, six in 1997, and none in 1998. The *Boston Globe* averaged five mentions of Robinson from 1990 through 1996, peaked at thirty-seven in 1997, and fell to nine in 1998.

11. Steve Sailer, "How Jackie Robinson Desegregated America," *National Review*, April 8, 1996, 42–44.

12. In the early 1940s, for example, New York Congressman Vito Marcantonio, a member of the radical American Labor Party, introduced a resolution to investigate racial prejudice in baseball. In addition to Tygiel's book, for sources on the progressive movement's efforts to integrate major league positions, see Tom Gallagher, "Lester Rodney, the *Daily Worker*, and the Integration of Baseball," *The National Pastime: A Review of Baseball History* 19 (1999): 58–64; Chris Lamb and Glen Bleske, "Democracy on the Field: The Black Press Takes on White Baseball," *Journalism History* 9, no. 2 (Summer 1998): 27–35; Bill Weaver, "The Black Press and the Assault on Professional Baseball's Color Line, October 1945–April 1947," *Phylon* 5 (Winter 1979): 17–22

13. The play was originally staged at the Old Globe Theater in San Diego in 1992. In another attempt to repair the city's relationship with Robinson, the Pasadena Playhouse staged *Mr. Rickey Calls a Meeting* in early 1997.

14. Ethnicity and ethnic identity have played an important role throughout the history of American baseball. Prior to Robinson's arrival, for example, a few teams hired Jewish ballplayers to attract Jewish fans. A decade before Robinson reached the majors, Hank Greenberg, the Detroit Tigers slugger, faced persistent anti-Semitism from opposing players and others. Greenberg was, not coincidentally, one of the major league players most sympathetic to and supportive of Robinson. Joe DiMaggio played a similar symbolic role among Italian Americans and also had to deal with negative stereotypes about his ethnic group. See Peter Levine, *Ellis Island to Ebbets Field: Sport and the American Jewish Experience* (New York: Oxford University Press, 1992); and G. Edward White, *Creating the National Pastime: Baseball Transforms Itself, 1903–1953* (Princeton, NJ: Princeton University Press, 1996).

15. In contrast, blacks comprise only 5 percent of fans attending major league games.

16. Aaron Rosenblatt, "Negroes in Baseball: The Failure of Success," *Transaction* 3 (September 1967): 58–62. Another study found persistent though declining discrimination against black players from the 1950s through the mid-1980s. See Andrew Hanssen, "The Cost of Discrimination: A Study of Major League Baseball," *Southern Economic Journal* 64, no. 3 (1998): 603–627.

17. Richard Lapchick with David Stuckey, "Professional Sports: The Racial Report Card," in *Sport in Contemporary Society: An Anthology*, 4th ed., ed. Stanley Eitzen, (New York: St. Martin's Press, 1993). Also see Lawrence Kahn, "Discrimination in Professional Sports: A Survey of the Literature," *Industrial and Labor Relations Review* 44, no. 3 (April 1991): 28–36.

18. Dusty Baker of the San Francisco Giants, Don Baylor of the Colorado Rockies, Cito Gaston of the Toronto Blue Jays, and Felipe Alou of the Montreal Expos.

19. Another black, Leonard Coleman, served as National League President, a position he inherited from another black, former big leaguer Bill White.

20. William Dawson of Chicago and Adam Clayton Powell of New York City.

21. See John Egerton, *Speak Now Against the Day: The Generation Before the Civil Rights Movement in the South* (Chapel Hill: University of North Carolina Press, 1994); Harvard Sitkoff, *The Struggle for Black Equality: 1954–1992*, rev. ed. (New York: Hill & Wang, 1993); Richard Kluger, *Simple Justice* (New York: Vintage Books, 1975); Gunnar Myrdal, Richard Sterner, and Arnold Rose, *An American Dilemma: The Negro Problem and Modern Democracy* (New York: Harper & Row, 1944).

22. Unionized whites and blacks not only earn roughly the same wages, they both earn more than workers without union representation do. According to the Economic Policy Institute, unionized black males earn 15.1 percent more than black people in comparable nonunion jobs; for whites, the union "wage premium" is 14.9 percent more; 18.7 percent more for Latinos. See Lawrence Mishel, Jared Bernstein, and John Schmitt, *The State of Working America 1998–1999* (Ithaca, NY: Cornell University Press, 1998).

23. Douglas Massey and Nancy Denton, *American Apartheid: Segregation and the Making of the Underclass* (Cambridge, MA: Harvard University Press, 1993); Stephan Thernstrom and Abigail Thernstrom, *America in Black and White: One Nation, Indivisible* (New York: Simon & Schuster, 1997); Andrew Hacker, *Two Nations: Black and White, Separate, Hostile, Unequal* (New York: Charles Scribners' Sons, 1992); and Orlando Patterson, *The Ordeal of Integration* (Washington, DC: Civitas/Counterpoint, 1997).

24. G. William Domhoff and Richard Zweigenhaft, *Diversity in the Power Elite: Have Women and Minorities Reached the Top?* (New Haven, CT: Yale University Press, 1998).

25. Dan Gillmor and Stephen Doig, "Segregation Forever?" *American Demographics* 35 (January 1992): 35–41; Massey and Denton, *American Apartheid*; Paul Jargowsky, *Poverty and Place: Ghettos, Barrios, and the American City* (New York: Russell Sage Foundation, 1997).

26. A U.S. Census Bureau study using 1990 data found that 60 percent of black residents of metropolitan areas—compared with 26 percent of whites—lived in poverty neighborhoods (those with at least 20 percent living below the poverty line). Most poor whites live in working class or middle class neighborhoods and areas removed from the large concentrations of poor people in central cities. See "Poverty in the United States: 1990," *Current Population Reports, Population Characteristics*, Series p-20, No. 450 (Washington, DC: Bureau of the Census, 1991).

27. Jackie Robinson, *I Never Had It Made* (New York: G.P. Putnam, 1972).

28. On the business side of baseball, see John Helyar, *Lords of the Realm* (New York: Villard, 1994); and Andrew Zimbalist, *Baseball and Billions* (New York: Basic Books, 1992). Good one-volume histories of American baseball include: White, *Creating the National Pastime*; Charles Alexander, *Our Game: An American Baseball History* (New York: Henry Holt, 1991); and Benjamin G. Rader, *Baseball: A History of America's Game* (Urbana: University of Illinois Press, 1994).

29. This was true of Robinson and many of his teammates.

30. Peter O'Malley is the son of Walter O'Malley, the team owner who moved the Dodgers from Brooklyn to the West Coast.

31. In the past, team owners often named baseball parks after themselves, such as Comiskey Park in Chicago, Briggs Field in Detroit, and Busch Stadium in St. Louis. There are still some recent examples of this phenomenon, such as Turner Field in Atlanta and Jacobs Field in Cleveland.

32. The first major strike occurred in 1972, lasting for 86 games.

33. Flood wrote a letter to Commissioner Bowie Kuhn that said, in part: "After twelve years in the major leagues, I do not feel that I am a piece of property to be bought and sold irrespective of my wishes." Flood filed a $1.4 million suit against Kuhn, the league presidents, and the twenty-four team owners. He was attacked in the press as being ungrateful for the fame and money baseball had brought him. Flood's challenge to baseball's establishment destroyed his career and his financial situation. The case dragged on for three years before reaching the U.S. Supreme Court. Close to bankruptcy, Flood signed a contract with the Washington Senators, but played only thirteen games, during which he received several death threats, and then quit. Flood later said: "I am pleased that God made my skin black, but I wish He had made it thicker." The discussion of Flood and the reserve clause draws on Moffi and Kronstadt, *Crossing the Line*; White, *Creating the National Pastime*; Alexander, *Our Game*; and Zimbalist, *Baseball and Billions*.

34. Some observers attribute the ballplayers' rising pay scale to supply-and-demand economics. In this view, the nation's 760 major leaguers are highly skilled, almost irreplaceable athletes, which gives them enormous leverage at contract time. This "labor shortage" theory may apply to the few dozen superstars and the next hundred top players—those with high name recognition, a big following of fans, and a consistent track record of high-quality performance. Even so, the majority of major leaguers are journeyman ballplayers who last less than five years in the majors. Despite their high yearly salaries, they have little long-term job security. Unless they have a college education and another occupation to fall back on, their economic future is not as secure as the glamour of their baseball careers.

35. Robert Frank and Philip Cook, *The Winner Take All Society: Why the Few at the Top Get So Much More Than Rest of Us* (New York: Penguin USA, 1996).

36. This doesn't mean that if more American workers were unionized, their pay scales would be even close to those of major league players. It does mean, however, that their pay and benefits would increase, as the figures on the union "wage premium" indicate.

37. Melvin Oliver and Thomas Shapiro, *Black Wealth/White Wealth* (New York: Routledge, 1995).

38. Economic trends are drawn from the following: Edward N. Wolff, *Top Heavy: A Study of the Increasing Inequality of Wealth in America* (New York: Twentieth Century Fund, 1995); John E. Schwarz, *Illusions of Opportunity: The American Dream in Question* (New York: W.W. Norton, 1997); Frank Levy, *The New Dollars and Dreams: American Incomes and Economic Change* (New York: Russell Sage Foundation, 1998); Mishal, Bernstein, and Schmitt, *The State of Working America*; and Reporters of the *New York Times, The Downsizing of America* (New York: Times Books, 1996).

39. Baseball owners play a similar game of playing cities and states against each other to get the best deal to construct new ballparks. And like the flight of business from central cities, a number of major league ballparks have been built in the suburbs. See Mark S. Rosentraub, *Major League Losers: The Real Cost of Sports and Who's Paying for It* (New York: Basic Books, 1997).

40. The U.S. government promoted this flight with national tax policies that encouraged businesses to relocate to new sites (rather than modernizing and expanding their plants and equipment in cities) and with foreign policies that propped up Third World governments that suppress dissent.

41. Robert Peterson, *Only the Ball Was White* (Englewood Cliffs, NJ: Prentice Hall, 1970). The revival of scholarship about the Negro Leagues began with Donn Rogosin, *Invisible Men: Life in Baseball's Negro Leagues* (New York: Atheneum, 1983). Subsequently, there have been many biographies and autobiographies of Negro League players, histories of Negro League teams and their owners, and analyses of other aspects of the Negro Leagues. The most comprehensive source on the Negro Leagues is Dick Clark and Larry Lester, eds., *The Negro Leagues Book* (Cleveland: The Society of American Baseball Research, 1994).

42. See Arnold Rampersad, *Jackie Robinson: A Biography* (New York: Alfred A. Knopf, 1997), 320ff.

43. This information was gathered for several articles about the players' union, including Peter Dreier and Kelly Candaele, "Pitchers and Pickets: Baseball's Labor Day Lessons," *Boston Sunday Globe* (September 4, 1994); and Kelly Candaele and Peter Dreier, "Baseball Players Must Act Like a Labor Union," *Los Angeles Times*, Opinion section (May 19, 1996).

44. In fact, surveys show that a majority of American employees want union representation. But they won't vote for a union if they feel their jobs are at stake. Any employer with a clever labor attorney can stall union elections, giving the boss enough time to scare the living daylights out of potential recruits. And according to one study, one in ten workers involved in an organizing drive is fired. The lucky ones get back pay and reinstatement five years after the fact. American employers can require workers to attend meetings on work time where company managers and consultants give antiunion speeches, show antiunion films, and distribute anti-union literature. By contrast, unions have no equivalent rights of access to employees. To reach them, union organizers frequently must visit their homes or hold secret meetings. The rules are stacked against workers, making it extremely difficult for even the most committed and talented organizers and workers to win union elections. Our nation's cumbersome labor laws deprive workers of elementary rights of free speech and assembly in an atmosphere free of intimidation. Fixing these crusty laws is key to providing American workers a democratic voice in the workplace. Reforming the nation's outdated labor laws should also be a key part of the progressive agenda for racial progress.

3

THE BEAUTY OF THE GAME

Dusty Baker

THOSE OF US IN BASEBALL HAVE SIMILAR STORIES BUT THEY ARE ALSO ALL A BIT DIFFER-
ent, and that's what makes baseball so beautiful. I really didn't grow up wanting
to be a baseball player—I just wanted to be a player. That's why I couldn't make
up my mind which sport I was going to play as a kid. So I played them all.

On the baseball field my dad was my little league coach. But when I was
eight years old, he cut me from his team, saying I had a bad attitude. Then he
cut me when I was nine, because I didn't learn quickly enough. And he cut me
again when I was ten. At that time I didn't know or think about the importance
of practice—you know, doing your homework, like one does in school, in order
to improve yourself.

At that time I had a number of heroes—I had Tommy Davis in baseball, who
wore number twelve and played with the Dodgers. I had Elgin Baylor, who
played with the Lakers. Nate Thurman played with the Golden State Warriors,
which were then the San Francisco Warriors. I had Bob Hayes in track and Jim
Brown in football. I wore their respective numbers, and played all their sports
when I was young. I dreamed of being a professional, and if I was going to be a
professional baseball player I was going to play for the Dodgers and I was going
to wear number twelve, and play left field, and I was going to bat third. It's
strange how as a kid you typically play a hero, and you dream about playing
somewhere in the big leagues.

But my story was somewhat different. I might have had a dream but I had no
clue that I would actually end up playing where my baseball hero played, wearing his number, meeting him, becoming good friends with him, and still wearing his number to this day. I was supposed to play basketball at Santa Clara
University, or at some other college, but my parents divorced and I was the
oldest of five. So I kind of sneaked away.

I was a twenty-fifth-round baseball draft choice when my mom and I signed
with the Atlanta Braves in 1967. They had flown me to Los Angeles, where they
were playing the Dodgers at the time. I said my prayers the night before because
I didn't know what to do. I remember that day, working out with the Braves. I

was eighteen years old and at Dodgers Stadium. I had no number on my back, and I had a little gym bag. Everybody on the team was there. The kids in the stands were calling out, "Hey no-number, what's your name?" I was going to tell them, but I knew they wouldn't know me. One person who did know me, though, was Bob Kennedy, who was observing all of this from his position as third base coach.

Paul Richards, the Braves general manager at that time, called my mom and me up to his room. I wasn't sure what I was going to do. He said he had to take a shower, and he threw this wad of money with a big rubber band around it on the dresser. I was looking at this bundle and thinking, "Damn, that's a lot of money." So, I ended up signing. It was a matter of faith that I signed. That's what baseball and life are all about, really. We're here on faith; we think we know what's going to happen, we think we know where we're going, but we really don't until we get there. You have to keep going in a positive direction until you see where you're headed.

My dad didn't like it too much that I signed. When I got back that winter, he took my mom and me to court. We had a dispute over the child prodigy law, which says that your parents can't spend your money. But I couldn't spend my money, either, unless I attended college, which my parents were big on. I was fortunate to have great parents, who pushed me to take Spanish and algebra and geometry, and all the tough courses, throughout high school. I told my mother, "I don't want to be this genius you want me to be."

I went into Double A baseball, and played my first game in Little Rock, Arkansas, and then went to Austin, Texas, our home base. This was a very, very rough time; tensions were high. The Vietnam War issue was hot, for example. I had been living in Sacramento, and I would go to San Francisco, to the Haight-Ashbury, to Golden Gate Park, to the Fillmore West, when those places were alive with protest. The Black Panthers were strong in Berkeley and Oakland. There was a lot of turmoil, unrest, and nonconformity, especially around race issues. I remember hearing about the racial segregationists, Lester Maddox and George Wallace. And, here I was, eighteen years old, away from home, and in the Deep South.

On my first day in Little Rock, I dropped the first fly ball hit to me. Some people watching began calling me all these names. I thought I'd been called some names before but I never heard names like these. Apparently these fans were from a nearby mental institution, which arranged a trip for them every Thursday. But even so, they were bad. And I got called other names, too, by people who were not insane. I began to realize that I was really in the South now, in the Deep South. I realized what had happened, and what I had done. Cito Gaston came over, seeing that I was upset, and he said, "Hey, man, I'll take care of you. Come hang with me."

There was no turning back. At that time there was a Jim Thorpe law that said if you were a professional in one sport you were a professional in every sport. You couldn't play professional baseball and also go to college and play basketball. So that was a major decision for me. I guess I had more of a negative motivation: I just didn't want my dad's opposition to baseball to be right. I didn't want to go home and be a failure and have somebody tell me, "I told you so." So I worked hard and was fortunate to get to the big leagues the next year, in 1968.

To tell you the truth, baseball was not my first choice. Baseball was hard for me compared to the other sports. I had to practice more to accomplish the same thing. I didn't love baseball at the time. I was playing for the wrong reason: I was playing for the money. That's why I signed. Then in my second year in professional baseball, Orlando Cepeda was traded to the Braves. Orlando, Hank Aaron, Rico Carty, Clete Boyer, Bob Tilden, Joe Pepitone—these were some of the guys I played with. These guys took me under their wing. Even back on the day I signed with the Braves, Hank Aaron told my mother that if I had enough confidence that I could get to the big leagues by the time my class graduated from college, then sign. If not, then I should attend college.

Later, Orlando let me hang with him every day. The first time I went to his room I discovered that Orlando was a real dude, with all these congas and bongos. He was sharp. He taught me how to dress. So Orlando says, "Hey man, come to the club with me tonight."

I said, "You mean it?"

He said, "Yeah."

So I think, damn, I'm going out with Orlando Cepeda. I just watched him on television the year before, when I was in high school, and now this. So I went down to his room and I'm ready to go. He says, "I changed my mind. You can't go."

I said, "What do you mean I can't go, man?" I was disappointed: I had called home and told my homeboys I was going out with Orlando that night.

Then he gave me this book and said, "I want you to read this book." Read a book? Man, you sound like my mama. Read a book? I'm ready to go party. He said, "You read this book and you report back to me tomorrow and tell me what it says. Then you can go out with me."

The book he gave me was *The Power of Positive Thinking*, by Norman Vincent Peale. I had no idea what it was about. But it meant so much to me at the time. I really didn't know that this and similar books would help me later on in life and in my career—that they would help me be positive and have faith, and allow me to call upon a Higher Power to help me not only in my game but in my life. I thank Orlando and Hank. That's the beauty of the game. When they take a young kid in and make him feel at home, make him feel comfortable, make him feel needed and wanted, it can take you a very, very long way. That's what happened to me.

After that, Orlando left the team and things got a little tough. Hank also left, and things got even tougher. You know, we were always partners, we were always friends. Orlando had taken me to Puerto Rico to play on his team, and I also played in Venezuela and Mexico. Aside from the Latinos, I was the only one who knew how to speak Spanish, and I was thanking my mom for that. Culturally, the way I was raised in different environments, really helped me in baseball. Now I get paid to speak to different groups about diversity, about how to get different races to get along. But this is nothing more than what we went through in baseball. Nothing more than going to Puerto Rico or to Mexico. Nothing more than being raised in a black, mostly Latino neighborhood in Riverside and then moving to an almost all-white environment in Sacramento, where there were only two blacks in my high school: me and my brother.

When I got to baseball, I could call upon my own past to determine exactly how to be and how not to be. Sometimes you have to play a political game you'd rather not play. Sometimes you have to keep your mouth shut when you don't want to. Other times, when somebody is intruding on your inner dignity, you have to take the risk, and do whatever you feel, as a man, you have to do to stand up for yourself.

Baseball was almost taken away from me. I used to think that working out was a matter of playing a little basketball. If I wanted to work out I'd play basketball for two or three hours. But then I hurt my leg in the winter playing basketball, and I had a serious knee operation the first year I got to the Dodgers. I was tired of being in the South and was happy to be back out West. But I wasn't in Los Angeles a week when I hurt my leg playing basketball. And that's when I really fell in love with baseball: when it was almost taken away from me. You never appreciate what you have until it's almost taken from you, and my career almost went down the drain. So, I was very fortunate to come back and have a great career in Los Angeles.

Later, I came to the Giants and then played with the Athletics. Bill Rigney was mainly responsible for getting me on the A's for the last two years of my career. I remember him watching me in spring training and saying, "Hey, you can still hit." This is, again, the beauty of the game. You meet great people along the way.

When my playing career ended, I really didn't want to get into coaching or managing. But then, all of a sudden I faced divorce—just like my mom and dad—and so I came back to northern California. At that time, Al Campanis made some derogatory racial remarks on television that surprised all of us. Campanis had been one of the best men I'd met in the game. He seemed to be among the fairest, especially when it came to race relations and dealing with minorities. But when Al said those things, all of a sudden organized baseball started looking for minorities to fill some positions. At the winter meeting in Dallas, Bob Kennedy came up to me and said, "Remember me?"

I said, "Yes sir, you're Bob Kennedy."

He said, "No, do you really remember me? Because I'm the man twenty years ago who talked Paul Richards into signing you and giving you more money when you were a twenty-fifth-round draft choice. Now, I'm the same man who thinks you would be a very good coach."

And I said, "Thanks." It had come full circle. I didn't know that this man knew me, I didn't know he knew anything about me.

Before making my decision, my brother and I went to Lake Arrowhead so I could decide what I wanted to do. So I'm checking into the hotel, and I find former Giants owner Bob Lurie right behind me in line, and he says "Dusty, you need to come join us."

I turn around and I said, "Man, what are you doing here?"

He says, "What are you doing here?"

So, I went and called my dad. I said, "Pops, what do you think?"

He says, "Son, that's a pretty good sign. You got this guy right in line behind you. That's a sign from God, even if it's not one I wanted to see." So that's how I made my decision and that's why I went into coaching, and then into managing.

I'm sometimes asked why many ballplayers want to play for me. Well, I don't know if they do. But in dealing with my players I just try to recall some things from my life as a young player, and try not to forget how hard the game is, even though they make it look easy. I expect a lot but I also realize that in this generation, a number of guys have come from single-parent homes, where their mothers and fathers might have been quarreling with each other, and where the kids are caught in the middle. They might have been lied to by their parents or others along the way, and been promised things that never happened. Most of them distrust authority figures. So I came up with a simple rule. Just don't lie to me. There's a good chance I've already tried any number of things they might try to pull on me. The next thing I tell them is to show up at work on time, and while at work, give me all you've got—no alibis, no excuses, just come out and play. I just try to understand the best I can, and remember how I felt, and how I wanted to be treated. I learned from the managers I played under, and some taught me as much about how not to behave with the players as anything else.

The game of baseball has remained basically the same over the years. But one thing that's a bit different is the reduced competition for the jobs. When I first came into baseball there were only sixteen teams, and more Americans playing baseball, proportionally, than now. You couldn't get hurt, or someone would take your job. People don't realize how sacred those positions were at that time. The days of Wally Pipp, who lost his job to Lou Gehrig, are gone. Multiyear contracts changed that, as compared to the old one-year contracts, when you could be gone after a year. And I don't mind the big money. I think the players should make big money. But all I ask of my players is that they try to earn the money. Give me 100 percent. The money doesn't make you play any better. Once I fell in love with baseball, I began to see things I had never seen before. Hank and Orlando used to say to me, "Do you see it?" And I'd say, "Oh yeah, I see it." But I didn't really see anything. The key is to have as much total recall as you can, to retain what you're taught. That's the key to success. If you retain what's taught, then someday you'll understand and apply it.

When I first came up, the players hung out with each other more. Most of the black players couldn't stay in the same hotels as the white players. We had to depend on other black and Latino players to take us out in the town so that we could feel safe. You end up in the wrong area in some of these towns, and you'd meet people who felt it was their God-given right to direct you back to the other part of town with their shoe in your butt. At that time, everybody took care of each other. Orlando Cepeda took care of me. Joe Morgan took care of young players in Cincinnati. And Billy Williams in Chicago. And Cleon Jones and Tommy Agee in New York.

But now I can't really blame the current players for having different attitudes. Today there's so much more individualism in society. The slogan of the 1980s was to take care of number one. Screw everyone else. Look out for yourself. So people have been trained to have this kind of attitude and it can make my job tough. I have to try to deal with selfishness sometimes. But there are still lots of good guys around. I try to tell my players not to "possess" the knowledge they have because it's not theirs to possess. Give it to somebody the way it was given to you. Pass it on.

People have asked me about Jackie Robinson's legacy. In 1998, Jackie's number was retired for all major league teams. But a lot of modern baseball players, including black players, apparently didn't know who Jackie Robinson was. It's a problem. More players now know about Robinson but most have still never heard of Curt Flood, despite his contributions to baseball and the players' standard of living. The problem is that organized baseball does a poor job of teaching players about baseball history. We need some history classes in baseball. If players are not taught, then how are they supposed to know? They wouldn't unless they had parents who are aware of it, such as mine, who used to talk at home about Robinson's accomplishments. But not that many people have parents like that.

In the same vein, I've been asked about Joe Morgan's recent article, which criticized organized baseball for ignoring a generation of inner-city, predominantly African-American, kids as ballplayers and fans. Morgan believes that we're going to have increasing difficulty not merely recruiting blacks as managers, coaches, and executives but also as players. Too many inner-city kids are drawn to other sports, or simply ignored. Morgan is rightfully concerned about keeping the promise baseball made to Jackie Robinson. Unfortunately, sometimes when you're an African American and you say what's on your mind, especially if it's your version of the truth, you're called "angry" or are accused of "sour grapes" or of having "a chip on your shoulder."

But sometimes people need to hear the truth. Morgan's concern makes all the sense in the world to me. I know, I lived that reality once myself. And history repeats itself especially if people don't study it and prevent these things from happening again. As Morgan suggests, city kids are not playing baseball nearly as much. Part of it is economics, and a lot of the money is going to build talent in Latin America, where you can sign kids for very little. That's part of it, and the rest of it is that we might not want to face the truth about certain racial and economic realities, because you're not going to be very popular saying it. And if you're black and saying it, you risk being written off as a troublemaker. But I'm glad that Joe Morgan is talking about it; I think it's about time.

When I first started coaching, Bill Rigney came up to me and said, "You won't be coaching long."

And, I'm saying to myself, "Damn, how does he know?"

And then he says, "You're too bright and too ambitious to be doing this for too long." He meant that I'd be managing soon. Baseball has had some problems, but I marvel sometimes about everything that has happened to me in the game. Baseball doesn't owe me anything. I owe baseball. It's a beautiful game. I try to tell my players to respect the game, to respect what they're doing. Enjoy yourself while you're here. Work as hard as you can while you're here. Enjoy the company and friends you're going to make in baseball because they are going to be some lifelong friends. Guys like Orlando Cepeda and Bill Rigney—both very much responsible for me being in baseball and for me being where I am in the game.

4

SAMMY SOSA MEETS HORATIO ALGER

Latin Ballplayers and the American Success Myth

Samuel O. Regalado

In 1867, Horatio Alger, the famed novelist, saw the release of his "Ragged Dick" series. And in one of his stories, *Fame and Fortune*, the author wrote that boys who sold newspapers and shined shoes were, at this level, upon the first rungs of the tall ladder of success. Indeed, with enterprise, hard work, and perseverance, triumph—according to Alger—was inevitable; a virtual certainty. These, and other tales, became a banner for the American prototype of the nineteenth century.

Though the author died in 1893, his idealism resonated well beyond his anticipated audience. And one of those areas of indirect impact was in the Caribbean. Alger, of course, never did visit Latin America during his lifetime. Nor is it likely that any of Alger's works ever made it into the hands of Caribbean youth of that era or of Sammy Sosa's generation. Yet, there existed a relationship between the two in that of the idealist and ideals. For it was very much the myth of "rags-to-riches" success, which Alger and his contemporaries promoted, that the ball-playing Latin youth of the twentieth century came to adopt in their own desire to climb baseball's ladder into the professional diamonds of El Norte. Long before Alger penned his first novel in 1867, generations of Americans accepted the national myth of opportunity and success. The Puritans' "City Upon the Hill" premonitions about America foreshadowed an avalanche of rhetoric that advanced the notion of unlimited possibility in the New World.[1] But it was the precocious Horatio Alger, a minister turned writer, who accelerated this myth.

Born in 1834, Alger grew up during one of the country's most difficult periods—amid the antebellum regional conflict, the slavery abolition issue, and the Civil War. Moreover, the unsettling Reconstruction period was overshadowed only by the rise of large-scale industrialization, which among other things, bred institutions and ideologies that challenged long-held traditions of individualism. The corporate atmosphere of that era, to a certain extent, ran counter to the entrepreneurial spirit that attracted people like Alger.[2] Having abandoned the cloth in 1864, the Massachusetts-born writer sought sanctuary in those traits that he believed stressed enterprise and rewards. Hence, Alger's theme in his 119 books was consistent: mixing hard work and perseverance was the chemistry for success.

The materialistic philosophies of his era, to be sure, accentuated these beliefs. Rewards, to many, were no sheer accident. After all, did not Andrew Carnegie, a poor Scottish immigrant, come to dominate the steel industry? Did not Richard Kyle Fox appear on American shores with only five dollars, then take the *National Police Gazette* and make it one of the most popular journals of its day? And what of the great boxer John L. Sullivan? Who better to provide evidence of tenacity and achievement? His efforts, like others in his time, were proof that even the humble could rise to the level of champion in America.[3]

Professional sports, of course, had long been regarded as a symbol of democratic opportunity. In theory, at least, ethnic background, skin color, and position in society took a back seat to talent. Men, they felt, competed on an equal basis and, in turn, paved a path out of poverty by virtue of their skill and determination. And over and over, Americans lauded their sports for this reason. Baseball, of course, held a special position among mainstream Americans. Its rise to prominence in the late nineteenth century carried with it all of the elements of the American myth of opportunity. "I tell you that baseball is the very watchword for democracy," bellowed one-time Pennsylvania governor John K. Tener in that era.[4]

Hence, it seemed no great surprise that, by then, a large number of baseball players were of Irish and German ancestry—mostly children of poor immigrants.[5] Blacks, of course, also heeded the call, but learned the hard way that the myth of egalitarianism in American sport was, indeed, a myth. The opportunity to succeed in professional sports, sadly, did not apply to them.

Still, in an age when the media became the mass media, when nationalistic promoters saturated the global public with tales of opportunity in America, and when novels such as those written by Alger offered a chemistry for success in the land of *E Pluribus Unum*, consumers of this marketing who lived in less than desirable circumstances were taken in by the specter of fame and achievement. Moreover, the notion that Americans valued merit added to their excitement and hope.

By the 1890s, expansionists trumpeted this myth to the regions that had come under American hegemony. Though the chief goals in these neocolonial ventures were to secure military bases as a means to promote American economic interests, American values, too, were imported. A form of cultural imperialism to some people, Latinos—while harboring spiteful attitudes toward their occupiers—were also intrigued with the wealth one might achieve using the tools outlined by Alger. Indeed, if hard work was the sole criteria to achieve a goal, lower-income Latins were already masters of that virtue. Unfortunately for many of them, rewards for their enterprise were rarely forthcoming. But, in America, many conceivably reasoned that even a shoeshine boy could flourish.

Overall, the pitch of promoting success succeeded. Immigrants poured into the nation between the 1880s and 1920s. Most were peasants who were poor, unemployed, or victims of religious or political persecution. Many turned to America as a sanctuary of hope. These practical concerns, coupled with the American mystique of uninhibited opportunity, provided a magnet too great to resist. Hence, they came from Japan, the Baltic, Eastern and Southern Europe to work in the fields, coal mines, steel mills, and textile industries. And some even came from the ball fields of Latin America.

From 1911, Latinos began to appear in the majors with minimal regularity. Driven by what Octavio "Cookie" Rojas called their "special hunger," they bought into the American pitch of achieving success by virtue of merit. These were the Horatio Alger characters of the twentieth century. And, while only light-skinned Latinos donned big league uniforms prior to 1947, Jackie Robinson's heroics thereafter brought baseball considerably closer to the description that, generations earlier, Tener had given it. And Robinson's accomplishment also had an important fallout in the Caribbean and Mexico, for Latinos of color now had the opportunity to join the ranks of achievers.

If poverty ranked high as a "push" factor for immigrants to leave their homelands for America, the "pull" was, among other things, the myth, which by its very definition held the promise of financial security and national prestige. For the prospective ballplayer, success in baseball, accompanied by achievement in the "city upon a hill," also fueled his Latino incentive. The United States, for many of them, was the place where dreams became real. "This was something I thought about, dreamed about, since I was a little boy playing baseball on the field on my father's farm," claimed Cuban Tony Oliva in 1961. "And now, here I was, actually going to America to become a professional baseball player."[6]

But racial discrimination was also real in the land of democracy. Since 1896 racial segregation was legal. But it did not take a law to make it perfectly clear to black Latins that, in certain areas, they were not wanted. Baseball did not want them either, until after 1947. And in the many regions where they commenced their careers, the welcome mat was also not always forthcoming. This was the era of civil rights clashes, a period when resistance to racial integration was as intense as those who wanted to eliminate it. And for Latins who bought into the myth, their level of tenacity, after their arrival, faced several stern tests.

"Wherever I looked during the frequent bus stops in Mississippi, Alabama, Georgia, and Florida there was always a sign that I couldn't read but which I was beginning to grasp the awesome power of," recalled Dominican Felipe Alou of his early days in the United States. "It screamed at me from everywhere: COLORED."

Like Alou, Puerto Rican Felix Mantilla also learned some hard lessons. "I remember times when the white players used to go to the good hotels and we had to find some flea bag somewhere to stay."

And Panamanian Manny Sanguillen said, "I tried to stay at the Howard Johnson's in Bradenton, Florida, and they told me I had to have a letter from the governor of the state."[7]

The racial components compounded their struggle to adapt to other facets of American culture. Moreover, the inability to communicate in English magnified their already isolated circumstances. "It was a unique sensation to realize that I was in a land I had heard so much about but which held not a single known friend," Felipe Alou remembered.

"I couldn't speak English. Not to speak the language . . . that is a terrible problem. Not to speak the language meant you were different," said Roberto Clemente.[8] And that difference served to fuel the aching loneliness that haunted all incoming Latinos.

Latin players, to be sure, rarely landed in a town that held vestiges of Spanish-speaking culture. And this disadvantage set them apart from other newcomers to the United States—most of whom gravitated to enclaves that housed others like themselves. The Little Italys, Chinatowns, Japantowns, and other such ethnic neighborhoods, came into existence for two chief reasons: to offset the racial discrimination these groups encountered from mainstream Americans, and as a means to re-create some semblance of the Old World and its folkways. They were sanctuaries that gave comfort and security to their inhabitants while on a foreign soil. Sadly, for the Latin players, this degree of comfort was all too rare. For they could not find fried bananas in Yakima, Washington; salsa in Danville, Virginia; or a copy of *El Mundo* in Butte, Montana.

It was not uncommon for Latins, while in the minor leagues, to sometimes not speak to their teammates for entire seasons, because of language difficulties. And not until the mid- to late-1970s did major league clubs begin using programs designed to orient incoming prospects. "I had no one to talk to," said Tony Taylor about his 1954 initiation to America via the minor leagues in a small Texas town. "The only English word I knew was 'okay,' and I would order meals by pointing at the food." He went on to say, "If I had ten more dollars I would have quit. I was so homesick. But the fare to Havana was seventy-two dollars. I looked in my pocket. I had only sixty-two dollars so I stayed."[9] And, eventually, he enjoyed nineteen years in the big leagues.

The circumstances were anything but easy for those who persevered. Their determination, however, was evident. "I knew it was going to take a lot of hard work, desire, and determination to succeed," said Dominican Manny Mota.

"When I came to the United States to play professional baseball, I wanted something that nobody was going to give me. I had to go and get it myself."[10] And he did, to the tune of twenty years in the majors. And as a big leaguer, Mota set the all-time record for career pinch hits.

And others, like Juan Marichal, Orlando Cepeda, Miguel Cuellar, Fernando Valenzuela, Tony Perez, Tony Oliva, to name a few, all overcame humble beginnings and a difficult adaptation to a foreign land to triumph in the United States. By the mid-1990s, Latins captured seventeen batting titles, seven Most Valuable Player awards, three Cy Young awards, countless Gold Glove awards, and proudly displayed five of their own in America's Baseball Hall of Fame.

And then in 1998, there was Sammy Sosa. His climb to the top was the classic Horatio Alger tale. As a boy he shined shoes and sold oranges to help his family survive. Later, still malnourished, he showed up for his tryout with a borrowed uniform and holes in his spikes. After reaching the majors, he worked hard to polish his game. And, after having launched sixty-six home runs, he rushed home to his hurricane-torn country with supplies for the needy. No better prototype could exist for the American myth of yesteryear.

So Horatio Alger, meet Sammy Sosa, for it is Sosa, his cultural peers, and their predecessors who were all, in many respects, the shoeshine boys of your myth. And despite the obstacles, it is—and was—they who, through their hard work, courage, and tenacity, turned that myth into reality.

Notes

1. Richard Weiss, *The American Myth of Success: From Horatio Alger to Norman Vincent Peale* (New York: Basic Books, 1969), 4–5.

2. Ibid., 114–115.

3. Irvin G. Wyllie, *The Self-Made Man in America* (New York: Free Press, 1954), 4–5; Michael T. Isenberg, *John L. Sullivan and His America* (Urbana: University of Illinois Press, 1988), 93–94.

4. Harold Seymour, *Baseball: The Early Years* (New York: Oxford University Press, 1989), 83.

5. Benjamin G. Rader, *American Sports: From the Age of Folk Games to the Age of Spectators* (Englewood Cliffs, NJ: Prentice-Hall, 1983).

6. Samuel O. Regalado, *Viva Baseball: Latin Major Leaguers and Their Special Hunger* (Urbana: University of Illinois Press, 1998).

7. Ibid., on Alou, 79; on Sanguillen, 80.

8. Ibid., 91.

9. Ibid., 96.

10. Ibid., 2.

5

From Hardball to Hard Time and Back

Orlando Cepeda, with Herb Fagen

A CAPACITY CROWD OF 62,056 FILLED SAN FRANCISCO'S CANDLESTICK PARK FOR THE *third game of the National League Championship Series {in 1989} between the Chicago Cubs and the San Francisco Giants. The series was tied at a game apiece. Manager Roger Craig's Giants were battling for their first National League flag since 1962.*

A fifty-two-year-old man walked slowly to the mound to throw out the ceremonial first pitch. When the Giants last played in a World Series in 1962, Orlando Cepeda had been one of baseball's frontline stars, the inimitable "Baby Bull," San Francisco's very own, who just a year earlier had paced the National League with forty-six home runs and a still-standing team record of 142 runs batted in.

Since then the vagaries of life had led him through the best of times and the worst of times. He had known wealth and fame, a celebrity status only few attain. He had also known disgrace and degradation as a fallen baseball hero, a tarnished idol.

From the late 1950s through the 1960s he was one of baseball's very best, the only man in the game's history to be unanimously chosen both Rookie of the Year and League MVP. But by the late 1970s and into much of the 1980s, he was an outcast here at home and a pariah in his native Puerto Rico. His life had come full circle, from hardball on the baseball diamond to hard time in a minimum-security prison. He had lost everything: money, pride, family, dignity. He said publicly that he hated baseball, that he wanted no part of it anymore. But privately, it meant everything to him. It always had and always would.

Now, on this night, the cheers from the stands brought tears to his eyes. The Baby Bull was back, and the partisan crowd of more than 60,000 welcomed him home in thunderous ovation. He thought about many things: his mother, Carmen, whom he had so adored; his father, Perucho, his hero and perhaps the greatest Puerto Rican baseball player of them all; his wife, Mirian, who stuck with him through the hard times with love and devotion; and his Buddhist faith, the spiritual force that helped soothe his pain.

When he'd begun practicing Buddhism in 1985, his friend and mentor Al Albergate told him that some day it would all turn around, that he'd be back in baseball and he'd hear those cheers once again. He could hear them now.

Today Orlando Cepeda is a contented man, at peace with himself and the world. His work as community-relations ambassador for the San Francisco Giants has earned him respect and admiration throughout the Bay Area of Northern California and in schools, communities, and neighborhoods the country over. {And in 1999, the Veteran's Committee elected Cepeda to the Baseball Hall of Fame. Here's part of his story.}

The Santurce Crabbers [in my native Puerto Rico] were a great team. [In 1953] I was just a kid working out with ballplayers who were like gods to me. In addition to [Willie] Mays and [Roberto] Clemente there was George Crowe of the Milwaukee Braves at first; Don Zimmer, a scrappy young shortstop and second baseman with the Brooklyn Dodgers; catcher Harry Chiti of the Chicago Cubs; and Bob Thurman, a veteran of the Negro Leagues who had joined the Cincinnati Reds in 1955.

The pitching staff was anchored by my boyhood hero, Ruben Gomez. Ruben still remains the winningest pitcher in Puerto Rican history, recording 174 winter league victories over twenty-nine seasons; and Sad Sam Jones, soon to become the strikeout king of the National League. He had one of the most wicked curveballs I ever saw, though I learned to hit him rather well.

I was Perucho Cepeda's son, and I was learning from some of the best in the business. For three months my father followed me from game to game. He made sure I went to school, and before every game he'd meet me at the ballpark with my uniform.

Pete [Zorilla, the Santurce owner] had taken me under his wing. A mentor and sponsor in the best sense, he convinced my parents that he could arrange for me to have a tryout with the New York Giants along with four other promising Puerto Rican youngsters. He would enclose a letter to the Giants promising each of us $500 if the Giants signed us. If we weren't signed, we would return home.

Five hundred dollars doesn't seem like much in today's millionaire market. But for a seventeen-year-old from the Puerto Rican slums, it seemed like a million dollars. Perucho agreed to let me go, somewhat reluctantly at first. He knew I had ability and the necessary baseball tools. But perhaps I had his temper, too. I would be playing baseball, but the culture and the language were different. How would I handle the racism and bigotry that was certain to come my way?

One thing was uppermost in his mind. If I could cut it, professional baseball in the United States offered me an opportunity to escape the slums and poverty of the Puerto Rican ghetto.

My father's health was failing. The malaria had taken a huge toll on him. He was stubborn and didn't take his medicine regularly. He was a strong man, he reasoned, and he could survive without medication. He had always survived the toughest of times.

Perucho had never been able to shake his shadow. He was caught in a trap. I watched as my father grew old before his time. But maybe I could escape. Perucho gave me his blessing. I hugged and kissed my parents goodbye at the San Juan Airport. Many things were on my mind.

In today's world of jet airliners and supersonic travel, a flight from San Juan, Puerto Rico, to Miami would hardly merit a mention. So it might be difficult to imagine what it was like for a group of five kids whose only world had been the Puerto Rican slums and barrios.

The flight to Miami seemed to take forever, though it was just a four-hour flight then. I was frightened. There would be language and cultural barriers to tackle. My father's fears of racism now seemed very real to me. How would I handle it? But the plane ride went well, and we arrived in Miami on time.

Then the fun started. We missed our bus. Roberto [Clemente] had to report immediately to Fort Myers to join the Pirates' training camp. So five wide-eyed Puerto Rican kids were left to fend for themselves. We asked a guy to phone the Giants' minor league camp in Melbourne, but he refused. Finally, someone at the Greyhound station called the police. This was the segregated South, and civil rights legislation was still a decade away. A few black officers arrived to escort us to the spring training barracks.

We arrived in Melbourne at 4:30 in the morning, dead tired from lack of sleep. We managed to close our eyes for two hours. Then we were suddenly shaken out of our beds. It seems that we were deposited in the white section of the barracks in the early morning hours. We were told to move promptly to the black quarters on the second floor and far to the corner.

My biggest obstacle was language. When I arrived in the States, I knew only one word that could pass for English, and that one word was *beisbol*. I don't think people can really grasp the difficulty of coming from a Latin country to play baseball in the United States back then. Today it's a lot easier. Then it was close to impossible. But if you made it, you would have more than you could ever have at home.

Dave [Garcia] and Alex Pompez were the only people who spoke fluent Spanish in the entire camp. Dave was in my corner all the way, and he helped all the Latin ballplayers. When we'd get down or lonely, he'd come up to our rooms and do card tricks, anything to take our minds off our problems. I hoped that Dave would take me to Mayfield with him. What I didn't know was that black ballplayers were not allowed to play in the Kitty League.

As I understand it, Dave even suggested to Jack Schwarz that because Dave spoke fluent Spanish and I had a Latin name, maybe Orlando could then be a dark-skinned Spaniard. It didn't work. Instead, Schwarz told Dave that there was an independent club in Salem, Virginia, that he was talking to about me and that he should keep me for a few days until something might be arranged. Dave told the manager at Salem, John Crosswhite, that I could play, that I could run, hit and throw. Crosswhite told him to send me up to him. Here's how Dave tells the story:

> Jack Schwarz told me to go to Cepeda's room and tell him that he was going to Salem. The tears just poured out of his [Cepeda's] eyes. He had no idea why he wasn't going with me. I didn't want to tell him that blacks weren't allowed in the Kitty League.
>
> The same thing happened with Felipe Alou. When he came up he was sent to Lake Charles, Louisiana. They found out he was black, and he had to go elsewhere. He was given twelve hours to get out of town.

Traveling from Melbourne to Salem, Virginia, was a nightmare. Charlie Weatherspoon, Frank Lee, and I went by Greyhound bus. We were all blacks. Charlie was supposed to look out for me because of my language barrier, but he became so confused by everything that I ended up looking out for him. The blind leading the blind, as they say.

We changed buses in Jacksonville, Florida, then made stops in Birmingham, Alabama, and Jackson, Mississippi. It was a full house, and the back of the bus was packed. I could barely move or sleep. One morning I saw an empty seat and sat next to a white girl. She started talking to me. She asked where I was from and what I was doing.

The driver got so mad that he pulled over and stopped the bus. He yelled so hard at the girl that she began crying. He let her off the bus right in the middle of downtown Birmingham.

We pushed on to Virginia, where the driver managed to miss the Salem stop. He let us out in the next town, and we had to wait for another bus to take us back to Salem. We arrived at noon on Sunday. In the confusion I lost my suitcase. I was dead tired and had worn the same clothes for three days. The first game I played in for Salem I struck out three times.

Everything there was black and white. I wasn't used to this. I went out to walk around that night about 8:00. I was looking through the store windows, gazing at all the merchandise and imagining what I would buy first once I became a rich baseball star. All of a sudden the police grabbed me and said that blacks had to be with their own people.

Perucho had worried and warned me about such incidents. Later, we took our first road trip by bus, out to West Virginia. Each time we stopped I couldn't get out. I couldn't communicate, and I didn't understand. Nothing made any sense at this point. The other black players could at least speak English. We arrived in West Virginia and waited for the black driver to take us to a guesthouse. The Jim Crow laws were on the books, so we were not allowed to stay at a "white" hotel with the rest of the team.

As soon as we returned to Salem, Pete Zorilla called me long distance. He had tracked me down to tell me that my mother wanted me to come home. Perucho was very sick. I caught the first flight I could. When I arrived, he was in a coma. He died a short time later.

My father's death hit me hard. I remembered that the last time he saw me play baseball I hit a home run. It made him so proud. But his death devastated me. He was only forty-nine years old. I used the $500 I had received when I signed my contract to pay for my father's funeral.

[My brother] Pedro had joined the army, and my mother was all alone. I gave serious thought to quitting baseball, about giving it all up. I didn't want to leave my mother alone and return to Salem, not for baseball, not for anything. But my mother wouldn't hear such talk. She insisted that there was nothing for me in Puerto Rico except poverty. It had been Perucho's dream to see me play professional baseball. I knew she was right. I stayed three or four days, then returned to Salem to resume my baseball career.

It was one of the saddest times of my life. In the evenings and on Sundays I'd sit alone in a room in the black section of town, listening to the sounds of gospel music from the church across the street. When I'd think about my father, my eyes would swell with tears and I would sob.

Looking back, I don't know how I did it. I couldn't hit anything. My father was on my mind. Every time we made a road trip, I'd be by myself. I never knew such loneliness. Once in Bristol, Tennessee, I was walking down the street and I saw three or four girls, white girls, speaking Spanish. They were Cuban, I could tell. I wanted to talk to them so badly. I hadn't spoken Spanish for two months. But they ignored me completely. They wouldn't give me the time of day. That's how entrenched segregation was in the South back then. How little I really knew, and how little I understood.

We returned from that road trip on Sunday. Monday morning Salem released me. It's no wonder. In 26 games I hit .247 with just one home run. That afternoon Pete Zorilla called me. He told me not to give up. I said, "Pete, I want to go home. I've had it!" He said to hold on. A friend of his had a team in Kokomo, Indiana, and the third baseman was hurt. Pete suggested that I go there for ten days, make $100, take the money, and return home. I needed the money so I agreed to go.

Dave Garcia was working behind the scenes on my behalf. The contact man was Jim Tobin, a former major league pitcher who umpired in the Caribbean

during the winter months. Jim owned the Kokomo club in the Mississippi-Ohio
Valley League. Dave told me later how he had helped me:

> There were three players we were going to recommend to Jim Tobin: Orlando
> Cepeda; Charlie Weatherspoon, a right-handed catcher; and a little shortstop
> named Al Rodriguez. Tobin said, "You can send them to me, but only if they're
> not black or Catholic." I didn't understand. Then Jim reminded me that
> Kokomo, Indiana, was Ku Klux Klan country.
>
> I told him I didn't know anything about that nonsense, but these boys had
> three things in common: They were black, at least two were Catholic, and all
> were good ballplayers. Jim agreed to take them.

So I caught the noon train to Kokomo. That, too, was an ordeal. Nobody had
told me where to go exactly. There'd be no one to pick me up when I arrived as
far as I knew. I spent all day, all night, and all morning awake on the train. My
bags had been lost on the way to Salem. I was afraid someone might steal them
if I went to sleep. I told the conductor who clipped the tickets to let me know
when we got to Kokomo. Each time the train stopped, I'd yell, "Kokomo?" And
he'd yell back, "No Kokomo. I'll let you know!"

I arrived there at five in the morning. Believe it or not, my bags managed to
get lost once again. My father always told me to carry my baseball glove and
shoes with me at all times because those were the two things you always needed
to play ball. I was lucky. At least I still had my mitt and my spikes.

It was pitch dark when I got off the train. I tried to ask somebody where the
Kokomo Giants were located, but the man I asked didn't know. So I started
walking. I was tired, and I finally saw a hotel and walked into the lobby. I can
still picture it vividly. People were drinking their early morning coffee. I said,
"Please, could I get a room?" I was told it was too early and I would have to wait
for the manager to arrive.

I waited and waited. Finally the manager, a woman, came in. "No, no," she
told the desk clerk. "We don't have rooms for these types of people." So they
kicked me out. This time I finally got the message.

So I began walking through town. A police officer drove by and saw me. He
stopped and in my broken English I said something like, "Me a baseball player!"
The officer made a phone call to Jim Tobin. Then he told me everything was all
right and that he'd drop me off in the black part of town. Another black player,
Chico Cardenas, was there. I had met him briefly in spring training, and we'd
clicked as friends. That made me feel a lot better.

It was a good time to be young and to be chasing a baseball dream. I went to
spring training in 1958 as a nonrostered player without a contract. I ended the
season as the National League Rookie of the Year and was named the San Fran-

cisco Giants' most popular player and club MVP. I fell in love with San Francisco, and the city embraced me like a native son.

How can I ever forget that spring of 1958? It was special. The flight from San Juan to New York took four hours, then another twelve hours from New York to Phoenix. I was traveling with Ruben Gomez, one of my boyhood heroes. Ruben had won seventeen games for the Giants in 1954 and fifteen games in 1957. He was a big Puerto Rican star whom I had admired for years.

Many things crossed my mind during that flight. I remembered my father and thought how nice it would be if he could see me play now. I knew he'd be proud. I thought of my mother, alone now, living in slumlike conditions. I was excited at the thought of playing alongside and against the greatest baseball players in the world—and being paid for it! I had followed a dream, and it was about to come true.

Yet I knew that there were people out there who weren't exactly wishing me well. Surprisingly, some of them were in Puerto Rico, people who had revered my father and thought I was trying to upstage him. One was a man who had played with Perucho, who said publicly that I would never make it in the major leagues.

Many people in the United States had a negative impression of Latin players, thinking that we were lazy, moody, and difficult to work with. And this showed up everywhere. I won the Triple Crown for St. Cloud in 1956 and led the league in almost every department, but I wasn't even named my team's most valuable player that year. Jack Schwarz, the Giants' farm director, was slow to promote me even with the strong numbers I put on the board every year.

Phoenix was not in the South, but once we left the ball field it was not a comfortable feeling. In the movie theaters blacks and Latins had to sit in sections separate from whites, in designated rows. When we broke [spring training] camp in Phoenix [in March 1958], we barnstormed through minor league cities in Texas, Oklahoma, Iowa, and Nebraska, before flying to San Francisco on April 13. Such barnstorming tours were common practice in those days.

We traveled with the Cleveland Indians to Houston, Dallas, San Antonio, Tulsa, and Oklahoma City, playing them in a series of exhibition games. In Texas we had to stay in black houses outside of Houston. We also had some problems on the train—they didn't want to let the black players eat in the dining car. But the Latin blacks were treated even worse than the American blacks. There were three types of people on the train: whites, blacks, and them. We were the "them."

I was confident. I knew I could play ball. I knew that one way or another I was going to make it. San Francisco was a long, long way from the ghettos and barrios of Puerto Rico. It was a dream come true.

One night around that time I was lying in bed. It was about 11:30, and I was half-asleep. I looked up and saw Perucho. As clear as can be, I saw my father. He stood there, then he put his arms around me and smiled. Then he left just as quickly as he had appeared. I knew then that things would be just fine. I was a Major League Baseball player.

[My first Giants' manager] Bill Rigney knew how to bridge the ethnic and cultural diversity on the team. Many were the times he chewed me out for making dumb mistakes, especially on the basepaths. But that was to help me become a better ballplayer and enable me to reach my full potential. [Subsequent Giants' manager] Alvin [Dark], on the other hand, managed with a vendetta and a meanness that was detrimental to all of us.

We were never a unified team, in spite of our incredible numbers. That cost us pennants. We were a club made up of three distinct groups: whites, blacks, and Latins. And even among the black players, there was animosity between American blacks and Latin blacks. When I was traded to the Cardinals in 1966, I realized for the first time how well a team could work together both on and off the field.

One of the first things Alvin did in spring training was to try to stop the Latin ballplayers from speaking Spanish in the clubhouse. I'll never forget that day. He called us behind second base and said we had to stop speaking Spanish in the clubhouse because other players were complaining that they didn't know what we were talking about. I said, "Alvin, I won't do that. I'm Puerto Rican, others are Dominican, and I am proud of what I am. This is a disgrace to my race." I went on to tell him that I didn't know who it was that was doing the complaining, but if some players really had complaints, they should have the guts to tell us directly and not be sneaky about it. Whether or not there were really complaints, let's remember that no other team had as many Latin players. For many of us, our native tongue was the only way we could converse coherently.

Alvin had little respect for Latin players. I don't think he liked black players in general. He brought the attitudes of the Old South to the ballpark with him. Others who might have thought the same usually left these thoughts at home. Whenever there was a meeting in the clubhouse he'd avoid the Latin ballplayers— that is unless he had a reason to yell at us. I love music, as everyone knows. It's been a big part of my life from the beginning. I was "Cha Cha, the Dancing Master." Everyone knew that.

Alvin decided I shouldn't play Latin music in the clubhouse. He wouldn't even let me carry my record player with me. One day I was about to leave for the airport when our clubhouse man, Eddie Logan, told me point blank that I couldn't take my record player along. I made it clear that if I couldn't, I would just stay home. I took that record player with me.

On the road the blacks, whites, and Latins each dressed in a separate corner of the clubhouse. When Alvin made his rounds, he'd growl out a thing or two.

Once when we were in St. Louis for a series, Harvey Kuenn and Don Larsen got drunk and made some noise. Somehow Alvin managed to blame the noise on the Latin players instead. More than once he said that blacks and Latins were dumb. If he'd chew out the team, he'd make sure the black and Latin players got more than their proper share of the blame.

Things are much different for today's Latin players. Managers like Tony LaRussa and Dusty Baker either know enough Spanish or have people who can readily communicate with the Latin players. But back then Latin ballplayers who came to the United States were susceptible to anything.

I was still just a kid myself. I probably was a little too hotheaded and sensitive for my own good. I had to grow up. Instead of just going out and playing my game, I let Alvin's remarks throw me too often. But again, ours was a different culture. Alvin never took the time to try and understand these problems and work them out for the betterment of the entire team.

Latins generally have a need to be loved. We want to like people and want people to like us. Our culture is clear on this. We are warm people, but we can't be demeaned as men.

Lots of times it wasn't easy. In cities like St. Louis, Cincinnati, Chicago, and Pittsburgh, we stayed in the nice hotels but couldn't eat in the nice restaurants. We either had to eat in our rooms or in the black section of town. Felipe [Alou] and I might have been authentic big league stars, but that didn't stop people from calling the police on us in Chicago.

The team stayed at the Edgewater Beach Hotel on Chicago's Lake Shore. Back then the north side of Chicago was almost totally white. So there were Felipe and I, walking down Sheridan Road. We were dressed in jackets and ties. Ballplayers were expected to dress that way then. Someone happened to see two black guys speaking Spanish and came to the conclusion that we must be up to no good. We went to a restaurant and waited nearly two hours without being served. We finally got up and left far hungrier than when we arrived.

Sometimes you had to have a sense of humor to survive. During a road trip in Pittsburgh, Felipe and I had finished working out. We were dressed well and decided to stop in a restaurant for lunch. We walked in and waited to be seated. Somebody came by and apologized warmly. We were told there were no more kitchen jobs available. If we were looking to wash dishes, we might try the place down the street. We had to laugh about that or we would have cried.

But a lot had happened. Alvin Dark was fired by the Giants after the 1964 season. The big rap against him was that he not only divided the team along racial and ethnic lines but that he had done everything possible to exacerbate the problem.

He had told a *Newsday* columnist earlier that year that he was having trouble with the club because there were too many black and Latin players on the team.

He said that the Negro and Latin players did not have the same pride as the white players, that we were not able to perform with the same mental alertness as the whites.

[Among the people I remember], [t]here was a burning intensity in Curt Flood. His mind was always working overtime. I'm reminded of Curt when I look at Michael Jordan or Mark McGwire: that look of intense concentration. You saw it in the clubhouse and you saw it on the ball field. But when you met him personally there was nothing but sincerity and warmth. It made no difference to him if you were famous or not, if he was a major league ballplayer and you were just an ordinary guy.

The unfortunate thing is that, if you did not know Curt, it was possible to misjudge him. Because he was sensitive, he carried a lot of pain with him. It was harder for him to shake off the injustices of the past than it was for some other fellows.

Curt challenged the baseball establishment when he refused to be traded to the Philadelphia Phillies. At first I didn't understand what he was doing. I was confused. But Curt was very upset with Bing Devine for trading him. He had established roots in St. Louis.

It was a mission with him. That's how Curt was. Trading ballplayers is part of the game. How well I understood that. But what the public at large never fully recognized is that being traded, especially midseason or during the spring, changed everything.

Curt couldn't accept the premise that he belonged to one particular owner or one particular club in perpetuity. He challenged this in court and he lost. In 1971 he tried a comeback with the Washington Senators but was unsuccessful. That spring we played an exhibition game in Virginia. He told me, "Charlie," (he always called me Charlie) "if I had to do it, I'd do the same thing all over again. Maybe someday it will help other ballplayers."

We lost a wonderful man and a loving friend when Curt Flood died in 1997. In addition to being an outstanding baseball player, Curt was an excellent artist. He painted a beautiful portrait of my son that still hangs proudly in my front hall.

Before he died, Curt wrote a note to his wife in which he told her to make sure I was one of his pallbearers. I did so with honor. The funeral was held in Los Angeles. Bill White, Bob Gibson, Lou Brock, Maury Wills, and Steve Garvey were among those who attended.

As a kid growing up in the slums and ghettos of Puerto Rico, it was baseball that saved my life. Of that I am sure. Without baseball, the dark side of my upbringing began to surface. That same shadow my mother had warned me about, the shadow I thought I had left behind, began playing catch-up.

Even as a baseball star, some of my boyhood pals were never far away. They liked the good times. They were bums and hangers-on, I suppose, but they were friends, or at least I thought they were. They liked the limelight they could touch when they associated with me. It gave them a phony sense of respectability and importance.

Sometimes they came to San Francisco to hang around with me. People were surprised to see me with them. Once my baseball career ended, however, the tables turned. I began following them, and following them down the wrong path.

I can't say for sure when the bad times started. My release from the Red Sox in 1974 is as good a guess as any. I became bitter and angry. Worse than that, I used my anger as an excuse to do things I would have been better off not doing.

Many ballplayers find it tough when they leave the game. You may not court the limelight, and maybe you don't even want it. You play baseball because you love it. But fame and celebrity can be seductive. They get their hooks in you whether you like it or not.

For years we are cheered, and booed. The media court us. The crowds roar. Then one day it's gone, over. Part of your identity remains planted firmly on the baseball diamonds [but there's] no roar from the crowd to hear anymore. A part of you remains empty.

For years after my career was over, when I'd watch a ballgame, I'd want to cry. When you're playing you take it for granted. Every day is a new day. When you stop, everything stands still.

I was thirty-six years old. I had money in my pocket, and my old friends were always there and ready for a good time. I went to discos, dated lots of good-looking girls. I was having fun. I wasn't a drinker, and the only drug I did was marijuana. I had smoked the weed as a kid, then started again in 1965.

Rock bottom began when I flew to Colombia to put on a baseball clinic. I met some people and smoked some weed. Colombia was the best for that. The clinic was on a weekend. I was shipping two big boxes full of rugs and handmade dresses back to Puerto Rico for Nydia. A friend asked if he could enclose a five-pound bag of marijuana in the box. That way they could get it through without any hassle. I saw nothing wrong with it at the time, so I agreed.

How quickly we fall from grace, especially in Puerto Rico. If it had happened in Los Angeles or New York, I would have been put on probation and received no jail time. The probation people in Florida assured me of that.

But with Roberto Clemente's tragic death, I had become Puerto Rico's reigning baseball hero. I had been arrested for importing marijuana with the intent to distribute it. In the eyes of many Puerto Ricans, I had disgraced my people and the memory of the great Perucho.

When I got out [of prison] some baseball people wanted me to coach in Puerto Rico. I coached Bayamon in the winter league. I worked with some good players: Dickie Thon, who went on to star with the Astros and the Phillies;

Dave Bergman, also with the Astros; pitcher Ed Solomon; and former major leaguer Luis Arroyo.

Emotionally and mentally I was far from healed. There were lots of lingering scars. The ordeal of being arrested, convicted, and imprisoned for almost a year had taken a big toll on me. Moreover, Puerto Rico was far from friendly to me. In fact, my life was still a nightmare.

My mother was gone. My wife and children had left. I was bitter and angry, and my self-respect had vanished. I'd occasionally go to a baseball game when some of my old friends, like Tony Perez, were playing against the Dodgers. One afternoon in 1984 I was on the field at Dodger Stadium talking to some of the players. Someone upstairs took notice and sent a security guard down to ask for my field credentials. They knew who I was. When I said I'd never needed field credentials before, I was told I had to leave the ballpark immediately. The Dodgers even sent a memo to all their ballplayers forbidding them to have any contact with me.

I returned to my apartment as close to a broken man as I have ever been. Many things passed through my mind. The possibility of ending my life seemed quite real, at least for a minute or two.

I needed something bigger, stronger than myself. This I knew. I had been introduced to the practice of Buddhism a year earlier. Buddhism had helped me over some tough times, but I hadn't embraced it with the necessary zeal. Suddenly I knew I had to pursue it with totality and dedication. It would take work, real work—maybe even more work than becoming a major league ballplayer.

As a youngster headed for trouble in Puerto Rico, it was baseball that saved my life. Now, as an adult, it was Buddhism that would give me the tools to change my life's direction. I am fortunate that it was there. And with practice and patience, things started turning around.

The story of my life cannot be written without paying deference to Buddhism. More than baseball, more than the home runs and runs batted in, more than the Rookie of the Year Award and the National League MVP, Buddhism helped make me what I am today. I say this because all the records and cheers and the celebrity do not, and did not, create inner peace. Buddhism saved me spiritually and gave me the tools to turn my pain into medicine. It has helped me make myself a far better human being. And in doing so, it has made me a better husband, father, and friend.

It is not an easy practice, make no mistake. Nor does it work overnight. It takes a long time, because the necessary changes must come from inside. Through practice and guidance you feel the happiness from within. Anyone can feel happy when life is going well. But there is also real happiness in learning how to deal with problems as they unfold.

Today my practice is very serious to me. It's number one. The first five years of serious Buddhism are usually very rough. You're cleaning your own life, purging yourself of negativity and weakness. Today I chant every morning for an hour and a half, then maybe half an hour in the evening. It's become a ritual. It gives me a joy that is difficult to explain and a contentment I never experienced before.

[In 1985] I told Al [Albergate] I was through with baseball. Baseball had rejected me, and I wanted to return the favor. He helped me see that I could never be through with baseball. Baseball was what I loved. Baseball was how I'd always made my living. It was what I did best.

He assured me that with the proper work and practice, I could turn my pain to medicine. Once that happened, I'd be back in baseball, back where I belonged. I'd feel the love and hear the cheers once again. Only this time I would appreciate them even more. It would require hard work on my part and a firm belief that this day would come. When that day came, he assured me, I would be ready.

I had worked hard to make things better, and better things were starting to happen. In Buddhism, our faith is based on experience. Faith almost always begins as hope or an expectation that something will happen. At the start of my journey, I was willing to try the practice and anticipate some result. Because these changes develop brick by brick, I have seen the actual proof of what my practice has given me.

My practice was bringing me inner peace, and it helped to make me receptive to a woman like [my wife] Mirian. Now it would finally help lead me back to baseball. I was on my way. Not just back to baseball but back to the San Francisco Giants, to the team where it had all started nearly thirty years ago.

One of the nicest things that's ever happened to me was being asked to throw out the first ball in the third game of the 1989 National League Championship Series against the Chicago Cubs. It was just as Al Albergate had said it would be a few years earlier. One day I'd hear those cheers again. One day baseball would welcome me back with respect and with honor. That day was October 8, 1989, and the cheers were from over 60,000 fans at Candlestick Park. There were tears in my eyes.

I was fifty-two years old, and I was back on my own field of dreams. The game would open shortly, and the Giants' Jeff Brantley would take to the mound against the Chicago Cubs' Rick Sutcliffe. But this one moment was mine. So many things crossed my mind. I thought of Perucho, "The Babe Ruth of Puerto Rico," one of the best ballplayers ever. He would have been so proud. I had come back. But even more important, I had beaten that ominous shadow that he hadn't been fortunate enough to escape. Then there was my mother, Carmen. How happy she would have been to see me back on track. Her tears might stop. I had finally outrun my environment. And this time it was for good.

The story of my life both in an out of baseball cannot be told apart from my culture and heritage. Unfortunately, the full, true story of the Latin ballplayer in the United States has not been written. Far too often the media has ignored us as a dynamic force in the history of Major League Baseball.

The bad rap many Latin players have had over the years has been unfair. Try to imagine a kid in the 1950s, a teenage boy in a new country. He hopes to compete against the best baseball players in the world, but he can't communicate in his new country's language. And if you were black during that time, the problems were amplified many times over.

When I first came to the United States, almost all the Latin ballplayers in the major leagues had been white Cubans. And no one was better than Dolf Luque, who made his major league debut with the Boston Braves in 1914. Called "The Prince of Havana," Dolf Luque pitched twenty years in the majors, winning 194 games and twice leading the National League in ERA. His best season was with the Cincinnati Reds in 1923, when he went 27–8 with an ERA of 1.93.

I was very disappointed when Ken Burns's PBS baseball special barely mentioned Major League Baseball's Latin connection. I'm not sure the name Minnie Minoso was even mentioned once. Minnie was as important to the Latin player major league aspirations as Jackie Robinson was to the black player.

We [Latin players] came along at a time when there wasn't big money in baseball. We were not given huge bonuses. While we were climbing the major league ladder in hopes of achieving major league status, we were usually just about at the poverty level. I never had a telephone. Calls to Puerto Rico were very expensive, and at times I didn't talk to my mother for as long as six months.

We also battled our way to the top with a different heritage and a different language. We were young and at times had no idea of what was really happening. When we fought back and got angry, we were labeled troublemakers, lazy, moody, undisciplined. The rap against Latin players has not totally vanished either. Many of the younger players will tell you this today.

For a Latin ballplayer in the U.S., there is still a great cultural gap to overcome. I can understand what some of these younger players must be feeling because I have been there. With the expanding role of Latin Americans in Major League Baseball today and the expanding fan base, a hard-hitting look at the problems of past and present Latin players is a story just waiting to be told soon.

If I have learned any lesson in life, it's that human decency and goodness do not begin and end with any particular race or group of people. As a general rule, people who respect themselves and respect others will find respect in return. It doesn't matter if you're black or white, Anglo or Hispanic; respect is a two-way street.

6

Borders and Shangri-La
Orlando (El Duque) Hernandez and Me

Andrei Codrescu

The true origins of baseball can now be revealed. The Transylvanian shepherds of my native Romania played a stickball game called *oina*. The field was roughly the shape of a baseball diamond. The bases were sheep tied to a stake that allowed them to roam in a small circle. When the ball was in the air, the stick-man made for the nearest sheep, which, being a moving target, was not easy to grab a hold of. The original Carpathian baseball was a bobcat or mountain lion furball. The winning team, which is to say the team that had fondled the most sheep, was awarded a number of sheep equivalent to the points they had made. The staked sheep were then eaten by the whole village. For most of the first half of the nineteenth century a team called the Carpathian Braves dominated the Transylvanian games. In 1838, a Romanian army officer visiting America taught the game to the natives of Cooperstown who, being somewhat puritanical, didn't allow the local sheep to be molested. They substituted them with some kind of pillows.

The substitution of pillows for sheep represents, in my opinion, a great loss for the game. Literally and metaphorically a sheep serves many purposes. For the Romanian people, the path described by sheep during their annual transmigration from the mountains into the valleys describes the natural borders of the country. Everything inside the path of the sheep is Romanian, everything outside of it is foreign.

There are some people who'd like to ascribe the same ritualistic significance to baseball. Americans are baseball-playing people, one might say, and then there are non-baseball-playing people, who are not Americans.

But baseball is obviously not as American as apple pie—even if apple pie was totally American, which it isn't. I had some pretty great apple pie in France. Baseball today is, in fact, more like pizza with everything on it, including pineapples and anchovies.

It is a shame also that bases are not composed of something edible. Food metaphors for nationhood have been with us at least since the Romanians landed in Cooperstown. You can study the history of American attitudes toward immigration from the "melting pot" to the "salad." The "melting pot" was a pretty a heavy-handed metaphor, more chemical than gastronomical. Not many cultures would survive this "boiling" with all or any of their parts, and that was how America, vigorously boiling, became a great nation. The problem was that some local cultures defied this metaphor and didn't boil at all, the prime example being Native Americans and African Americans. Europeans boiled pretty well because they came from Europe preboiled, not to mention pretty well shaken and ready to give up the Old World.

The nouvelle-cuisinish, gentler "salad," used now to describe the blending of non-Europeans into America, leaves much to be desired as well. First, there is the question of what force keeps the salad greens in the same bowl, and second, who and what eats the stuff. Personally, I much prefer a well-done leg of lamb to salad—and this after being a California-style vegetarian for seven years. Nor do I think that the Hispanics, Asians, and islanders now being made part of this "salad" have much use for salads over more substantial fare.

Baseball is a much more apt metaphor for the process of American-making than either "the boiling pot" or "'the salad." We know that African Americans, for instance, who didn't do very well in the boiling pot, did great in baseball. After a long struggle. And Hispanics, who grow most of our salad, also fare a lot better in baseball.

The imperative to be an American has lessened as the nation's identity crisis has. There is hardly a need now to loudly proclaim oneself American, though clearly there is still a sizable minority that has made an identity crisis its mission. There are identity crises of many kinds operating at many levels of our society, particularly within socioeconomic groups left behind by technology, but there is hardly a crisis of *national* identity. An American passport is the most desirable document in the world precisely because it guarantees the security of an identity without the terrors of ethnicity, religion, or race. There are exceptions and unfairnesses, of course, but the essential democratic fact of America remains acceptance and tolerance. The roving cosmic sheep that patrol our borders, the Atlantic Ocean, the Rio Grande, and so forth, do not, despite the efforts of the border patrol, keep most people out.

This, at least, is how the world outside our borders conceives of us, and how many, but not most of us conceive of ourselves. Borders remain crucial to this understanding. The borderless world and the global economy are hegemonic fictions made particularly grating by the fact that the hegemony in question, the United States, represents an ideal model. Tolerance, or at least the least repression, cannot but be an ideal in a world where people still kill each other over the content of kitsch songs. Songs about sheep, for the most part. The hegemonic fictions—the work of a common utopian gene—can best be studied in the regions of the border itself where border communities have come into being. The "border world" is neither inside nor outside the border; it takes its character from both sides and it makes something new. It is based on the movement of metaphorical sheep, which embody gentleness, good meat, good fur, responsiveness to dogs, the chief symbol for Christ, their well-known ability to provide disguises for wolves, and an affinity for being cloned. They are the first to be sacrificed, but they are also the first to prevail in terms of coats, weavings, and sentiments.

Which brings me back to baseball, one of the best border worlds operating today, a real laboratory for studying the workings of global fictions and what they have wrought. I am also going to try to make my way through this self-made forest of metaphors without losing a beat. Writing is sometimes more complicated than baseball.

I am going to accomplish this through the use of two examples: that of the emigration and apotheosis of Orlando "El Duque" Hernandez from Havana, Cuba, once a political outcast, now a star pitcher for the Yankees. And the second example: myself, who became an American when I understood baseball.

In the border world, the Cuban American subdivision is one of the richest. Problems between Cuba and the United States are more in the nature of a lovers' quarrel than anything else.

I went to Cuba in December 1997 just ahead of the Pope's visit there. Cuba was preparing for the Pope and I wanted to get there before the masses of reporters did—I was convinced they were coming to turn over every stone. I didn't know that Monica Lewinsky would burst onto the scene halfway through the Pope's visit—so that half the stones remained unturned when the reporters rushed back to the United States.

I went there with Art Silverman, a producer for National Public Radio, and David Graham, a photographer. We were joined in Havana by Ariel Peña, our translator. Every day, for the duration of our ten-day visit, the four of us wrote a collective poem called "Exquisite Corpse." This is done by writing a line, folding it over so the next person can't see what you've written, then they write something, fold it over, pass it on to the next person to write, and so on. When the page is all written up, you unfold it and there it is—an X-ray of the collective mind. This is what we wrote on December 21, 1997:

Exquisite Corpse
by Ariel Peña, Art Silverman, David Graham, and Andrei Codrescu

Ravens for the forklift.
The music tells us
where to burn
the black seeds
of our feelings.

There was a Christmas tree rigged with loudspeakers standing in the middle of a busy street in front of the Havana Psychiatric Hospital. It was blaring scratchy Christmas carols in Spanish. Behind the fence of the hospital a row of inmates on wooden chairs was rocking back and forth watching baseball practice.

We were looking for "El Duque," Orlando Hernandez, one of the greatest baseball players in the world, at the Havana Psychiatric Hospital where he had been punished to work every day as a physical therapy counselor. He had been banished from Cuban baseball for life for the crime his half-brother, Livan, had committed, in defecting to the United States.

El Duque wasn't working, but it wasn't hard to find someone to help us locate him. An inmate on a bicycle led us through a maze of streets in a modest Havana neighborhood to his house. People on the street nodded and greeted us as we passed, fully aware that these Yanks with microphones were on their way to meet their national hero. Most of them had not seen the World Series where Orlando's half-brother, Livan Hernandez, had led the Florida Marlins to the championship—the game had been blocked out on orders from the bearded one. But all of them knew that El Duque, their neighbor, was an even greater pitcher than Livan.

El Duque wasn't home but his pretty and young common-law wife, Noris, invited us to sit on the small front porch of their tiny house. She told us that she had seen the World Series games with El Duque, thanks to friends from CNN who had smuggled them into the Habana Libre Hotel to watch on cable television. "Smuggled," because Cuban citizens aren't allowed inside tourist hotels in Cuba.

El Duque came home shortly. A tall, handsome, self-possessed man, he emanated dignity and quiet strength.

We sat around the table in the one-room house with the dirt floor and started talking. It became evident that this was no mere sports star, but a remarkable person raised on baseball and family love.

"It is a pleasure to shake your hand, because I know it's one of the best in the world."

"Thanks, but I'm just like any other person."

"How long did you play in the Cuban National League?"

"I played for ten years. I have the best pitching record in the history of Cuba."

"It's extraordinary to have two brothers who are great ball players."

"When I was a child, my dad taught me to play. He was in the minor leagues. When I went to bed, I had a ball, a bat, and a glove, instead of toys. Livan and I played against each other, professionally, only once."

"You are both heroes in Cuba."

"I don't know. Many people thought that we were stars, but I don't think I'm the best. I want to be the only Orlando Hernandez, that's all. I think Livan would have been great if he stayed here."

"He's not great now?" We were talking about the 1997 MVP.

Orlando smiled.

"How did you feel when he left?"

"I felt really bad. I knew I wouldn't see him for a long time. I wouldn't be able to help him polish his technique. I'm not there to help him."

"Have you been able to follow his career?"

Orlando began to answer, but Ariel—our translator—sighed and her eyes filled with tears.

Orlando looked like he was choking up, too. His wife, who sat on a chair next to him, wiped her eyes with a handkerchief.

"Sorry," said Ariel.

Orlando smiled at her, a beautiful full smile.

"I support Livan from here. I talk and give him advice on the telephone. We are close. The only thing I can do is wish him happiness. Every one of his successes is mine. That makes me feel very, very happy. But I feel sad because I can't give what I know to the people of Cuba. I understand that I can't play. I have to pay for what my brother did."

"Seems unfair for you to pay for what your brother did. Even the Bible says that children shouldn't pay for the sins of their fathers."

"Well, there are two Bibles."

How could Castro's Bible be so cruel? It occurred to me that there was more than politics at work here. History might have been quite different if Fidel Castro, who had also played baseball, would have been drafted by a major-league team in the United States. As rumor has it, he nearly was. Was the frustrated pitcher inside the dictator taking it out on El Duque?

"What was the sequence of events after his defection?"

"The first and hardest one is I was suspended from baseball for life. Second, I cannot go out of the country and I can't represent Cuba as a player. It's a lot of humiliation. If there is something that keeps me alive, is my belief in God. I was never interested in playing baseball for money."

"What are you doing with your time now?"

"I work now at the psychiatric hospital. It's a humane job. But it's not what I want to do. I get paid nine and a half dollars a month."

"You're not only a great player, but a great human being. Thank you."

"You don't know how much good this interview has done for me. This is what keeps me alive. Because if some people think that I don't exist, I just remember these moments. I come to realize that I'm alive."

Ariel could barely translate this. Her eyes were full of tears.

When we left, El Duque gave me his baseball cap, which he took off his head, and inscribed it, "PARA ANDREI—El Duque—Hernandez, Habana, Cuba."

Four days later, on Christmas morning, Orlando, together with his common-law wife, Noris Bosch, and six others, hid aboard a fishing boat, and trusted themselves to the sea. Many others had escaped Cuba this way, but this group was not "others." Orlando "El Duque" Hernandez was a treasure, worth millions. He was also the first Cuban baseball player to escape in this perilous way. Others had just walked away from the team when it was playing outside Cuba.

Defecting Cuban baseball star to go to Costa Rica

SAN JOSE, Jan. 7 (AFP) — Cuban pitching ace Orlando Hernandez. and seven other Cubans who defected last week will arrive here Wednesday from the Bahamas, a Costa Rican government official told AFP.

"It is very probable that Hernandez and the others will arrive this afternoon on a private plane from the Bahamas," the source said.

Costa Rica's Migration Council approved visas for the defecting Cubans early Wednesday, the source said.

Hernandez, nicknamed "El Duque" (the Duke), and the seven other Cubans were taken to the Bahamas after being rescued from a raft at sea on December 30.

On December 31 the U.S. State Department granted Hernandez, his wife, and another baseball player, Alberto Hernandez, (no relation) permission to enter the United States.

Hernandez has reportedly been weighing the U.S. asylum offer as part of baseball contract negotiations.

On Monday the U.S. State Department said Hernandez would be given a "reasonable period of time" to decide whether he wants to come to the United States.

Cuban baseball star arrives in Costa Rica and asks for asylum

SAN JOSE, Jan. 8 (AFP) — Cuban baseball star Orlando Hernandez, and six other Cubans who defected last month arrived here from the Bahamas late Wednesday and requested political asylum.

"That's why we're here. In fact, we've already asked for it," Hernandez said after he and the other athletes were seen getting off a private jet at Costa Rica's international airport at 23:15 p.m. (0515 GMT Thursday).

The group's arrival came as a surprise because hours earlier the Costa Rican consul in the Bahamas said Hernandez and fellow baseball players were bound for Nicaragua.

"This is a dream come true. It's one of God's miracles. I lack words to express how incredible it all has been, because this is a great victory," Hernandez told reporters.

Hernandez, who goes by the nickname of "El Duque," or the duke, said he planned to stay in Costa Rica while he seeks to sign on with a professional baseball team.

"We want to be residents of Costa Rica. We will stay here. We will work here. In fact, I'm going to start training here and later we'll travel to play professional baseball," said Hernandez, whose brother, Livan Hernandez, is the star pitcher of the Florida Marlins, a relatively new baseball team based in Miami. Hernandez, Johel Pedroso Delgado, Osmani Lorenzo Rodriguez, Juan Carlos Romero Cabello, Geieys Gonzalez, Barreto and Lenin Rivero Hernandez arrived here accompanied by Joe Cubas, a baseball agent from the United States who specializes in scouting for Cuban talent.

The defectors were taken to the Bahamas after being rescued from a raft at sea on December 30. Their temporary permission to stay in the Bahamas ran out Wednesday.

On December 31, the U.S. State Department granted Orlando Hernandez, his girlfriend Noris Bosch, and another baseball player, Alberto Hernandez—no family relation—permission to enter the United States.

Noris Bosch left the Bahamas for Miami, sources said.

U.S. State Department spokesman James Rubin on Wednesday did not rule out the possibility that the two baseball players along with five other Cubans who left Cuba with them will come to the United States at a later time.

Orlando's sea journey was shrouded in mystery. Some of the newspaper reports mentioned rough seas and a leaky raft. There followed many twists and turns after the group's rescue from the deserted Bahamian island. The famous Joe Cubas, agent to defecting Cuban talent, was on hand to manage Orlando's future. The United States offered asylum to Hernandez but not to the others. Orlando refused to go without them. Instead of coming to the United States, he went to Costa Rica, but this, of course, was a strategic move to gain free agency.

The media fairy tale was filled, like all fairy tales, with perils and traps, false endings, and magical events, but it remained basically simple: after the perilous sea journey, the noble hero arrived in the United States, was reunited with his brother Livan, and signed a $6.6 million contract with the Yankees. The Yankees! One can only imagine the fury of Fidel Castro, who has railed against Yankee imperialism for years.

Still, Orlando remained only another Cuban defector, whose prowess was unproven, until the night of June 3, 1998 when he stood on the mound at Yankee Stadium and pitched against the Tampa Bay Devil Rays. At the press conference that followed his indisputable triumph, he charmed the armies of the media with the same modesty and sincerity that had made him beguiling to the few reporters who had known him earlier. The Yankees didn't send him back to the minors, where he had been waiting for his chance.

But there is more to the story of El Duque. While waiting for The Call, he played for the Columbus, Ohio, Clippers, a Triple A farm team for the Yankees. I flew to Columbus on a sweltering May morning to renew our acquaintance, four months after we had met in Cuba.

Columbus sits in an all-American Midwestern landscape of corporate buildings, malls, and highways under construction. The city is booming. In its plain-
ness, newness, car-driven culture, and lack of street life, Columbus is the antithesis
of the peeling, crowded, throbbing, bicycle-filled, and very human city of Havana. The only thing they have in common is Columbus himself, who discovered Cuba, and now, for a short time, they also shared El Duque.

The Clippers stadium was surrounded by bulldozers and cranes that stirred
up a fine red dust that made it hard to breathe. There was no escaping the sun on
the hot bleachers looking on to the Astroturf. The Clippers were practicing:
they had begun the season with the worst record in their history: 2–18, until the
arrival of El Duque. Since then, they'd been practically unstoppable.

When I tried to clear time for an interview, a grumpy pitching coach said
that Orlando didn't have any time. It was somewhat understandable. Journalists
had been swarming and it cut into practice. Still, I felt that I had a special claim.

On his way back from the bullpen, I managed to get Orlando's attention. A
big grin broke on his face. We high-fived and I told him that I'd come to talk
with him, but I could only stay in Columbus for one day.

He said that he had a lunch appointment and that most of the day was taken,
but that he needed to go shopping for clothes the next day in the morning.

"Where, Orlando?"

"To the mall," he said.

And so it was that next morning, on another hot and windless day, I accompanied Cuba's greatest pitcher and new millionaire, Orlando "El Duque"
Hernandez, to a Columbus, Ohio, shopping mall that was physically and psy-
chologically very far from the Havana Mental Hospital.

Orlando drove his small rental car zestfully, singing along to a tape of Cuban
salsa music, answering my questions and simultaneously talking on his elegant,
palm-sized cellphone. During our next few hours together, he spoke on that
phone about a dozen times, mostly with family and friends in Cuba, and about
three times with Noris, who was in Miami. By the time we reached the mall, he
had already expanded thousands of words into the world, near and far. He reminded me of a cheerful bird who can't contain its morning song.

This was not the man I had met in Havana. That one had been worried, sad,
and under pressure. The new Orlando looked younger, acted younger, and seemed
determined to enjoy himself. As a former refugee from a communist paradise
myself, I could sympathize. One becomes younger in America. Freedom is, among
other things, cosmetic.

When I asked him if he would return to Cuba if the system changed, he said:
"I will continue to play here. I am Cuban. I will always be Cuban. If things
were normal, there wouldn't be any problem. Miami is closer to Cuba than
Columbus."

That was a political irony that Orlando's little cellphone, with its distance-erasing ability was trying to overcome. If the past was a land rich in personal significance, the present was a dazzling playground.

Orlando attacked the mall like a tiger. Our first stop was a shoe store. He stood among the bewildering varieties, studying their swirling shapes and colors, their wings, their panthers, and their wild bird logos. He picked up a pair of Nikes and looked at them long and hard. There was something religious about it, as if the object wasn't a mere shoe but the spirit of capitalism.

Orlando's taste in clothes ran to blue and black jeans and red T-shirts. In the clothing store, he headed for the jeans racks and tore through them as if they were Christmas presents. Wrappers flew everywhere. Like Nikes, denim was a totemic material to Cubans, just as it had been for Eastern Europeans. Not many years ago, in Bucharest and Moscow, one would be offered treasures for one's pants. For a time, denim was a currency in the communist world. Ironically, the workers' paradise turned out to be a shopping mall. Orlando still had about him the innocence of his country and, to him, these objects *were* Christmas presents. He had braved the seas on Christmas Day to get to them.

The original "El Duque" had been Orlando's father, also a ball player, who had been renowned for his tastes in clothes and jewelry. Orlando had inherited the moniker, but he had a way to go before equaling his father's prerevolutionary elegance.

"My first day in America we had a family reunion. Next day I went out with Livan and we had a very good time. He knows all the best places."

With packages safely in the trunk, we headed for the only Cuban restaurant in Columbus. The place turned out to be more Mexican than Cuban, and Orlando doesn't like anything spicy.

"I am a finicky eater," he said. "I didn't even eat conch on Anguilla Cay."

With that, El Duque told me the story of his escape from Cuba, in minute detail. The fishing boat he and his companions had been hiding in had reached the deserted Bahamian island of Anguilla Cay without incident. Rough seas had been predicted, and a storm rained on the Florida coast, but a "miraculous hand" smoothed the water in front of them. Their stay on the island was part camping adventure, part efficient labor-division. Some fished, some prepared the conch, some made a shelter with branches. Their provisions had included bread, some Spam, and water. Orlando ate thin slices of bread and left the conch and the seaweed to the others. On the island, they found cooking utensils and the abandoned camps of other Cuban defectors who had come before them. Twice, a reconnaissance plane flew overhead and they hid from it, fearing it was one from the Cuban air force. The first night they slept on the ground and watched the stars. On the second night it rained, and they took shelter, improvising a gas lamp from a piece of gauze and lighter fluid.

"It was bad when we ran out of Marlboros," Orlando said. "The captain's wife had some Cuban 'Popular,' but I wouldn't smoke them."

Orlando "El Duque" Hernandez will, no doubt, be the beloved hero of a fairy tale that will not stop before it is made into a major motion picture. (The Anaheim Angels had, in fact, offered a movie deal as part of their bid for Orlando). He is uniquely a hero of our time, someone who defies tired political systems, crosses borders, is not afraid to upbraid a dictator. He is also supremely confident in his lucky star: the shine of it is in his eyes when he speaks. It has guided him, it has smoothed the waters, it has brought him riches and fame.

But this hero is hardly unidimensional. He is complex. Certainly, he is self-effacing, boyish, and heroic. He is thoughtful, though, when he advises other Cuban baseball players to think hard about escaping the way he did. "I didn't do it because I'm a hero," he said, "but because I'm crazy." What's more, this is a hero-in-the-making. He has brought with him modesty and confidence, but he is now in the land of excess and temptation. How he deals with the overwhelming demands of our country, the flattery, and his own legend, will truly prove his mettle.

Cuba sí, Yankee no. Not. In Romania, the dictatorship collapsed shortly after the Olympian gymnast Nadia Comanici defected to the West. There isn't an obvious connection, of course, but history isn't obvious and it does repeat itself. In any case, history has thrown Castro a wicked curve ball.

Orlando's story is obviously not that of your typical immigrant. Mine is, more or less—at least as far as baseball is concerned.

I became an American when I understood baseball. I lived for a time in the 1970s on Melville Street in Baltimore (named after an obscure city councilman, not the writer) in the shadow of the old Memorial Stadium. On game nights, Melville Street was lit up like a stage by the stadium lights. Neighbors sat on stoops with their transistor radios and you could hear the clamoring of the crowd on radio a fraction of a second before the sound of the real crowd reached us. I was writing a book called *In America's Shoes*, and I used the crowd as an editor. When they booed, I crossed out what I'd just written. When they cheered, I admired my acumen.

I didn't set foot inside Memorial Stadium until my son, who was already an American and played Little League, took me to a game. I was impervious to the charm of the evening for nearly five innings, because the crowd scared me. I was born Jewish in a provincial, former Austro-Hungarian city at the edge of Europe where crowds spelled trouble. An ancient and unbridgeable hostility divided guys with muscles from guys with glasses. There was little more terrifying than walking home with a book under my arm into the path of an angry crowd coming from a game lost by the home team. I was fresh meat, a four-eyed scapegoat, responsible, I knew, for the team's loss and for every other historical misfortune that had afflicted the natives.

But Memorial Stadium was not the soccer stadium of my youth. By the fifth inning I began to enjoy the rumble of the crowd, the smell of hot dogs and beer, the good-natured roar in the stands, the velvety feel of the summer night, and my son's unabashed joy in the Orioles' hits and runs. I allowed myself to relax and I understood the difference between the democratic ease of America and the still-simmering resentments of Europe. As the game unfolded, I was grateful to the summer night crowd for being there for pleasure not politics, and I had the foresight to say a little prayer of thanks for the fact that they were calling for pitches instead of, let's say, Jewish blood. I understood the difference between a crowd and a mob. Under certain circumstances, any crowd can become a mob, but democracy stood between them, preventing it.

I have been in many American ballparks since then, both lovely, old, intimate spaces like Wrigley Field, and new domes like the New Orleans Superdome, and have always felt secretly grateful, after some initial apprehension. American stadiums define in many respects the character of their cities, more so than the teams themselves. These days, few players in the major leagues were born in the cities whose pride they supposedly uphold. Most of them were traded and sold, and have no qualms about playing for their traditional enemies. That local pride survives under these circumstances is testimony to the power of advertising and to the desperation of people to belong to a community, but also to the physical fact of the stadiums themselves.

Tiger Stadium in Baton Rouge, for instance, is a monument to the Southern religion of college football, but also to the grandeur of Southern politics. Governor Huey P. Long, the emperor-like ruler of Louisiana in the 1930s, wanted to build a stadium but had federal money that could only be used for public housing. So he combined them. He built the housing in a horseshoe shape and topped it with bleachers. *Voila*, a stadium!

If American stadiums are still, for the most part, apolitical spaces, the same can't be said about stadiums in other countries. In Chile, during General Pinochet's dictatorship, thousands of political prisoners were held starving in the soccer stadium in Santiago, then taken to their deaths by military police. And who can forget the stadium built in Munich by Hitler for the Olympic games of 1936?

Large structures like stadiums are intrinsically ambiguous. As Michel Foucault proved in his book, *The Birth of the Clinic*, such spaces cannot stay unoccupied for long.[1] They demand to be used. Thus, in seventeenth-century Europe, when leprosy mysteriously vanished, the old leprosariums were used to house mentally ill people, thus giving birth to the modern institution of the asylum. While American stadiums are happily filled with the citizens of a democracy resolving their conflicts in sport, it isn't a stretch to conceive of other uses for them. The New Orleans Superdome recently became the world's largest emergency shelter during Hurricane Georges. The citizens were grateful, though it didn't stop them from making off with a few chairs. Happily, they didn't spill into the streets, calling for blood.

All of which should be taken as evidence that baseball is democratic because, in a fashion I have not yet been able to understand, American democracy is an intrinsic part of the game and, conversely, baseball is an intrinsic part of democracy.

Note

1. Michel Foucault, *The Birth of the Clinic* (New York: Pantheon, 1973).

7

California Baseball's Mixed Multitudes

Joel Franks

ALL SORTS OF CALIFORNIANS PLAYED ON THE MARGINS OF PROFESSIONAL BASEBALL during the first four decades of the twentieth century. Carey McWilliams, who wrote tellingly in the 1930s and 1940s about these diverse Californians, called them the "mixed multitudes": Californians of both sexes, of varied racial, ethnic, and social identities. Their need for a sense of community amid enormous social, economic, and demographic changes was often great.

Seventy years ago, as today, California stood out as a magnet for migrants from places like Italy and Japan, Iowa and Oklahoma. And the state expressed no little amount of either hostility or generosity toward newcomers. Therefore, Californians lived on cultural crossroads. Baseball and its child, softball, could make at least temporary sense for a people experiencing substantial and not always very positive transformations. These people and their offspring might find through baseball the ability to connect to their pasts, gain wider social acceptance, link to other communities, achieve control of their lives, show pride in their communities, and just have fun.

While Californians' interest in watching others play baseball flagged at times, the "mixed multitudes" expressed a constant love of playing the game themselves. But, as elsewhere, this love of baseball was often nurtured within the context of changing power relationships in California and nationally. In baseball, social reformers often saw a way to divert poor, often immigrant, youths from gambling, substance abuse, prostitution, and crime. In baseball, employers often saw a way to divert laborers from trade unions. In baseball, civic boomers often saw a way to make money at the expense of neighboring towns and cities. In baseball, school administrators and student bodies often saw a way to assert their school's supremacy at the expense of other schools.

Class and Commerce

Working people in California might well have used baseball as a means of diverting themselves from hard, boring, and even dangerous jobs. Sometimes, however, baseball teams were organized by private companies partly to channel employees from trade union activities. Sometimes, private businesses formed teams as a way of advertising themselves. And sometimes, private and public organizations encouraged baseball simply to furnish badly needed, healthy fun to working people. Regardless, teams representing trade unions or private businesses occasionally furnished opportunities for culturally diverse Californians to display their love of and skill in baseball or softball.

In Santa Clara Valley during the Progressive era, workers actively played baseball. In August 1902, the *San Jose Mercury* reported on a game between a team of mill men and painters. The former won the game and the opportunity to play a nine representing Santa Clara's American Federation of Labor on Labor Day. A number of companies in and around San Jose formed baseball teams. For example, the Fredericksburg Brewery had a nine in the 1900s, as did the New Almaden Mines. Spanish-surnamed players were featured on both teams, but especially on the nine from the New Almaden Mine, which employed a significant number of Latinos. A Martinez played second base for the Fredericksburg Brewery team in 1908. Chris Estrada starred as pitcher for the New Almaden Mine team, backed up by teammates with the surnames of Lopez, Rodriguez, and Torres.[1]

In the 1910s, a team representing employees at the Agnews State Mental Hospital in Santa Clara forged one of the most formidable amateur or semiprofessional teams in the Santa Clara Valley. They would play home games on the grounds of the hospital and supposedly provide a useful distraction to the hospital's "inmates."[2]

During the 1920s and 1930s, baseball and softball leagues proliferated in California. This was particularly the case during the thirties when Californians seemed to need healthy outlets from the pressure cooker atmosphere of the Great Depression. Many of these teams were amateur. Others were semiprofessional in that team members were offered financial inducements such as a piece of the gate money or jobs with the firm sponsoring their team.

Fifty years earlier, when baseball began, young men employed in offices felt they needed baseball as a recreational outlet. That need persisted in the 1920s. For example, a Banker's League was organized in San Francisco in August 1920. Donating the trophy to the winning team was San Francisco's leading banker himself, A.P. Giannini, founder of the Bank of Italy, which would become the Bank of America. Among the nines in this league were teams representing the Federal Reserve, First National Bank, Bank of California, Bank of Italy, Mercantile Trust, Wells Fargo, and Anglo-California Trust.[3]

At about the same time, an Industrial Baseball League formed in San Francisco. The teams were sponsored by some of the largest corporations in the city—Union Oil, Zellerbachs, MJB Coffee, and the Southern Pacific Railroad. The

San Francisco Chronicle called the league a big success in 1922 and maintained that several of the players were one-time professionals. Ten years later, the Industrial Athletic Association ran a baseball league in San Francisco. In August 1931, the MJB Koffee Kids beat the Southern Pacific nine for the league championship.[4]

In the mid-1920s, plenty of baseball teams in the San Jose area represented various private and public organizations. Relatively small businesses such as Carroll-Bishops' cigar store and California Billiards sponsored nines, as did larger organizations such as Pacific Gas and Electric and Agnews State Hospital. In Los Angeles, a firm called Spiegelmann Company sponsored a semiprofessional nine, with Spanish surname players such as Gonzales, Estrada, and Carrillo in the lineup.[5]

Twilight leagues were formed in towns and cities such as Sacramento and Los Angeles in the 1920s. Games were held in the summer and late in the afternoons and early evenings so that working people could participate or just watch. By the 1930s, however, lights were installed at many Golden State community diamonds. In Corona, business people organized the Southern California Baseball Association to stage night games in the late 1920s. By 1929, the Southern California Baseball Association consisted of three eight-team leagues and attracted impressive crowds.[6]

In San Jose during the 1930s, a Night Ball Association was formed. Included in this association were teams of women sponsored by local companies. These female athletes threw, caught, and batted a ball that was nearly as small as the ball used by men, and the pitchers threw the ball overhand. Some of the teams in the Night Ball Association were the Valley Auto Girls, sponsored by an auto dealership, and the Sunsweets, sponsored by the Sunsweet Prune Company. One of the best players in this association was Alice Hinaga, a Japanese American and top-notch pitcher and hitter. Among the teams she played for in the 1930s were the Premier Paint Girls, Red and White Store, California Prune and Apricot Growers, and the Muerson Label team. Playing on the Red and White team with Hinaga was Asaye Sakamoto. In Fresno's Municipal Night League, another Japanese American woman, Maria Kawakami, starred as pitcher and at first base for the Golden State Bakery team.[7]

California men, of course, also played for private company-sponsored teams. In San Jose, the Garden City Chevrolet auto dealership sponsored a junior team in the mid-1930s. Among the players on this team was an apparently Japanese American lad, Yutaka Iso, along with Latinos Joseph Gomez and Able Rodriguez, and a Portuguese player, Alphonso Gomes. Five years later, Sunnyside Market in San Jose sponsored a nine with two players possessing the Japanese last name of Shimizu. Meanwhile, Franco's Market sponsored a team on which Latinos "Pep" Martinez and Bobbie Rodriguez starred. In Southern California, movie studios sponsored baseball teams. Paramount Studios, for example, were represented by a baseball club in 1941.[8]

Racial and Ethnic Communities

Among the more interesting developments in California baseball was the enthusiasm with which the state's Asian American communities embraced the sport during the first half of the twentieth century. Californians of Japanese and Chinese, as well as Filipino, ancestry produced community baseball and softball teams, which played other Asian American and non–Asian American clubs. In so doing, team members frequently crossed what had been substantial cultural borders. Yet California's anti-Asian movement remained relatively unmoved by the spectacle of young men and women of Asian ancestry playing America's "national pastime."

During the early 1900s, the progressive impulse to reform misdirected and potentially misdirected youth found adherents and targets in California's Asian American communities, which were dynamic sites of social and economic transformations. The Chinese Exclusion Act, advocated without regret by many Californians, had reduced the Chinese American population in California during the Progressive era. Nevertheless, by the 1910s, Chinese American communities in California had developed something of a second generation. Japanese immigration may have been hindered by the Gentlemen's Agreement, but a Nisei or second generation had emerged even more impressively among Japanese Americans. Meanwhile, people constantly migrated in and out of these Asian American communities, which were points of destination for legal and illegal immigrants and points of departure for jobs in agriculture, cannery work, and railroad construction. Finally, while separated by an ocean from the politics of their homelands or their parents' homelands, the people living in these communities could not help but be affected by, for example, the efforts to modernize China and Japan either through democratic or not-so-democratic means.

For Asian American reformers in California, sports such as baseball could serve multiple, but related, purposes. To divert younger members of their communities from widely frowned upon and illegal pastimes not only had intrinsic benefits, it also demonstrated to suspicious non-Asian Americans that people of Chinese or Japanese ancestry possessed an appropriate sense of morality. Moreover, it discouraged the growth of cultural practices and institutions that Asian American reformers regarded as baggage the Chinese and Japanese people, no matter where they lived, had to denounce if they were to adapt to the modern world.[9]

In San Jose during the 1910s, Japanese American leaders were concerned about young men in their *nihonmachi* embracing gambling and crime too warmly.

Mas Akizuki, one of these community leaders, recalled much later that a base-ball team was organized in San Jose's *nihonmachi* as a way of providing young men a relatively healthy, wholesome, and widely accepted recreational outlet. The fact that baseball was already a relatively popular sport in Japan undoubt-edly helped matters, as was the prevalence of baseball playing among Japanese Hawaiians. Indeed, San Jose's team was called the Asahis, as was the first Japa-nese Hawaiian club organized in Honolulu in the early 1900s. According to Akizuki, the Asahi club achieved lukewarm support from the San Jose *nihonmachi* initially. By 1920, however, the Asahi baseball field attracted large crowds of Japanese San Joseans.[10]

The San Jose Asahis was not the first Japanese American nine organized in California. In 1903, the Fuji club was established in San Francisco by *Issei* or first-generation Japanese Americans. Subsequently, Issei nines were formed in California during the progressive years. Los Angeles likewise had an Issei team by 1905 and an Issei league by 1910. In 1915, the *Sacramento Bee* reported that the local Japanese team lost to the Victor Brothers College nine, 8 to 7. More than two years later, the *San Jose Mercury* said "a Jap team from Los Angeles" traveled north to play the Agnews State Hospital nine and lost, 21–0.[11]

By 1920, Chinese American nines had surfaced. In 1912, the *Sacramento Bee* reported an impressive celebration of the newly formed Chinese Republic by Chinese Californians in the Colusa area. This celebration included an automobile parade, speakers such as noted Chinese American journalist and reformer, Ng Poon Chew, and a baseball game between a picked nine from Colusa and Colusa's Chinese band. In the 1910s, San Francisco Chinese had organized the Chinese Athletic Club to provide healthy and wholesome physical recreation to mem-bers. In 1918, according to the *San Francisco Chronicle*, the Chinese Athletic Club had formed a baseball nine. About this time, a group of University of California students of Chinese ancestry had organized a baseball team known as the "Sing Fats." Headed by a former Cal football player, Son Kai Kee, they trekked down to San Jose in 1919 to take on a local semipro club and were routed by the San Jose Bears, 19–0, before a large crowd. Given the score, the *Mercury* unnecessarily noted that "the Chinese made a poor showing."[12]

While organizing baseball teams helped to strengthen Asian American com-munities in Progressive-era California, there were other ways baseball played a part in asserting Japanese American and Chinese American community pride. In the 1900s and 1910s, California was visited by Japanese university baseball nines, as well as the University of Hawaii's Chinese Hawaiian club. According to newspaper accounts, these nines received considerable support from local Japa-nese American and Chinese American communities. When, for example, the Waseda University team played in Los Angeles in 1905, many of the spectators possessed Japanese ancestry and rooted enthusiastically for the university nine.

Seven years later, under the headline of "Orientals Await Opening Game," an article in the *Sacramento Bee* reported on the Chinese Hawaiian team's visit to California's capital. It declared that the local "Young Chinese Association" planned on giving their "countrymen" a big reception. All of Sacramento's Chinatown, moreover, was expected at the game. Even the city's Japanese community was supposedly interested, because the Chinese Hawaiian nine had beaten the Waseda University and the Keio University nines in Honolulu. Indeed, the fact that these Japanese and Chinese Hawaiian teams could beat or, at least, hold their own against white teams apparently reinforced Japanese and Chinese Californian community pride in their achievements.[13]

The inter-war years witnessed a proliferation of Asian Pacific American community baseball and softball teams. Japanese American teams were the most active. However, Chinese and Filipino Americans participated as well in community baseball and softball.

San Jose's Asahi club was just one of several Japanese American nines organized in California during the 1920s. While the U.S. Congress explored ways to restrict Japanese immigration to the United States, San Jose's Asahi club forged links to European Americans living in and around Santa Clara County. According to a *San Jose Mercury* sportswriter, "The Japanese boys," who played for Asahi, "have proved to be thorough sports and are highly spoken of among the other teams playing in the winter leagues." The popularity of Japanese American baseball in San Jose's *nihonmachi* was demonstrated when a team called the All Hawaiians came into town to play the Asahis. The *San Jose Mercury* reported that a large crowd gathered at the Asahi's home field to watch the Hawaiians edge the home team, 1–0. The daily, moreover, presented readers with a detailed and respectful inning-by-inning account of the game.[14]

California's Central Valley became a hotbed of Japanese American baseball during the 1920s. In 1924, a baseball team from Japan's Meiji University toured the United States to raise money to rebuild the university destroyed by an earthquake. On a diamond in West Sacramento, this team met a local Japanese American nine. The *Sacramento Bee* declared, "The local Nippon nine is one of the fastest Japanese clubs in this part of the state and play excellent baseball." In 1925, Marysville's Japanese American community petitioned the city council for help in constructing a second ballpark in the town. The petitioners claimed that one park would not fit the needs of European American and Japanese American young people alike. The petitioners, however, assured the council that white youngsters could use the proposed park as well.[15]

The Japanese American Yamato Colony in the Central Valley was represented by a ball club that faced such local opponents as the semiprofessional Lodi nine in 1926; a game that the Yamato team lost, 1–0. In Sacramento, a team called the Nippon Cubs played in the city Municipal League in 1927. During the

Great Depression, the Church Division of Sacramento's Twilight League had clubs called the Japanese Baptists and the Japanese Presbyterians who played nines representing the First Evangelicals and the Church of Latter Day Saints. Around 1934, a Central Valley Japanese League was formed. Eight teams representing central California communities such as Lodi, Livingston, and Walnut Grove belonged to this league. Japanese American churches and businesses took the initiative of sponsoring these nines.[16]

To the south, Japanese Americans headed by Kenishi Zenimura were active in developing community baseball in Fresno. Born in Hiroshima in 1900, Zenimura was a true pioneer of Japanese American baseball. Like many Japanese immigrants, he spent some time in Hawaii before coming to the mainland in 1920. Once in California, he worked at a small restaurant in Fresno and then as a mechanic. Zenimura established a ten-team Nisei League in Fresno and played for a team called the Fresno Athletics, a Japanese American nine that played in Fresno's Twilight League in the 1920s.[17]

Zenimura also organized a Japanese American all-star team, which played out of Fresno. This team competed against and beat top-notch college and university teams in California such as Stanford, St. Mary's, University of Southern California, and Fresno State. It also toured Japan, Korea, and Manchuria in 1924, 1927, and 1937. While in Japan in 1927, the team played against the Negro League's Philadelphia Royal Giants.[18]

Japanese American nines were active in other parts of California during the 1920s and 1930s. According to the *San Francisco Chronicle*, a team called the Alameda Japs lost to a nine representing the Eisenberg Shoe Store, 9–5, in June 1928. Japanese Americans were represented by baseball teams in Watsonville and in nearby Salinas. In 1930, the *Los Angeles Times* published a box score of a team from Hollywood with Japanese surnames. Competing in the semiprofessional Southern California Manager's Association in the fall of 1939 were the Los Angeles Nippons, described in the *Los Angeles Times* as a strong club. Indeed, when the Japanese attack on Pearl Harbor was made public in Los Angeles, the Nippons happened to be playing a team representing Paramount movie studios. According to the *Hollywood Reporter*, FBI men headed to the ball park where the Nippons were playing, but allowed the game to go on until the Paramount nine won, 6–3. Then, according to the *Reporter*, "the G-men rounded up the Jap contingent."[19]

Oakland's Chinese American community was well represented in the 1930s by a tough semiprofessional nine called the Wa Sungs. They were coached by Al Bowen, who, as Lee Gum Hong had, pitched briefly for the Oakland Oaks in 1932. Three of the Wa Sungs were either Lee Gum Hong's brothers or cousins and a few, such as a shortstop with the last name of Chan and a speedy outfielder, Allie Wong, were considered professional material. According to the *Oakland*

Tribune in 1932, "The Wa Sung club has one of the biggest followings of any baseball team in the East Bay." Two years later, the *San Francisco Examiner* declared that the "Bowen quartet, cousins and brothers, are a splendid attraction." Oakland was also a Chinese American softball center. Among the most notable nines in the 1930s was the Dragonettes, a powerful female nine, led by pitching star Gwen Wong. According to *Chinese Digest* sportswriter Herbert Eng, Wong was "a left-handed Amazon." In Sacramento, the Chinese American Chung Wah Association was represented by a baseball team in the early 1930s.[20]

Filipino baseball clubs and leagues were organized in the San Francisco Bay Area, as well as in Los Angeles during the 1920s and 1930s. In 1927, the Filipino All Stars club competed in San Francisco's semiprofessional, mid-winter league. Eight years later, the Filipino Merchants Club played in the Bay Area, as did the Filipino Athletic Club. In Depression-ridden Los Angeles, Filipinos organized an Indoor (Softball) Baseball League with 100 participants representing the Ilocos Sur Association of America, Filipino Patriotic Association, Pungasian Youth, La Union Association, Catholic Filipino Club, Filipino Youth, and the Sons of Cebu.[21]

Other racial and ethnic groups were represented in California by baseball teams. Among these were white ethnic groups. In 1900, the *San Jose Mercury* reported that a number of young men of Portuguese ancestry had formed a baseball team in Santa Clara.[22]

The *Los Angeles Times*, in 1912, briefly described an indoor baseball game at a local recreation center between a team of "Mexicans" and a team of "whites." The latter team won 6–3. In Santa Barbara during the 1920s, a Mexican American *mutualista* or mutual-aid society, *La Uniona Patriotica Mexicano Independiente*, sponsored a championship baseball team. Early in the 1930s, the Mexican Athletic Club had a baseball team in Sacramento. In 1933, one could read in the *Sacramento Bee* that the Mexican Athletic Club of Sacramento beat Stockton's Mexican Club, 15–10. Among the "sandlot" clubs playing in the Bay Area during the mid-1930s were the Mexican Athletic Club of San Francisco.[23]

In *Labor and Community*, historian Gilbert Gonzalez points out the importance of baseball to people of Mexican ancestry living in various Orange County labor camps. Among the nines formed in the 1920s was a La Habra club called *Los Juviniles*. Gonzales writes, "*Los Juviniles*, like other village teams, primarily played other Mexican teams in an informal league. Although recognition for the best team was generally forthcoming, no one was crowned champion."[24]

In 1915, an African American team representing Los Angeles's "Colored YMCA" played the Manual Arts High School nine. The correspondent for the *California Eagle*, an African American newspaper published out of Los Angeles, maintained, "This is the first time so far as I can remember that a colored team of any sort has had a game with the first team of any of the leading high schools."[25]

California's African American communities were represented by several baseball teams between the wars. According to the *San Francisco Chronicle*, a black semipro team, the Vernet Giants, played out of San Francisco in 1925. Also in 1925, the *Sacramento Bee* reported that the Oakland Colored Giants trekked up to Eureka to lose to the Humboldt All Stars.[26]

During the Depression, African American community nines seemed to proliferate. Another team called the Colored Giants played out of Marysville. The *San Jose Mercury's* Henry Hicks described the Colored Giants as "the finest negro club ever organized in the northern part of the state." He reported that that the team consisted of players from Sacramento, Richmond, and Oakland, as well as Marysville. The Colored Athletic League was represented by a team in Fresno's National League. In 1934, the *San Jose Mercury* referred to the ball team representing the Athens Colored Elks of Oakland as "one of the finest colored baseball teams on the Coast." Calling them "the Oakland darkies," the *Mercury* claimed that the "Colored Elks" played a "flashy type of baseball," highlighted by "clockwork teamwork." Their stars were Jim Lane, designated by the *Mercury* as the "bronze Babe Ruth," and Wilson Record, who played Negro League ball with the Detroit Stars. Playing in Santa Clara in 1938, was another baseball team called the "Colored Giants" and a softball team called the "Colored Ghosts." Toward the end of the 1930s, an organization called the Los Angeles Colored Athletics had a team. Early in 1941, the *Los Angeles Times* reported on a game in southern Pasadena between the Los Angeles Colored Giants and the Rosabell Plumbers. Led by former Pacific Coast League (PCL) star, Lou Novikoff, the Plumbers won 9–0.[27]

School Days

Schools, colleges, and universities furnished opportunities for children and young adults to play baseball and softball during the first four decades of this century. By the dawn of the twentieth century, most school officials recognized baseball and softball as healthy forms of recreation for their pupils. High school and postsecondary school officials often considered baseball, as well as other competitive sports, a means of engendering school spirit. Clearly, however, for older students in California, football was the leading competitive sport by the 1920s, if not earlier.

Educational institutions generally reflected the cultural distinctions in California. Earlier in this chapter, we mentioned the game between the Colored YMCA in Los Angeles and Manual Arts High School. The pervasive character of racial exclusion in the Golden State minimized contacts between whites and non-white students on and off the baseball diamond. Nevertheless, through baseball, racial, ethnic, and sometimes gender, borders were crossed in California schools.

The Progressive era witnessed several examples of California school-aged ballplayers crossing racial and ethnic borders. In 1906, Poly High School in Los Angeles had a player with the last name of Lane on its roster. The *Los Angeles Times* described him as "a hard hitting colored man." In 1915, according to the *Times*, Los Angeles High School had "Sangi . . . the Japanese . . . pitcher." The next year, the *Times* reported that Sam Sakamoto was the "demon ballplayer of Los Angeles High." Meanwhile, Occidental College, an institution lying between Los Angeles and Pasadena, claimed a pitcher on its baseball team known as Montijo, "the Mexican marvel."[28]

San Diego High School fielded a girls' indoor baseball or softball team in the 1910s that played against similar teams representing National City, Coronado, and Long Beach High Schools. To the north, indoor baseball attracted the participation of female students at the University of California and Mills College in Oakland. Harold Seymour reports on the game between the two schools in 1915 and periodically afterward. In 1912, the *Sacramento Bee* provided an account of a baseball game in Chico between female students from the Training School and the Normal School. The *Bee* declared, "Some of the bloomer girls declare that if it were proper, they would try out for the boys' team."[29]

The number of school-aged players crossing gender, racial, and ethnic borders in California seemed to expand in the 1920s and 1930s. In 1922, the *San Jose Mercury* reported that a pitcher with the surname of Hernandez competed on the San Jose High School boys' nine and Luz Chavez pitched for the Hester Grammar School girls' baseball team. San Jose High School had a girls' team, too. The *Mercury* reported on April 6, 1922, that it defeated a nine representing Castroville's Washington High School, 12–6. At about the same time, girls' baseball teams represented both Sunnyvale Grammar School in Santa Clara County and nearby Mountain View Grammar School. On April 9, 1922, the *Mercury* published a box score of a game between Cambrian and Orchard Grammar Schools. Hispanic and Japanese surnames were evident on both teams. In the spring of 1924, two Santa Clara County grammar schools played boys' teams and girls' teams against each other. A girl with the Japanese surname of Takimoto played on the Los Gatos Grammar School team against the Berryessa and Penitencia Union Grammar School girls' nine. In Southern California in 1925, Los Angeles High School was represented by two girls' baseball teams. Ten years later, young women representing El Monte High School won the Valley League Indoors Baseball championship.[30]

In the mid-1930s, the star player on Pasadena's Muir Technical High School was a soon-to-be-famous Jackie Robinson. In 1936, Robinson was named to the annual Pomona tournament all-star team, along with two other future greats, Ted Williams from Hoover High School in San Diego, and Bob Lemon from Long Beach's Wilson High School. After graduating from Muir, Robinson starred on the Pasadena Junior College nine, although he preferred playing basketball and football.[31]

At about the same time, the University of California, Los Angeles (UCLA) started to gain national prominence in intercollegiate athletics. Among the big reasons why was Kenny Washington, an African American from Los Angeles whose all-around athletic skills were rivaled by few at the time. Washington, the son of a prominent Negro Leaguer, Ed Washington, gained his greatest fame at the Westwood campus as a superbly versatile football player. However, Washington could also play baseball and he starred at shortstop for the UCLA nine, which competed with other Pacific Coast university teams representing the University of California, Stanford, and UCLA's keenest rival, the University of Southern California. A powerful hitter, Washington awed spectators with a long home run against Stanford and achieved a career batting average of over .400.[32]

In 1939, Washington would be joined at UCLA by another African American with amazing talent in football, as well as in basketball and track. Jackie Robinson had electrified Los Angeles–area sports fans as a multisport hero at Pasadena Junior College. Raised in Pasadena and the brother of an Olympic broad jump medal winner, Robinson, like Washington, was best known as a football player. In the fall of 1939, Robinson teamed up with Washington to make UCLA one of the most exciting football teams in the country. By the time Pearl Harbor was attacked, Robinson would play baseball for the UCLA nine, but at that time the National Pastime seemed to attract relatively little of his interest or passion compared to other sports. Indeed, his batting average dipped below .200 and most contemporaries considered Washington the better prospect in baseball.[33]

Other California college and university diamonds also hosted ballplayers transcending social barriers between the wars. In 1923, the *San Jose Mercury* declared that Fred Koba, who starred at shortstop for the San Jose Asahis, roamed the infield for the Stanford University nine. Social scientist, Eliot Mears, claimed that in 1925 the Occidental College baseball team elected a Japanese American named Tanaka as captain. One of the Occidental Players volunteered the information that "T . . . may be yellow on the outside . . . but he is white on the inside." Playing third base for San Francisco State College in the early 1930s was Joe Lee, who played for the Wa Sungs of Oakland. African American Johnny Allen starred on the San Jose State College nine in the late 1930s, as well as the college's basketball and football squads.[34]

Native Americans in California also played plenty of baseball. Active in Southern California's baseball diamonds during the Progressive era was a Native American nine representing the Sherman Institute, a federally funded boarding school situated in Riverside County. Generally consisting of young men from the Cahuilla reservation, the Sherman Institute team played white high school and college teams. In the early 1900s, John Tortes played for the Sherman Institute nine. Later, he would play and star with the New York Giants as "Chief" Meyers.

In 1905, Tortes was on the team that defeated the University of Southern California, 7–4. A *Los Angeles Times* correspondent expressed surprise. According to this writer, it was common knowledge that American Indians could play football, but there were many sports experts who doubted they could play baseball: "Various managers passed 'the Indian' up, fearing he would not know enough about the rules to run the right way around the bases." In any event, in beating USC, the Sherman Institute players performed as if "a ghost dance or a scalping party was on hand." Sherman baseball players may have outplayed whites, but the *Times* writer indicated that their "savage" backgrounds followed them onto the baseball diamond.[35]

Over the years, California school nines scheduled games against opponents of diverse racial and ethnic identities. Some of the games were played in California, and some were played in places like Hawaii and Japan. One of the more interesting of these games occurred in 1905 when the Waseda University nine met a contingent from Sherman Institute in 1905. Writing for *Sporting Life*, Roger Ransom observed of the Waseda-Sherman contest:

> The meeting of the little brown men from the realms of the Mikado and the red men from Sherman Institute . . . marked an epoch in the history of our National Game, which is deserving of more than passing mention in the columns of America's greatest baseball paper. For the first time a baseball game was played by teams whose players were from two races that have adopted a sport heretofore distinctly that of white men. . . .
>
> The Orientals from Japan had it over the aborigines during all stages of the game. With the exception of the sixth inning, when the Sherman Braves with a whoop broke from the reservation and went tearing madly about until the six of them had scored before coach and trainer Field Marshall Hashido and his aides drove them back.[36]

Ransom's blend of contempt and respect for these athletes of color was not unusual. When the Waseda nine played Stanford in a game in San Francisco, the *San Francisco Chronicle* described the Waseda ballplayers as "the remarkable little brown men." When Santa Clara College traveled to Hawaii in 1908, *San Jose Mercury* readers read similar sentiments: "The Island teams are made up of Chinese, Japs, Americans, and Hawaiians. They were in the field it is said to be inferior to the average American team's work, but they are good batsmen."[37]

The coming of the aforementioned University of Hawaii's Chinese nine frequently stirred ambivalence in California baseball circles. The Chinese Hawaiians arrived in California in the spring of 1914 and promptly defeated nines representing Stanford University and St. Mary's College in the San Francisco Bay Area. They then trekked to Southern California to play against Occidental College. The *Los Angeles Times* announced their arrival by printing stereotype cartoons in its sports pages. One cartoon showed white players stepping on the queues of Chinese base runners. The caption read, "A practical way to stop a base stealer." Yet a more respectful text accompanied the cartoons. The *Times* stated that "sensational base running and perfect fielding were featured" on the Chinese Hawaiian team.[38]

After the game, a *Times* headline declared that "nine little Chinamen" beat the Occidental team. An accompanying cartoon used stereotypical images to portray the Chinese Hawaiian ballplayers. But the actual text of the story reporting on the game reveals Chinese Hawaiians unbounded by racial stereotypes. The victorious Hawaiians beat Occidental and aggressively and joyfully rode the umpire and the opposition. When the Occidental catcher tried to fool a Chinese Hawaiian base runner with the hidden ball trick, one Chinese Hawaiian player yelled, "I thought we were going to learn something about baseball by coming across the Pacific Ocean. I didn't expect to see anyone try such a bush league trick at least a century old."[39]

University baseball in the Progressive era disclosed some of the class-associated conflicts found in other parts of America's sporting world—indeed in other aspects of American life. Americans of middle- and upper-class origins frequently disagreed over the role of sport in education and this disagreement easily invaded university athletics at such institutions as Stanford and the University of California, Berkeley. In the nineteenth century, college and university sports were supposed to express the ethos of amateurism. Clearly, that ethos had weakened considerably by the end of the nineteenth century. It simply could not wall itself off from the commercialization of modern, capitalist American culture.

The problem of amateurism and college and university sports persisted into the twentieth century and, one can now safely say, beyond. By the twentieth century, American-style (as opposed to soccer- and rugby-style) football had become the most popular competitive sport on most male and coed college and university campuses. The sport's competitiveness and violence produced vociferous fans on and off the campus, and added to the deterioration of genteel amateurism, in which fair play was supposedly more important than victory.

During the first decade of the twentieth century, both the University of California and Stanford banned American-style football from their intercollegiate sports program. One justification was that the sport had become too professionalized—too wrapped up in victory for its own sake. Another was that the sport engendered too much violence and serious, even fatal, injuries. Many other colleges and universities on the Pacific Coast followed Cal's and Stanford's lead. In 1911, Benjamin Ide Wheeler, president of the University of California, and David Starr Jordan, president of Stanford, began to express dismay over intercollegiate baseball. Critics probably thought that such attention was long overdue. In 1905, for example, William "Heinie" Heitmuller, a Cal baseball and football star, was declared ineligible to play baseball for the university. Heitmuller was accused of playing for an Oakland professional team under the assumed name of Constantine. Heitmuller countered that he never played the game under an assumed name and did not take money for doing what he considered a favor for the Oakland club. His amateur status, therefore, remained pure. Heitmuller, nevertheless, lost his eligibility just as Cal was going to meet the rival Stanford nine.[40]

In 1911, Cal's Wheeler reacted with anger when Cal rooters ridiculed an opposing pitcher. A lover of baseball, Wheeler conceded that he would not ban the sport, but declared, "I do not think that college men should undertake to battle the pitcher." In other words, Cal students should not have behaved like ordinary, noncollege students at the ballpark. Meanwhile, Stanford's Jordan sought to exile baseball from his campus. According to the *San Francisco Examiner*, "It was the vulgar and persistent attempts to rattle the pitcher that most affected Jordan's attitude." Jordan was appalled by the kind of insults flung by Stanford students at opponents. Intercollegiate baseball games, he believed, did not seem to bring out the best in Stanford students. Jordan decried the game's "muckerism" and maintained, "Baseball is played on a low plane."[41]

Baseball, unlike American football, endured Jordan's animosity. The national pastime remained on the Palo Alto campus while American football was banned. However, Jordan and the others who supported a genteel amateurism could not have been happy that California's college and university baseball teams had become breeding grounds for the professional leagues. Cal, for example, dispatched Orvie Overall and "Heinie" Heitmuller to professional baseball in the early 1900s. The notorious Hal Chase went to the Los Angeles Angels in 1904 from Santa Clara College. In the first few decades of the twentieth century, Harry Hooper, along with Joe Oescher and Eddie Burns, left St. Mary's for the professional ranks.[42] Thankfully, perhaps, David Starr Jordan was no longer president of Stanford in the 1920s. Otherwise, he would have witnessed Ernie Nevers, an awesomely versatile athlete, not only become a professional football player after his stint at Stanford, but a professional baseball player as well.

The "Bushes"

Whether they competed for company, ethnic group, or town, whether they played hardball or softball, and whether they were men or women, semiprofessionals comprised an important part of California's baseball scene in the first four decades of the twentieth century. San Diego, for example, did not have a PCL team until the late1930s, but according to historian Frank Norris, its residents could play and watch plenty of baseball in the 1910s:

> The numerous teams represented businesses, navy ships, neighborhoods, or rival towns. As might be expected a few teams remained intact for ten years or more, while countless others stayed together for only a single season if that long. The situation, therefore, was largely similar to the present situation extant in the park leagues of San Diego and nearby towns.[43]

Harold Seymour contends that Southern California was a hotbed of semipro baseball during the 1930s. Several semipro nines performed in and around Hollywood. Meanwhile, Southern California communities from Ventura and Bakersfield to the north, San Diego to the south, and Riverside to the east supported many semipro teams.[44]

There were several factors encouraging diverse Californians to play in semiprofessional and amateur baseball and softball leagues. One, obviously, was that California's climate allowed men and women, as well as boys and girls, to take to the diamonds throughout the year. Harold Seymour writes, "The salubrious West Coast climate provided a receptive avenue for softball."[45] A second factor was that amateur and semiprofessional baseball, often called "bush league" baseball, was widely seen as an incubator for top-notch, professional talent. The *San Francisco Chronicle's* Harry Smith wrote in 1937, "If we didn't have the 'bushers,' we wouldn't be developing our stars for the minor leagues, and if the minors didn't have talent, the majors would hardly amount to much."[46]

Indeed, the sandlots and bush leagues of San Francisco seemed to propel one good ballplayer after another into the Pacific Coast League and the majors during the 1910s, 1920s, and 1930s. Frank Ish, part owner of the San Francisco Seals remarked in 1912 that "we have found that right here in California the bushes are loaded with youngsters who can play rings around the men we import from the East at big expense." The DiMaggio brothers, Harold Peterson points out, learned to play baseball on San Francisco's Russian Hill, near the Fisherman's Wharf area: "Their field was the asphalt and tar North Beach playground, their bases bits of concrete, and home plate was a flattened tin can. . . . A sawed off oar from Papa Joe's fishing boat served as the bat."[47]

Third, as one can gather from Peterson's remarks, playing baseball and softball frequently required as much, if not more, imagination than money. Historian Susan Cahn maintains that softball's popularity in California and elsewhere during the 1930s was significantly dependent upon it not costing too much to play and watch:

> As a relatively inexpensive outdoor sport, it seemed perfectly fitted to Depression-era recreational needs. For a minimal admission charge, if any, fans could

gather in the twilight of weekday evenings or for long, sunny weekend afternoons and watch friends and neighbors play a modified version of baseball
that, with its softer ball and shorter basepaths, seemed more accessible to athletes of modest ability.[48]

Fourth, bush-league baseball was good for business. As mentioned earlier,
private businesses promoted themselves by sponsoring teams. What is more, in
Hollister, a town in San Benito County, the Southern Pacific Company owned
the local baseball park in 1920.[49]

Finally, bush-league baseball could inspire neighborhood and town boosters
when professional teams were unavailable. Rivalries between neighborhoods and
towns were played out on baseball diamonds in the early decades of the twentieth century. In 1900, the *San Jose Mercury* reported that a fierce competition had
developed between Willow Glen, a middle-class district in San Jose, and the
nearby town of Los Gatos. A game between nines representing Willow Glen and
Los Gatos was played at San Jose's Cycle's Park. Apparently, a fight interrupted
the game and the deputy sheriff took it upon himself to stop the game entirely
before someone got seriously hurt. Five years later, according to the *San Jose
Mercury*, "Baseball is very strong at Lodi and Stockton. A small sized battle being started at Lodi on Memorial Day as a result of somewhat personal newspaper
comments made by baseball writers of the two towns." In 1919, the *Mercury's*
Jack Graham declared that San Jose baseball fans wanted to see a game between
the San Jose Merchants or the San Jose Bears against a team from Stockton. He
stated, "There are a lot of fans who would like to see a good local team wallop
the best that Stockton has just for old time's sake." And twenty years later, the
San Jose daily insisted that a big rivalry persisted between semipro nines from
San Mateo and San Jose.[50]

For bush-league followers such as Jack Graham, local nines ought to have
represented their towns and cities and not simply promote private businesses.
He wrote in August 1919, "It is the advertising of the city that we are after in
baseball circles and not some company who is advertising its manufacturing
business." He urged, then, that baseball supporters in and around San Jose encourage interest in nines clearly representing and promoting San Jose and nearby
Santa Clara, Sunnyvale, or Los Gatos.[51]

Obviously, California baseball supporters frequently took bush-league baseball seriously. For example, club managers were willing to pay players, although
not enough to make them full-time professionals. In the 1920s, semipro league
organizers were apparently concerned about overpaying the players. In 1923,
according to the *Sacramento Bee*, the Sacramento Valley Baseball League consisted of semipro teams representing towns such as Woodland, Colusa, Williams, and Dunnigan. But league organizers were worried about keeping "wages"

down. One of the managers, R.P. Wallace, who also served as auditor for Yolo County, complained, "Fancy wages have broken up most of the semipro leagues, and we don't propose to make the salary blunder in this league." Meanwhile, the San Joaquin Valley League sought to solve the problem of overpaid players by limiting clubs to $2,300 each for labor costs.[52]

Just as the professionals, semipros in California and elsewhere signed contracts, and players and other teams were expected to honor those contracts. In 1920, Mission League managers were disturbed when the Salinas team signed a contract jumper. The signing was voided by the Mission League, which, in turn, sought to ban the player from competing in other leagues. Later in the year, Madera of the North Valley League signed Hal Chase and Harl Maggert. Chase had just been exiled from the Mission League for involvement in a PCL fixing scandal, to which Maggert was directly tied. The management of the Chowchila team subsequently protested Madera's actions.[53]

Even if one didn't get money to play bush-league baseball or softball, a ballplayer could still do fairly well. In the spring of 1941, Lou Novikoff played softball in the Southern California area. The *San Francisco Chronicle* claimed that Novikoff could get in about twenty to twenty-five hours of play during the week for a team sponsored by an industrial firm which, in turn, would offer the long-time professional baseball player a cushy job.[54]

The bush league teams representing California's smaller cities offered some opportunities for individuals to both patrol and cross racial and ethnic borderlands. In 1902, the San Jose Amateur Club got a chance to play a team the *San Jose Mercury* dubbed the "Colored Champs." It was an opportunity the San Jose nine generally enjoyed as it won easily, 18–5. According to the *Mercury*, "The crowd was large and enthusiastic and they cheered for the visitors, especially the colored spectators who had turned out in force to see the game." The same year, the *San Francisco Examiner* reported on a Valley League game between Hanford and Bakersfield. Hanford beat Bakersfield, 15–6. And "Sandow and Chico, the Mexican battery, who played with the Hanford team made an excellent showing." The Spanish surnamed Oscar Chavez managed the Santa Barbara semiprofessional nine in 1907, while a Robles played on the Pastime amateur nine in San Jose in 1908, and a Martinez suited up for a semipro team representing San Jose in 1909. In Santa Cruz, former full-time professional Abel Arrelanes managed the local semipro nine. On the team as well, were Joe Arrelanes and E. Arrelanes. In the early 1910s, an American Indian pitcher named Luther "Indian" Smith caught the attention of the PCL's Portland Beavers by dominating batters in Northern California semiprofessional circles. In 1916, the *San Francisco Chronicle* reported that the Lodi semiprofessional club had a Japanese player named Tokio. The *Chronicle* declared, "He is said to be some player and puts lots of life in the game with a wonderful amount of pep." In the 1930s, Russell

Hinaga captained the Milpitas semiprofessional team. And George Berrysea, "a young Indian," pitched for the Langendorf Royals, sponsored by Langendorf Bakery Company and playing out of the East Bay.[55]

Allie Wong was considered one of the standout semiprofessional players in the Bay Area. In the late 1938s, he played on a nine called the Moffett Packers and was a member of an East Bay semiprofessional all-star team, which tangled in an exhibition game against a team of major leaguers. Wong got two hits against John Babich, who pitched for the Boston Braves. Wong, according to the *Chinese Digest*, was "the greatest Chinese exponent of baseball today."[56]

Softball and the 1930s

We have explored softball earlier, but we should probably look into it in greater depth. This variation on baseball has, indeed, been a prominent recreational and, to some degree, spectator sport in California. The Great Depression years, as both Susan Cahn and Harold Seymour point out, witnessed a considerable spurt in the sport's popularity in the Golden State, especially among culturally diverse, working-class Californians. Cahn cites a survey conducted in 1938 of the Los Angeles area. According to this survey, 9,000 softball teams existed within a 100-mile radius. Of these 9,000 squads, 1,000 were female teams. Softball, Cahn maintains, attracted a multicultural group of players and supporters: "On the West Coast, Mexican and Asian immigrants took up the sport with help from ethnic businesses, schools, and service agencies. Japanese Americans, for example, organized teams through Japanese language schools and Buddhist associations." In Oakland, according to Seymour, softball and badminton were the most popular recreational sports during the 1930s among adults. Three lighted diamonds were opened in 1936. In 1937, 4,000 people in Oakland played softball, while throughout Alameda County about 500 teams had been organized.[57]

In Southern California, women's softball teams possessed colorful—although often patronizing—names and exciting players. On August 28, 1936, the *Los Angeles Times* ran a picture in its sport section of Jo La Fargue, who starred at third base for a team sponsored by Mark C. Bloom's tire company. The team was unsurprisingly called the Bloom Girls. Meanwhile, movie actor and former boxer, Maxie Rosenbloom sponsored a team called Maxie Rosenbloom's Curvaceous Cuties. Other softball teams in the area were known as the Balia Ice Cream Cuties, the Bank of America Bankerettes, and the Columbia Picture Starlettes.[58]

Men, of course, played softball too. San Benito County softball fans were treated to an all-star game in 1937. The Gilroy All-Stars were led by African American pitcher, Lee Wilkinson. Another African American pitcher, Dick Fields, led the Hollister All-Stars.[59] In Southern California, Pasadena ran an Owl League,

which played softball by baseball rules. One of the top teams in the Owl League
was a club called Floracombe, which was commercially sponsored and made up
of members of the African American North Pasadena Athletic Club. Starring at
shortstop for the team was a teenager named Jackie Robinson.[60]

One of the big softball events in California was a jamboree held at Los Angeles's
cavernous Memorial Coliseum. During the softball jamboree, six games were
played at one time. One of the most interesting teams participating in June 1940
was Grants' All-Stars. This squad included two of the best athletes in America—
Kenny Washington and Jackie Robinson.[61]

Conclusion

Between the Pacific Coast League teams and the vast number of Golden State
semiprofessional and amateur squads, Californians could survive without the
major leagues. Yet what made the semiprofessional and amateur nines particularly important is that they conveyed the hopes and passions of California's "mixed
multitudes." It was not always easy, but those who played on the lower rungs of
California's baseball ladder consistently contested the notion that baseball belonged to any one group or geographic region.

Notes

1. *San Jose Mercury* (August 25, 1902), 8; *San Jose Mercury* (August 4, 1908), 5; *San Jose Mercury* (August 17, 1909), 3.

2. *San Francisco Chronicle* (January 20, 1917), 10.

3. *San Francisco Chronicle* (August 17, 1920), 1hj; *San Francisco Chronicle* (April 12, 1921), 1h.

4. *San Francisco Chronicle* (August 12, 1922), 3h; *San Francisco Chronicle* (August 30, 1931), 2h.

5. *Los Angeles Times* (March 9, 1925), pt. 1, 10; *San Jose Mercury* (May 10, 1926), 17.

6. *Los Angeles Times* (February 7, 1925), pt. 1, 7; Larry G. Bowman, "Kansas City Monarchs and Night Ball," *The National Pastime* 16 (1996): 80.

7. *San Jose Mercury* (September 18, 1934), 14; *San Jose Mercury* (July 1, 1935), 13; "Diamonds in the Rough: Japanese Americans in Baseball," *Nikkei Heritage* (Spring 1997): 18–19.

8. *San Jose Mercury* (September 2, 1934), 19; *San Jose Mercury* (September 5, 1939), 5; *San Jose Mercury* (September 11, 1939), 7; Otto Friedrich, *City of Net: A Portrait of Holly-wood in the 1940s* (New York: Harper & Row, 1986), 102.

9. Yuji Ichioka, *The Issei: The World of First Generation Japanese Immigrants* (New York: Free Press, 1988.)

10. Steven Misawa, ed. *Beginnings: Japanese Americans in San Jose* (San Jose: Japanese American Community Senior Services, 1981), 14.

11. "Diamonds in the Rough," 6; *Sacramento Bee* (March 1, 1915), 10; *San Jose Mercury* (August 6, 1917), 8.

12. *Sacramento Bee* (April 1, 1912), 6; *San Francisco Chronicle* (February 16, 1918), 24; *San Jose Mercury* (August 23, 1919), 5; *San Jose Mercury* (August 25, 1919), 5.

13. *Sacramento Bee* (April 1, 1912), 6; *Sacramento Bee* (April 5, 1912), 10.

14. *San Jose Mercury* (February 19, 1923), 9.

15. *Sacramento Bee* (May 3, 1924), 25; *Sacramento Bee* (July 2, 1925), 18.

16. *Sacramento Bee* (March 5, 1927), 2; *Sacramento Bee* (July 2, 1933), Sports Section, 2; *San Francisco Chronicle* (October 5, 1926), 24.

17. "Diamonds in the Rough," 8.

18. Ibid.

19. *San Francisco Chronicle* (June 12, 1928), 4h; *San Francisco Examiner* (June 9, 1935), part 1, 21; *Los Angeles Times* (January 27, 1930), 10; *Los Angeles Times* (October 11, 1939), part 1, 18; Friedrich, *City of Nets*, 102.

20. *Oakland Tribune* (September 20, 1932), 18; *San Francisco Examiner* (March 6, 1934), 24; *San Francisco Examiner* (September 20, 1932), 16; *Sacramento Bee* (July 10, 1933), 15; *Chinese Digest* (March, 1938): 18

21. *San Francisco Examiner* (June 4, 1935), 20; *San Francisco Examiner* (June 9, 1935), 21; *San Francisco Chronicle* (March 1, 1927), 2h; Bencio Catupusan, *The Filipino Occupation and Recreational Activities in Los Angeles* (Saratoga, CA: R&E Research Associates, 1975), 34.

22. *San Jose Mercury* (August 9, 1900), 7.

23. *Los Angeles Times* (April 7, 1912), part vii, 7; Albert Camarillo, *Chicanos in a Changing Society: From Mexican Pueblos to American Barrios in Santa Barbara and Southern California, 1846–1930* (Cambridge, MA: Harvard University Press, 1979), 152, 154; *Sacramento Bee* (November 14, 1932), 14; *Sacramento Bee* (July 3, 1933), 4; *San Francisco Examiner* (June 9, 1935), 21.

24. Gilbert G. Gonzalez, *Labor and Community: Mexican Citrus Worker Villages in a Southern California County, 1900–1950* (Urbana: University of Illinois Press, 1994), 94.

25. *California Eagle* (January 23, 1915), 5.

26. *San Francisco Chronicle* (April 12, 1925), H3; *Sacramento Bee* (Sept. 1, 1925), 28.

27. *San Jose Mercury* (July 7, 1935), 32; *San Jose Mercury* (September 1, 1934), 15; *San Jose Mercury* (August 3, 1938), 17; *Sacramento Bee* (July 10, 1933), 15; *San Francisco Chronicle* (July 1, 1934), Fresno and Valley Section, A; *Los Angeles Times* (October 1, 1939), 18; *Los Angeles Times* (February 3, 1941), part 2, 10.

28. *Los Angeles Times* (June 3, 1906), part 3, 1; *Los Angeles Times* (March 14, 1915), part 7, 8; *Los Angeles Times* (April 4, 1916), part 3, 3; *Los Angeles Times* (April 1, 1916), part 3, 1.

29. Barbara Noonkester, "The American Sportswoman from 1900–1920," in *Her Story in Sport*, ed. Reet Howell (West Point, NY: Leisure Press, 1982), 186–194; Harold Seymour, *The People's Game* (New York: Oxford University Press, 1990), 472; *Sacramento Bee* (April 2, 1912), 10.

30. *San Jose Mercury* (April 1, 1922), 12; *San Jose Mercury* (April 6, 1922), 12; *San Jose Mercury* (April 13, 1922), 15; *San Jose Mercury* (April 9, 1922), 20; *San Jose Mercury* (April 10, 1922), 8; *San Jose Mercury* (March 1, 1924), 16; *Los Angeles Times* (November 20, 1915), pt. 5, 6; *Los Angeles Times* (March 14, 1925), pt.1, 11.

31. Arnold Rampersad, *Jackie Robinson: A Biography* (New York: Alfred A. Knopf, 1997), 18–62.

32. *Los Angeles Times* (March 16, 1938), part 2, 1.

33. Rampersad, *Jackie Robinson*, 18–62; *Sporting News* (March 15, 1950), 14.

34. *San Jose Mercury* (February 18, 1923), 24; *San Jose Mercury* (January 10, 1940), 12; Elliot G. Mears, *Resident Orientals on the Pacific Coast* (Chicago: University of Chicago Press, 1928), 366; *San Francisco Examiner* (April 17, 1934), 22.

35. *Los Angeles Times* (May 4, 1905), part ii, 3.

36. Cited in Albert Spalding, *America's National Pastime* (Lincoln: University of Nebraska Press, 1992), 397.

37. *San Francisco Chronicle* (May 1, 1905), 8; *San Jose Mercury* (August 4, 1908), 5.

38. *Los Angeles Times* (March 10, 1914), part 3, 2.

39. *Los Angeles Times* (March 15, 1915), part 7, 7.

40. *San Francisco Chronicle* (April 5, 1905), 8; John E. Spalding, *Always on Sunday: The California Baseball League, 1886–1915* (Manhattan, KS: Ag Press, 1992), 98.

41. *San Francisco Examiner* (April 4, 1911), 1; *San Francisco Examiner* (April 4, 1911), 2.

42. *San Jose Mercury* (April 5, 1903), 2; *San Francisco Chronicle* (April 17, 1901), 9; *San Francisco Chronicle* (October 2, 1940), 35; Paul J. Zingg, "The Phoenix Fenway: The 1915 World Conferences and Collegiate Connections to the Major League," *Journal of Sport History* 17 (Spring 1994): 35–56.

43. Frank Norris, "San Diego Baseball: The Early Years," *Journal of San Diego History* 30 (Winter 1984): 8.

44. Seymour, *People*, 272.

45. Ibid., 372.

46. *San Francisco Chronicle* (February 12, 1937), 2H.

47. *San Francisco Chronicle* (September 3, 1912), 9; Harold Peterson, *The Man Who Invented Baseball* (New York: Scribner, 1963), 170.

48. Susan K. Cahn, *Coming on Strong: Gender and Sexuality in Twentieth-Century Women's Sport* (New York: Free Press, 1994), 141.

49. *San Jose Mercury* (July 17, 1920), 8.

50. *San Jose Mercury* (May 7, 1900), 8; *San Jose Mercury* (June 2, 1905), 12; *San Jose Mercury* (August 24, 1919), 14; *San Jose Mercury* (August 7, 1938), 20.

51. *San Jose Mercury* (August 26, 1919), 8.

52. *Sacramento Bee* (April 14, 1923), 26; *San Francisco Chronicle* (March 5, 1923), H3.

53. *San Jose Mercury* (July 9, 1920), 20; *San Jose Mercury* (August 14, 1920), 2.

54. *San Francisco Chronicle* (March 15, 1941), 3H.

55. *San Francisco Chronicle* (June 11, 1916), 39; *San Francisco Chronicle* (March 19, 1934), H16; *San Jose Mercury* (August 25, 1902), 8. *San Jose Mercury* (August 3, 1908), 10; *San Jose Mercury* (April 17, 1909), 12; *San Francisco Examiner* (April 14, 1902), 7; *Los Angeles Times* (August 12, 1907), 13; *Los Angeles Times* (November 25, 1915), part 3, 3; *San Jose Morning Times* (August 23, 1909), 8.

56. *Chinese Digest*, March 1938, 18; June 1938, 17

57 Cahn, *Coming On Strong*, 142; Seymour, *People*, 371.

58. *Los Angeles Times* (August 28, 1936), 9; Seymour, *People*, 274.

59. *San Jose Mercury* (July 10, 1937), 16.

60. Rampersad, *Jackie Robinson*, 44.

61. *Los Angeles Times* (June 19 1940), 7.

8

THE ROAD TO COOPERSTOWN
Japanese American Baseball, 1899–1999

Kerry Yo Nakagawa

THE NISEI (SECOND GENERATION JAPANESE AMERICAN) BASEBALL LEAGUE EXHIBIT has earned a place in the Baseball Hall of Fame at Cooperstown, New York. The league has played a significant role in the history of American baseball, crossed paths with some of the great heroes of the sport, and promoted this all-American sport internationally.

Nikkei (Japanese American) baseball generally parallels, in many respects, the development of American baseball. Beginning in the early 1900s, Japanese American baseball leagues began to sprout up in towns and cities throughout Hawaii, California, Washington, and in the Rocky Mountain states of Colorado, Wyoming, and Utah, and also in Nebraska. Despite the discrimination and racism experienced by Japanese Americans during that time, on the baseball field they could feel equal to anyone else. Some of these players were the first Americans to play ball in Japan and they helped promote the game of baseball in that country. They were ambassadors and bridge builders not only internationally but also within their own communities.

These young men truly played for the love of the game. Discipline, teamwork, loyalty, humility in victory, and dignity in defeat empowered them. There was no financial windfall from playing on a Nisei team, but monetary gain was not the goal of these great ballplayers; they simply wanted to compete and competitors they became. They played on church teams, in city and county leagues, won regional and state championships within the Nisei league, and dominated university teams in the United States, Japan, Korea, and China. Their world-class skills allowed them to play alongside professional baseball legends like Lou Gehrig, Babe Ruth, Joe DiMaggio, Ted Williams, and Jackie Robinson. The Nisei truly brought out the best in each other and in those who opposed them. Their self-esteem, family, and community pride were at stake and often fueled their driving passion for excellence.

Players, coaches, and fans shared many special moments and afternoons in this very social sport. Their incredible fellowship lasted on and off the field from

1903 to 1972, and the legacy they created continues today in the fourth and fifth generations of Japanese Americans who continue to love and play the great American pastime.

The Genesis of Nikkei (Japanese American) Baseball

While many Nisei considered baseball all-American, it was their immigrant parents, the Issei, who transported the sport from Japan to their communities in the United States. The sport of baseball was first introduced to Japan in 1873 at Kasei Gakko (now Tokyo University) by an American teacher named Horace Wilson. This was only four years after America's first professional baseball team, the Cincinnati Red Stockings, took the field in 1869. Wilson stressed the spiritual aspects of baseball, drawing parallels to the Japanese deference to authority, teamwork, responsibility, discipline, honor, sportsmanship, and conditioning. The game quickly spread throughout the country and became the most popular team sport in grade schools, high schools, and universities in Japan.

The emergence of Japanese American baseball in California can be traced to 1903, the year of the first official major league World Series. That year, the Fuji Club of San Francisco was organized; it included the players Aratani, Matsui, and its founder Chiura Obata, who was to become a prominent artist and art professor at the University of California, Berkeley. San Francisco rivals, the KDC (Kanagawa Doshi Club) Issei team, was led by Shohei "Frank" Tsuyuki. Between 1903 and 1915, a number of Japanese American teams formed in California, Colorado, Washington, and Wyoming. The players on these teams were primarily immigrants (Issei) who had learned the game in Japan.

All-Nisei teams were organized in 1912–13. In 1914, 1918, 1920, and 1923, the Seattle Asahis and Mikados ventured to Japan for the first of many goodwill baseball tours with the universities. Hawaiian Japanese teams toured Japan in 1915 and 1920. In the early 1920s, when players from Hawaiian teams traveled to the mainland to play the local Nisei teams, Nisei baseball progressed to new levels, enabling various all-competitive state and nationally recognized leagues. In Hawaii, there was a greater talent pool; the size of the population in the Islands increased the competition and skill level of its players.

The popularity of baseball spread throughout California's San Joaquin Valley during the 1920s and eventually there was a team in every Japanese American farming community. If there were not enough players to field an entire team in a community, neighboring towns would join together to form a squad. The Nisei Baseball League consisted of three divisions: division A was the highest level and was often compared to semipro level, division B was high school, and division C was for the junior high school level. Observers of the time remember the skill level being very high.

The Dean of Nisei Baseball

If there is one person identified with Nisei baseball, it is Kenichi Zenimura, the "Dean of Nisei Baseball" and founder of Fresno's Central California All-Star team, the Fresno Athletic Club. Beginning in 1919, he spent fifty-five years in competitive baseball and his team would attain state and national recognition.

Born in Hiroshima, Japan, in 1900, Zenimura moved to Hawaii a short while later. Introduced to the game of baseball at Mills High School, he mastered the sport and served as a player and coach for a team that won the Island championship. In 1920, Zenimura moved to Fresno. Working at a small restaurant and as a mechanic, he eventually established a ten-team Nisei league. He managed, coached, and played shortstop. Later, his all-star club, the Fresno Athletics, played in the integrated Fresno Twilight League. It became so dominant that when Babe Ruth and Lou Gehrig arrived in town on a barnstorming tour in 1927, several players, including Zenimura and the "Nisei Babe Ruth," Johnny Nakagawa, were invited to play.

Zenimura's teams dominated such college clubs as Stanford, St. Mary's, University of Southern California, and Fresno State during exhibition play. Internationally he organized six-month tours in 1924, 1927, and 1937 to Japan, Korea, and Manchuria. These goodwill all-stars compiled a 40–8–2 record over the "Big Six" universities in Japan. Another powerhouse from the Negro Leagues, the Philadelphia Royal Giants, met the Fresno Nisei's in three classic contests in Japan and in the United States in 1927.

Zenimura's sons would go on to play professionally for Japan's Hiroshima Carp. Fibber Hirayama, another Fresno Nisei graduate, would join them later. Hirayama played ten years with the Carp and is still involved with player development today. Zenimura became the first Japanese American elected to the Fresno Athletic Hall of Fame in 1979. Other prominent members of this sacred house include Olympic decathlon champion Rafer Johnson, Hall of Fame pitcher Tom Seaver, and Fibber Hirayama.

The Golden Era of Nisei Baseball

The development of Nisei baseball was highlighted by opportunities to play with established baseball stars and to travel within the United States as well as internationally. For example, in Gehrig's and Ruth's 1927 "barnstorming" tour through eight West Coast cities, Zenimura was on Lou Gehrig's team that beat the Babe's 13–3. According to the *Fresno Bee*, Zenimura said, "The first time I got up, I got a single. I was very fast and took my usual big lead off first. Ruth glanced at me and said, 'Hey, son, aren't you taking too much of a lead?' I said, 'no.' He called for the pitcher to pick me off. The pitcher threw and I slid behind Ruth. He was looking around to tag me and I already was on the sack. I think this made him mad. He called for the ball again. This time he was blocking the base and he swung his arm around thinking I would slide the same way. But this time I slid through his legs and he was looking behind. The fans cheered. Ruth said, 'If you do that to me again, I'll pick you up and use you as a bat, you runt.'"[1]

A photo of Ruth, Gehrig, Zenimura, and several Nisei players appeared in the Japanese newspapers. Shortly after, Zenimura received a call from Japan asking if he could get Ruth to travel to Japan to play. Several years later, Ruth did travel to Japan and was a huge hit. Lefty O'Doul, who accompanied Ruth, was another of the Japanese fans' favorites.

All-star teams consisting of Nisei players from central and northern California toured Japan, Korea, and Manchuria in 1937. Shig Tokumoto, a pitcher on the 1937 tour, recalled that they traveled by train and played teams along the coast from Pusan, Korea, to Port Arthur in Manchuria, and played them again on the return trip. The Nisei players accepted the hospitality of host families or roomed in hotels paid for by a sponsoring company. Despite a tour that lasted for six months, with the team playing sometimes three times a day, the Nisei team finished with an official 41–20–1 record.

In 1934, Harry "Tar" Shirachi, star pitcher of the Salinas Taiyo was a member of an all-star Nisei team that toured the Midwest, playing against semipro teams and even against the famous House of David team. At a tournament in Wichita, Kansas, one of the pitchers was Negro League star and future Hall of Famer Satchel Paige. Shirachi, now 88, remembers that in the Midwest, Nisei caused a stir just by showing up. For many of the fans, it was the first time in their lives they had ever seen a Japanese person and especially one who might speak English better than they did. Talent once again transcended the xenophobic attitudes, and as the Nisei displayed their athletic abilities, the tour and the diamond became an education both for the ballplayers and fans. By World War II, there were about fifty Nisei teams throughout California.

Nisei women also played baseball. Alice Hinaga of the famous Hinaga brothers baseball clan, (Russell, Chickie, and George) was the pitcher and top hitter for the Night Ball Association of San Jose. From 1934 to 1938, Alice was the star of four different teams: the three-time champion Premier Paint Girls squad, Red and White Stores, California Prune and Apricot Growers, and the Muerson Label team.

Nancy Ito was voted an all-American thirteen times and helped her Orange Lionettes win four national softball championships. In 1982, she was voted into the National Softball Hall of Fame in Oklahoma City, Oklahoma. Marion Kawakami of Fresno played for the Golden State Bakery team of the Municipal Night Circuit League. She was a defensive standout at first base and was the power hitter of the squad. Her brother Shiro was playing for the professional Dairen Manchuria team that same 1937 season. In Jerome, Arkansas, Jane "No Hit" Ota was fanning them left and right on the internment camp team. Houston Astro scout, George Omachi, once said that, "Jane could pitch on any Division college in America, and probably start."

Baseball During the Internment

Zenimura's passion and expertise in the game were outstanding, but his vision and leadership during the xenophobia that marked the relocation and resettlement of Japanese Americans were equally notable. World War II hysteria brought 5,000 internees to the animal stalls at the Fresno Fairgrounds. But within weeks, a baseball stadium was constructed under Zenimura's supervision. Six months later, his family was moved to the desert wastelands of Gila River, Arizona. Once again, this field general began designing, organizing, and constructing what became known as Zenimura Field. Amid the desert wasteland and desolate vastness of sand and sagebrush rose a masterpiece field of dreams (which still stands today on a Pima Indian reservation). When completed, this stadium had dugouts, bleachers, a grass infield, and an outfield fence complete with castor beans similar to Wrigley Field in Chicago.

Padding for cushions came out of mattress ticking and bases were made out of wood. Funding for most expenses incurred by the Nisei baseball team came from the community. The best bleacher seats were purchased at premium prices. Money was raised by passing the hat after games, from raffles and from donations by the "BBC" (Baseball Crazy) Issei, who were known to engage in the practice of betting on ballgames. The Issei funded bus trips from Gila River to play camp teams in Heart Mountain, Wyoming, and also in Poston and Jerome, Arkansas. Baseball during internment transformed these so-called "enemy aliens" into traveling goodwill ambassadors.

The passion for baseball can be seen in the fact that Gila River—one of the internment camps during World War II—had three divisions and twenty-eight teams. The involvement of parents, family, and friends is illustrated by the number of people who watched the games. It is said that at the "A" division games in Gila River, fans would sometimes stretch all around the field, with 4,000 to 5,000 people watching and cheering on the team. Zenimura was known to have spent more than $2,000 on equipment and uniforms for the teams.

Ironically, for Japanese Americans interned during World War II, playing, watching, and supporting baseball—the American game—behind barbed wire brought a sense of normalcy, created a social and positive atmosphere, encouraged physical conditioning, and maintained self-esteem despite the harsh conditions of desert life and unconstitutional incarceration. The civic pride and dignity fostered within many communities that had organized teams helped the Issei and Nisei survive this ordeal. Internees young and old demonstrated that talent transcends prejudice and extinguishes the demonization of Asian immigrants. The Nisei baseball organization, through its positive identity and image, helped nurse the deep wounds of the barbed wire. George Omachi said, "The baseball experience was one of those elements that allowed me to develop as a person and an individual, plus it gave me opportunities."[2]

After World War II, the Nisei baseball teams enjoyed continued success. For example, in May 1949, the Nisei All-Stars defeated the Fresno State Bulldogs by a score of 13 to 6. Although outhit 6 to 11, the All-Stars executed a number of perfect bunts and stole ten bases to win the game.

Also, players Fibber Hirayama and Kenshi Zenimura were the first postwar U.S. mainlanders to play in Japan. Hirayama became a two time all-star and competed alongside Hall of Famers Mickey Mantle, Whitey Ford, Casey Stengel, and Stan Musial when their teams traveled to Japan. When Hirayama and Zenimura first landed in Japan in 1956, 100,000 fans greeted them at the Hiroshima Train Station.

Nisei also played a role when American major league teams and players traveled to Japan. For example, Cappy Harada arranged for Joe DiMaggio to give batting clinics to all the professional teams in Japan when the Yankee Clipper was there on his honeymoon with Marilyn Monroe.

Baseball Unites the Generations

Baseball served as a "bridge" between the Issei and Nisei. It was easily accepted and comfortable for the Issei because of its popularity in Japan. Many Issei introduced the game to their peers in Sunday school as a fun and social sport that was genderless. Boys and girls participated and competed together and also formed teams. The girls' Lumbini team in Fresno, for example, played and competed with other churches in the Valley.

A close-knit community was essential for Japanese Americans from the 1920s through the 1950s. It was the primal protection of numbers that cemented their faith, relationships, and family. Church and ballpark (not necessarily in that order) were strong symbols of their faith. They quietly expressed and pledged their love for God, Buddha, Jesus, or whomever they worshiped under the church's roof. In the ballpark bleachers, the Issei expressed themselves in ways that were atypical of their reserved and nonverbal manner. On these hallowed grounds, the Nisei could, in fact, feel the love of their parents cheering them on to victory. Where else could Issei go to express their support and love and verbally demonstrate their passion by hollering, heckling, screaming, shouting, and on some occasions, betting with their friends? They could exhibit parental pride as part of the crowd. Elation, suspense, disappointment, excitement, success, and failure could all be felt in one afternoon. That's exactly why baseball became the all-time favorite sport with them.

All genders could participate, and once organized teams were formed, the Issei became a league of their own. Many Issei would look to game days as "BBC Day." This seemed to shed new light on the complex and multiple ways in which an immigrant community adapted and contributed to the larger society. Sports have played a long and important role in Japanese American communities. In response to the racial prejudice that barred most Nikkei from European American leagues, they organized and played among and against themselves. "The importance of identity and community participation was very crucial to the survival of Japanese Americans pre-war and especially during camp," according to University of California, Berkeley professor Jere Takahashi.[3]

Fibber Hirayama has recently said:

> I would hope . . . the young kids of today realize that there were people like Mr. Zenimura who were able to get together a number of Nisei and play a game that was a lot of fun, and people enjoyed, but also provided for other people: the fans. And I think this had an effect on the upbringing of the younger generations. The Nisei realized what was involved with the hard work. They were able to impart that on our younger generation. I hope our younger generation never forget what the Issei and Nisei folks did to make it a better place to live in. And baseball was a part of it.[4]

Nisei Stars

Aside from the players already mentioned, Nisei baseball has had many standout competitors. For example, Ken Nushida signed with the Pacific Coast League's Sacramento team in 1932. From Hawaii, Henry Tadashi "Bozo" Wakabayashi traveled to Japan to enter the professional ranks with the Hanshin Tigers. He played sixteen seasons as a professional, including seven as a player-manager. He was inducted into the Japanese Baseball Hall of Fame in 1964. George Matsuura, star player of the Los Angeles Nippons, toured with his teammates to Japan in 1931, then went back in 1936 to play professionally with the Nagoya team.

In Nevada City, California, Herb "Moon" Kurima struck out twenty-one Grass Valley batters for the Elk Grove Legions semipro team win. Moon averaged twelve strikeouts a game. Kiyo Nogami lettered in baseball at the University of California, Berkeley, in 1933. He toured with the Alameda-Kono All-Stars that went to Japan in 1937. He was signed by the Hankyu Braves and played for two successful seasons. In 1937, Lefty Nishijima, pitcher for the Santa Maria Junior College baseball team and his catcher, Tashi Hori, faced Jackie Robinson of

Pasadena Junior College—Jackie took Lefty deep twice to right field.

George Hinaga played one year of professional baseball with the Vancouver Asahis (a semipro squad that played against farm teams of the major leagues) in 1939. Henry Honda tried out with the Brooklyn Dodgers in 1943 but was not offered a position because they said he would soon be drafted into the army, and ironically he was. In 1947, he was offered a contract with the Cleveland Indians, but had to pass it up because of a torn tendon in his arm.

At the Fort Snelling, Minnesota, Army Camp, Bill Tsukamoto faced a twenty-one-game winner for the Yankees, Spurgeon "Spud" Chandler. Two years earlier in the 1943 World Series, Spud pitched and won two games. Spud hung a curve ball over the plate and Bill sent it deep, a spectator grabbed the ball and limited Bill to a triple instead of a homer. The almost all-Nisei team won 4–2.

In 1952, Fresno State star, Fibber Hirayama, signed with the Stockton Ports Pacific Coast League team. He played one year, then moved on to a ten-year career with the Hiroshima Carp in Japan. His record of five stolen bases in one game at Fresno State was tied recently by Tom Goodwin of the Kansas City Royals. Kenshi and Kenso Zenimura lettered at Fresno State and played with the Hiroshima Carp. They were the first and only brother combination to play together. Kenshi played five years and was a two-time all-star.

Cappy Harada is the only Nisei to become general manager of a professional baseball organization—the Lodi Crushers in 1966–67. He promoted goodwill baseball games during the postwar occupation in Japan with General MacArthur, and worked with Horace Stoneham for twenty-three years with the San Francisco Giants. He signed the first Japanese major leaguer, Matsunori Murakami, to a Giants' contract. Cappy pioneered the licensing of major league logos around the world with Baseball Commissioner Bowie Kuhn.

George "Hats" Omachi, was a Houston Astro scout, Nisei player, and legendary coach of the Fresno Niseis. George discovered Hall of Famer Tom Seaver and helped coach many other future major leaguers. Wally Yonamine, played for the San Francisco 49ers in 1947. A wrist injury ended his football career but his baseball abilities sent him to Japan's Hall of Fame. He left baseball with one of the highest lifetime batting averages, .311.

Kats Shitanishi of Fresno played in the Boston Red Sox farm system in 1967. In 1975, Ryan Kurosaki became the first American of Japanese ancestry to play in the major leagues. He was a pitcher alongside teammates Bob Gibson and Lou Brock of the St. Louis Cardinals. Len Sakata, World Series champion with the 1983 Baltimore Orioles, is the only Sansei (third generation) to wear a World Series championship ring. Len presently coaches professional baseball in Japan. And on May 13, 1995, Shig Tokumoto was presented with a baseball field named in his honor at Hanford, California. This eighty-two-year resident, is a former ballplayer, coach, and crusader for youth baseball.

Bridge Across the Pacific

Beginning as early as 1914, Japanese Americans have traveled across the Pacific to play baseball in Japan. They helped to pioneer and innovate the game of baseball with an American spirit of style and play. Seattle and Hawaii Nisei teams played the universities in Japan from 1914 to 1923. California teams from Fresno, Stockton, San Jose, Los Angeles, and Alameda made yearly tours from 1924 to 1937.

In 1934, an American Hall of Fame team led by Babe Ruth and Lou Gehrig came to Japan. The all-Japan team was selected from the best players from college and amateur squads. With these members as its core, the first professional team of Japan was formed. The Dai Nihon Baseball Club was organized at the end of 1934, and by 1936, seven professional teams had been established.

Hawaiian all-stars Henry "Bozo" Wakabayashi, Jimmie Horio, and Kaiser Tanaka became legends in Japan with their professional play. Eighteen prewar players went from Hawaii and California to play professional ball in Japan. Professional baseball rapidly grew into Japan's most popular spectator sport in the postwar years, with an annual attendance of more than 14 million. Televised baseball games became top-rated programs. Since the early 1950s, twenty-two Japanese American players have played professionally in Japan. Only three Japanese players have come from Japan to the United States to compete on a major league level.

Besides Wakabayashi, Wally Yonamine, Ryan Kurosaki, and Len Sakata have also gained fame in Nisei and professional baseball in Japan. Wakabayashi and Yonamine have been inducted into Japan's Hall of Fame, Kurosaki became the first Sansei (third generation) to pitch in the major leagues, and Len Sakata of the 1983 Baltimore Orioles won a world championship as their utility player that year. Don Wakamatsu was the first fourth generation Japanese American to enter the "Show." He started with the Dodgers and went to the Reds and currently coaches the Arizona Diamondbacks AA team.

Passing the Torch

There is a significant resurgence of the Japanese American baseball tradition in central, northern and southern California. Fourth generation (Yonsei) Japanese Americans are continuing the tradition of competitive baseball in mainstream America. Division I Colleges throughout California have Yonsei players on their starting rosters. Our Nikkei landscape is well represented in professional levels of science, medicine, business, law, and the arts. But a relative void exists for us in professional sports. Baseball, however, can be the vehicle for many to excel and to inspire our younger generations to reach for the American dream.

A number of current players already have major-league baseball potential. They include farm-system stars such as Orin Kawahara, pitcher and thirteenth pick for the Seattle Mariners; Chris Miyake, second baseman for the Pittsburgh Pirates; Todd Takayoshi, infielder for the Anaheim Angeles; Kurt Takahashi, pitcher for the San Francisco Giants; and Ken Morimoto, outfielder, and Onan Masaoka, pitcher, both for the Los Angeles Dodgers. Many other prospects will also likely emerge in the coming years.

If we were to dissect a Nikkei baseball, the center would epitomize the core members and pioneers of the Issei and Nisei organization. The fibers and strings would represent the communities that tie their identities, loyalties, and cultural affinities around the team's players. The leather skin would represent the physical and mental toughness developed by the Issei and Nisei during immigration, internment, and resettlement. The stitching bonds the generations together and seals these family spirits for future generations.

This symbolic baseball is being handed to new generations with the knowledge, history, and pride of their ancestors. They in turn will hone and polish their skills, developing their own discipline, courage, determination, and sportsmanship that will sparkle on and off the fields of green. With this legacy of Japanese Americana, they will become "diamonds in the rough."

The history of baseball is becoming increasingly relevant, as more and more players emerge from Japan, Korea, the Dominican Republic, Cuba, Mexico, and the sandlots of our ethnically diverse ballparks in America. Baseball is internationalizing rapidly across the world, and as our national pastime spreads, so should our bridges of goodwill and brotherly love.

Afterword: A Gila River Pilgrimage

In 1998, I helped organize a pilgrimage to Arizona for a couple of former baseball players and former detainees of two of the internment camps that housed Japanese Americans during World War II. The Poston and Butte detention camps were the third and fourth largest cities in Arizona during the 1940s. Among those housed at the camps was the Hollywood actor (and costar of *The Bad News Bears*), Pat Morita, and the former baseball star, Kenso Zenimura. With their stories about life in the camps, they joined me and Gary Otake—a curator for the National Japanese American Historical Society—on two symposium panels at the Arizona Hall of Fame Museum in Phoenix. Our appearance was hosted by the museum's curator, Jacqueline Miller, and by the Arizona humanities coordinator, Rick Noguchi. The public was invited to listen to us, and to other historical accounts provided by other former internees. Among other things, this meeting provided a touching reunion, after almost sixty years, for Kenso and James "Step" Tomooka. The two played baseball together at the internment camp's Zenimura Field, named after Kenso, whose family organized and built it. As Step recalled, "Once the word got out that Zenimura was building a baseball diamond . . . almost a hundred volunteers [from the camps] came out to clear the sagebrush and rocks."

After the symposia, we traveled forty miles into the desert on—ironically— the Pearl Harbor Freeway to visit the Butte Camp, located in the Gila River Indian community. There we joined Mas Inoshita, a volunteer caretaker of the Butte Memorial site and a Nisei resident of Glendale, Arizona. He has been unofficially adopted into the Pima Indian Tribe. Mas took us to the Gila River Indian Community Center to meet the tribal council and the Pima governor, Mary Thomas, who serves as both the tribe's political as well as spiritual leader.

On behalf of the Nisei Baseball Research Project (NBRP), which I direct, I presented Governor Thomas with an autographed, tribute baseball and a NBRP T-shirt. She reciprocated with official Gila River pendants and olive oil from Zenimura Field. Thomas explained how the Gila River Indian community is totally self-sufficient. It includes the Gila River Farms (producing olive oil, oranges, wheat, and alfalfa), the Gila River Casino, a resource center and museum, a fire department, a waste management facility, and a (leased out) portion of Falcon Field, an airport on their land. Thomas had recently returned from Xian, China, the site where the now famous terracotta warriors were excavated. Also at that site was an ancient hut that was an exact duplicate of the huts built by the Pima Indians. This provides additional credibility for the apparent migration of Native Americans from Asia, through the Bering Strait, into North America. It also fortifies the sense that our cultures have been spiritually infused.

When Governor Thomas asked Morita and Zenimura why they had come to the Gila River, they mentioned their desire to reconnect with their own past. In response, Thomas took their hands and began to cry. She said, "Babies were born on our land and some of your people died here. You are part of our community and we apologize for what happened." Very emotionally, Pat said the Gila River Indian community was not responsible for the internment of Japanese Americans; instead, the encampments were forced upon Indian lands. Thomas was a child at the time but felt a lot like some of our Nisei, "We should have resisted the government's demands." Tears flowed throughout the room like the ancient Gila River and I found it remarkable that baseball was really what had brought us together. Among their experiences in the camps as detainees, Pat and Kenso had remembered baseball the most vividly. In pursuit of those memories, baseball had emerged as a cultural phenomenon linking Japanese Americans not only with each other but with Native Americans as well.

We toured the Resource Center and the relics of Camps 1 and 11. Broken china, rusted toys, and old jewelry filled bins at the camp dump sites. At the Butte Camp site memorial, permanent plaques memorialize not only the detainees but also the Japanese Americans who fought and died in World War II, even while many of their families remained interned back home. From this site, we could see miles and miles of foundations and overgrown weeds and sagebrush covering the camp landscape. Kenso found his former barrack space and reflected back on his stay. "We lived right here in apartment 13 C. My Mom, Dad, and brother Kenshi stayed here. Next to us was my grandmother and her family."

As we stood in front of what used to be the mess hall, Pat said, "I remember they used to ring the bell for us to come to eat."

A short distance from block 28 was Zenimura Field, the old baseball field, and now an olive orchard. I broke out the mitts and a baseball so Kenso and Pat could have a catch again. I got chills watching them tossing the ball back and forth on Zenimura Field, for the first time in fifty-six years.

In stark contrast, we were all back, that evening, behind home plate at the Bank One Ballpark—the home of the Arizona Diamondbacks—where we watched the roof of the $350 million stadium open up to Pat Morita's rendition of the national anthem. Fifty thousand fans cheered his performance. Our group was treated to the owner's suite at the ballpark, arranged by Madeline Ong Sakata. Her father, Wing Ong, was a U.S. Congressman, who served two terms from Arizona during the prewar days. Helping us cheer on the Diamondbacks was the honorable Bill Lam Lee, state legislator Barry Wong, and superior court judge Brian Ishikawa, who even caught a foul ball.

While at the stadium, I couldn't help recalling our experiences earlier in the day. I had images of sagebrush and desert sand transformed by passion, labor, and community spirit into a field of dreams—the Zenimura ball field, built to pursue America's great game and to numb the sting of a cruel internment. Almost six decades later, the field has now become a productive olive orchard, and down the road, at a much higher cost, another field of dreams has been built. From sagebrush and sandlot baseball to major league baseball, from barbed wire to olive branches, Pima Indians and Japanese Americans. Through baseball, we've discovered our new relatives in Arizona.

Notes

1. Tom Mechan, "Ken Zenimura, Dean of Nisei Baseball in U.S., Recalls Colorful Past," *Fresno Bee* (May 20, 1962), 8.

2. Interview with author, July 17, 1993.

3. Interview with author, May 6, 1994.

4. Interview with author, August 15, 1998 for documentary film, *Diamonds in the Rough*.

9

FROM SAN FRANCISCO SANDLOTS TO THE BIG LEAGUES
Babe Pinelli

John J. Pinelli

MY GREAT GRANDFATHER, RAPHAEL PAOLINELLI, OWNED A FOOD STORE ON FILLMORE Street in San Francisco. On his way to the store on April 18, 1906, a falling telephone pole permanently removed him from our family; this happened during the great 1906 San Francisco earthquake. One of his sons, my grandfather, Rinaldo Angelo Paolinelli, was thrust that day from the innocence of childhood to the trappings of adulthood. He was ten years old and forced to drop out of grammar school to help his mother and siblings eke out a living. From this scary and stark beginning, Rinaldo Paolinelli—better known as Babe Pinelli—would move from the sandlots in San Francisco to the major league diamonds both as player and umpire.

Babe was born in San Francisco on October 18, 1895, to Raphael and Ermida. He had an older brother, Lando, and a younger sister and brother, Cora and Fiore. Despite the abrupt change in his life at the mere age of ten, Babe would eventually go on to complete eight years as a minor league player and eight more years as a major league player. After his playing years ended, he would umpire in the Pacific Coast League for two years and complete his tenure in professional baseball with twenty-two years as a National League umpire. Since he never missed a game in all those years, former National League umpire Tom Gorman called Babe "the Lou Gehrig of umpires, our Iron Man."[1]

During his playing and umpiring days, Babe's entire family supported him and knew he would succeed. His brothers, Lando and Fiore, often spoke of his genuine ability on the San Francisco diamonds. His sister Cora, who is still living, enjoyed watching him play baseball. She never doubted that he was one of the greatest umpires in baseball history. Babe's mother always approved of his career, and always had a pasta feast waiting for him when he was in town.

As a youngster, my grandfather, [Babe, contributed four and a half dollars a week to the family by selling newspapers on San Francisco street corners. He kept fifty cents for himself. He was a "newsie."] During these times, he would play on various sandlots in San Francisco and at his neighborhood playground, Hamilton Park, on Post and Steiner streets. His obstinacy in following his older brother Lando and his friends to these sandlots got him the nickname "Babe." He would insist on playing baseball with them and when they said no, Babe would start crying and screaming. He was a "Babe," and the name stuck. On the sandlots Babe began honing the baseball skills that would eventually lead him to the big leagues. He also began the long road to controlling his wild temper. As he often said, "I had firecrackers in my blood!"

In his teens, he not only played recreational baseball but also played for "organized" teams such as the North Beach Outlaws, a sort of little league team. From 1910 through 1916, Babe played with a number of semipro clubs including those in Sonoma, Petaluma, and Sebastopol in California, and in Bandon, Oregon. While playing for these clubs, he also was working on a relationship with a pretty young woman, Mabel McKee. He married her in December of 1916. Their first son, Roy, my father, was born in July 1917, and a second son, Ray, came along in 1919. During this period, Babe graduated from being a newsie to a variety of jobs including delivery boy and sign painter. Indeed, throughout his life he remained a meticulous painter.

Before joining the minor leagues, Babe met up with a childhood friend, Sammy Bohne, at the Arthur Company Utah Copper League, an independent circuit near Salt Lake City. Babe enjoyed Utah and thought the league had many promising players. He also played at Marysville in California for the so-called Trolley League.

One night during the off-season while back in San Francisco, Babe and Sammy stopped in at Dreamland Rink, where boxing matches were being held. Many of Babe's friends encouraged him to fight the big shot of the night, Pickles Martin. My grandfather not only had a fierce temper but he could fight. Whether it was a street fight or an amateur boxing match, he was tough. That toughness and his readiness to fight came from his experience having to fight for street corners to sell newspapers as a young boy. He lost a few fights, but not many. As Babe got into the ring, Pickles made the mistake of saying he would knock Babe's head off. It was all over for Pickles. As my grandfather would say, "Two punches and school was out."

After that fight, the matchmaker, Frank Schuler, wanted to schedule Babe as a regular fighter. Knowing that both his mother and Mabel would be upset, Babe agreed to fight but only under the name "Battling Joe Welch." Although Babe was a terrific boxer, his days in the ring would quickly end. While he worked out as a boxer, both he and Mabel felt that baseball, not boxing, would be his true career. Boxing was soon over, but his short fuse and willingness to fight still remained.

Babe made the move from semipro ball to the minor leagues in 1917, when he began playing for the Portland Beavers. In 1918, the Portland team moved to Sacramento but the Pacific Coast League temporarily went out of business because of World War I. Thus, Babe was immediately called up to the big leagues. He joined the Chicago White Sox to finish out the 1918 season, a year before some of his old Chicago teammates would become embroiled in the Black Sox scandal of 1919. In a few short years, my grandfather had gone from semipro to the minor leagues and finally to the big leagues. He described the moves as monumental, especially going up to play in the big leagues.

But in 1919, Babe found himself back in Sacramento and nearly thrown out of baseball. He was at bat and the plate umpire, "Singing Lord Byron," called a strike. An argument ensued and as Byron removed his facemask it accidentally struck Babe on the jaw. Babe's reaction was immediate and unfortunate. He swung at Byron, knocking him to the ground. Striking an umpire is probably the worst offense in baseball. After the game, Babe told Byron that he had not swung at him deliberately. Byron understood and said it was as much his fault. Still, Babe had hit an umpire. But, Al Jolson, who would end up a good friend of Babe's, sent a telegram to the Pacific Coast League president, William McCarthy, explaining the circumstances and asking for leniency. Later that day, Jolson told Babe about the telegram. Babe was grateful. Babe and Byron were eventually questioned by McCarthy who, because of the special circumstances, later dismissed the case. Lucky grandpa—and a new lesson on curbing his temper.

In 1920, my grandfather signed a contract with the Detroit Tigers. Imagine! He was going to be a teammate of one of his heroes, Ty Cobb. Cobb and Babe had a few brushes early on, but in the end remained friends for life. In retirement, they stayed in touch and occasionally played golf together. But Babe found himself back in the Pacific Coast League with Oakland in 1921. He thought he had another year with Detroit sewn up but the stars weren't with him. Nevertheless, he had a good year with Oakland, batting .339. Then, in 1922, Babe was sold to the Cincinnati Reds, a team he would stay with for six seasons.

During those years with the Reds, Babe began to think about the future. He had been playing professional baseball since 1917, but it wouldn't last forever. He wondered whether he should consider coaching, management, or even umpiring. It didn't take long to decide. He felt that managers and coaches come and go with a team's success, but an umpire could last a long time. While he knew his major league career would probably end after Cincinnati, he figured he could stay in baseball as an umpire. So, in the midst of his playing career, in 1925, he was already thinking about becoming an umpire! It would be ten years before he got a National League umpiring contract, but it was ten years of studying the rules, learning the profession, and getting a grip on his temper.

In 1926, he met and spoke with the great umpire, Bill Klem, who gave him advice on umpiring and on controlling his temper. He remembered this advice throughout the rest of his career. The more Babe pondered the thought of becoming an umpire, the more he discussed it with Mabel, and the more he thought it was the right decision. First, he'd have to become an umpire in the minor leagues, but he didn't want to end his baseball career there. Perhaps with diligence and perseverance he could develop a long and stable career with one of the two major leagues. That was his goal: stability. In 1926, at the age of only thirty-one, he envisioned a new career in baseball.

My grandfather lasted with the Reds until 1927. Then, from 1928 through 1932 he was back in the minors, where he played with the Oakland and San Francisco teams in the Pacific Coast League. He had some glory days there. On July 4, 1929, for example, while playing for the San Francisco Seals, he had six hits, including three home runs, two of which were grand slams. That day, he tied the minor league record of twelve runs batted in! What a day! When Babe returned from Cincinnati to California he came back as a sort of hero—the first Italian American from San Francisco to ever play in the National League (Ping Bodie was the first in the American League). But being Italian American actually caused my grandfather a lot of strife in both the minor and major leagues. Most of the time, he handled the situations very well, but there were instances when name calling got his fists flying.

Babe was able to put most of the "kidding" behind him, especially as he began contemplating a future career as an umpire. Another five years as a minor league player gave him a total of sixteen years in professional baseball and still more time to study the art of umpiring. He gained some hands-on experience during the off-season by umpiring for local Bay Area colleges and universities, and even some high schools. While he was with the Reds and in his last years with Oakland and San Francisco, he worked diligently on taming his temper. He knew an umpire would never make the pros if his actions were influenced by a short-fused disposition. He also learned to sell himself as his reputation as a scrapper preceded him. He would have to convince the people "upstairs" that he could handle himself in a fair, controlled, and dignified manner as an arbiter on the field. He succeeded.

In April of 1933, Babe received a contract with the Pacific Coast League. He managed the transition from a fiery player to a self-controlled umpire. It took him eight years. Mabel stood by his side, learning baseball rules herself, and quizzing him daily. Babe soon realized that being an umpire was quite different from being a player. To begin with, it was lonely. For example, before or after a game, he could not fraternize with the players. It could be perceived as favoritism or even as a conspiracy. He would have none of that. No one roots for the umpire, and for what team could an umpire's wife root? Babe would have to adjust to this new career. Bill Klem taught Babe to umpire for the ball only. He would say to himself, "What's the ball going to make me do?" He quickly became a well-respected minor league umpire and began preparing for that day when he would step onto the big league diamond as the man in blue. This day would come soon.

In 1935, Babe received an umpiring contract from the National League. His time had come. He would remain with this league for twenty-two years. The move from the minor leagues to the major leagues would be as dramatic for him as an umpire as it had been as a player. The managers and—more important— the players had ever-growing egos. To deal with this, Babe studied them all very carefully. He learned their habits, dispositions, and temperaments. This helped him become one of the most respected umpires of all time.

My grandfather told me and my brothers and sisters many stories from these days. In one of my favorite stories, Babe was arguing with Leo Durocher, who was with Brooklyn at the time. Leo charged onto the field ranting and raving about something. When he neared my grandfather, who was amused at the situation, Babe leaned over and asked Leo what kind of after-shave he was wearing! "It smelled wonderful!" Babe said. Leo grinned and walked away. Another time, my grandfather called Babe Ruth out on a called third strike, and for the second time in the same game. Ruth turned to Babe and said that everyone in the park knew the pitch was a ball, and then called him a "tomato head." My grandfather told Ruth he might be right but that as the umpire his was the only opinion that counted! That was Babe.

Umpires have many tough decisions to make in the major leagues. Babe described these four as the toughest: the tag at second, the half swing, the double play pivot, and the shoestring catch of a line drive by an outfielder. He considered the balk to be the most technical of all calls. It would seem that the umpire's task behind the plate is particularly difficult, especially calling balls and strikes. It is crucial that the umpire be an expert on this, and Babe was considered one of the best. His greatest moments were when he was doing just that.

In 1956, Babe was calling balls and strikes, and acting as the chief umpire in the fifth game of the World Series—his last game behind the plate. Only he and the league president knew he was to retire in two days. The game was in Yankee Stadium and Don Larsen was pitching for New York. Twenty-seven batters came up and twenty-seven consecutive outs were registered. In the ninth inning, Dale Mitchell pinch hit for Sal Maglie of the Dodgers. The first pitch was a ball. The second was a strike and so was the third. Babe called the fourth pitch a strike and history was made: the only perfect World Series game in baseball history! What a way for Babe to retire!

Many have agreed that the ball was actually a little high and outside. This stirred great debates, right from the beginning, which have lasted to this day. But with a count of one and two on possibly the last batter in a World Series game, with so much on the line, a hitter has to swing at anything close. My grandfather's call was not only right but also just. When he and I would discuss the call, Babe told me again and again that he never had second thoughts about it. He paid no attention to the ridicule. He was the final and only arbiter and he was right. And, as Stephen Jay Gould has written, "Babe Pinelli, umpiring his last game, ended with his finest, his most perceptive, his most truthful moment. Babe Pinelli, arbiter of history, walked into the locker room and cried."[3]

Of course, this is only the short history of my grandfather's baseball life—his triumph over both the odds and his temper that allowed him to join the ranks of the big leaguers as player and as umpire. It is the story of a boy who was fatherless by the age of ten but who nevertheless succeeded with the help, as he always said, of his God, his country, his family, and baseball.[4] He went from playing ball on San Francisco's sandlots to swinging the bat on major league diamonds and finally to calling the shots as a National League umpire.

Although Babe died a number of years ago, his influence on me has remained great. I admired and adored him, as did all of his grandchildren. He entertained us with innumerable baseball stories. He passed on to me the importance of having God in your life, of struggling to better yourself no matter the circumstances, of being honest and truthful, and of possessing strong morals and ethics. My grandfather was tough but also a very warm and caring man; his emotions ran high. He loved his family dearly and spent at least a couple of days each week with his children and grandchildren after he retired. He moved from San Francisco to his beloved Sonoma in the late 1950s, while keeping his hand in baseball through scouting and various speaking engagements.

Many other stories about Babe Pinelli could be told. He was a tough act for a grandson to follow.

Notes

1. Tom Gorman, *Three and Two!* (New York: Scribner, 1979).

2. Larry R. Gerlach, "Babe Pinelli: Mr. Ump," *Society for American Baseball Research Annual* (1995), 43–45.

3. Stephen Jay Gould, *The Flamingo's Smile* (New York: W.W. Norton, 1985).

4. Babe Pinelli, with Joe King, *Mr. Ump* (Philadelphia: Westminster Press, 1953).

5. Ralph Pinelli, "I Call Things As I See Them," in *This I Believe*, ed. Edward R. Murrow (New York: Simon & Schuster, 1952), 137–138.

THE COMMON DREAM EXAMINED

William Edwards

LONG BEFORE THE FIRST HINT OF SUMMER IN MOST OF THE COUNTRY, THE "BOYS OF summer" begin the annual pageantry that is commonly known as the national pastime. Perhaps no team sport is as anxiously awaited as baseball. Fans across the country anticipate the umpire's clarion call to "Play ball!" And, with the first pitch, baseball and the country renew an ancient love affair. What is there about baseball that somehow seems to transcend sport and come to symbolize a nation? Why has baseball come to symbolize the national pastime?

Baseball is more than sport; it is a metaphor for American society. It has always been a sport through which American society affirms, in part, its creed that any boy can rise above the lowliest situation to become a national hero. Baseball has been, and continues to be, society's great experiment in social mobility.

Baseball seems incomparable for its stories of upward mobility. There is no shortage of narratives of immigrant boys who rose from the ranks of poverty to capture national headlines with their skills as baseball players. Baseball players were not simply athletes; they were symbolic representations of entire ethnic communities. They were the embodiment of the American dream. What other symbol captured the possibilities of success, as did baseball? It was a contradiction to the harsh realities of long hours in the factory where one's labor was extracted for low pay and where working conditions were often deplorable. Just as American society offered opportunities for upward mobility for countless thousands who came to this country from abroad, baseball embraced the common man's rise to heights of greatness.

The history of baseball has always had its links to the working class, and through the game, working-class aspirations could become national dreams fulfilled. While baseball transformed dreams into possibilities, it forged communities into a sense of collective consciousness. A team and a community were woven into a collective identity. The game was an occasion to express that collective sense of identity. The triumph of the team was a reward to a community. Each team victory affirmed the possibilities of yet greater success. A team victory was also a triumph of the spirit as ethnicity and class could be suspended in the "field of dreams." After a victory, workers could return to the routine of the factory or the everyday life of the community emboldened by the heroics of "our team."

If baseball was a metaphor for social mobility, the national pastime mirrored the role that race played in the larger society. If we were to think of baseball as nothing more than a game, it would matter less that its mirror image cast a shadow over racial exclusion. Baseball was a medium that echoed to the nation the extent to which race would come to limit the possibilities of the American dream. The sport that came to symbolize a national identity reflected its social practice with respect to race. Throughout its early years, baseball preserved its role as an arbiter of which communities would represent the national pastime. In the spirit of the Supreme Court's 1896 decision in *Plessy v. Ferguson*, the national pastime would remain separate and unequal.

Defying Social Stigma

Baseball has given this country some of its most enduring metaphors. "Digging in," "hitting a home run," "playing until the last out," are part of the lingo that characterizes the game, but these phrases also have come to signify social cues to success. Consciously or otherwise, we have borrowed certain social lessons from baseball. Of course, baseball is not the only sport from which metaphors have been borrowed. Another way in which baseball has affected the social fabric of this society is through defining its participants and what they symbolize. The 1998 season was a stellar period in major league baseball as the world celebrated the unparalleled performances of Sammy Sosa and Mark McGwire. Each player came to represent loftier goals than those usually associated with baseball players. Their *personas* were elevated to heights that few players ever realize. Sammy Sosa in particular defied social stigma.

The legacy of baseball is built upon the heroic feats of individuals who, otherwise, would be subject to society's worst social stigmas. The contributions of Jewish, Irish, and Italian players during the early years of baseball belie the underlying eugenic movement in this country. During the 1920s especially, eugenics enjoyed its greatest influence. Promoting the idea that human worth was related to genetic endowment, eugenicists were eager to prove that Jews, Irish, and Italians, among others, were members of an inferior genetic stock. While players from each of these groups performed with superior skills, it was difficult to sustain the notion of their genetic inferiority unless one argued that they were merely endowed with the "natural" talent to be baseball players. To be sure, these players were unable to bury all aspects of ethnic enmity, but they were often embraced as national symbols. Moreover, their example made the American dream possible for many others.

Baseball, as a national sport, was a significant arena to defy social stigma. On the field, victory was reserved to the best athletes on that day. As champions were crowned, records set, and performances dazzled millions across the country and abroad, a new social acceptance was inspired. If social stigmas remained, the country would nevertheless have to tolerate at least some of its ethnic contradictions. And that it did: major league baseball maintained a closed-door policy to the country's largest minority population while remaining a game for whites only.

The Jackie Robinson Phenomenon

Others have chronicled the importance of Jackie Robinson's entry into major league baseball. I will not repeat their accounts but only suggest that the breaking of the color barrier was more than the story of one man's success. By the 1940s, baseball had earned its title as the national pastime. But, while the nation reveled in the growth and popularity of major league baseball, the history and contributions of black players rarely earned more than a footnote. As early as the Reconstruction Period, the color line was drawn in professional baseball. Racial exclusion would remain for nearly a century before Jackie Robinson signed a contract with the Montreal Royals, an International League affiliate of the Brooklyn Dodgers.

Barred from participation in the early formation of professional baseball, black players formed their own leagues. An irony of the early racial discrimination against black players was that their excluded teams, which banded together to comprise the first National Association of Baseball Players, were not from the South but rather the North. While the Civil War was being fought, it was the North that drew the color line in professional baseball. Before the *Plessy v. Ferguson* case, professional baseball declared its own policy of racial separation. Organized baseball was no exception to the legal and social barriers that characterized the nation as a whole.

The signing of Jackie Robinson by Branch Rickey in 1945 was acknowledged then and now as a daring social experiment. Rickey knew, as did countless numbers of white players, that skills were not the defining factor that excluded black players from the major leagues. Those who followed baseball knew about the quality of the players in the colored leagues and in the Negro League. Diversity in major league baseball would mean defying the color line, but most important, changing the nature of the game itself. On April 10, 1946, baseball history was made and the future of the game changed forever as Jackie Robinson became a member of the Brooklyn Dodgers. There were signs that the magnitude of this change would resound throughout the country. History is replete with stories of the reaction to Robinson's joining the Dodgers.

Branch Rickey never claimed he was a great sociologist, but his selection of Jackie Robinson was calculated in part based on Robinson's ability to transcend the barrage of personal attacks that were sure to come. He could not be just another player. He would become a part of a community of players and fans who collectively shared an identity in common. To break the color line was to open the door to new social possibilities. At the same time, Robinson carried on his shoulders the weight of an entire race. Like Jesse Owens in the 1936 Olympics, Jackie Robinson symbolized the degree to which race, sport, and national identity were intertwined. The great challenge to major league baseball was not Robinson's ability to play the game, but how the relationship between race and national identity would merge. Would major league baseball, as the national pastime, truly embrace all of its people? The answer to this question was not long in coming. Larry Doby signed a contract to play with the Cleveland Indians in July 1947 and became the first black player in the American League.

Diversity and the Universality of Baseball

Baseball is a universal sport. By its very nature it is shared by millions of people throughout the world. Many writers, in other contexts, have captured the widespread appeal of baseball. While it has been a sport dominated by the participation of men, women have also made their mark, although their story may be less well known. Baseball, as sport, has been one of the most important vehicles for the building and sharing of community. In communities throughout the world, players and fans gather to share the fun and frivolity of a game, and at the same time share in a cultural experience expressed in the flare and manner in which the game is played. Historically, baseball was seen in this country through the eyes of whites who popularized the sport, but they were hardly the only ones attracted to the game. The allure of baseball is as much a part of the culture in Latin America and Japan as it is in the United States. And women also had a league of their own.

The story of the universality of baseball is one that frequently misses the underlying sense in which baseball galvanized groups of people and afforded them a sense of communal expression. For example, through his Nisei Baseball Project, Kerry Yo Nakagawa (see his essay in this volume) has collected an array of pictures that tell a poignant story of the Japanese American legacy in baseball. Among the photos are some taken during the internment of Japanese Americans. With gun towers in the background, we can see a baseball game in progress while the internees are restrained behind barbed wire fences. Their faces portray a mixture of joy, laughter, and excitement as they cheer Japanese

American players. These are the faces of the captured, but the pictures tell us much more about baseball, community, and the human spirit.

The same is true for Samuel Regalado's story (see his essay in this volume) of the Horatio Alger dream that motivated so many Latin American players. Regalado tells of young Latin players imagining themselves in similar roles to American players. To a great extent they envisioned baseball as a means to rise above poverty. They shared a common reality with black players in this country: racial exclusion. But, instead of being deterred, the Alger dream appealed to their own sense of possibilities. Dusty streets and overgrown pastures became their fields of dreams. Neither the United States nor their dreams of major league success seemed that far away. In their own way, the Latin players added their cultural imprint to the game of baseball.

What each of these stories reveals is a common link between the game of baseball and the heights to which the human spirit can aspire. Baseball occupied an important place in the life and culture of Japanese Americans. Although restricted from participation in major league baseball, they played in leagues of their own. Baseball was shaped by the cultural traditions common to Japanese Americans. Competition was largely restricted to the West Coast, but games outside the country also existed. On rare occasions, Japanese American players joined major league professionals and a few Negro League players, as they "barnstormed" together. The entry of Jackie Robinson into the major leagues in the late 1940s was not overlooked by Japanese American players even though their recent internment, still fresh in their minds, made such access for them seem slim.

Baseball crossed the barriers of language and nationality to unite players who shared a love of the game. As baseball closed the gap between race, ethnicity, and nationality, the national pastime took on a new demeanor. The Negro League dissolved as major league baseball opened its doors to black players. Latin players came to the United States and have become fixtures on every major league team. Japanese and Korean players are gradually making inroads into major league baseball. Baseball has achieved a diversity unimagined more than a century ago. The recent acclaim received by Sammy Sosa attests to more than baseball's achievement of diversity. Sosa became as much a national symbol in this country as he did in his native Dominican Republic. Off the field, Sosa has also inspired the nation: his persona has revitalized a sense of community that many saw as otherwise vanishing in American society. Sosa's personality became infectious in a country that has been questioning the role of athletes as national symbols. He rose above being simply a baseball player. Sosa was the perfect medicine for helping the country feel good about itself.

The 1998 World Series almost seemed anticlimatic after the dramatic last two weeks of the regular season. The nation watched with great expectation as

Sammy Sosa and Mark McGwire rewrote baseball history, and in the process demonstrated a mutual admiration that won the hearts of millions. Two players, one white and the other Latino, transcended race, ethnicity, and national origins to represent the best that baseball could hope to offer. In those moments when the players were seen embracing each other or cheering each other's home runs, it was hard to recall when such a scene would not have been possible. Dreams fermented in distant lands had come together in Chicago and St. Louis. Emotions ran high as fans packed ballparks around the country to see the new sultans of swing inaugurate perhaps a new day in baseball. It even became fashionable to become an honorary Dominican. The flag of the Dominican Republic flew alongside the American flag in Chicago in tribute to Sosa's contributions. At least in those moments baseball truly became a field of dreams.

Old Dreams, New Markets

Baseball has extended its reach far into the global market. Baseball camps can be found in countries where dreams of playing in the major leagues are made. Young players can be seen wearing the jersey of their favorite player. Baseball broadcasts reach into countries where anxious fans can follow the game. Local heroes have become international heroes. The baseball community is international. Ethnic communities in this country that gave baseball its early "boys of summer" must share the stage with newcomers. As these newcomers make their mark in the game they extend the community of the sport.

The United States has come to learn that the passion for baseball runs very deep in many countries. Dreams that were once played out on the streets of New York, Chicago, and Boston, are being re-created daily in places like Cuba, Puerto Rico, the Dominican Republic, Central and South America, Japan, and Korea. Communities of interests are drawn together as competition crosses national and international lines. It seems hardly noticeable today that at one time the color line was the division that separated players.

Time alters one's perspective. Today's game of baseball affords an ample distance from the early days to provide that perspective. By countless measures the game has changed, but one aspect is constant. Baseball is not a product for which only one country can lay claim. The dreams that give the game its attraction to so many seem impervious to social, political, and economic barriers. From the sandlots to today's multimillion–dollar sports arenas, baseball retains its capacity to appeal to a diverse population.

The great social experiment launched by Branch Rickey in 1946 has brought forth a harvest that has defied social convention. Little could he have imagined at the time how the common dream of playing major league baseball would be realized by so many. In retrospect, his choice of Jackie Robinson proved prescient. Robinson's role as a pioneer opened doors that had been closed, but in the larger sense he gave baseball the chance to prove that common dreams can meet on the playing field in mutual respect and competition. Today, new dreams are being shaped as the battle for inclusion and diversity in baseball has given rise to new aspirations for management and ownership. We can only hope that they will soon be realized.

PART II

Material Dreams:
Class, Economics,
and Baseball

LEFT CAPITOLA FOR A FATE UNKNOWN

Harry Hooper

Paul J. Zingg

ABOUT TEN YEARS AGO, AFTER HAVING WRITTEN A BOOK AND SEVERAL ARTICLES ON intercollegiate athletics, I thought it was time to write a history of American sport more generally. As an American historian, the irresistible focus of such a work was baseball. I decided I wanted to examine how baseball became respectable as middle-class entertainment and as a middle-class profession, and to do this through a biography. Aside from the story I eventually told, the path I took to write this book reveals much about the joys and surprises of the historical research process.

To pursue a biography, I had two criteria for selecting the subject. First, the person had to have been an outstanding ballplayer, so good, in fact, that he had to be in the Baseball Hall of Fame. Second, the person had to have gone to college, although not necessarily be a college graduate, but that would have been a nice bonus. In other words, I sought someone whose college experience would have given him a number of career options besides baseball, rather than merely a blue-collar or day-laborer job. Among the half dozen or so candidates I considered, I eventually narrowed the choice to Harry Hooper.[1]

Hooper was a great star of the Boston Red Sox and the Chicago White Sox, from 1909–25. Playing with Babe Ruth in Boston, he convinced the Boston management to shift Ruth from a pitcher to an outfielder and everyday player. He was the captain of two World Series championship teams in Boston, including the last Red Sox champion in 1918. An extraordinary defensive player, he was more "Everyman" than "Superman" but highly respected for his baseball skills and leadership qualities.

When I began my research on Hooper in 1988, I discovered that he had three children, and that they were all still living. I contacted each of them, but was particularly interested in his oldest son, who lived in Capitola, California, near Santa Cruz. I went to visit Harry, Jr., who was happy to show me lots of photographs and clippings, and other quite ordinary memorabilia—balls, bats and hats, World Series pins, and so forth. But he really didn't tell me a whole lot about his father. Basically he had newspaper clippings about Harry hitting a home run, Harry making a great catch, Harry getting a new set of luggage by the grateful citizens of Boston, and so forth.

Since I was looking for something more personal, I was a little disappointed. But he didn't know me, and thus was not likely to turn over much of what he had anyway. Before I left, he suggested that I might want to have a conversation with his brother, John, who lived in Baytown, Texas, not too far from Houston. So I hopped on a plane and went to see John, the youngest of Harry Sr.'s children.

Initially, my conversation with John began much as it had with Harry Jr. John showed me gloves, balls, bats, photos, and clippings. They were nice, but nothing exceptional. We weren't really connecting very well. He wasn't quite sure what I wanted either, and I wasn't quite sure how to ask him for something a bit more personal about his father. But as I was looking through the photos, John finally reached to the top of a bookcase and pulled down an old, worn book. He said, "I don't know, maybe this will interest you." It was his father's diary.

It's the diary his father kept during his first year playing for the Boston Red Sox. It began: "Left Capitola on the 11:20 A.M. train for a fate unknown." It was an absolute gold mine, for in that diary were the recordings of this twenty-two-year-old ball player leaving California and heading east, to try to make a go of it in major league baseball. He recorded everything: not only how he played on the field but also the life and times of a major leaguer in that era. It's also a record of the transition of baseball from infancy to early adolescence. The sport was becoming more established as an entertainment form, and certainly much more established as a legitimate career path.

Barely containing my excitement, I asked John if he had anything else like this. "Yes," he said, "I think I've got some letters around here." Eventually he came up with about five hundred letters that his father had written to his sons, to his wife, and to himself as a series of reminiscences. They were so powerful, so warm, and so rich that they created in me a deep sense of obligation to tell Harry's story and, hopefully, to tell it well.

I was suddenly responsible for the public memory of Harry Hooper, so I could not present him in a way that painted a false picture. This, as much as anything else, is the challenge of a biography. Do you have the materials to tell the story? Is the story interesting? Can you tell the story well? Is it believable? Will people appreciate it? Filmmaker Ken Burns did. Burns asked me to work with him on innings three and four of his PBS-TV *Baseball* documentary. These innings focused on the ballplaying of the 1910s and 1920s, in particular. Burns recognized that Harry's story was a good one, and thus he put a five-minute segment on Hooper into his film, and a short excerpt from Harry's diary into its companion book.[2]

Back in 1909, a rookie outfielder named Harry Hooper reported for spring training with the Boston Red Sox. He was a college man, and he began to keep a diary of the often-dreary life on the road:

Tuesday, March 9: I played left field for Regulars against Yannigans. We beat them 10–7 in seven innings. Caught off first going to third in mud.

Thursday, March 25: Played the bench. Came near getting into game when [Tris] Speaker got hit sliding home, but he stayed in the game. Harry Wolter and myself take in moving pictures in evening.

Friday, April 16: Walk to top of Washington Monument with Nickerson. . . . Play left field in afternoon. . . . Get two hits in four, one single, 3 [putouts, and] one assist to plate.

Monday, April 19: President Taft sees game.

Monday, April 26: Doc Powers [catcher Mike Powers], who took sick at the finish of opening game, died today. We sent $25 for a wreath.

Monday, May 10: Rained all day. Sat around in hotel.

Tuesday, May 11: We are all invited to the Opera House to see *The Broken Idol*. It is very good.

Wednesday, May 12: We are invited to the Burlesque at the Empire. Good show—for its kind.

Sunday, June 27: Hot as Hell. Take walk around lake behind Washington Monument.

Monday, June 28: Beat Washington. Got hit off [Walter] Johnson which scores winning run.

Harry Hooper's life illustrates the interrelationships between the California dream and the American dream. It is a story about one man's opportunity: a chance not to be bound by some predetermined pathway, or restricted by geographic location. Hooper's California roots represent the merger of the East and West, both in baseball and in the broader American society.

Hooper's story emerges from the history of California and West Coast baseball. We can trace it back to townball, which was both an urban and a rural antecedent of baseball that was first played—in an organized way—in New York, Boston, and other East Coast cities. A version of townball first came to the West Coast with the Forty-Niners and the Gold Rush. Tens of thousands of people came out West from the major East Coast cities, bringing their sporting passions, interests, and pastimes with them. The earliest record of baseball being played on the West Coast appeared in a San Francisco newspaper in 1852. It observed "spirited games of town ball" being played on one of the town squares.[3]

Soon thereafter, formal ball clubs came into existence. The first organized West Coast ball club was the Eagles Baseball Club, which began in 1859. Others quickly followed, such as the Pacific Baseball Club, founded in 1862. The

Civil War had profoundly influenced the popularity of baseball because it was a major recreation of the young soldiers who fought in that war. They played the game either in their own camps or in prison camps and took that experience with them back to their hometowns after the war. Some came out West, thus enhancing the spread of the game to California that had begun with the Gold Rush. Some played for the great eastern teams, such as the Brooklyn Excelsiors and the New York Knickerbockers, and then left—with baseball—for California.

An important turning point in American baseball history was the 1869 national tour taken by the Cincinnati Red Stockings, the first openly all-professional, that is, salaried, team. The Red Stockings came to California on the transcontinental railroad, which had been completed only months before. The Red Stockings represented Cincinnati, although only two of the players actually came from that city. They served as an important example: they were extremely good and they were paid. The lesson was not lost on civic boosters, who began to realize that the only way they would get a good team would be if they hired players and provided them with a sufficient salary so that they could play the game basically full time. For the new teams, the great objective was to beat the hired teams from other cities, just as Cincinnati had targeted the teams from Chicago and St. Louis.

The Red Stockings came to San Francisco on their West Coast tour and played five games against the Eagles and the Pacifics. In those games, Cincinnati beat the San Francisco teams by a combined score of 289 to 22. Anybody who thought West Coast baseball was already pretty good suffered a rude shock by the time the Red Stockings left town. But the experience encouraged the California teams to become more professional.

By the turn of the century, one of the hallmarks of minor league and professional baseball was the sense of shared space and community identity that ballparks provided. These ballparks were literally carved out of the often odd-shaped, available space of city blocks. Today, there are not many ballparks left like them, with Chicago's Wrigley Field and Boston's Fenway Park as the most notable examples. There's been a slight resurgence in those kinds of parks, such as with Jacobs Field in Cleveland, and Camden Yards in Baltimore. They are attempts to revive the city around the ball field, much like the early ballparks did.

The ballparks on the West Coast were no different in this respect than those in the East and Midwest. In San Francisco, people were proud of Seals Stadium, and in Los Angeles people debated which was the better ballpark: Gilmore Park or Wrigley Field. Within cities and from one city to another, fans debated which ballpark was more a celebration of the game, and also a celebration of the host city. It was critical to these debates that these ballparks were literally built in the middle of the city, near the neighborhoods of the fans and the players. Often, the players wouldn't dress at the ballpark but rather at their boarding house, where they were renting rooms. They'd walk to the ballpark in their uniforms, meeting people along the way. It's hard to imagine that happening today. But that kind of identity and intimacy represented by these ballparks was a distinctive feature of turn-of-the-century baseball, and of the teams in the Pacific Coast League in particular.

When the Pacific Coast League (PCL) was featured as an exhibit a few years ago at the Oakland Museum, it ran for two and a half years. And it traveled to all the major PCL cities: Seattle, Portland, Oakland, Los Angeles, San Francisco, and Sacramento. The book I wrote for that exhibit went into a second edition only three months after the exhibit opened.[4] The tremendous interest shown in the exhibit reflects the PCL's huge popularity even to this day. That appeal has stemmed in large part from the PCL's great stability. The teams and playing schedules remained virtually identical from 1931 to 1958—the same eight teams for twenty-eight seasons.

It's instructive to examine some of the West Coast ballparks and players from this era. It illustrates the environment from which someone like Harry Hooper emerged. In San Francisco, one of the ballparks was at the bottom of the Haight-Ashbury district, an area that later became famous in the 1960s for its counterculture lifestyle. Championship games were played at the Haight Grounds in the 1880s and 1890s. It was not much more than a basic grandstand but people turned out in large numbers.

There was another ballpark in San Francisco at Folsom and 25th streets. These recreation grounds sat about 12,000 people. It was the first enclosed ballpark on the West Coast. Later it was expanded to accommodate 17,000 fans. Across the San Francisco Bay, in Emeryville, was Oaks Park, on the corner of Park and San Pablo avenues. Now, only a little plaque remains for the ballpark that housed the PCL's Oakland Oaks. This is where, reputedly, the longest home run in professional baseball history was hit by a player named Roy Carlyle, who wasn't even the team's main home-run hitter. The ball supposedly traveled 680 feet.

Seals Stadium in San Francisco was located at 16th and Bryant. It was the class ballpark of its era. It sat 25,000 people, and attracted Ty Cobb to throw out the first ball in 1931. Besides being the home of the PCL Seals team, it was also the home of the San Francisco Giants for one year. There's a used car dealership there now, and a couple of old neighborhood bars, including the Shortstop, which has a lot of Seals memorabilia. During the last game at Seals Stadium, fans ripped up seats, tore down fences and pulled up chunks of turf. Some people probably still have these souvenirs.

Sacramento had a professional team in the 1890s, which was in one of the California leagues that predated the PCL. This team, the Gilt Edge, was quite successful. By this time they were no longer playing with the softer ball. Most players were wearing gloves to field the now well-established hardball. By this time, baseball had become more established and more regularized, and the ball could go a lot farther than the old townball did. That increased fan interest. You could throw it harder, you could hit it harder, and all of this added to the skill level and excitement of the game.

In the first decade of the twentieth century, St. Mary's College was one of many colleges with baseball teams. St. Mary's had particularly good teams, and perhaps some of the very best in the history of collegiate baseball. In 1907, for example, St. Mary's was undefeated, including wins over the Chicago White Sox and a traveling Japanese team. Hooper attended the St. Mary's grammar school beginning in 1903, and then played on the St. Mary's College team in 1907 and 1908.

There were great baseball heroes in California. None provided more local pride than the DiMaggios, including not only Joe, but also his brothers Dom and Vince, both of whom also played in the major leagues. But first they played in the PCL, with the Seals and the Hollywood Stars. Buzz Arlett of the Oakland Oaks was a superstar. In fact, in 1984, he was voted as the greatest minor league ballplayer in American baseball history by the Society for American Baseball Research. He holds just about every offensive record for the PCL and many overall minor league records. He didn't make it to the major leagues until he was thirty-two years old, and by that time he was well past his prime, although he did bat .313 for three seasons.

In addition to Arlett, players such as Frank Shellenback, "Old Folks" Herman Pillett, and many others, played on PCL teams for ten, twelve, fourteen, twenty years. Sometimes they chose to stay on the West Coast, even preferring it to the majors. The Pacific Coast League was playing sensational baseball, and was often described as the "third major league." Also, the salaries it paid were often more than players would have earned on the East Coast, even in the major leagues. Many West Coast players also didn't want to be away from their families for six to eight months, which is what it meant to play back East, especially in the days limited exclusively to train travel. Of course, safe air travel changed all of this in the late 1950s, when the majors arrived on the West Coast and the old PCL met its demise.

Harry Hooper came out of this California ball-playing tradition. Both of Harry's parents were immigrants to California from the East, his father coming from Canada, his mother coming from Pennsylvania. Both arrived in the West, not knowing anyone but hoping to make it. They met at a farm below San Jose and made their lives as sharecropper farmers. They never owned their own land and always worked for others. Out of that poverty, they thought at least one of their children should have the opportunity to have an education, and they chose Harry.

Hooper had first been exposed to the game when his mother took him to Brooklyn to visit relatives in the late 1890s. He fell in love with baseball. He came back and found variations of baseball—one-a-cat and stickball—were being played in his school. He had the skills and the temperament for baseball, and thus when he went on to St. Mary's High School he served as the college team's mascot, and played the game himself quite seriously. As a result, he earned the equivalent of an athletic scholarship to stay at St. Mary's and play for its college ball team.

Hooper graduated from St. Mary's with an engineering degree, and went to work for a railroad in Sacramento. He did railroad work from Monday through Friday, and played baseball on Saturday and Sunday. He got paid $80 a week by the railroad and $85 a week to play baseball. So, he figured there might be more money in baseball than in engineering. And, it gave him the opportunity to play baseball all summer. He led the California League in hitting, which got the attention of the Boston Red Sox scouts, who sent him off to spring training in Hot Springs, Arkansas, in 1909.

Hooper made it to the majors with Boston and played his first World Series in 1912. In that championship, he made a sensational one-handed catch of a potential home run to seal the win for Boston. Like many ballplayers, he used his first World Series check to buy a new car, a Stutz Bearcat. He was also the leadoff hitter and standout right fielder for the 1915, 1916, and 1918 World Champion Red Sox teams. He won the final game of the 1915 World Series with two home runs. He also put together a World Series record of eighteen consecutive games with a hit. He was a great defensive star: he had a great arm and also perfected the sliding catch. Hooper, Tris Speaker, and Duffy Lewis were the star outfielders for the Red Sox throughout the 1910s. Hooper played seventeen years in the majors, and ended his career with the Chicago White Sox in 1925.

Hooper went on to become the postmaster for Capitola, California for more years than he played major league baseball. In 1971, after a long wait, Harry was inducted into the Baseball Hall of Fame. He was eighty-three years old, and was surrounded on induction day by such people as Stan Musial, Joe DiMaggio, and Roy Campanella—not a shabby representation of the game's best. And not a bad ending for a California boy whose roots go back to the early days of West Coast baseball.

Notes

1. Paul J. Zingg, *Harry Hooper: A Baseball Life* (Urbana: University of Illinois Press, 1993).

2. Geoffrey C. Ward and Ken Burns, *Baseball: An Illustrated History* (New York: Alfred Knopf, 1994), 115.

3. *Daily Alta California* (January 14, 1852), 2.

4. Paul J. Zingg and Mark D. Medeiros, *Runs, Hits and An Era: The Pacific Coast League, 1903–58* (Urbana: University of Illinois Press, 1994).

Past [Im]Perfect
Mythology, Nostalgia, and Baseball

Suzanne Griffith Prestien

*F*IELD OF *D*REAMS, THE POPULAR 1989 FILM BASED ON THE NOVEL *S*HOELESS *J*OE BY W.P. Kinsella, purports to be a movie about the game of baseball. But we all know that appearances are deceiving, and by the end of the film, we have learned that *Field of Dreams* is also about several other themes that baseball helps tie together. Foremost, the film is about the coming together of a father and son and about conquering demons from the past.

The film also asks the question: "What makes a hero?" It answers with several possibilities: Ray Kinsella, who built the magic field and who brings these forces together; Moonlight Graham, who sacrifices his dream to save lives; and Terence Mann, a "make love, not war," radical writer from the 1960s, who finds the strength to start living again. While they all constitute legitimate heroes, I will look instead primarily at another candidate: Shoeless Joe Jackson, an illiterate farm boy who became one of Major League Baseball's true stars, until he was banished from the game for allegedly throwing the 1919 World Series.

In *Field of Dreams*, Shoeless Joe is portrayed as a hero of mythological proportions, albeit a toppled hero who must be replaced on his rightful pedestal. Through Jackson and the game of baseball, Kinsella and Phil Alden Robinson—the film's director and screenwriter—express a longing for an idealized past, a version of America that never existed. Arguably, Kinsella and Robinson do not really want us to conquer our demons from the past. Instead, they want us to recall them, whitewash them, and make them part of our present. *Field of Dreams*, therefore, uses the archetypal hero and baseball—America's national pastime—to remind us "of all that once was good and could be again."[1]

To discover the elements of myth within this work, we must first decide: what exactly is a myth? In its most primitive form, a myth is a story that tries to make sense of human existence, to bring order out of the disarray that is life. Simply put, myths try to explain difficult, universal concepts. We feel the need to understand those things for which we have fear or awe: birth, death, tragedy, and natural phenomena. So we tell stories to try to come to terms with our world and to harmonize our lives with reality.[2] In *The Power of Myth*, Joseph Campbell claims, "Myths tell us how to confront and bear and interpret suffering, but they do not say in life there can or should be no suffering."[3] They teach us certain values by glorifying heroes who embody the desired qualities.

Myths, however, do not exist only to teach us how to endure. According to Campbell, they also "inspire the realization of the possibility of your perfection, the fullness of your strength, and the bringing of solar light into the world."[4] Campbell believes that myths help us learn how to "follow our bliss." Thus, myths cover all aspects of life, good and bad; they "formulate things for us."[5]

Myths also give us roots, and more important, hope. These stories are such a part of our culture that they become an assumed part of our daily lives, "silently gathering meaning until someone prophetic comes along and renders them conscious in a new form. The story, then, part of the past but new in the present, takes on new life and continues to form the life of mankind." In this way, these stories are timeless, as they help make sense of the present by keeping us connected to our past. They translate what we have been through into what we are now. Myths are part of a process of self-understanding and self-protection that makes our often dreary lives more livable;[6] they renew and reassure us by telling us that although things end (life, relationships, the seasons), they often begin again.

Around the world, the myth of the hero is the most common and best known. Although hero myths may vary in detail from culture to culture, some common traits characterize all heroes, and we see them in the real person of Shoeless Joe Jackson and in the character of the same name in *Field of Dreams*. Experts in mythology, like Campbell and Joseph L. Henderson, tell us that, over and over again, the various hero myths describe the hero's humble birth, his early proof of superhuman strength, his rapid rise to power or prominence, his triumphant struggle with the forces of evil, his susceptibility to hubris, and his fall—through betrayal or a "heroic" sacrifice that ends in his death.[7] Indeed, the hero may be "swallowed and taken into the abyss to be later resurrected" when most needed.[8]

Campbell claims that the first requirements for a heroic career are the virtues of loyalty, temperance, and courage,[9] and that "the hero is one who comes to participate in life courageously and decently . . . not in the way of personal rancor, disappointment, or revenge."[10] In fact, in *The Power of Myth*, when Campbell discusses the hero's need to journey within, he neatly makes the connection between athletes and heroes for us: "The athlete who is in top form has a quiet place within himself, and it's around this, somehow, that his action occurs,"[11] just like the hero who must find within himself the strength to face his adventure.

Publicly, the hero functions as an inspiration to society. We look up to these individuals because they do what we cannot. Campbell says a hero is someone who has "done something beyond the normal range of achievement and experience."[12] Certainly we all can appreciate overcoming tremendous odds—we love to root for the underdog—and we need people who can master those odds to encourage us, to keep our hope alive. Thus, the hero is not only acting for himself; he has given his life to something bigger. So whenever "a person becomes a model for other people's lives, he has moved into the sphere of being mythologized."[13]

Again, when pointing out the danger of simply allowing others to perform great deeds for us as we idly sit by, Campbell cites athletics as an example: "The one who watches athletic games instead of participating . . . is involved in [only] a surrogate achievement."[14] Not that we don't need heroes today; for we desperately need someone to, as Campbell explains it, "pull together all these tendencies to separation, to pull them together into some intention."[15] It's just that today, the people we look up to tend to be celebrities instead of true heroes in the mythological mode.

Many writers have noted the way baseball functions as myth in Kinsella's books, including this one. We can compare the various journeys that occur in *Field of Dreams* with Joseph Campbell's quest of the hero. This journey has three stages: separation/departure, initiation, and return, which reflect the rites of passage in most cultures.[16] All legendary heroes have followed this path to spiritual transformation—Jason, Aeneas, Moses, and—in *Field of Dreams*—Shoeless Joe Jackson. When we apply this model to Shoeless Joe and *Field of Dreams*, it helps us see baseball as a mythological source of transformation.

So, we might consider Joe's ignominious ouster from Major League Baseball as his separation. His initiation, which involves an ordeal by fire, could be the Black Sox scandal and the subsequent trials and our belief in the hero's guilt. This stage of the journey also includes an apotheosis, during which the hero "becomes free of all fear, beyond the reach of change."[17] Physically, at least, Joe is little changed when he surfaces in a cornfield in Iowa; he is still in his baseball-playing prime. The return stage of the quest is, of course, obvious in terms of Shoeless Joe and *Field of Dreams*. What was incomplete before the journey is now complete. And certainly Shoeless Joe, along with a number of other characters in the film, has found his idea of heaven through the mythological journey and the mythology of baseball.[18]

Besides conforming to the quest, some of the film's characters also fit Campbell's and Henderson's definitions of the hero, with Shoeless Joe Jackson, in particular, fulfilling the role of archetypal hero. Joe's character in *Field of Dreams*, and in real life in fact, conforms rather neatly to the paradigm just presented. Jackson was an uneducated boy with a dream of being a great ballplayer, a dream he worked hard at and eventually fulfilled. In the film, Ray tells us, "Ty Cobb called [Shoeless Joe] the greatest left fielder of all time." They called Joe's glove "the place where triples go to die." In the novel, Ray adds, "[Joe] never learned to read or write. He created legends with a bat and a glove."[19]

By overcoming his underprivileged background and by heading straight for the big leagues, Jackson undertook a kind of hero's adventure by opening himself up to possible failures. That he succeeded most of the time is a testament to his concentration, determination, and courage—the kinds of virtues Campbell has associated with heroes. After the 1919 Black Sox scandal, Jackson willingly risked the jeers of jaded fans so he could continue playing baseball with semi-professional teams in the South. As Ray mentions, his father saw Joe playing "under a made-up name in some tenth-rate league in Carolina. [Joe had] put on 50 pounds and the spring was gone from his step, but he could still hit."

Shoeless Joe also displays his loyalty, another important characteristic of the hero. His loyalty is first and foremost to the game of baseball. In real life, Jackson was somehow able to get past the tragedy of being banned from baseball and continued to play. In the film, he comes back from the dead just to be able to feel "the thrill of the grass" and have the smell of the ball and the glove in his nostrils. He is depicted as courageously and quietly accepting his fate. His reverence for the game is still obvious, when we hear Joe say, "I loved the game. . . . I'd have played for food money. I'd have played free and worked for food. It was the game, the parks, the smells, the sounds."[20] And now, through his mythic and literal rebirth in the paradise of this baseball field, Joe has a chance to play again. He and "the others" are reborn.

For Ray, Shoeless Joe has always been a hero, one who connects him to his deceased father. In the film's opening montage and voice-over, we learn that Ray's father was a die-hard Sox fan who put his son to bed with stories of "the great Shoeless Joe Jackson." Ray enthusiastically recites stats and stories about Shoeless Joe to his wife Annie and daughter Karen. When he tells the story of how Joe got his nickname, Ray does it in the same way people tell the story of George Washington and the cherry tree—as a myth, as a legend. Ray obviously admires and respects Jackson, as we see when Shoeless Joe first appears on the ball field.

Not only is Ray in awe of the ballplayer, but we too are made to feel awestruck by the way the scene is shot. Film director Robinson highlights Joe (played by Ray Liotta) in his bright white uniform against a midnight blue sky. He shoots him from a slightly low angle, to make him look larger than life, heroic. Joe's somber attitude and the serious look on his face keep Ray and the camera and thus, the audience, at a respectable distance until Jackson is ready for closer contact. Only then do we get eye-level close-ups of him, when our initial wonderment has worn off a bit and our curiosity has kicked in.

In reality, while Jackson never did lose his love of the game, he also never seemed resigned to his fate. Only thirty-three at the time he was banished,

Jackson sued Charles Comiskey—the infamous owner of the Chicago White Sox, and later refused to cooperate when Judge Kenesaw Mountain Landis—the baseball commissioner who handed him and seven other White Sox players their lifetime ban—asked him to testify in another investigation. Said Jackson, "I owed nothing to baseball."[21] He also said, "Sure I'd love to be in the game, love to have something, anything to do with it. But I'd rather be out than in and bossed by a czar. . . . If you ask me, I got the dirtiest deal any man in organized baseball ever got."[22]

That doesn't sound like a man who is taking his lumps lying down, but in *Field of Dreams*, Shoeless Joe is presented instead as the dignified fallen hero, whose quiet perseverance and undying love for the game entitle him to exoneration. While in reality Jackson may have placed himself above the commandments of baseball, in the film the game that Comiskey and Landis run—the business of baseball—is clearly a fallen world, a world unable to appreciate true worth and purity of spirit. That's why they cast our hero into the abyss, leaving him to be resurrected by a man (Ray) and a world that needs true heroes.

Thus, for Ray—a child of the 1960s—Jackson is just the cause he needs to keep him from "turning into [his] father," a fate that, at the beginning of the movie, is akin to death in Ray's eyes. Ray considers Shoeless Joe an unjustly toppled hero, "a symbol of the tyranny of the powerful over the powerless."[23] While he admits that Joe may have taken some money in the Black Sox scandal, he refuses to admit that his hero threw the game. He tells Karen, "No one could prove he did a single thing to lose those games." Once he actually hears Jackson himself speak of the game they both love so dearly, Ray is convinced that building the baseball field was the right thing to do: The hero must be pulled from the abyss and given a second chance, or as Harlan Jacobson calls it, a Second Coming.[24]

The reality of Shoeless Joe and the Black Sox scandal differs somewhat from the way *Field of Dreams* presents it. Jackson's attitude is one difference. The clarity of his case is another. Ray is right: Joe did receive $5,000 to throw the World Series. Jackson admitted this himself, although he also says he didn't want to keep the money and tried to give it back. But there are conflicting stories about whether Jackson actually played to throw the games (the situation is not as clear-cut as the movie would make it).

Much of the confusion comes from Jackson's own testimony. On one hand, as Ray excitedly points out early in the film, Shoeless Joe had a terrific Series. He got more hits than any player on either team; he had sixteen putouts, one assist, and no errors.[25] On the face of it, as *Field of Dreams* makes clear, any relationship between his record and the accusation that he played to lose seems far-fetched. In his testimony before the grand jury in 1920, however, Jackson admitted he had agreed to take part in the fix, and said, "We went ahead and threw the second game."[26] But in that same testimony, he also vows that he played to win throughout the entire Series.

So the issue of our hero's innocence is far from resolved, except in the film, where a falsely accused hero is needed to make the plot turn. In fact, Robinson's movie tries to wish away (and wash away) the harm done to Shoeless Joe. Jackson is "dip[ped] in magic waters" which cleanse him of any possible wrongdoings and return him to us, to the innocence of some idealized past.[27] After all, America regularly purifies its history and its heroes.

Shoeless Joe functions as a hero for a culture that now lacks true heroes. But in both the film and in real life, Jackson—through his connection to baseball—also helps Robinson connect us all to America's mythological past. With *Field of Dreams*, Robinson reconstructs the childhood of most middle-aged white males who, as boys, chose their heroes from American generals, Saturday matinee cowboys, or baseball players whose progress they followed on the radio or in the newspaper box scores.[28] Baseball serves as a link between fathers and sons. As the poet Donald Hall points out, "Baseball is continuous . . . an endless game of repeated summers, joining the long generations of all the fathers and all the sons."[29]

Baseball can make these links because it has a timeless quality, as it transcends the material world. When we go to the ballpark, we enter a realm beyond everyday concerns, a world unfettered by time; it seems possible that a game could last forever.[30] In an interview, author W.P. Kinsella claimed, "Baseball . . . still retains a mythic proportion, since the game has a sort of infinite dimension: there's no distance that the slugger cannot theoretically surpass, that the fielder cannot theoretically cover."[31] According to August Fry, baseball—like myth—helps us understand a reality that is rooted in our past, while also addressing issues about how time treats us in the present: "The one who 'enters' the game, steps out of normal time into (re)created time, into time moving toward completion or apocalypse, time made 'prophetic' by play."[32] Obviously, Joe Jackson steps out of time into Iowa, a clear link to this mythological past that seems so attractive to Kinsella and Robinson, and indeed, to many of the rest of us.

Baseball is also continuous, stable; the particulars may change somewhat, but the basics rarely do. Although the game has been around for over a hundred years, the rules have changed very little and the few alterations (like the designated hitter, night games, and higher salaries) have hardly affected how the game is actually played.[33] Baseball statistics—often compulsively compiled—closely connect baseball's present to baseball's past, as we compare Albert Belle's home run output, for example, with The Babe's. While the baseball business differs somewhat from when the game first began, and while the America outside of the ballpark has undergone tremendous transformations over the years,

Bryan Garman notes, "The game that is played between the foul lines has remained relatively stable."[34] In other words, baseball's continuity connects us with history and constantly reminds us of what we like to believe was a stable and steady past.

Baseball also links us to this fabled past through a cyclical pattern of regeneration. In its beginnings, baseball removed city dwellers from the dreary grime of industrial, urban America into a pastoral setting, reminiscent of an American farm landscape. Today, nostalgic ballparks, like Cleveland's Jacobs Field, still serve as a brief intermission from the hectic plots of our lives, taking us back to a slower, less complicated time.[35] The game, as Ken Burns' *Baseball* documentary showed us,[36] came out of the people; we were formed by the game, "and through it received structures for our own hope and failure, of our crucial good and evil, and finally of a beginning and an ending."[37]

The very structure of the baseball season speaks to us of rebirth. Baseball starts in early spring, the natural time of regeneration, and continues into the fall, when nature is in decline. As Garman points out:

> Three long months later, fans are again willing to forgive the failures of their heroes, and the cycle begins anew when they enthusiastically embrace the hope of yet another baseball season. Because these cyclical traditions are reinforced by their ties to the natural growing season, they constitute a powerful regenerative ritual, which is not present in any other major sport.[38]

Thus, unlike other sports, baseball is circular, both in its playing field and its goals (that is, to run around the bases, to leave home only to hopefully return home again). So, too, is *Field of Dreams* circular: the film starts with Ray's father and baseball, and ends with Ray's reunion with his father and baseball. Like Ray's father and Shoeless Joe, our national pastime has always demonstrated the ability to regenerate itself and come full circle.

In *Field of Dreams*, we see baseball's ability to transcend the material world and put us in touch with another time—a time screenwriter Robinson and author Kinsella seem to believe was perfect, almost Edenic; a time, as Jacobson puts it, before America lost control,[39] and before athletes lost control. Ray's homemade ballpark is a paradise on earth, as it returns us to the irresponsibility of youth and forces the problems of the everyday world (like bankruptcy and foreclosure) to recede.[40] As August Fry illustrates, it seems to be re-creating Eden before the fall or more literally, America before the Black Sox scandal: it gives the eight men accused of throwing the World Series another chance at perfect happiness. Fry claims that:

> Those who were excluded from this Eden, finally and forever, are quite correctly from a mythological point of view the ones who most properly should

be the first ones who are permitted to return and to continue to play. For the courts had cleared them of blame, while the baseball commissioner . . . called in from outside the sport to purify it, had banned them for life from ever playing again in organised baseball. The angels had been set at the four gates of Eden. . . .[41]

In this new Eden, Robinson's vision of the perfect America, those unjustly accused can keep playing, since they have been dipped in those "magic waters" and made pure again. Shoeless Joe asks, "Is this heaven?" and he's not far off, for as Frank Ardolino suggests, *Field of Dreams* is "an Elysian manifestation of baseball, America as pastoral paradise."[42]

The descriptions and images of Ray's baseball field in *Field of Dreams* reinforce the idea of the ballpark as heaven on earth, as a perfect place that reminds us of seemingly perfect times past. In his novel, Kinsella takes great joy in describing in detail the magical baseball games, but in the film, Robinson shows us the images that truly convey the beauty and pure delight of the game and this place: Shoeless Joe, white uniform highlighted by green corn and green grass, eagerly waiting for a ball to come his way; Ray and his dad finally playing catch against a sunset watercolored in gold and pink; and the scene that best represents what it means for the former players to be able to play again—Shoeless Joe's teammates whooping out of the cornfield, dancing and laughing onto the sunny, emerald green diamond, conveying pure happiness at being in a ballpark again.

The field achieves a mythic quality when Shoeless Joe and the other long-gone players miraculously appear. Its magic is emphasized by the beautiful way the field is shot, with high key sunlight, accenting the brilliant colors, or bright artificial lights towering against a blue/black Iowa sky. The field's gravel perimeter bounds its magic—players who cross it cannot reenter: they leave our glorious past for an uncertain future. Through some breathtaking cinematography and some skilled actors, Robinson makes us feel that baseball is more than just a game.

Field of Dreams preserves the mythic values of America's pastoral past, and in doing so, battles corporate America as represented by Ray's brother-in-law, Mark. If Shoeless Joe is the archetypal hero, Mark plays the role of the mustache-twisting, whip-cracking villain in the film and the book. He just cannot wait to get his hands on Ray's land and turn it into another mechanized, corporate farming consortium. As he tells Ray in the novel, "The days of the small farmer are gone forever. You're an anachronism."[43] Indeed, Ray's livelihood is being challenged, in large part because the baseball field is eating up his valuable acreage, but he believes there is a spiritual solution to his worldly travails. His spiritual solution—closely related to baseball—represents a return to a premechanized

America that values a close connection to the land. It also disdains the dehumanizing technology of corporate America,[44] which Ray neither understands nor accepts and, as Robinson is suggesting, perhaps we need not accept so readily either.

The timelessness of baseball allows us to continually relive an innocent and idyllic past. *Field of Dreams* reflects this by having players from various eras forming teams and playing together harmoniously in Ray's ballpark. The players who come to Ray's field appear the same as they did in their prime, when they played in major league ballparks around the country, thus further suggesting a game being played beyond time. Fry notes that:

> The time created out of time must still be somewhere else in some kind of eternal present where the game continues to be played, or where it is continually playable. Such elegance and beauty cannot be lost forever, and its . . . purity insures that in some vale of the shades the great players of the past replay, over and over again, the nine innings of their eternity.[45]

Baseball's continuity gives it the power to reassure us through constant connections to the past. In the film, Terence Mann sums up this idea:

> The one constant through all the years has been baseball. America has rolled by like an army of steamrollers. It has been erased like a blackboard, rebuilt and erased again. But baseball has marked the time.

Thus, baseball can actually transcend time and in *Field of Dreams*, so, too, can the players.

The movie conveys this timelessness and connection to the past in an even more obvious way. Here, Robinson actually transports us back in time. Ray and Terry Mann go to Chisholm, Minnesota, a sleepy little town that hasn't changed much in decades, in search of a former player named Moonlight Graham. While there, Ray is magically whisked back to 1972 for an encounter with Graham, who by that time had already had a long career as a physician after his playing days. Ray is taking a walk when suddenly a wind blows and he begins to notice anachronisms such as a theater marquis that reads: "*The Godfather*, 'One of this year's ten best,'" and a license plate registration sticker that reads "'72." Ray has traveled into the past to give Doc Graham another chance at his past—baseball. And Robinson's movie gives us a chance to reclaim a small-town lifestyle and all it stands for.

Finally, we know that all the tourists who somehow find their way to Ray's Iowa farm at the end of the film will indeed be transported back to that idealized past. A trip to the ballpark will revive even the cynic "who gave up the sports page for the Dow Jones Average when he was twenty-one," as Kinsella says in the novel.[46] Terence Mann explains:

> The people who come here will be drawn. . . . They'll turn up your driveway, not knowing for sure why they're doing it, and arrive at your door, innocent as children, longing for the gentility of the past . . . they'll pass over the money without even looking at it—for it is money they have, and peace they lack. . . . They'll watch the game, and it will be as if they have dipped themselves in magic waters. . . .

These people will remember the simplicity of their childhoods here. The magical game will connect them with the myths of the past, and thus make them feel reborn, a rejuvenation Robinson and Kinsella obviously believe many of us "post-moderns" need. And then there's Joe, for whom rebirth is perhaps more compelling than for most of us, and who is the hero we need to buoy us up and keep us going, believing that if we're good enough, we can all be forgiven. In other words, Jackson is the modern hero who tries to bring light into our dark, mythless world.

So, with Shoeless Joe's appearance, Ray can wipe away the sins of baseball's history and return the game to its mythological innocence. But Phil Robinson and W.P. Kinsella are also trying to convince us, through baseball and Shoeless Joe, that America had an idealistic past which, although it never really existed, can nevertheless be relived by a lucky few in the present, at least in this film.[47] Is that so wrong?

Perhaps not. Evidently, since *Field of Dreams* is so popular, the American public longs for a hero like Shoeless Joe and for a history based on a strong code of ethics, honor, and forgiveness. We want to believe in "the world of baseball" too. So we see the Kinsellas, a happy little family, live a relatively simple life in America's heartland; they are people of the earth, farmers, good citizens who get involved and believe in the Constitution and our national pastime.

In *Field of Dreams*, Shoeless Joe and the baseball field remind us of a time when a wife stood by her husband, even if he was bringing the family to the edge of financial ruin. Thus, stalwart Annie tells Ray, "If you really feel you should do this, then you should do it." As we've seen, Terence Mann sums up this nostalgic philosophy near the end of the film, while the sun shines and the "amber waves of grain" flutter gently in the background: "This field, this game, is part of our past. It reminds us of all that once was good and could be again." So what if Joe took the money? He has suffered bravely, he has been loyal to the sport, he deserves a second chance. Perhaps.

So what if the game was never really innocent, if capitalism has actually been a part of baseball since the Cincinnati Red Stockings were incorporated back in

1869?[48] The Black Sox scandal wasn't the first time a game had been fixed; it was only the first time in the World Series. But surely baseball learned its lesson; it deserves to be returned to a state of grace. Maybe.

And so what if *Field of Dreams* wants us to return, as Harlan Jacobson suggests, to "those innocent days of white baseball, when there were no stains on American honor, no scandals, no dirty tricks. When everything was white, pure and clean and simple and . . . well, white. When the Sox stayed white."[49] By emphasizing the term "white," Jacobson reminds us that in the past this film longs for, there were no black major league ballplayers. There weren't even integrated restrooms or restaurants. Robinson tries to atone for Kinsella's disregard for people excluded from our "perfect" past by making the character of J.D. Salinger in the novel into a black writer—Terence Mann, played by James Earl Jones in the film.[50] This, along with his nostalgic and mythical use of baseball and Shoeless Joe, allows Robinson to make our imperfect past: "past perfect."

Notes

1. W.P. Kinsella, *Shoeless Joe* (New York: Ballantine, 1982); *Field of Dreams*, directed and screenplay Phil Alden Robinson (1989).

2. Paraphrase of Bill Moyers quote in Joseph Campbell, *The Power of Myth* (New York: Doubleday, 1988), 4.

3. Campbell, *The Power of Myth*, 160.

4. Ibid., 148.

5. Ibid., 155.

6. August Fry, "The Return of Joseph Jefferson Jackson, A Study in American Myth," in *A Centre of Excellence*, ed. Robert Druce (Amsterdam: Rodopi B.V., 1987), 90.

7. Joseph L. Henderson quoted in Linda S. Joffe, "Praise Baseball. Amen. Religious Metaphor in *Shoeless Joe* and *Field of Dreams*," *Aethlon* 9, no. 2 (1992): 153–160.

8. Campbell, *The Power of Myth*, 146.

9. Ibid., 153.

10. Ibid., 66.

11. Ibid., 161.

12. Ibid., 123.

13. Ibid., 15.

14. Ibid., 131.

15. Ibid., 134.

16. Joseph Campbell, *The Hero with A Thousand Faces* (Princeton, NJ: Princeton University Press, 1949), 30.

17. Ibid., 157.

18. Brian Aitken, "Baseball as Sacred Doorway in the Writing of W.P. Kinsella," *Aethlon* 8, no. 1 (1990): 69–70.

19. Kinsella, *Shoeless Joe*, 5–6.

20. Ibid., 13.

21. Harvey Frommer, *Shoeless Joe and Ragtime Baseball* (Dallas: Taylor, 1992), 174.

22. Ibid., 175, 177.

23. Kinsella, *Shoeless Joe*, 7.

24. Harlan Jacobson, "Shot in the Dark," *Film Comment* 25 (1989): 78; Daniel Gropman, *Say It Ain't So: The True Story of Shoeless Joe Jackson* (New York: Carol/Citadel, 1995), 171.

26. Ibid., 262.

27. Bryan K. Garman, "Myth Building and Cultural Politics in W.P. Kinsella's *Shoeless Joe*," *Canadian Review of American Studies* 24, no. 1 (1994): 46.

28. Ibid., 48.

29. Donald Hall quoted in Joffe, "Praise Baseball," 159.

30. Timothy C. Lord, "Hegel, Marx, and Shoeless Joe: Religious Ideology in Kinsella's Baseball Fantasy," *Aethlon* 10, no. 1 (1992): 46.

31. Kinsella quoted in Aitken, "Baseball As Sacred Doorway," 63.

32. Fry, "The Return," 92–93.

33. Garman, "Myth Building," 49.

34. Ibid, 50.

35. Garman, "Myth Building," 47.

36. Ken Burns, *Baseball* (PBS, 1995).

37. Fry, "The Return," 92.

38. Garman, "Myth Building," 48.

39. Frank Ardolino, "Ceremonies of Innocence and Experience in *Bull Durham*, *Field of Dreams*, and *Eight Men Out*," *Journal of Popular Film and Television* 18 (1990): 46.

40. Lord, "Hegel, Marx and Shoeless Joe," 46.

41. Fry, "The Return," 99.

42. Ardolino, "Ceremonies of Innocence," 45.

43. Kinsella, *Shoeless Joe*, 62.

44. Lord, "Hegel, Marx and Shoeless Joe," 49.

45. Fry, "The Return," 99.

46. Kinsella, *Shoeless Joe*, 46.

47. Garman, "Myth Building," 44.

48. Ibid., 52.

49. Jacobson, "A Shot In the Dark," 78–79.

50. Robinson could not legally use Salinger's name in *Field of Dreams*, as both Kinsella and James Earl Jones indicated in interviews, since Salinger's attorneys were making threats even before the film went into production. Obviously, however, Robinson could have chosen to make his fictitious author white, so his decision to cast Jones in this role was not likely motivated merely by the legal system.

THE SHOT HEARD 'ROUND THE WORLD

America at Midcentury

Jules Tygiel

At 3:58 P.M. ON OCTOBER 3, 1951, NEW YORK GIANTS THIRD BASEMAN BOBBY Thomson launched the most famous home run in baseball history. With two men on base in the bottom of the ninth inning of the third and final game of a playoff series between the Giants and their interborough rivals, the Brooklyn Dodgers, Thomson drove Ralph Branca's second pitch into the left field stands lifting New York from a 4–2 deficit to a 5–4 victory, capping perhaps the most dramatic pennant race ever staged. The feat instantly entered the nation's folklore as a symbolic signpost for a generation of Americans. "It was likely the most dramatic and shocking event in American sports and has since taken on the transcendent historic character of Pearl Harbor and the Kennedy Assassination," observed journalist George W. Hunt in 1990. Anyone alive then and vaguely interested can answer with tedious exactitude the question, "Where were you when you heard it?" Roger Angell calls it "Baseball's grand exclamation point." Novelist Don DeLillo used it to introduce *Underworld*, his fictional inquiry into the meaning of modern America. "Isn't it possible," mused DeLillo, "that this mid-century moment enters the skin more lastingly than the vast shaping strategies of eminent leaders, general steely in their sunglasses—the mapped visions that pierce our dreams?"[1]

On the day after the home run, the *New York Daily News*, recalling Ralph Waldo Emerson's patriotic hymn, called Thomson's hit "The Shot Heard 'Round the Baseball World." A *New York Times* editorial invoked the same imagery, dubbing it "the home run heard 'round the world."[2] The two similar phrases merged in the popular memory, forever celebrating Thomson's triumph, in Emerson's exact phrase, as "the shot heard 'round the world."

Labeling Bobby Thomson's home run in this manner endowed the moment with several enduring, yet unintended ironies. In one sense it reflected American postwar arrogance about the nation's centrality in world affairs, that people across the globe cared about all things American, including its idiosyncratic national pastime. Yet, it also reflected Cold War reality. Hundreds of thousands of American military personnel stationed "'round the world," in Europe and Asia, heard "the shot" via Armed Forces Radio. Millions of others, who experienced the event as it occurred, also literally *heard* it on radio broadcasts beamed not merely across the New York metropolitan area, but throughout the nation. Significantly, still others *saw*, rather than *heard* the shot in homes, in bars, or standing on the street outside store windows with television sets, many of them watching their first televised baseball game. Thus, Thomson's home run, the last great moment of radio sportscasting, simultaneously offered the first nationally televised sports highlight. These radio and television witnesses included untold numbers of African Americans drawn to a contest pitting the National League's two most racially integrated teams—the Jackie Robinson Dodgers and the Willie Mays Giants. Thus, baseball's "home run heard 'round the world"— stroked against Cold War and civil rights backdrops, situated at a crucial communication crossroads, and occurring at a juncture of critical changes in both baseball and society—offers a revealing glimpse of midcentury America.

For many fans and historians, the 1951 playoffs mark the premiere highlight of a golden age of baseball that extended from the arrival of Jackie Robinson in 1947 to the uprooting of the Dodgers and Giants from New York a decade later. To a great extent, the retrospective romance of the era reflects the centrality of New York in both the baseball and American universe at midcentury. Although perhaps not as dominant as its provincial residents believed, and increasingly challenged by developments in Washington, D.C., Los Angeles, and other large cities, New York City in 1951 remained the center of radio, television, publishing, and recording and theatrical culture. Events taking place in New York assumed an often-exaggerated significance. Furthermore, in no other era would New York baseball teams achieve the success they had over these eleven seasons. Between 1947 and 1957, a New York team appeared in the World Series every year but one. Seven of the eleven World Series pitted the Yankees against either the Dodgers or the Giants. The 1951 playoffs possessed a particular resonance. Despite baseball folklore about the great Giant-Dodger rivalry, the two teams had rarely battled for a pennant. Only in 1920, when the Dodgers finished first by seven games and 1924 when the Giants edged the Brooks by a game and a half, had the teams finished in the top two slots in the National League. Played against the backdrop of the Jackie Robinson experiment, these New York matchups proved a formative signpost for an entire generation of New Yorkers.

There remains much to commend this idealized view. The game in 1951 seemed, both figuratively and literally, closer to the fans than later editions. Until 1954, when the Boston Braves moved to Milwaukee, baseball retained the limited geographical configuration established a half century earlier. Ten cities, none further south or west than St. Louis, hosted sixteen teams. Teams played in stadiums built in the teens and early twenties, located amidst urban neighborhoods, within walking distance or streetcar and subway rides of most fans. The ballparks, most of which, like Ebbets Field, held between 30,000 to 40,000 fans, brought fans close to the action.

The players themselves were less remote and more accessible. Bobby Thomson and Ralph Branca, the two pivotal figures in the final game's final play, epitomized this link. Both came from large immigrant working class families; both had been raised and lived in the New York area, and according to legend, had kissed their mothers goodbye when they left for the game that morning. Thomson, born in Scotland, had come to the United States at the age of two. His family had settled in Staten Island, where he still lived. On the day of the game he commuted to Manhattan on the Staten Island Ferry. Branca, one of thirteen surviving children of an Italian father and Hungarian mother, had been born and raised and resided in Mount Vernon, New York. A local boy who made good, Branca was even engaged to marry the boss's daughter (Ann Mulvey, whose father owned 25 percent of the Dodgers) at the end of the season.[3]

Other Dodgers and Giants also had direct links with the metropolitan area. The Dodgers routinely scouted local prospects at the Parade Grounds, a local complex of twenty-six baseball diamonds not far from Ebbets Field. As a goodwill gesture, the Dodger club routinely signed about ten Brooklyn boys a year to play in its farm system. While few of these aspirants ever made the Dodgers, those who did became local heroes. Reserve outfielder Cal Abrams, a graduate of James Madison High School and veteran of the Parade Grounds, was a particular favorite among the Jewish fans who honored him on a special "night" during the 1951 season.[4]

Even those who did not hail from the New York metropolitan area often seemed a part of the community. Players tended to live during the season, and sometimes all year, in the cities in which they appeared, rather than in affluent suburbs. Their salaries, although higher than the average workingman, rarely placed them out of the working class. Most sought off-season employment to supplement their incomes. Physically, as well as financially, they weighed in only slightly above average. Relatively few exceeded six feet in height or 200 pounds in weight. Reporters described former Cleveland third baseman Al Rosen at five feet ten inches and 175 pounds as "big" and "burly."[5]

Like Thomson and Branca, the athletes on the 1951 Dodgers and Giants captured the polyglot make-up of postwar urban America. In addition to the distinctive racial mix, the teams included players representing a wide variety of ethnicities. A majority of the players hailed from the American South and Midwest. But the Giants' lineup with Whitey Lockman, Don Mueller, and Larry Jansen had a substantial contingent of German extraction. Sal Maglie, Carl Furillo, Branca, and Roy Campanella were the sons of Italian immigrants. Clem Labine was of French-Canadian heritage; Andy Pafko, Hungarian; Ray Noble, Cuban. Along the bench sat players with ethnic surnames like Hermanski, Palica, Miksis, Koslo, and Podbielan. Many had served in the military during World War II. Several, like Gil Hodges, Irvin, Cox, and Furillo had experienced active combat.

Yet the roseate glow adhering to these seasons obscures other more sobering truths. It is telling that the third game of the 1951 playoffs, despite the massive hype surrounding it, attracted only 34,320 fans, filling only two thirds of the seats at the Polo Grounds. Baseball, at least when measured at the box office, experienced a staggering decline in the early 1950s. From 1947 through 1949, the major leagues had drawn approximately twenty million fans a season. In 1951, the sixteen teams barely topped the 16 million mark (a figure which would further sag to 14.3 million in 1953.) The New York teams were not immune to the plague. Whereas 5.6 million people had attended Yankee, Dodger, and Giant games in 1947, in 1951—despite the great pennant race—only 4.3 million fans went through the turnstiles. Crowds were surprisingly small at several key junctures of the season. On August 28, after the Giants had won sixteen straight games to propel them back into contention, only 9,000 fans appeared at the Polo Grounds to see if they could extend this streak. At the home finales for the two clubs on September 22, only 19,000 people appeared at Ebbets Field; a scant 6,000 at the Polo Grounds.[6]

Commentators have advanced many explanations for baseball's midcentury attendance woes. Suburbanization drew fans away from the old ballparks, with automobiles replacing streetcars for many as the primary mode of access. With few stadiums equipped with adequate parking (Ebbets Field had only 750 spaces)[7] and most games now played at night and often televised, suburbanites found a trip to the ballpark a chore, rather than an escape. Historian Ben Rader also attributes the decline to a "fundamental shift in urban leisure patterns," in which the suburban home, centered around the television, "became a self-sufficient recreation center," and the rapid growth of the suburbs drew people not just distant from inner-city ballparks, but into rival leisure pastimes. Charles Alexander notes that while in 1948 urban Americans spent two-thirds of their recreation dollars on baseball, just two years later baseball accounted for less than half of these expenditures.[8]

Often lost in these discussions is the uniqueness of the post World War II baseball boom. Before 1945 major league teams had never drawn consistently large crowds. Game attendance during the boom years of the 1920s averaged only 7,531 fans. During the Depression years it dropped to 6,578. In 1945, as the war drew to a close, the 10.8 million fans who attended games established a new record. In 1946 baseball, a symbol of the euphoric postwar celebration, nearly doubled its attendance as 18.5 million people flocked to ballparks. The figure rose to 19.8 million in 1947 and 20.8 million in 1948. Average game attendance between 1946 and 1949 jumped to an unprecedented 16,027.[9]

In retrospect, this bulge, which created new standards for major league attendance, was clearly an aberration rather than a new yardstick. The decline of the 1950s represented a correction to baseball's postwar bull market. Nor did this drop necessarily mean a corresponding decline in devotion. As Roger Kahn has noted, "The crowds watching television baseball multiplied and grew. Interest as opposed to attendance never flagged."[10] Even in 1953, when fan support slipped to its lowest level in the postwar era, attendance hovered almost one-third higher than in 1945 and fifty percent higher than most wartime and prewar seasons.

Yet major league owners drew several lessons from the attendance dip: most cities could not maintain more than one team; many of the older stadiums needed to be replaced, preferably with arenas with easier access to the suburbs and adequate parking; and cities outside of the sacred circle of the Northeast and Midwest could offer new markets and larger crowds. In 1954, the Braves migrated from Boston to Milwaukee launching an era of relocation and expansion that would transform not just the map of baseball, but the game itself. By 1958, both the Dodgers and Giants would be in California. Although they did not realize it at the time, the fans watching and listening to the final game of the 1951 playoffs were bearing witness to the end of an era.

Two memorable artifacts of Thomson's shot have left the game indelibly etched in the nation's soul. The first is the sole remaining newsreel footage of the game, showing Branca's pitch, Thomson's swing, Dodger outfielder Andy Pafko standing at the wall looking up, and Thomson jubilantly romping around the bases, stomping on home plate into the jubilant arms of his Giant teammates. The second is a recording of Giants' radio announcer Russ Hodges' famous home run call:

> Branca throws again . . . there's a long fly . . . it's gonna be . . . I believe . . . the Giants win the pennant . . . the Giants win the pennant . . . the Giants win the pennant . . . the Giants win the pennant.

This description has been replayed so often as to create the illusion that most Americans who experienced the Thomson home run did so through Hodges' impassioned exclamations. In reality, if not for the improbable actions of a Dodger fan, Hodges' broadcast would long since have been forgotten. Neither teams nor radio stations routinely taped or preserved broadcasts in the early fifties. Thus no full record of Hodges' work in the radio booth on October 3, 1951 has survived. However, Lawrence Goldberg, a Dodger fan listening to the game in

Brooklyn, confident of a Dodger victory, decided to record Hodges call of the final half inning so that he could relive Hodges' anguish in defeat. Placing a primitive tape recorder next to his radio, Goldberg instead captured the classic home run call. A lesser man, or more devious Dodger diehard, might have destroyed the tape, but Goldberg called Hodges the next day. "I want you to have this tape," explained Goldberg, unwittingly creating a piece of Americana.[11]

If not for Goldberg's recording our memories of Thomson's home run would be quite different. Only a small proportion of those experiencing the game did so via Hodges' broadcast. Indeed Americans in general, and New Yorkers in particular, had an unprecedented range of options for partaking in the playoffs. The *New York Times* called the decision about which version of the game to tune in on, "the great schism of 1951. . . . The metropolis went quietly mad trying to figure out which radio station to listen to. . . ."[12] In New York City, the playoffs were broadcast by Hodges and Ernie Harwell on WMCA, the Giants' station, while Red Barber and 23-year-old Vince Scully handled the Dodger accounts on WMGM. A group of radicals at the City College of New York heatedly debated the issue of Barber versus Hodges, finally compromising by alternating stations after each inning. Those opting for neutrality could settle for national broadcasts on the Mutual Network with "Brother Al" Helfer, a former Dodger and Giant announcer.[13]

Television offered yet another alternative. The first playoff game, played at Ebbets Field, had been televised by the Dodgers on Channel 9. The second and third games, at the Polo Grounds, were televised on Channel 11, the Giants' station. Hodges and Harwell alternated the radio and television announcing chores. As the senior announcer, Hodges covered the middle three innings on television, allowing him to deliver the more crucial first and last three innings on the radio.[14]

As Yankee announcer Mel Allen later noted, the early 1950s were an experimental era for radio and television. "In '51 and '52 they were both giants—both hating each others guts, and the competition was conducive to baseball because they were both great vehicles for the game," commented Allen.[15] For those in the New York area, television had lost some, though not all, of its uniqueness by 1951. Many, if not most New York homes, possessed televisions. Others could partake in the "World Series special" offered by General Electric allowing them to buy a 17-inch television for just $299.95 with weekly payments as low as $2.72. Those who did not own sets could watch with neighbors or relatives or in a variety of other venues. Bars and restaurants had long since discovered that televisions broadcasting sports events attracted patrons. As early as 1947 an estimated 3,000 New York City bars and grills had added televisions, prompting *Newsweek* to observe, "Television is the best thing to happen to the neighborhood bar since the free lunch." Many watched the game in small crowds around televisions placed in windows of appliance and other stores. One 12-year-old New Jersey boy later recalled watching the Thomson game on a television set up in a local Passaic bank.[16]

Nor was televised baseball a novelty. New Yorkers had watched the World Series on television since 1947. All three New York teams broadcast many of their home games during the regular season. In August 1951 the Dodgers had even experimented with color television. Ten thousand viewers received color wheels, allowing them to convert the images on their screens. Red Smith, who watched the game at CBS headquarters, found "the reproduction . . . excellent, striking, and only faintly phony." Gil Hodges' well-muscled arms "were encased in a pelt of somewhat lovelier tone—about the shade of medium roast beef—than Gil wears in real life." Dodger Manager Charlie Dressen's white uniform appeared "as immaculate as a prom queen's gown," until when walking along the grass, "he turned green, like cheap jewelry."[17]

Outside of New York City, fans had fewer, but a nonetheless impressive array of options. The dramatic expansion of television in the postwar era obscures the corresponding boom in radio broadcasting. The number of local radio stations in the nation doubled between 1945 and 1950. Baseball became a major staple of radio programming on the local, regional, and national levels. Several major league clubs, including the Dodgers and Giants, had established regional networks to carry their games. The St. Louis Cardinals, whose network encompassed over 120 stations in nine states, dispatched Harry Caray to call the game live from the Polo Grounds. The Giants network broadcast games over 38 stations to an estimated audience of three to four million people.[18]

The Dodgers, in addition to a local regional network that reproduced Barber's broadcasts, had established a second innovative Dodger Network in 1950. This network broadcast Dodger games recreated by announcer Nat Allbright in a Washington, D.C., studio. It primarily targeted the South, where the Dodgers, as the pioneers of baseball integration, attracted a wide audience primarily, although not solely, among African Americans. "They were . . . even in the South, almost a matter of life and death," recalled Allbright. "You had whites who were praying for Big Newk and Jackie Robinson to lose. You had blacks who wanted them to win." In Washington, D.C., broadcasts over the Dodger Network garnered higher ratings than Senators games on radio.[19]

On the national level, most fans absorbed their baseball on one of two networks: the Mutual Broadcasting System and the Liberty Broadcasting Network. In 1949 Mutual, the nation's largest network with 350 affiliates, contracted with major league baseball to air a Game of the Day every afternoon of the baseball season except Sundays. During the 1951 season, Mutual carried 145 major league games over 520 stations, many of which had signed on specifically to carry its baseball programming.[20] Liberty was the creation of Texan Gordon

McClendon. Beginning in 1949 McClendon, who dubbed himself "the Old Scotchman," bypassed major league licensing by purchasing game transcripts from Western Union and recreating his own Games of the Day from his studio in a Dallas suburb. By 1950 McClendon had established a network of 430 stations, mostly in the South and Southwest. Unlike Mutual, Liberty aired games on Sundays, and in 1950 added a "Game of the Night."[21]

McClendon became an institution in the postwar American South. Willie Morris, who grew up in Yazoo, Mississippi, recalled, "By two o'clock almost every radio in town was tuned in to the Old Scotchman. His rhetoric dominated the place. It hovered in the branches of the trees, bounced off the hills, and came out of the darkened stores." McClendon experimented with various sound effects to make his games more natural. One out of four weeks each month, Liberty would broadcast live from a major league ballpark. In 1951 the *Sporting News* named McClendon its broadcaster of the year. By that time his empire had grown so large and his baseball coverage so extensive that McClendon had begun to limit his own on air time to major events, turning over the Game of the Day and Game of the Night broadcasts to young announcers like Lindsay Nelson, Jerry Doggett, and Buddy Blattner. On October 3, however, McClendon manned a mike at the Polo Grounds broadcasting live to his devoted following. Indeed, more Americans may have heard McClendon's home run call than either Hodges' or Barber's or Helfer's on Mutual. Like Hodges, McClendon barked out, "The Giants win the pennant!" Then after several moments of crowd noise, the Old Scotchman added, "Well, I'll be a son of a mule."[22]

Television, not radio, however, had emerged as the major media issue facing baseball in 1951. Four years earlier, New York Yankee General Manager Larry MacPhail, who had pioneered radio broadcasts, had unsuccessfully attempted to block the sale of television rights to the 1947 World Series fearing that telecasts would drive down attendance. World Series attendance nonetheless remained high, but Dodger President Branch Rickey concurred in his arch rival MacPhail's assessment of the impact of television on the gate. When offered $150,000 to televise Dodger games, Rickey rejected the proposed deal. "Radio stimulates interest. Television satisfies it," pronounced Rickey predicting an erosion of the fan base. Yet, within a short time both the Yankees and Dodgers (as well as the Giants) had capitulated to the lure of television revenues. From a business standpoint, the choice was not hard to make. By the mid-fifties the Dodgers earned more than $750,000 for television and radio rights, a figure which exceeded the player payroll by $250,000. "We were in the black before Opening Day," allowed Dodger executive Buzzie Bavasi.[23]

Yet baseball, at least in the short run, had entered into a Faustian bargain. Many observers blamed television for the decline in attendance in the early fifties. Veteran sportswriter Grantland Rice opened the 1951 season with a *Sport* magazine broadside entitled, "Is Baseball Afraid of Television?" identifying television as "by all odds the greatest problem baseball has faced in these 75 years." The following season prompted articles by St. Louis Brown owner Bill Veeck and sportswriter Dan Daniel, both of whom had advocated baseball telecasts in 1948, entitled "Don't Let TV Kill Baseball" and "TV Must Go—Or Baseball Will." "All we've got to sell are seats," argued Veeck. "If our ballparks are empty, what good does a TV sponsor's fee mean." Veeck also presciently predicted that "television would help widen the inequality that has existed for too long in baseball . . . the rich are getting richer and the poor are getting poorer."[24]

The 1951 Dodger-Giant playoffs added a new dimension to these debates. Prior to 1951 television shows could not be transmitted live from coast to coast. Programs produced in New York were filmed and then flown to California for western distribution. This hardly diminished the appeal of most early television, but proved a poor substitute for live sports events. Several months prior to the playoffs, however, American Telegraph and Telephone had installed a co-axial cable allowing nationwide broadcasts. The 1951 World Series, scheduled to begin on October 2, was to be the first nationally televised sports event. Taking advantage of the new technology, the Dodger-Giant playoffs supplanted the Series as the pioneer broadcasts. This development was so unexpected that CBS televised the regular Dodger broadcast of the first playoff game from Ebbets Field on October 1 nationally without a commercial sponsor. For games two and three from the Polo Grounds, however, Chesterfield cigarettes, the Giants' regular sponsor, agreed to pay the coast-to-coast transmission costs in exchange for commercial rights over NBC.[25]

The playoffs thus found a ready national audience. *Time* reported that in Los Angeles, where people "never used to get excited about the World Series," television purchases skyrocketed. Denver, according to *Time*, was experiencing not only its first live World Series, but its first television of any kind. Denver's Grand Palace department store installed sets in its show windows and hotels placed televisions in their lobbies for the week. Other cities replicated the pattern found in earlier years in New York. When the Series began, "TV watchers . . . clotted around dealers show windows, jockeyed cunningly for position at bars, ate with their eyes upraised in restaurants which had a video screen." Police erected barricades to control crowds watching the games.[26]

It is difficult to gauge how many people in the United States watched the third game of the 1951 playoffs on television. Many people still lived in areas that could not receive television transmissions and most Americans outside of the New York metropolitan area probably did not own televisions. Media reports focused primarily on the World Series, rather than the playoff television experience. *Look* magazine, in an article entitled "The World Series Stare," estimated that 70 million people watched the first game of the 1951 World Series.[27] A lesser, but nonetheless unprecedented number, probably saw Bobby Thomson instantaneously dash the Dodger pennant hopes, undoubtedly whetting their appetites for more televised baseball.

The phrase "shot heard 'round the world" possessed yet another irony. Although the vast majority of people in the world paid no heed to the events at the Polo Grounds, baseball—like the nation as a whole—seemed unusually focused on world affairs. The entire 1951 season had been played out against the backdrop of Cold War and Korean War tensions. The season opened on the day that General Douglas MacArthur, recently relieved form his command in Korea by President Harry S Truman, arrived in the United States for his triumphal farewell tour. Thomson's home run coincided with President Truman's acknowledgment that the Soviet Union had detonated a second atomic bomb, confirming the end to the American nuclear monopoly.

These concerns never seemed far removed from the baseball diamond. MacArthur delivered his famous "Old soldiers never die" speech on April 19, the third day of the baseball season. He then faded not away, but into the midst of the first Dodger-Giant series of the season. On April 20th, as President Truman threw out the first ball in Washington, D.C., to a chorus of boos, New York City held a massive ticker tape parade honoring MacArthur. At the Polo Grounds the Giants delayed the starting time for their first game against the Dodgers by one hour to accommodate parade goers and recruited a Marine wounded three times in Korea to throw out the first ball. MacArthur, who upon arrival in the United States after a two-decade absence, had listed baseball among the things he missed most, made a well-publicized appearance at the Polo Grounds on April 21. Forty six thousand fans watched the General's son Arthur, seated alongside him, throw out the first ball.[28]

MacArthur became a familiar figure at New York City ballparks, attending games at Yankee Stadium and Ebbets Field as well as the Polo Grounds. In May, Dodger publicist, Irving Rudd, orchestrated MacArthur's Brooklyn debut with a lavish ceremony featuring the World War II Nisei "go-for-broke" battalion and MacArthur materializing in full-dress uniform out of a limousine driven through a gate in the right field fence. MacArthur told the crowd, "I have been told that one hasn't really lived until he has been to Ebbets Field. I am delighted to be here." Nor was this mere rhetoric. The deposed general returned to Ebbets Field twelve more times in the course of the season and attended the playoff series as well. Major league owners also joined the MacArthur mania, floating his name as a replacement for Commissioner Happy Chandler who, like MacArthur, had been dismissed when he failed to please his superiors. When MacArthur declined, the owners offered the job to MacArthur's colleague, Major General Emmett "Rosey" O'Donnell. President Truman, however, refused to release O'Donnell from active service.[29]

Cold War themes reverberated throughout the 1951 season. Sportswriters took to calling Giant second baseman, Eddie Stanky, who in 1949 had set a National League record for walks, "Gromyko" for the Russian diplomat who stormed out of the United Nations. When Dodger Manager Charlie Dressen chastised pitcher Erv Palica for lacking guts, a *New York Post* editorial challenged this "unfortunate statement." "The public does not readily associate courage with a game that children can play, especially when they turn the page and read the latest casualty lists from Korea," commented the *Post*. Dressen later blamed the Dodger collapse, in part, on the shortage of reserves created by the Korean War draft, which had claimed 190 players out of the Dodger system. Those recalling the playoffs often did so within the context of the war. One group of Dodger fans watched the first game on TV while waiting to give blood for American combatants. A group of anti-war protesters at the City College of New York unanimously voted to adjourn their strategy meeting to listen to the third game.[30]

The *New York Times* also joined the Cold War chorus. The *Times's* lead editorial on October 4 dealt with "The Russian Bomb," calling it "news of gravest import in the whole world." The *Times* immediately followed this dire pronouncement with an editorial beginning, "Well, the Giants exploded a bomb, too," invoking the image of a "home run heard 'round the world."[31]

The notion that events in baseball might have bearing on the Cold War had already been introduced by the game's unfolding racial drama. Only four years had passed since Jackie Robinson's historic breakthrough and major league desegregation had progressed grudgingly. Only three teams in each league fielded black players in 1951. Yet many observers grasped upon the imagery of an integrated game as a potent propaganda weapon. In 1949 when Paul Robeson had questioned whether African Americans would participate in a war against the Soviet Union, the House Un-American Activities Committee recruited Robinson to rebut his charges.[32] A group of promoters proposed a world tour by the Brooklyn Dodgers and the Cleveland Indians—the most integrated team in the American League. They considered it "most important that the Negro race be well represented, as living evidence of the opportunity to reach the top, which America's No. 1 sport gives all participants regardless of race."[33]

The 1951 Dodgers and Giants symbolized baseball's, and America's, impending racial revolution. The two New York squads accounted for all but one of the black players in the National League. (Sam Jethroe, the 1950 Rookie of the Year whom the Boston Braves had acquired from the Dodgers, was the sole black player on the remaining six teams.) Both the Dodgers and Giants fielded several African Americans, almost all of whom had played critical roles in the pennant drive. During spring training both clubs toured the South, breaking down color barriers in many cities, while attracting overflow crowds of both black and white fans. It was not lost on contemporary observers that the two most integrated teams in the National League had finished in a dead heat for the pennant.

According to most accounts, racial harmony prevailed on both clubs. But the unique element of race always percolated just beneath the surface of the Giants and especially the Dodgers. The Giants began the season with four Negro League veterans: Monte Irvin, who would emerge as the team's leading slugger; Hank Thompson, the erratic and alcoholic third baseman; backup shortstop Artie Wilson; and journeyman Cuban catcher Ray Noble. Several key Giant performers, including team leaders Stanky, Alvin Dark, and Whitey Lockman hailed from the South. Nonetheless, maintains Irvin, "We got along with those guys just fine . . . there was absolutely nothing racial on the ball club."[34]

Several incidents, however, illustrated the uncertain dynamics of the newly integrated game. Announcer Ernie Harwell claimed that the "fun-loving" Eddie Stanky took to calling Noble "Bushman." The catcher warned manager Durocher, "I'll kill him if he calls me that again."[35] Giant personnel decisions raised the specter of a quota system limiting the number of blacks on the team. In late May the Giants management promoted African American sensation Willie Mays to the major league club. The Giants had purchased Mays' contract from the Birmingham Black Barons of the Negro American League in 1950 and Mays had advanced through the Giants farm system at an unexpectedly rapid rate. Assigned to the Minneapolis Millers in 1951, just one step below the major leagues, Mays assaulted American Association pitching at a .477 rate while astounding eyewitnesses with his spectacular fielding. Giants' Manager Leo Durocher demanded that Mays be added to his squad. When the promotion came on May 27, the Giants demoted Artie Wilson, one of the four other African Americans to make room for Mays. Several weeks later, the Giants sent slumping third baseman Hank Thompson to the minor leagues. For the third straight year, they bypassed Negro League great Ray Dandridge as a solution to their perennial third base problem. The Giants left Dandridge stranded on their Minneapolis farm club, and instead shifted outfielder Bobby Thomson, who had never played the position, to third.[36]

Had the Giants imposed a quota preventing them from keeping too many African Americans on the team? Many observers at that time and subsequent chroniclers of the 1951 Giants believe they had. "They'll deny it," Irvin later commented, "but I'm sure there was a quota system. . . . My feeling is they didn't want more than two or three blacks playing then."[37] Dandridge, arguably the greatest third baseman in baseball history and the American Association's Most Valuable Player in 1950, never made it to the majors.

The promotion of Mays injected yet another element into the racial mix. The twenty-year-old phenom captivated nearly everyone with his skills and exuberance. But responses to Mays, whose southern mannerisms and youthful naiveté often reinforced racial stereotypes, revealed much about attitudes and assumptions of the time. The Giants assigned Irvin to room with Mays and, in Irvin's own words, to "look after him." Announcer Russ Hodges recalled that Irvin, "a man of quiet dignity and great pride . . . realized at once that Mays, as a potential national figure, must also be a credit to his race." Leo Durocher delighted in his own relationship with the young Mays, who always called him "Mr. Leo." Yet, as Roger Kahn notes, "There was always an Uncle Tom in Durocher's view of Mays. . . . He was the straw boss and Mays the plantation hand." Newspapers endowed Mays with a Stepin Fetchit discourse. One 1951 cartoon depicted Mays in action exclaiming, "Ah gives base runners the heave ho!" and "Ah aims to go up in the world."[38]

Revealingly, the three most important cogs of the 1951 Dodgers: Roy Campanella—who won the National League's Most Valuable Player Award; 20-game winner Don Newcombe; and Jackie Robinson were also the squad's only black players. Four years after Robinson's debut, all of the reserves, other starting pitchers, and relief pitchers on the pioneer team of baseball integration were white. As always, the race issue on the Dodgers coalesced around Robinson. Robinson reigned at the peak of his playing prowess—batting .338, hitting a career high 19 home runs, scoring 106 runs, and setting National League records for second basemen in fielding percentage and double plays. On the final day of the regular season Robinson's heroics, including a game saving catch in the eleventh inning and a game winning home run in the fourteenth (prematurely dubbed by *New York Post* writer Arch Ward, the "shot heard 'round the baseball world") had forced the playoff series. In the aftermath of Thomson's home run, a *New York Times* editorial addressed Robinson's almost supernatural mystique, acknowledging that "even the great Jackie Robinson must bow to miracles."[39]

Robinson was also at the peak of his talent for generating antagonism and controversy. On May 2, National League President Frick chastised Robinson for his aggressive base running. When Robinson defiantly defended himself, Frick responded angrily, "I'm tired of Robinson's popping off. I have warned the Brooklyn club that if they don't control Robinson, I will." According to John Kiernan, Robinson, still unintimidated, countered "And I'm getting tired of being thrown at. Let Mr. Frick change the color of his skin and go out and hit against Maglie." Three weeks later in Cincinnati, Robinson received three letters threatening his life. After a close call at home plate and the ejection of Campanella in the ensuing argument cost the Dodgers a critical September contest against the Braves, newspapers falsely accused Robinson of smashing in the door to the umpire's dressing room. As Robinson later complained, the report led "millions of baseball fans to believe . . . that I am a foul-tempered character."[40]

One particular episode involving the Giants and Dodgers illustrates the pent-up racial undertones of the campaign. At Ebbets Field only a thin wall separated the clubhouses between the home and visiting teams. Losing players could hear the revelry in the other locker room. After one Dodger victory over the Giants, Robinson deliberately taunted his archrivals, tapping his bat against the wall and yelling insults. The enraged Giants began cursing back. Stanky shouted, "Stick that bat down your throat, you black nigger son of bitch," only to find his teammate Irvin standing next to him. For Irvin, it was a delicate situation. He had never been close to Robinson and the Dodger-Giant rivalry, rather than any racial solidarity, dominated his thoughts. Angered by Robinson's tirade and anxious to retain harmony on the Giants, Irvin reassured his teammate. "That's just fine with me, Eddie," he told Stanky, later explaining, "I could have gone along with anything they said; I was that mad."[41]

The presence of Robinson, Irvin, Mays, and other black players reflected more than social transition, but a profound change in the game on the field as well. As one sportswriter has noted, "Baseball in 1950 stood at the end of the era built by Babe Ruth," who had died two years earlier. It poised on the brink of an age forged by Robinson and, especially significant in 1951, Willie Mays. Mays, with his indisputable excellence, convinced all but the most stalwart resisters to integration, of the need to recruit African Americans. The Ruthian game had been characterized by what Bill James has described as a "one-dimensional offense . . . the baseball of the ticking bomb."[42] Black players would transform major league play. Led by Mays, they added the speed and flair that had characterized the Negro Leagues without sacrificing the power introduced by Ruth.

Indeed, in the fall of 1951 baseball, like America, seemed poised on the brink of change in many areas. In the nation's capital, a House subcommittee launched the first Congressional investigation into baseball's monopolistic practices, ending the game's isolation from government scrutiny. The season marked the first in which Walter O'Malley, who would emerge as the dominant personality of baseball's elite, guided the fortunes of the Dodgers. He had wrested control from Branch Rickey, architect of both baseball integration and its minor leagues, the symbol of an earlier era. The game also had a new commissioner, Ford Frick, named to the post just one week before the playoffs began. Frick, unlike his predecessors Kennesaw Mountain Landis and Happy Chandler, was a man drawn from the ranks of the game, not a politician. He would restore command over the game to the owners. In one of his first actions, Frick limited unauthorized radio re-creations of the game, dooming McLendon's Liberty Network. "Tonight, a chapter in the life of the American dream closes," lamented McLendon in his farewell broadcast.[43]

Another more subtle challenge to the traditions of the game was in evidence at the third game of the 1951 playoffs, though few people realized it at the time. Baseball, for all its fascination with statistics and record keeping, had always pursued a stalwartly unscientific and unsystematic course. Field managers guided the destinies of their teams "by the book," an unwritten compendium of arcane strategies and intuitive impulses. The two colorful, controversial managers at the Polo Grounds on October 3, 1951, Leo Durocher of the Giants, and his former protege, Charley Dressen of the Dodgers, personified this approach. Dressen, renowned for taking credit for victories but blaming his players for losses, summed up his leadership philosophy as, "Stay close to 'em. I'll think of something."[44]

Dressen rarely paid attention to an innovative young Canadian who had labored for the Dodgers since 1947. Allan Roth had approached then Dodger president Branch Rickey with a hobby he had developed as a child, tracking the game pitch-by-pitch and keeping detailed records of each player's strengths and weaknesses. Rickey, always attuned to the scientific approach, employed Roth and encouraged his efforts. With pencil and paper, Roth began to compile the most detailed analysis of baseball ever undertaken. "Back then my system was unique," he later explained. "I would record the types of pitches and location. I even had averages for players when they were ahead or behind on the count. My system showed the record for a hitter against a pitcher for the year and over his career." Roth's efforts, especially with the introduction of computers in the 1970s, would provide the basis for modern baseball statistics. Unfortunately, in 1951, his was a craft in the wilderness. "Charley Dressen didn't want to see it," said Roth. "The man didn't want help from anybody. He thought he could do it all himself."[45]

In the bottom of the ninth inning, with two men on base, the Dodgers leading 4–2, and Bobby Thomson scheduled to bat, Dressen made a pitching change. He called in Ralph Branca. Dodger publicist Irving Rudd turned to Roth. "Allan, Allan, what are the statistics on Ralph Branca pitching to Thomson?" asked the anxious Rudd. Roth did not even have to check his numbers. Branca, who had allowed just seven home runs to the rest of the league, had surrendered ten to the Giants. Five of his eleven losses had come against the Giants. Thomson had stroked two of those homers, including one two days earlier in the first game of the playoff series. Roth, staring out at the field, just shook his head sadly. Moments later, Thomson struck "the shot heard 'round the world."

Notes

1. George W. Hunt, "Of Many Things," *America* (January 27, 1960); *USA Today* (October 3, 1991); Dom DeLillo, *Underworld* (New York: Scribner, 1997), 59–60.

2. *New York Daily News* (October 4, 1951); *New York Times* (October 4, 1951).

3. Ron Fimrite, "Side by Side," *Sports Illustrated* (September 16, 1991), 66–77; Bobby Thomson with Lee Heiman and Bill Gutman, *The Giants Win the Pennant, The Giants Win the Pennant* (New York: Zebra Books, 1991); John Drebinger, "Bobby Thomson, Scotland's Gift to Baseball," *Baseball Magazine* (October 1947), 379–381; Roscoe McGowen, "Branca,

Boy Behemoth of the Brooks," *Baseball Magazine* (October 1947), 365–367; Roger Kahn, "The Day Bobby Hit the Home Run," *Sports Illustrated* (October 10, 1960), 37–42.

4. Carl Prince, *Brooklyn's Dodgers: The Bums, the Borough, and the Best of Baseball, 1947–1957* (New York: Oxford University Press, 1996), 120–122; Peter Levine, *Ellis Island to Ebbets Field: Sport and the American Jewish Experience* (New York: Oxford University Press, 1992), 124–125.

5. Peter Gammons, "1950 vs. 1960: A Tale of Two Eras," *Sports Illustrated* (April 16, 1990), 26–32.

6. Harvey Rosenfeld, *The Great Chase: the Dodgers–Giants Pennant Race of 1951* (Jefferson, NC: McFarland, 1992), 105.

7. Ibid., 74.

8. Benjamin Rader, *Baseball: A History of America's Game* (Urbana, IL: University of Illinois Press, 1992); Charles Alexander, *Our Game: An American Baseball History* (New York: Henry Holt, 1991), 220.

9. On average attendance figures, see Rader, *Baseball*, 173.

10. Roger Kahn, *The Era: When the Yankees, New York Giants, and the Brooklyn Dodgers Ruled the World* (New York: Tichnor & Fields, 1993), 286.

11. Russell P. Hodges and Al Hirchberg, *My Giants* (Garden City, NY: Doubleday, 1963), 112; Curt Smith, *Voices of the Game* (South Bend, IN: Diamond Communications, 1987), 65.

12. *New York Times*, October 1, 1951.

13. Cecil Powell, "Of Willie Mays, Joe McCarthy, and Bobby Thomson," *Massachusetts Review* 32, no. 1 (Spring 1991): 106; Smith, *Voices of the Game*, 117–127.

14. Thomson, *The Giants Win the Pennant*, 354–355.

15. Smith, *Voices of the Game*, 128.

16. Kahn, *The Era*, 288; Dave Berkman, "Long Before Arledge . . . Sports and TV: The Earliest Years, 1937–1947 as Seen by the Contemporary Press," *Journal of Popular Culture* 22, no. 3 (Fall 1988): 49–63; Rosenfeld, *The Great Chase*, 253–254.

17. Red Smith, "What It's Like on Color TV," *Baseball Digest* 10, no. 10 (October 1951): 23–25.

18. Rader, *Baseball*, 160; Smith, *Voices of the Game*, 136–138; *New York Times* (October 1, 1951).

19. Smith, *Voices of the Game*, 138.

20. Ibid., 116–127.

21. Ibid., 112; Jim Harper, "Gordon McLendon: Pioneer Baseball Broadcaster," *Baseball History* 1, no. 1 (Spring 1986): 42–51.

22. Smith, *Voices of the Game*, 127; Harper, "Gordon McLendon," 45–46.

23. Dan M. Daniel, "Television Opens Up Fantastic Avenues for Baseball Revenue," *Baseball Magazine* 80 (May 1948), 17–21; Branch Rickey and Robert Riger, *The American Diamond: A Documentary of the Game of Baseball* (New York: Simon & Schuster, 1965), 194; Kahn, *The Era*, 285.

24. Grantland Rice, "Is Baseball Afraid of Television?" *Sport* 4, no. 4. (April 1951): 12–13; Dan Daniel, "TV Must Go or Baseball Will," *Baseball Magazine* 84 (November 1952): 6–8; William Veeck, Jr., "Don't Let TV Kill Baseball," *Sport* 6, no. 6 (June 1953): 10–14.

25. Thomson, *The Giants Win the Pennant*, 54; Bob Oates, "Thomson's Homer Just a Single in L.A.," *Baseball Digest* 18, no. 10 (October 1959): 59–61; "The World Series Stare," *Look* (October 1951), 29; Ray Robinson, *Home Run Heard 'Round the World* (New York: Harper-Collins, 1991), 16.

26. *Time* (October 15, 1951).

27. "The World Series Stare," 29.

28. Thomas Kiernan, *The Miracle at Coogan's Bluff* (New York: T.Y. Crowell, 1975), 61.

29. Irving Rudd and Stan Fischler, *The Sporting Life* (New York: St. Martin's Press, 1990), 99–102; Ron Briley, "Amity Is the Key to Success: Baseball and the Cold War," *Baseball History* 1, no. 3 (Fall 1986): 10.

30. *Time* (April 28, 1952); Rosenfeld, *The Great Chase*, 30, 210; Charley Dressen, as told to Stanley Frank, "The Dodgers Won't Blow It Again," *Saturday Evening Post* (September 13, 1952); Powell, "Of Willie Mays," 106.

31. *New York Times* (October 4, 1951).

32. Ron A. Smith, "The Paul Robeson-Jackie Robinson Saga and a Political Collision," *Journal of Sport History* 6, no. 2 (Summer 1979): 27–35.

33. Jules Tygiel, *Baseball's Great Experiment: Jackie Robinson and His Legacy* (New York: Oxford University Press, 1983), 334–335.

34. Thomson, *The Giants Win the Pennant*, 182–183.

35. Rosenfeld, *The Great Chase*, 84.

36. Tygiel, *Baseball's Great Experiment*, 263.

37. Thomson, *The Giants Win the Pennant*, 179.

38. Gerald Eskenazi, The Lip (New York: William Morrow & Co., 1993), 249; Hodges and Hirchberg, *My Giants*, 98; Rosenfeld, *The Great Chase*, 54; Kahn, "The Day Bobby Hit the Home Run"; Tygiel, *Baseball's Great Experiment*, 305.

39. *New York Post* (October 1, 1951); *New York Times* (October 4, 1951).

40. Thomson, *The Giants Win the Pennant*, 164–165, 169; Kiernan, *The Miracle at Coogan's Bluff*, 68; Rosenfeld, *The Great Chase*, 184–189.

41. Rosenfeld, *The Great Chase*, 36; Thomson, *The Giants Win the Pennant*, 254.

42. Gammons, "1950 vs. 1960," 26–32; Rader, *Baseball*, 163.

43. Smith, *Voices of the Game*, 133; Harper, "Gordon McLendon," 48.

44. Frank Graham, Jr., *A Farewell to Heroes* (New York: Viking Press, 1981), 231.

45. Thomson, *The Giants Win the Pennant*, 266, 307.

46. Rudd and Fischler, *The Sporting Life*, 105.

BEYOND THE DUGOUT
Reassessing the Baseball Dream

George McGlynn

Yes, I HAD ACHIEVED THE DREAM OF THOUSANDS OF POOR AND MIDDLE-CLASS KIDS IN America. I had been signed, at the age of eighteen, to a bonus contract with the St. Louis Cardinals. It was the early 1950s and I was attending Syracuse University on an athletic scholarship. Most college players then had mediocre skills and played a limited schedule. Professional scouts told me I was wasting my time playing college ball. So I decided to accept an offer to play professional baseball. I signed on the condition that I would not join the team until the end of each spring semester. It was a decision I did not regret later.

At this time no other sport seriously challenged baseball's supremacy as the national pastime. The sport had gained status and acceptability among all social groups. To be identified as a professional baseball player conveyed automatic status and social acceptability. Unlike most vocations, sheer natural ability coupled with a strong dedication to the game—for its own sake—could propel one to the top. Achievement in baseball was unambiguous. The game, with its rich traditions and history of baseball heroes, provided a sense of continuity and stability in a rapidly changing and uncertain society. No other sport seemed to catch the essence of the nation's character as baseball did.

Baseball stars were better known than major politicians and corporate magnates. Only Hollywood stars competed with them for celebrity status. Like a number of other young boys during the 1930s and 1940s, I grew up in this euphoric atmosphere, spending hours learning the game's fundamentals, listening to the major league broadcasts, and dreaming of one day becoming a professional baseball player.

I remember the exhilarating experience of being transported into another world when I first walked onto the playing field of a professional baseball park, wearing that famous St. Louis uniform emblazoned with the red cardinals perched on a bat. The beautifully cultivated green grass, the white boundaries outlining the playing field, the commercial billboards on the outfield fences and the hundreds of seats that would soon be filled with fans who had paid to come and see me pitch. I was now a professional player and relished the adulation from my peers, fans, and relatives.

But during my first year in the minors, my dreams began to unravel as I confronted the realities of life as a minor league player. Long road trips, night games in poorly lit parks, cheap hotels, crowded and filthy locker rooms, and indifferent managers were the norm. In addition, my fellow teammates seemed solely concerned with their own batting and earned run averages. The major possibility that they might not make the grade meant having to return to the factory floor or to hundreds of other dead-end jobs. None of my teammates had attended college or even anticipated higher education. Their tenuous position precluded any chance they had of initiating real friendships. These conditions produced an artificial social atmosphere and a strange ambivalence among the players about their team's overall performance. Yet even with these limitations, my motivation remained high and I maintained my commitment to realizing my potential as a professional baseball player.

My baseball career, however, was interrupted by a serious injury and then— following a successful convalescence—by three years as a Marine Corps officer in the Far East. During my time in the service, I began to reflect on my future goals and on the role baseball might play. The thought of returning to baseball with a low salary and uncertain status after being away from the game for more than three years raised a number of doubts for me. My motivation to get back into the game had fallen to an all-time low. In part, I attributed this feeling to an awareness I developed in my early years: what was important in life and for my future, like for others of my generation, was subject to the social control of my environment. The sociologist, C. Wright Mills, once warned that what interests people is not always what is in their best interest. I gradually began to realize that my early interests and the things I valued in the past no longer seemed important. Continuing in baseball would unnecessarily delay my future plans.

Nevertheless, to put my feelings to the test, I decided after being discharged from the service to return to the minor league team I was assigned to by the St. Louis Cardinal organization. After a few weeks my feelings were confirmed. The need to prove myself had evaporated. Other goals, such as completing graduate school and launching a university teaching career now took precedence. Much to everyone's surprise, I asked for my release, which the Cardinals granted, and I left baseball for good.

As I look back on professional baseball during my playing days, and compare the game then to what it has become today, I am concerned about its future in a society where sport has become identified as a business—technically organized, ruthlessly competitive, and profit oriented. What I sensed about baseball, in making my decision about leaving the game, has escalated over the past forty years.

Professional baseball is one of the major businesses in the United States today. The business end of baseball serves as a model for business in society, and reflects the power and control that exists in the business world. Wealth and power are associated with baseball just as with any business. Like any American business, the public is absent from the decision-making process. Banks decide which stadiums will be built, television networks decide which games will be sponsored and viewed, the press decides which teams or individuals will be celebrated, municipal governments decide which clubs will be subsidized, and the federal government—through favorable tax rulings and exemptions from the law—helps develop and maintain sports entertainment.

Professional baseball is also America's last true monopoly. Owners decide whether or not to stage their games, when, where, and how to do so. Ownership gives them the power to dictate the game's development (or nondevelopment), the life and working conditions of the players, and franchise relocations and television contracts. The pursuit of profit underlies all of these decisions.

Professional baseball is a business, but ironically, a romantic one. Baseball has always had a unique place in American custom. Inherently, it has the potential to uplift us, to provide heroes and role models and values that exhibit the best in America. The game carries with it a mythology of commonly shared values that connects strongly to the emotions and psyche of the average American, which may explain its popularity over the decades. These factors, to some extent, have clouded some of the game's darker characteristics.

Before television, most people had never seen a major league game from beginning to end. Newsreels showed only clips, and then only for important games. For most fans, their only contact with professional baseball was viewing a minor league game. Television literally revolutionized baseball. But in the process, it destroyed the minor leagues. The minor leagues were forced to succumb to the greed of the major-league owners. Alone, the minor leagues could do nothing to stem the intrusion of big-league telecasts in their home territory. Starting in 1949, the number of minor-league clubs plummeted 68 percent by the late 1950s.

Professional baseball has flourished partly because it long enjoyed an extremely favorable legal, social, and political environment. In addition, the owners have, over the years, relocated and expanded franchises, and built a number of new stadiums. They have not hesitated to experiment with the basic nature of the game in hopes of increasing revenues.

For example, in 1963 the owners increased the strike zone, requiring umpires to call strikes that were formally balls, in hopes of speeding up the game. Early twentieth-century games lasted an average of one and a half hours. By the 1960s, the average game was two and a half hours. Pitchers worked more slowly, batters stepped out of the box more often, managers had more conferences and replaced pitchers more frequently. As a result of the reduced strike zone, baseball was transformed into a series of defensive contests reminiscent of the early twentieth-century deadball era.

In the 1970s, the owners tried to undue the damage and reduce the decline in hitting by lowering the pitching mound from fifteen inches to ten inches, thus making the curve and the slider less effective. They also ordered the umpires to reduce the strike zone from the knees to the armpits to the knees to belt. They also instituted the designated hitter to replace the nonhitting pitchers. In 1987, to reduce the number of home runs, the owners again enlarged the strike zone and cracked down on cork-filled bats.

The major sports media have played an integral part in promoting professional baseball. Sports such as baseball are used to promote more newspaper sales, to sell advertising space, and to win lucrative contracts for radio and television time. The media helps sell spectator baseball and the attendant sports-related consumer products to the public. They provide a very selective vision of the game. They present baseball in terms of general values, and avoid social values that do not serve their economic interest.

The media seldom confront the game's larger social issues, such as racism, violence, profit taking, union busting, reactionary practices, and corporate power and malfeasance. Instead, the public is fed a steady diet of trivia, slogans, titillation, personalities, and an obsequious catering to owners. In the process, they help confine the social imagination of the fans, focusing instead on personal needs and aspirations that help reinforce the established social order. Severe limitations are placed on those with unorthodox views.

Some sportswriters and broadcasters soon realize that certain beliefs and criticisms can be pursued only at one's own risk. But the media's domination and the propagation of conventional values occurs so naturally that media sports people, many with good motives, convince themselves that they are objective in reporting events. The constraints are so powerful that alternative views of sport are hardly imaginable.

The public funding of baseball facilities is another problem that has only been marginally addressed. Cities that host professional baseball teams are often victimized by owners who demand publicly financed stadiums, tax breaks, and increased percentages of parking and concession revenues from municipally owned stadiums. While local governments lack funds for schools and infrastructure, and lay off public workers and slash welfare rolls, spending on new sports facilities is booming at a pace unheard of since the early 1970s.

More than half of the major league baseball teams are either planning new stadiums or are already playing in one, almost all built at public expense. Sports subsidies, despite local politicians' claims to the contrary, wind up in the pockets of team owners and a few players. New stadiums are being built on the backs of those least likely to be able to afford to attend games. The increase in prices has sharply reduced working-class fans. As one new stadium spokesperson has said, "Our main concern is catering to the wealthy fan and corporate elite who inhabit the high-priced seats and luxury boxes. Those who can't afford the prices can always watch the game on television." Also, once stadiums are built, they are fixed in place, but the teams that use them are potentially mobile and often leave or threaten to do so.

Like other U.S. industries, baseball has become "delocalized," and no longer dependent on a particular community but rather ready to pounce on the most profitable deal, whether it means moving a dress factory to Indonesia or a baseball team to Florida. Just as other corporations have threatened to relocate to extract tax breaks and favorable labor policies, some baseball owners have strong-armed cities into surrendering valuable resources to either retain or attract a franchise. Contrary to claims made by stadium boosters, economic studies show that cities usually spend more than they gain from courting a sports team.

The plight of the player also receives insufficient attention. Seven out of every eight professional players are currently under minor-league contracts, where salaries often dip below $1,000 a month. Minor league players still labor under conditions reminiscent of indentured servitude. The few, exceptional players who make it to the majors nevertheless enjoy only brief careers, usually lasting less than five years. The baseball disputes during the mid-1990s showed the owners' callous attitude toward the players. Incapable of sharing revenues among themselves, the owners wanted to redistribute the players' wealth to smaller market teams. Management's unwillingness to bargain in good faith revealed their actual objective: not to reach a settlement but rather to destroy the players' union.

Americans who watch baseball understand how the sport reflects our changing values. Fans have become accustomed to complaining, salary disputes, temper tantrums, clubhouse lawyers, training violations, criticism of managers, attacks on umpires and fellow players, and bad mouthing of the media and teammates. Such incidents are common and increasing in American baseball, even though they remain untolerated in Japanese baseball.

Baseball has been a special part of American life for more than a century. It provides millions of fans with a well-deserved break from the rigors of everyday life. It has been a bridge of tradition and nostalgia that connects the past with the present, and parents with their children. Professional baseball is an integral part of American popular culture. What occurs on the baseball field does have an impact on society. Unfortunately, while the game remains a simple pleasure, the business of baseball has become complicated and, at times, cutthroat. As a consequence, the fans have become increasingly disenchanted. Millions of fans have begun to realize that corporate greed may be destroying the game they love. And some players, like me, are becoming disillusioned, too. What I saw beginning to happen in baseball during my playing days, many years ago, has vastly intensified over the years.

Baseball is a great game. It is drama at its highest level. Its greatest attraction lies in the vicarious experience it imparts to its fans. It is truly heroic, at once glorious and tragic. Baseball's lure lies in its genuine element of uncertainty and suspense. The goals are clear and the ambiguities are few. We don't want to think badly, or perhaps even think at all, about what we treasure. This is a prevailing attitude in the American love affair with baseball. But unless we explore more than the surface, unless we go beyond media stereotypes, and unless we critically evaluate the game, we will remain entrapped in our own orthodoxy. We'll be unable to understand baseball and help direct the future of the game we love.

AMERICA'S TWO REALMS

Randy M. Torrijos

Ghost of Shoeless Joe: Is this Heaven?
Ray Kinsella: No, it's Iowa.

—from *Shoeless Joe* and *Field of Dreams*

IN A RECENT TELEVISION INTERVIEW, ESSAYIST RICHARD RODRIGUEZ CLAIMED THAT what makes someone American is a belief in self-determination. This is a simple enough notion: that people have the ability to chart their own paths in life, that their obligations should be only those they themselves choose, and that they have the opportunity to achieve their goals if they just work hard enough. This idea underlies the American Dream, and promises that we can improve our lives through hard work, and that we will fail only by not trying. The Dream is sustained by a belief in rugged individualism: that the life one has is of his or her own making. No one is responsible for the condition of your life, and you are not responsible for anyone else's. The Dream is advertised as the ultimate freedom: living by your own decisions, enjoying the fruits of your labor, controlling your own destiny.

In theory, America as an organized nation exists to facilitate the efforts of its people. The law exists to insure everyone equal opportunity and to allow people to achieve their personal destiny. It guarantees that people really can, if they desire, be left alone. All of this, the Dream promises, allows us the freedom to be our own person while living a successful, or at least better, life.

The promises of this Dream have some validity, despite the countless people who find themselves jobless, or the victims of exploitative wages, or other hardships. After all, we often hear about immigrants and "against-all-odds" dreamers succeeding through hard work and innovation. Indeed, my parents came to this country with little money and less education, growing up under conditions that in America would be considered unlivable. To them, the images of children in open-guttered shantytowns (so often used by charitable organizations to raise funds) draw as much sympathy as a picture of a Midwestern farm town would to most Americans. The frame of reference for immigrants like my parents is not one in which such poverty is an unimaginable nightmare but rather where it's part of their history.

By believing in the American Dream, my parents and people like them actually have achieved a higher standard of living. In the country they came from, their new level of material wealth would be considered gluttonous. In America, it's merely middle class. Such advancement would be unthinkable in their home country, where jobs and education are based on class and names. The only way to reach a decent standard of living is to be born that way, or to get married into a family that already enjoys such security. Protection under the law amounts to who you can pay off and for how much. As such, it is easy to see why America is a comparative paradise to some people. To the lucky few who do get everything the Dream advertises, there should be happiness and fulfillment.

Yet inherent in the very core of America's ideology of rugged individualism is a degree of competition that seems almost warlike. This seems a logical result of a lifestyle that promotes the competing self-interest of every individual in an environment of limited resources. In a culture where one's own desires are paramount, some people are sure to lose out. In the United States, this is acceptable as long as the most talented and hard working rise to the top, and add to the strength of the greater society. American culture exists as a continuous zero-sum game: you either have or have not, you either win or lose to the competition. Competition has become the most sacred value in American life. It excuses greed and selfishness. It makes it tolerable that people sleep in the streets. In business, it forgives companies for putting Americans out of work for the sake of more profits. For consumers, it justifies the purchase of products from companies that exploit slave-wage labor.

In his critique of American society, *From Freedom to Slavery*,[1] Gerry Spence uses the example of one man amassing a warehouse full of canned beans, more beans than one could possibly eat, while people starved outside his door. The bean owner justifies this, saying he worked for the beans, and that he therefore deserved them. The starving people could get their own beans. This brings to mind megarich corporate owners, each with more money than they, or their children, or their grandchildren, could reasonably spend.

Whatever virtues they may or may not have, people such as these are hailed by Americans as being great solely because they have accumulated so much wealth. This reigns dominant over everything else, since gaining the most material wealth proves that you have beat out all the competition; doing so means you are a good human being. It's not that Americans don't like people who help the poor or people who succeed ethically; it's just that it doesn't really matter to them either way. Caring and morality are private matters; they shouldn't be used to judge your importance as an American.

Thus, we have the American value of life, dictated by how good you are at what you do, with the very best making the most money. This leaves many Americans out. But what about those who have achieved the American Dream, and some level of material wealth? What kind of security do they have? For many of them, even when they were relatively poor, security used to come from their human relationships. They once put a high value on other people, no matter their economic value, and they could count on their family and community to be there every day. How certain are such things in America, however, where families split apart for the sake of careers, and where communities are torn down and built over as dictated by prevailing economic conditions?

In his novel about the American Dream, *The Tortilla Curtain*,[2] T. Coraghessan Boyle describes the large cultural gap between a dirt-poor immigrant couple from Mexico and a rich white family in Southern California. The immigrants depend far more on each other because it's all they have. These cultural gaps do not disappear once such families actually improve their standard of living. A survival instinct tells them to sacrifice for extended family and friends while the American culture around them tells them to live and work for themselves, to be rugged individuals. A conflict emerges between the value they hold in the collective community and the value they learn about being the best and making the most money for themselves.

Similar conflicts play out elsewhere as the lure of the American Dream unfolds in diverse areas of U.S. life. Among the most poignant reminders of this can be found in the dreams that millions of Americans have held in relation to the national pastime, baseball. We see these dreams in real life, and they are also replayed in endless fictional accounts—in both books and films. Even far-fetched stories can tug at our common American values.

Take, for example, W.P. Kinsella's novel, *Shoeless Joe*,[3] which later became the hit film, *Field of Dreams*. A colleague of mine thinks Kinsella's story is too "hokey" and unbelievable. Yet consider the scene in which a dead player appears magically from a cornfield to play ball on a diamond made by a farmer who takes orders from voices in the air. Rather than hokey, I find it instead to be very realistic. To criticize a story like this for being hokey is akin to criticizing a horror story for being too scary.

Kinsella's tale is about dreams, and specifically about the kind that have slipped by us but that we get a second chance to grab. It's a premise that demands that we see the impossible. The story touches many people—even many non-baseball fans—because it shares a value so many Americans hold: that dreams are the stuff of life that makes us who we are, and that those who keep believing in them are really holding on to their humanity.

The first part of this message seems self-evident. Who among us has not been shaped by hopes for the future? Who doesn't regret the desires we never got to fulfill? But the more contested part of this message is the notion that dreams are worth chasing and worth holding onto forever. In his novel, *Man on Spikes*,[4] Eliot Asinof explores this presumption, and provides a revealing contrast to Kinsella's story. In both of these works, baseball represents a dream that man strives for, and in so doing, is revealed a message about life.

Baseball exists in two realms. One is the physical—recorded in statistics, newsreels, and old photographs. The other is the mythical—the legends passed down as folklore, the memories enhanced by nostalgic imagination, and the dramatic struggles of humans as played out by heroes in baseball novels. The physical and mythical are not, however, mutually exclusive. Baseball myth has always found its origin in some reality (no matter how slight), and the reality itself is affected by the myths that rise up as little boys and girls run onto baseball fields in hopes of becoming the next "great one."

Somewhere along this relationship of perpetual creation, the line dividing truth and fact becomes too faded to see, and in its wake comes a hybrid of both. When you step up to the plate, or walk into a ballpark and catch a glimpse of the great green expanse, you can feel it: the tugging feeling that alerts you to a momentary existence in a limbo where reality and fantasy are one.

It should be no surprise that the two realms of baseball would hold such a dependent relationship. After all, our notions of both baseball's reality and legend come from the same place: stories about great plays and players of the past. Perhaps it is because baseball has had such great true stories that it has inspired so many other, fictional ones. In any case, the fictional provides what the factual does not: an opportunity for clarity. But this clarity is not born out of some deeply profound insight into the truth, but rather by creating enough mythology around the facts so that the truth makes sense. Simply put, fictional stories are a vehicle for processing a reality we do not understand or want to accept.

A straight retelling of reality cannot perform in the same way, at least in any effectively honest manner. It does not have the luxury of creating dramatically meaningful moments to express clear successes or failures, of understanding wholly the motivations (whether good or bad) of its main characters. And reality cannot, if it's being honest, paint participants in events as simply heroes or villains. Unlike fiction, reality remains bound by the constraints of truth; it cannot stray too far from it and, at times, it must simply admit ignorance, despite the questions that may still linger. Such is life.

How does that play out in the stories at hand? In Asinof's book, we meet the "Man on Spikes," Mike Kutner, in the small mining town where he is discovered by a prominent scout. He is promised a large signing bonus and the chance to play in the minor leagues. The scout tells him—and he truly believes—he has the talent to make it to the majors. But he never gets the bonus and instead of a one-way ticket to the majors, he finds himself the victim of inter-team disputes and owner exploitation. His time as a minor leaguer drags on far too long, and yet somehow in an instant Kutner finds himself at the old "baseball age" of thirty-five—his boyhood dream still intact but nothing more than just a dream.

But through it all, he keeps the faith and puts his dream above all else in his life, believing always that one day he would make it. One of his first teammates describes Mike's dedication, and how it bordered on obsession:

> The kid lived nothing but baseball, day after day. Seven days a week he played his heart out. He drove himself through the season as if that was all there was to life. He never even went to movies for fear of straining his eyes. His diet was strict and measured, and he trained for every game. When he talked of the future, it was only the big leagues, like the world ended there and paradise was the goddamn Yankee stadium.

Indeed, the rest of Mike's life does suffer from his fixation on baseball. It drives him and his father—who always saw baseball as a waste of time—farther apart. Kutner even misses his father's funeral for the sake of chasing a batting title, bringing his mother great disappointment. His undying dream strains his marriage, and drives his wife to find comfort in alcohol while Mike is away at games. And he ignores the chance at other, profitable careers, toiling away in the minors at a measly $600 a month while working odd jobs in the off-season.

What makes his futile dream all the more tragic is that Mike is actually very good, good enough to make the majors and better than most who have gone up before him. Perhaps this is what kept him going, but determination after a certain point becomes foolish stubbornness, as his wife explains:

> You're good. Sure—so what! What's so important about that? . . . Lots of guys are good and don't make out. They don't ever make out. Not only in baseball, Mike . . . in everything. Show me where there are guarantees. I've never seen any. Don't you see? You have to be *more* than good. You have to be lucky; you have to be a bootlicker or part your hair the way some dumb manager likes it. You're none of them, Mike. You're just good, and that's not enough!

Of course, Mike ignores her wisdom and to the surprise of everyone but himself, he actually does make it to a major league team, a rookie at the age of thirty-five. But by this time he is already past his prime, wise with years of experience but unable, physically, to compete with the young players a few years out of high school who are comparative veterans in the big leagues. His first game in the major leagues turns out to be his last, and he leaves the game a failure.

But in his failing Kutner finally finds satisfaction when, at last, he can get on with the rest of his life. While the end result was positive, the undeniable truth is that he has sacrificed too much, suffered too long, and enjoyed life too little—all for a dream that in the end does not seem worth it. He finally finds fulfillment in his love for his wife, to whom he goes proclaiming his newfound freedom from his haunting ambition.

From *Shoeless Joe* and *Field of Dreams*, the character Ray Kinsella provides a contrast to Mike Kutner. Kinsella is a man who has lived a fairly normal life, who has a wife and daughter he loves very much. But Kinsella, like most people, had to sacrifice some of his dreams for practical reasons. By the time we encounter him, he is in the process of rediscovering those childhood dreams and the innocence that fostered them. Why else would someone relocate to Iowa to become a corn farmer?

Perhaps his searching state of mind makes him so sympathetic to the voice in the cornfield that tells him, "If you build it, he will come." Kinsella has a vision of a baseball diamond, and he begins to believe that he must build it so that the cheated hero, Shoeless Joe Jackson, can play baseball once again. During his rebellious youth, for the sake of hurting his father, Kinsella had scorned the legacy of Jackson—one of his father's favorites. Now, Kinsella believes that building a ballfield will grant him redemption.

After plowing under a good deal of his cropland and then building the baseball diamond, Kinsella discovers that Jackson was not the "he" the voice was talking about. He spends most of his time trying to figure out who exactly was supposed to "come" to this field he built. Through his odyssey, he allows some magical, even impossible, dreams to be fulfilled: the legendary Shoeless Joe Jackson, along with several other great players from the past, can once again play baseball. The writer Terence Mann (who's modeled after J.D. Salinger) reignites his passion for writing. And Doctor Graham gets to confirm that his true calling in life really was medicine, not baseball.

As wonderful as these wish fulfillments turn out to be, they are nevertheless only peripheral, since although the field hosts all these dreams, they still do not get to the real reason the baseball diamond had to be built. Only in the end do we discover the answer: the catcher for the baseball ghosts turns out to be Kinsella's father, with whom he never got the chance to reconcile before he died. Kinsella and his father get to have a catch again with each other, and for the first time the grandfather meets his granddaughter and daughter-in-law. The ball field was built to get his father to return. Father and son are reunited by the only thing that ever brought them together: baseball.

For all the great things Kinsella experiences and witnesses in this story (the redemption of a hero, the rebirth of a writer, and the reassurance of a man's life-changing choice) the most important is the peace he finds with his father. In this respect, *Man On Spikes* and *Shoeless Joe/Field of Dreams* are not so different. Despite the diverging roads taken by Kutner and Kinsella, and despite the different values they seem to put on the pursuit of dreams (with the former seeming to warn against it while the latter seems to endorse it), they end up in the same place. For when Mike and Ray complete their quests for the one driving dream in their lives, they realize that true fulfillment and understanding of life comes from the relationships we have with those we love. It's an important lesson to consider when contemplating the American Dream.

It has been said that baseball represents what Americans think they should be, that in its essence it eternally holds on to the values that we believe make us American. Perhaps this is why baseball serves as such a perfect metaphor for the dreams in both of these stories. And yet the specific characteristics are vastly different for the so-called dream each of them encounters. One sees all the dream's faults, as Mike Kutner finds fulfillment only in spite of pursuing his dreams, while Ray Kinsella finds peace through attaining his. Who knows which approach is better? I suspect the answer lies somewhere in between. Either way, it says something about how baseball can serve both of these messages, thus showing that the game is as dynamic and varied as the values people bring to it.

Even more telling, despite the differing interpretations of the dream, the two stories pretty much draw the same conclusion: our human relationships have the greatest value. Although we may disagree on the methods, many of the values Americans (and maybe people in general) hold about life are, ultimately, shared. After all, most Americans have a very similar notion of what Heaven looks like, and yes, I do believe it looks a lot like Iowa.

Notes

1. Gerry Spence, *From Freedom to Slavery* (New York: St. Martin's Press, 1995).
2. T. Coraghessan Boyle, *The Tortilla Curtain* (New York: Harper, 1996).
3. W.P. Kinsella, *Shoeless Joe* (New York: Ballantine, 1983).
4. Eliot Asinof, *Man on Spikes* (Carbondale: Southern Illinois University Press, 1998).

THE RING

Thomas J. Stillman

It was a few days before Christmas. I had just about finished my shopping and was heading back to my car through the heart of downtown San Francisco. We were in the middle of the coldest weather we have had in a decade. The head-lines of the sports page announced the demise of the American Basketball League, a lost chance at dreams for many young women, I thought. Baseball was the last thing on anyone's mind.

As I made my way through the crowds of last-minute shoppers, I went through my internal checklist. "All the gifts were bought, buy some more wrapping paper, try to get those cards mailed, and oh, that yellow notice." When I first received the slip, I thought it was a package from the Book of the Month Club. I wish I could remember to send those notices back on time. But when I looked up the zip code, I saw it was from Cotati, a little town south of Rohnert Park. "It must be from Sherry or Ariel," I mused. As I dodged more on-rushing shoppers with spending in their eyes, it hit me. "The Ring!!" I nearly screamed on Grant Avenue. I picked up my pace and hurried back to the car as quickly as the pedestrians and lights would let me.

The path of that ring and the dreams it symbolized began in February 1995. A group of eight investors, hoping to capitalize on the major league strike of 1994, decided to create an independent baseball league. This group of teams was to be modeled after the Northern League, an independent league that had enjoyed much success its first year in 1994. The Northern League was com-prised of teams in Minnesota and the Dakotas. Bill Veeck, Jr., son of the great baseball owner and promoter of the fifties, owned the St. Paul Saints, on which the television series *Baseball Minnesota* was based.

The new league was to be called the Western Baseball League and would have teams in Surry, British Columbia; Tri-Cities and Grays Harbor, Washing-ton; Bend, Oregon; and California representatives from Long Beach, Palm Springs, Salinas, and Sonoma County (Rohnert Park). Baseball fans were ready for a league that had no affiliation with Major League Baseball. They were disgusted with the strike, the cancellation of the World Series, and the big money that players and owners alike were getting.

My introduction to the Western League came in a radio report at the beginning of April 1995. There were two new teams coming to the San Francisco Bay Area: the Sonoma County Crushers and the San Francisco Spiders, an entry in the International Hockey League. I was about to begin a Master's program in sports administration. As this would be a career change for me, I needed as much experience as possible, so I applied for a position with both clubs. Fortunately, the Spiders (who lasted one year at the Cow Palace) never returned my phone calls. Bob Fletcher (who, with his wife Susan, owns the Crushers) did call and asked if I had a laptop computer. I would sure go out and buy one if it meant working in professional baseball. Bob told me the Crushers needed an official scorer (the person, of course, who rules on hits, errors, and earned runs).

On a rainy April morning, I headed up to Rohnert Park Stadium, former home of the Redwood Pioneers of the California League. Poor attendance forced the demise of that team. I entered the small building that housed the ticket office and administrative personnel. Bob told me that doctors, lawyers, and professionals from all walks of life had sent in their resumes to get a job with the Crushers. He wanted me to understand that there was no glamour involved in working for an independent baseball team. Even he would have to clean bathrooms if necessary, and everyone would be expected to do what it takes to provide a fun atmosphere for the fans.

Bob and Susan Fletcher had been longtime IBM employees. They took early retirement with no idea of becoming owners of a baseball team. But when the opportunity presented itself, they thought it would be a fun thing to do. Bob and Susan are unique as baseball owners. During each game, they go through the crowd to meet as many people as possible and listen to opinions—both good and bad.

After our interview, Bob took me out to the ballpark. Through the rain and the torn-up field (they were in the midst of putting in new turf), I could see I had stumbled upon a little piece of heaven. While it might be hyperbole, I really did expect Shoeless Joe Jackson to emerge from the center field fence. The stands were extremely close to the field, the farthest seat behind the plate being less than 100 feet away. Behind that, Bob showed me where my seat would be—the second seat from the right overlooking the field and next to the public address announcer. I left that day having an unpaid internship and I needed to buy a computer.

A few weeks later, I met my pressbox associates: Steve Bitker and Kevin "the Rat" Radich, who would be doing the radio play by play, and Dave Raymond, the director of public relations and public address announcer. All of us have been united by a common baseball dream.

Steve Bitker is the morning radio anchor at KCBS radio in San Francisco. After graduating from the University of California at Berkeley, he went to Japan to work for a year. He attended many baseball games and became quite proficient in Japanese. Steve is an avid baseball fan who has a special interest in the minor leagues. He's also enjoying critical acclaim for his book on the 1958 San Francisco Giants.[1] He came to work for the Crushers to fulfill his dream of broadcasting professional baseball. If a job with the San Francisco Giants or Oakland A's became available, he would certainly take it, but with the Crushers he can enjoy doing play by play, as well as being a dad and husband.

Kevin Radich is one of the morning personalities on KNBR, an all-sports station in San Francisco. He came to the Crushers with the dream of becoming an analyst on major-league broadcasts. Unfortunately, his early morning shows and other professional commitments made it impossible for him to attend all the Crushers games. After two seasons, Kevin graciously resigned from the organization.

Dave Raymond is a 1994 Stanford University graduate in communications. He grew up in Nebraska where he became an avid Huskers fan. We often joke with Dave about his love of teams with the primary color of red (Stanford and Nebraska). After graduating from "The Farm," Dave lived in his car for a year— traveling throughout the United States and the Bay Area. Dave would think nothing of driving to Denver's Coors Field from the Bay Area to catch a Rockies-Braves game. He worked for the Stanford athletics department broadcasting women's volleyball and working in the sports information office. Dave was hired by the Crushers as one of their first employees. His job was to do the radio play by play on road games and to serve as director of media relations. In the latter role, he writes meticulous game notes and provides Steve Bitker with a wealth of knowledge for his broadcasts. Dave's dream is to become a major-league announcer. Actually, his radio broadcasts are already of major-league quality but he'd like to be an announcer for a major-league team.

Besides the four of us in the booth, the original group also includes Kevin Wolski. He serves as director of sales and is responsible for the forty advertisements that appear on the outfield wall. He was instrumental in getting the fifty-foot Korbel bottle, which pops its cork every time a Crusher hits a home run. All of the many promotions that have become part of each Crusher game are his brainchilds. Like Steve Bitker, Kevin's dream is to have a job where he could have some fun. No one has more fun than Kevin, who loves baseball and loves interacting with the many fans that come through the gate at Rohnert Park Stadium.

The evening of May 19, 1995, was opening night of the first Western Baseball League season. The tiny building where I first met Bob was jammed with more than fifty people before and after the game. At game time, there were twenty people crammed in the pressbox. Everyone was excited by this new team and this new league. Confusion was everywhere. The software I needed for scoring had not arrived, people did not know where their seats were, the anthem singers did not know when to come on. Somehow, amid all the chaos, the

Crushers managed to beat the Salinas Peppers. Right away, however, it seemed that my dream was coming to an end.

After that first game, a strangely dressed, portly fellow was waiting for me in the office to tell me he disagreed with one of my scoring decisions. I politely acknowledged his opinion and told him that my original decision stood. It turned out this odd fellow was Paul Deese, the manager and part owner of the Crushers. During the second game, the trainer, on behalf of Deese, came up to the pressbox to tell me I had to change another scoring decision. The play involved a sharply hit ball to the Salinas pitcher. The ball was in the pitcher's glove and as he swung his arm back, the ball came out. I ruled it an error on the pitcher. I was too busy to argue with anyone and told the trainer to return to the dugout.

After the game, Deese was back in the office, still in his uniform and with steam coming out of his ears. He ranted and raved at me for what seemed like an eternity. One of his arguments was that the pitcher is not a fielder. That must have been a new rule for independent baseball. I calmly told Deese how I saw the play. If he continued harassing me I was going to take my computer and go home. The next day he apologized and the remainder of the season went without incident from him.

The Crushers languished in third place for most of that first season and missed the playoffs. Due to some incidents with a few players, Bob Fletcher issued a "No Jerks" edict for future hiring for the Crushers. He was also able to buy out Paul Deese's share in the team and hired longtime San Francisco Giant catcher Dick Dietz. Dick was the complete antithesis of Paul Deese. I thought it would be in both our best interests to discuss our relationship before the season started. I was happy to find that Dick was only concerned with winning and not in players' personal statistics.

Dick was hired in late February 1996 and was therefore handicapped in getting the players he wanted. The Crushers again finished 1996 out of the playoffs. One player Dick wanted did get a chance at fulfilling his dream, however. Benjy Gecy was a diminutive shortstop from Coker College in South Carolina. His size indicated that he would not be a power hitter. On one warm summer day, however, he looked like Babe Ruth. With the bases loaded, Benjy hit a towering drive to left field for the Crushers' first grand slam in their history. This event comes with an asterisk, however. The fence in left field is higher than in the rest of the park. Above the lower fence, a "Wine Wall" (for the many wineries in Sonoma County) was constructed. There is a small gap between the lower and upper wall. It was through this gap that Benjy hit his historic "home run." The umpire failed to see the path of the ball and since the ball landed on the other side of the fence, it had to be a home run in his opinion. Benjy finished up 1996 with the Crushers and did not return, but he will always be a part of the team's lore.

Tragedy shattered the dream of one of the most popular players the Crushers ever had. Late in a game against Long Beach, ace reliever Lee Langley was facing right fielder Kadir Villalona. Villalona hit one of Langley's hard fast balls right back to his face and Langley fell to the ground in a heap. After about thirty minutes of medical attention, Lee was taken to the hospital to have reconstructive surgery done on his eye socket and cheekbone. His vision never got better in the left eye, and after a few appearances early in 1997 with the Crushers and then with Moose Jaw in Saskatchewan, he decided to hang up his cleats.

The team finally got hot in 1997. David "Moose" Mowry hit twenty-three home runs and the Crushers signed local favorite Todd Pridy, who had led the Salinas Peppers to the playoffs the previous two seasons. The Crushers finished with fifty-nine wins against thirty-six losses and made the playoffs for the first time in three years. By this time, there had been considerable reorganization in the league. Surry had relocated to Reno. Long Beach had relocated to Mission Viejo. Palm Springs had suspended operations, and Chico was the new entry in the league.

Steve Nettleton, the owner of the Chico Heat, spent $1 million to upgrade Chico State's baseball park. Chico State won the 1997 National Collegiate Athletic Association Division II World Series and the Heat was drawing the largest crowds in the history of the WBL. They were the Crushers' opponents in the first round of playoffs in 1997. The season was divided into two forty-five-game halves. The winner of the Northern and Southern Division in each half would face each other in the playoffs. If the same team won the division title in both halves of the season, then the team with the next best record would be in the playoffs.

This is how Chico with its 45–45 record came to face the Crushers in early September 1997. Another anomaly of the playoff structure was that the best of three series started in Chico. Chico won the first game and the series then went to Rohnert Park for the remaining two games. Behind the brilliant pitching of John Patton and Eric Miller, the Crushers shut out the Heat 10–0 to tie the series at one game apiece. In game three, the Crushers were ahead 4–3 going to the top of the ninth. Ace reliever Eric Miller was on the mound and struck out Tim Cooper. John Coats then hit a drive deep to right center field to tie the score, and in the tenth inning Miller gave up an RBI single to Cooper which scored Mike Davis. Chico had won, and the magical season and the dreams of all the Crusher fans were put on hold.

Based on the previous season, the year 1998 brought great promise. Chico, with its attractive stadium and generous-to-a-fault (contrary to league rules, some say) ownership, strengthened their team incredibly. As September rolled in, the Heat and Crushers found themselves in reversed roles from the previous season. This time it was Chico who had won the first- and second-half Southern Division titles. The Crushers had needed two wins in their last three games to clinch their playoff spot. Even though they made the playoffs, the task of winning the championship looked daunting as the Crushers had been swept by Chico in five games in the final weeks of the regular season and had lost six in a row to the Heat.

After the Crushers' unceremonious exit in 1997, the league voted to change all playoff series to the best of five. The first two games would be played in the home park of the first half division winner, the second two would be played in the other team's park and the fifth game would be played in the park of the team with the best record. In 1998, however, three games were all that was needed. The Crushers managed to win the first two games at Chico, but the Heat was ahead 2–0 going to the bottom of the sixth inning of game three. With four walks and two hits, the Crushers scored three runs in the bottom of the sixth and one insurance run in the eighth to defeat the Heat 4–2 and head to the Western Baseball League championships. The victory was particularly sweet for Eric Miller who received the save in the game one year after yielding the winning run to the Chico Heat.

For those who remembered the loss the previous season, the upcoming championship series against the Western Warriors may have seemed anticlimatic. The Warriors' story of 1998 is another chapter in the lore of WBL history. After three plus seasons in the Western Baseball League, the owners of the Grays Harbor Gulls could not support their team any longer. The last game under this ownership was played at Rohnert Park on June 25th, and the Gulls were scheduled to play the Chico Heat next. If Grays Harbor folded, it would be three cheap forfeit wins for the Heat. Charlie Kerfeld was manager of the Gulls and had earned the respect of all his players. He told the Gulls' ownership that the team was not coming home and with the help of the other owners of the league, the Grays Harbor Gulls became the Western Warriors. Until financial backing was found, the team would be funded by the home team for hotel expenses and by the other teams for salaries and other expenses. This team, which had played some fifty-seven straight games on the road, had defeated Reno to earn their berth in the WBL Championships.

The Crushers won the first two games and at 8:13 P.M. on Sunday, September 13th, hero Eric Miller induced Mike Rendina to hit a groundball to second baseman John Casey who flipped a throw to first baseman Todd Pridy. The Crushers had won their first Western Baseball League championship in four years.

The players rushed on to the field but more important, Bob, Susan, Steve, Dave, Kevin, and I (the six originals) were there to enjoy it together. Immediately following the game, a spontaneous celebration occurred with players, staff, and fans outside the Crushers' clubhouse. Dick Dietz had fulfilled his dream of finally winning a championship. Dick had been in professional baseball since 1955 and this was the first championship he had won at any level. It brought a tear to one's eye as he danced with his life partner, Betty, to phantom music outside his office in the Crushers' clubhouse. The celebration ended with us getting measured for those championship rings that finally arrived in late December—the best Christmas present of all.

Besides the dreams held by players, managers, and staff, minor league baseball fulfills other dreams as well: those of the fans. Words cannot adequately describe the youngsters and their bright eyes, as they stand next to a Crusher player in his uniform or as they get a chance to meet Crusher the Abominable Sonoman, the team's furry, loveable mascot. Before each game, he rides out from the bullpen on his motorized three-wheeler and puts his arms around the umpires as the national anthem is sung. During the game, he pats children on the head, mocks the base coaches, and squirts the fans with a Super Soaker on very hot days.

The young fans also enjoy participating in the many promotions that are held between innings: the ball toss, the uniform race, "Race the Mascot," "Let's Make a Deal," the inner tube race, and "Bowling for Prizes." Of course, an experience at the park is not complete unless the kids run around the bases after the game and pretend they are their favorite players.

Adult fans enjoy how close the seats are to the players. The fans can talk baseball with the players before or after the game and they appreciate the athleticism without megadollars looming over the game. The team gives Rohnert Park and the North Bay a feeling of community pride as residents follow their team religiously on the road and at home.

After 183 consecutive regular season games and six consecutive playoff games, Bob Fletcher was wrong about one thing he told me in that initial interview. There is glamour in minor league baseball when I can walk into the park and all the fans greet me as I make my way up to the perch that gives me the best view of this corner of Heaven. Not to mention the ring!

Postscript

After the 1998 season, one of the original four—Dave Raymond—began announcing games for the Stanford University Women's Basketball team. Then, he was hired to do the baseball play-by-play for the Charleston, South Carolina, team of the South Atlantic League. This gets Raymond into the organized baseball stream, and puts him well on his way toward his dream of a broadcasting job in the major leagues.

Note

1. Steve Bitker, *The Original San Francisco Giants: The Giants of '58* (Champaign, IL: Sports Publishing, 1998).

LURING TEAMS, BUILDING BALLPARKS

Jeremy Howell

IN AN ERA OF MILLION DOLLAR SALARIES, TRANSNATIONAL CORPORATE OWNERSHIP, AND celebrity worship, sports can appear as a metaphor for all that is good and bad in our culture. Nowhere was this more evident than during the 1998 baseball season, forever marked by the dramatic battle between St. Louis slugger Mark McGwire and Chicago Cubs favorite Sammy Sosa as they closed in on Roger Maris's revered single-season home-run record. With each mighty swing of the bat, McGwire and Sosa made distant the memory of perhaps the game's bleakest moment, the cancellation of the 1994 World Series, an event that not even two world wars could previously bring about.

Over the promotional thoroughfares of drive-time radio, the saturated airwaves of television, the flickering electrical circuits of the computer, and the magazine shelves of the local bookstore, these two athletes led us to that most hallowed of cultural places from which only heroes emerge. Indeed, so great was the spectacle that many have anointed the 1998 season as one of baseball's most shining moments, a year in which the game again found itself in the nostalgic spotlight of the national consciousness.

It is against this quixotic backdrop and amid this newly found public euphoria that I wish to locate two other key dates in the annals of baseball history. The first marks major league baseball's structural roots and the second marks its structural future.

Sports historians and economists have told us that during baseball's period of early commercialism and professionalism, the game grew at an extraordinary rate. With expanding industrialization and urbanization, sped by the transformations in communication, transportation, and other technological innovations, baseball became entrenched as a popular spectator sport. The emergence of crowds at local club games and the desire of local entrepreneurs to promote their leading-citizen status and increase patronage of their shops, restaurants, or saloons, led to an estimated 850 baseball clubs being launched in the United States between 1869 and 1900. As one might expect, given this twilight period of industrial capitalism, the vast majority of these clubs went out of business within a few years of existence.[1]

But then, enter William Hulbert and my first key date. On February 2, 1876, a select group of baseball owners met behind locked doors at the New York Grand Central Hotel to create what we now know as baseball's National League. Led by Hulbert, owner of the Chicago club, the 1876 meeting was an attempt by a prestigious set of owners to stratify the marketplace and create order out of chaos. The market had to be tutored and this could occur only with the formation of a single major league.

The 1876 meeting would put into place the two key structures that have since come to define the economic structure of Major League Baseball (MLB). First, monopolistic practices in the marketplace would guarantee a limited number of entrants into the prestige league. The prestigious set of owners would decide what firms would be allowed to enter the league and what franchise territory they would be exclusively allocated. Second, monopsonistic practices concerning interteam competition for athletic labor would ensure teams the exclusive right to enter into a contract with a player and to reserve the rights to that player through a perpetually renewable contract. Players would be tied to their team indefinitely, thus preventing interteam bidding on labor.[2]

I begin with this otherwise rather innocuous historical date because over the past century the league has continued to operate under such cartelized economic conditions. Despite legal and collective bargaining challenges about interteam bidding for talent and franchise location and relocation, collusion and competition remain the name of the game. Teams collude by continuing to artificially construct market scarcity. Simply put, there are more cities that want teams than there are teams made available. When the league sees it in its own self-interest to grow and tap into newly emerging market (media) territories, it might grant an expansion franchise to a new set of prestige owners. For instance, the Arizona Diamondbacks were awarded a franchise by MLB in 1995 for $130 million (to be shared by the cartel), plus $20 million the team would not receive from future television contracts (that is, from fellow cartel members).

But teams also compete and obviously not all market territories are equally ranked. For instance, while baseball teams attempt to maximize joint profits by sharing many of the revenues the league generates (such as national television revenues, expansion fees, and licensing), they do not share all revenues (such as local broadcast revenues, signage, concessions, and luxury suite revenue). Under this scenario, the large market New York Yankees have annual media revenues of $70 million, an enormous figure when measured against the league average of $29 million, but even more extraordinary when compared to the small market Montreal Expos, and its annual figure of $19 million. Thus, the exclusive territory rights and the high fraction of revenue arising from the local market have encouraged teams to seek greener pastures. But these are few and far between, thereby leaving many teams to seek new ways to reignite their existing market-place.

This provides the context for the recent rash in ballpark melodramas unfold-ing in San Diego, Detroit, New York, Montreal, San Francisco, and Cincinnati. In an era of free agency, where top-quality baseball demands top-quality sala-ries, market territory can have an important impact on the dollars teams devote to athletic salaries. Citing attempts to offset the league-wide skewed payroll— the 1998 Baltimore Orioles and Montreal Expos had payrolls of $74 million and $9 million respectively—many teams now call for new ballparks so as to un-cover new competitive revenue streams. By 2002, at least seventeen of MLB's thirty franchises will be playing in stadiums built since 1991.[3]

Along with the increased luxury suite and plush entertainment boxes, many teams have turned to additional means of developing extra revenue. The newest profit center involves selling naming rights to ballparks. Long before it was built, San Francisco's downtown ballpark was named Pacific Bell Park, for which the power company paid $54 million over twenty-four years. Even older ballparks can be renamed for a fee. Jack Murphy Stadium, named for an infamous local sportswriter, became Qualcomm Stadium at the Jack Murphy Sports Complex for a fee of $18 million. This provides long-term brand recognition at a bargain price especially when integrated into additional marketing strategies of stadium signage and over-the-air promotions. And, in another innovative move, besides selling their stadium's name to Bank One for $66 million over thirty years, the Arizona Diamondbacks also generated roughly $7.2 million in 1998 conces-sions, with additional concessions deals paying as much as $10 million for long-term rights.

While we all know why an owner may demand a new stadium, it's far more debatable whether a city should devote public money to the funding of a new ballpark. With the increasing demise of the manufacturing economy and the con-sequent rise of the service economy, many postindustrial cities have tried to revi-talize their cores by developing an amenity infrastructure.[4] The vision of a city's core as a corporate headquarters center with a central business district of office buildings, specialized shops, restaurants, hotels, and luxury apartments appears to have dominated every American vision of downtown spatial management.

Considered more broadly, a clear relationship seems to exist between stadium development, franchise location, and broader strategies of pro-growth and ur-ban redevelopment. If economic impact studies are to be believed and the inclu-sion of a baseball franchise may add to the success of the downtown destination image—thus attracting additional tourist dollars into the community—then so much the better. More important, if its presence will "boost" other companies to make investment within that city's market and bureaucratic boundaries, then having a franchise becomes a civic mandate.

Of course, as recent ballpark referendums indicate, how we should "buy" into this conflation of public and private is the topic of vociferous debate. For some, public funding of a downtown-redeveloped space is appropriate and should be applauded. For instance, the aforementioned Arizona Diamondbacks received $240 million of public money for their new downtown stadium. The city is transformed into a commercial center out of which benefits will trickle down from private-sector economic growth to the community as a whole. But for others, this colonizing of the city into a strictly commercial space devoid of any real sense of organic place is disheartening. It allows the city's core to be themed as a somewhat ubiquitous downtown entertainment metropolis defined by the landscape, language, and imagery of consumption.

This leads us to my second key date in baseball history. In 1997, Australian media baron Rupert Murdoch paid $311 million to the Walter O'Malley family for the Los Angeles Dodgers franchise, as Michael Santoli indicates in his *Barron's* expose. For many the purchase price of the Dodgers was outrageous, particularly since *Financial World* magazine had only one year earlier valued the organization's worth at a high-water mark of $180 million. The problem is that such a valuation measures the Dodgers under the historical market conditions of artificial scarcity, as outlined above.[5] To Rupert Murdoch, chairman of News Corp. Inc., the Dodgers represent far more. That's what marks the sale's significance. It provides as much of a turning point as the 1876 meetings that created the National League because it marks the beginning of a new relationship between baseball, media distribution, entertainment programming, and television content—an alliance that is redefining the political economy of the game.

By owning the Dodgers, Murdoch can "sell" the local broadcasting rights to his own cable sports television station in Los Angeles. After all, his Fox Sports Network, in a joint venture with TCI's Liberty Media, already owns local broadcast rights to twenty-two of the thirty other MLB teams. Take, for instance, a Dodgers-Yankees game. It makes for interesting bicoastal viewing. This is especially so since in late 1998, Fox's WNYW purchased local broadcast rights for the Yankees in a two-year $40 million deal. Moreover, the rest of the country could watch the game on Murdoch's Twentieth Century Fox television network. He has a five-year $565 million national television contract with MLB.

But we should not be too parochial here. Should baseball continue to develop an international audience, Murdoch can broadcast Dodger games on his British Sky Broadcasting (Britain), Star TV (Asia) and JskyB (Japan) satellite systems. Maybe an English infielder and a Korean pitcher might add to the interest and spectacle. Should it be a pay-TV event, perhaps? In his home country of Australia, Murdoch has been known to demand changes to a sport so that it plays better on television. Of course, National Football League owners can say the same thing about American television.

But what if Murdoch or others seek changes that go beyond merely the rules of the game? What if they actually do involve the management of personnel? Who has more global value to the Dodgers, a Kevin Brown or a Chan Ho Park? And does that value have anything to do with actual performance? For a moment, imagine McGwire as a Dodger. Maybe there would be a global audience for a global star, and reports of his escapades would appear in the *London Times*, the *Baltimore Sun*, the *News of the World*, the *New York Post*, and the *Australian*, all of which are owned by Murdoch's News Corp. Inc. Could McGwire be turned into a cartoon character? Why not? He can even have his own show on Fox Kids Network or perhaps his own movie produced by 20th Century Fox Studios or Fox Searchlight Pictures. And just in case we need an official Mark McGwire autobiography, why not one published by Murdoch's HarperCollins book company?

Clearly, there is something new in this scenario. It differs markedly from an owner purchasing a team with the goal of winning a championship for the community, or even reaping the profits of a local franchise territory, or simply receiving a dose of ego gratification. For Murdoch buying a sports team gives him something far more important. Sports brings him the magical eighteen- to forty-nine-year-old consumer audience, the most courted segment of television demographics.[6] By owning the team, Murdoch can control both content and distribution. Add to this the ownership of the stadium, and the implosion of programming and promotion is complete.

The intertextual and cross-promotional opportunities are obvious. Does anyone remember whether the Walt Disney Company paid $50 million to the National Hockey League (NHL) for the right to create the Mighty Ducks of Anaheim before or after it produced the Emilio Estevez film, *The Mighty Ducks*? (The movie was actually made one year before.) And what of the fact that the NHL Ducks logo was a key plot in *D2*, the movie sequel? And now that Disney owns 25 percent of the Anaheim Angels, what are we to think of their reported offer to make a movie of Orlando (El Duque) Hernandez's life story as part of the Angels' unsuccessful bid for the exiled Cuban pitcher?[7] Now there is a global story. It's corporate synergy at its best. Each promotional message refers us to a commodity that itself is the site of another promotion. It will be a made-for-TV movie to be shown on Disney-owned ABC with sporting highlights on Disney-owned ESPN. Sign him up.

While such deals may be currently prohibited, just as MLB currently controls international rights to the game, one has to wonder how the game's structure may change in coming years. History has shown us that MLB as a cartel is only as strong as the relationship among the individual firms that make it up. Should Murdoch decide to rock the boat, then we may discover that the Dodgers were actually undervalued at $311 million. This is particularly true when we consider his current attempt to purchase the Manchester United Football Club, one of Europe's best supported soccer teams, for $1 billion. With the current crop of international stars playing in the English Premiership League (the broadcast rights to which Murdoch already owns) the global promotional opportunities are enormous.

One might ask, in this new promotional baseball economy, is winning important anymore? Maybe. But, in a celebrity culture where the sign value attached to both player and team in cross-promotional strategies is essential, winning just might be an addendum. This may be one of the unfortunate legacies of McGwire's record-breaking home run season. During his tour of cities in pursuit of the record, many purists bristled when fans booed their home team manager each time McGwire was walked. He simply was bigger than the game.

While many of us remember the young steward who gleefully returned McGwire's record-breaking sixty-second home run ball to him on national television, the most lasting image of the season—in this vortex of promotional culture—may be *Spawn* comic book creator Todd McFarlane's purchase of McGwire's seventieth home run ball for more than $3 million. An outrageous price, perhaps, but we should not forget the logic of commodity sign value. During his February 8, 1999 national press conference announcing his purchase, McFarlane spoke in front of a banner that had Todd McFarlane Productions spelled out 103 times. The linking of a commodity to the staging or recapturing of memorable experiences appears to be the promotional name of the game.

This returns us to ballparks. While some ballparks remain an object of loving nostalgia between community and team, most are now nevertheless immersed in this entertainment-spectacle masquerade. While new stadiums might try to recapture a spirit of place, heritage, and belonging, ivy-covered walls often end up as sixty-foot signage panels, concourses become a menu of entrepreneurial retail zones, promenades become interactive play areas, basements become museums, virtual game rooms, and childcare centers. Throw in a hot tub on the third base line, an eighty-foot Coca-Cola wooden contour bottle above the left field bleachers, and we are talking about the creation of the new baseball environment. If promotion is the new spectacle of culture, then sport is its agent and entertainment its currency. It's a new world for baseball.

Notes

1. Kim Schimmel, Alan Ingham, and Jeremy Howell, "Professional Team Sport and the American City: Urban Politics and Franchise Relocations," in *Sport in Social Development: Traditions, Transitions and Transformations*, eds. Alan Ingham and John W. Loy (Champaign, IL: Human Kinetics, 1993).

2. Ibid.

3. Bill King, "New Stadiums May Not Solve Old Problems," *Street & Smith's Sportsbusiness Journal* 14, no. 20 (December 1998): 13.

4. David Whitson and Donald Macintosh, "The Global Circus: International Sport, Tourism, and the Marketing of Cities," *Journal of Sport & Social Issues* 20, no. 3 (August 1996): 278–295.

5. Michael Santoli, "King of Sports," *Barron's* (September 21, 1998), 31–35.

6. Alan Deutschman, "Sly as Fox," *New York Times Magazine* (October 18, 1998), 68–72.

7. Joanna Cagan and Neil deMause, "Bizbrawl," *New York Times Magazine* (October 18, 1998), 66–67.

18

A NEW GOLDEN AGE?
An Evolving Baseball Dream

Leonard Koppett

WHEN I WAS GROWING UP IN NEW YORK IN THE 1930S, THE PHRASE "THE AMERICAN Dream" was seldom used. Then, and in the decade that followed (before, during, and after World War II), people had as many dreams as ever. But the stereotypical package—owning a home and car, financial security, children growing up to be better off than their parents, living in a "nice" (meaning homogeneous) neighborhood, college education open to all—came into common currency only after the war, when all of Europe and much of Asia were in shambles and 12 million Americans and their extended families focused on rebuilding civilian lives after their military experiences.

Our prewar dreams were more modest. The first item was to have a job—any job—at a living wage. That came out of the disillusionment following World War I and the Great Depression. The second item was sheer survival during World War II, for oneself and our loved ones. Item number three was to avoid destitution in old age. None of these seemed peculiarly "American."

American boys dreamed of being major league baseball players, well-paid and famous, since the only other lucrative sports possibilities were to be a prize fighter (too brutal) or a jockey (only for the exceptionally small, and city kids didn't relate to horses, anyhow). American girls dreamed of a "good" marriage, based on romantic love first and financial security second, in a "respectable" context.

Literature, along with conversation and private thoughts, reflected those dreams. Baseball became imbedded in the American consciousness early in the twentieth century. It had several important characteristics. First, it could be played, and watched, anywhere in a primarily rural country with abundant open space, at a time when even urban areas still had many empty lots. Second, professionals could develop its techniques to the highest degree. Third, there could be a game played, and news about it, every day. Fourth, the game itself was a unique blend of individual effort and team play that was closely in tune with the life experience of most Americans. And fifth, for immigrants and their children, especially those born here, baseball could be both the symbol and the emotional content of their Americanization.

The Baseball Dream, specifically, was fed by two sources: journalism (newspapers, magazines, and simplified histories) and fiction. Before World War II, almost all book-length fiction was in "boys' books," series like *Baseball Joe* and *Frank Merriwell*. The subject was always a game-play drama and an off-field interference with it (by gamblers or other villains). Short stories aimed at an adult audience, such as those by Ring Lardner and Paul Gallico, were exceptional. Short stories in pulp magazines (like *Street and Smith's Sports Story*) were a bit more sophisticated but always almost entirely game-oriented. A serious writer, like Thomas Wolfe (the one from the 1930s) or Ernest Hemingway, might write a baseball segment as a passing reference, but such instances were few.

In the 1930s, when radio broadcasts became common, the new medium spread existing attitudes and perceptions beyond the printed page, strengthening but not changing underlying viewpoints. Baseball movies were usually semi-slapstick comedies unconcerned with realism.

Only after World War II did serious baseball literature appear. By then, writers who grew up amid the universal consciousness of baseball began using its familiar themes as metaphors, symbols, references, examples, and evocations of broader aspects of life. They not only have their own emotional and factual base to draw upon, but also the assurance that readers have enough comparable associations to be receptive to the "larger meaning" of their baseball-related story. These became, accordingly, more serious baseball movies and plays, which in turn stimulated others.

So the Baseball Dream became a subdivision of the larger, solidified American Dream. But what about the future of the dream? In the 1980s and 1990s, baseball went through upheavals greater than any it had experienced since 1903. Expansion, realignment, season-interrupting strikes, explosive salary escalation, players changing teams as free agents, off-field drug and other problems—all tarnished baseball's image. Other sports grew and provided increasing competition for attention, especially through television, as did nonsports television more generally. More leisure time and dollars were being spent on other recreational choices. Baseball's hold on the American imagination—whatever that was— lost its exclusivity.

To look ahead, therefore, to see where this might lead, we can start by assessing baseball's status as the twentieth century ended. (It's very favorable.) We can identify its current weaknesses and pinpoint its instabilities and danger signs. (They're real, but not the way they are usually described.) We can delineate the sort of threats their rivals present, and suggest how these can or cannot be met. (Many can be met, but not all of them.) Only then can we speculate on what baseball's cultural impact will likely be in the new century, for new generations.

The key traumatic event was the baseball strike, which wiped out the end of the 1994 season, including the World Series, and made a shortened 1995 season begin late. Ever since, the conventional wisdom has focused on how long it would take to "bring baseball back," and what must be done to accomplish it. Fans and commentators assumed this was a terrible problem, and most baseball officials, from the very top down, expressed this view publicly and often, giving it an aura of a self-fulfilling prophecy.

But they were all wrong. The "recovery" took exactly one year, and by 1998, baseball was—by every standard—the best it has ever been. Attendance, which had reached a peak in 1992 and had gone still higher in 1993 and 1994 under exceptional circumstances, was right back to the 1992 level in 1996—the first full, poststrike season. It went higher still in 1997 and 1998, not reaching the artificial highs of 1993 and 1994 but far ahead of anything else in baseball's past. Baseball's revenue, on a per-club basis, was the highest it had ever been, and was guaranteed to go higher, with new television deals on the horizon.

Its competitiveness, in terms of spreading championships around, having more pennant races in more divisions, and a more even distribution of talent, was the greatest it had ever enjoyed. In the sixteen years ending with 1998, no less than eighteen different teams reached the World Series, only one (the Braves) as many as four times. In the hallowed Golden Age of 1949–64, only four teams (the Yankees, Dodgers, Giants, and Braves) took twenty-seven of the thirty-two World Series places. In 1932 through 1943, four teams took seventeen of the twenty-four places.

The abundance of glamorous stars has also never been greater. At least a dozen future Hall of Famers were still playing in 1998. Spectacular performances have proliferated—no hitters, home run records, a team winning 125 games in one year, the most prodigious base stealer in history adding to his total. Lou Gehrig's record of consecutive games played, once believed unapproachable, was obliterated by Cal Ripkin Jr. In 127 years of organized major league baseball, only two men had ever hit sixty home runs in one season—Babe Ruth's sixty in 1927, Roger Maris's sixty-one in 1961. Then, in 1998, Mark McGwire hit seventy and Sammy Sosa hit sixty-six.

For the last six seasons, beginning with 1993, scoring and all other hitting statistics have suddenly returned to the level that made baseball so popular between 1920 and 1960, after three decades of decidedly less offense. A livelier baseball has made this possible, just as it did then. Baseball authorities have not acknowledged this, but the evidence is unmistakable statistically and confirmed anecdotally by players, coaches, and managers, who make their living noticing such things.

Baseball's total television audience has been bigger than ever. While an individual network can complain about "lower ratings," they don't reflect the actual number of viewers. Cable, local and national, and direct satellite reception have fragmented what used to be a single national package, but the total number of people reached through separate outlets keeps increasing.

Until 1980, no baseball club had ever been sold for as much as $20 million. By 1983, the record price was $53 million, and by 1986 it was $95 million. In the 1990s, four teams changed hands for more than $100 million each, and in 1998, the Los Angeles Dodgers were sold for $330 million, while the Yankees were considering a $600 million offer. The entry fee for an expansion team, which was $2.1 million in the first expansion in 1961, and no more than $10 million as late as 1977, turned out to be $95 million in 1992 and $130 million in 1996. We know about inflation over the past twenty years, but not on the order of more than 1,000 percent. The value of all franchises has soared beyond anything ever imagined.

Player earnings, of course, have increased just as fast while taking a larger share of the total annual revenue. The last round of free-agent signings entering the 1999 season produced a top level of $13 million to $15 million a year. But the total player payroll was still only a little above 50 percent of the gross—less than in football and basketball. Thirty years ago, it had fallen to about 15 percent—less than half the percentage baseball had paid during the Depression years of the 1930s. That was when, and why, players began to take unionization seriously and worked to make it effective.

Then there's the physical plant. Most parks used before 1960 had been built in the 1909–15 era, with Chicago's Wrigley Field, Boston's Fenway Park, and Detroit's Tiger Stadium still in use in 1999. When expansion began, a new wave of "multipurpose" stadiums sprang up, most of which proved less satisfactory for baseball than for football. Since 1991, however, brand new baseball-only parks have been opened in Chicago (American League), Baltimore, Cleveland, Dallas, Denver, Atlanta, Phoenix, Seattle, San Francisco, Detroit, and Houston, with others under construction for use beginning in 2001 in Milwaukee, Cincinnati, and Pittsburgh. These are intentionally old-fashioned in their playing contours, and in their appearance and design, but replete with luxury boxes, other premium seats, the latest internal technology, enlarged and well-designed concession areas, and lavish clubhouses and practice facilities for the players. In addition, major renovation and modernization has been made on ballparks in Anaheim, Oakland, and Tampa-St. Petersburg, with strong demands for new ballparks in New York, Philadelphia, Minneapolis, Montreal, and Boston.

So if attendance, revenue, television exposure, star players and performances, high-level offense (which fans have always preferred), competitiveness, franchise values, player salaries, and modern facilities are at all-time highs, it's fair to say that baseball, in the poststrike years of 1996–2000, has never been in better shape. Nevertheless, real problems exist, some more widely discussed than others, and all capable of getting worse.

Scheduling, for example, can never be satisfactory with thirty teams, sixteen in one league, fourteen in the other. (Two fifteen-team leagues would require at least one interleague game every day). With or without interleague play, members within each division meet too seldom to maximize rivalries and pennant-race fever.

The revenue gap between the biggest-market teams and the rest, which always did exist, has gotten out of hand and must be addressed. Weaker franchises, now more numerous than before, need places to move, or better revenue-sharing formulas, or richer owners. The salary spiral is also out of control, and must somehow level off.

The interests and agendas of several huge corporations that own some clubs increasingly conflict with the needs and views of the "baseball only" private ownership groups, and the differences are widening. A way to define true "gross revenue" must be found if any labor peace is to be maintained through future collective bargaining agreements. Corporate ownerships make this more difficult.

The formation of a fan's intensity, which must occur in childhood or not at all, was neglected for a full generation by catering to television's demand for prime-time exposure of the most important games (the playoffs and World Series) and by abandoning many programs that brought youth groups to actual games (the old "knothole gang" phenomenon). The effects will not be fully felt until this cohort reaches middle age, and shows only a meager ticket-buying impulse. Unlike others who aim sales at young demographics, the baseball promoter's goal must be the creation of a lifetime attachment.

Finally, the shift to a dependence on upscale, affluent, and corporate customers, at the expense of traditional blue-collar and working-class customers, is dangerous. A scandal or economic downturn may make many luxury-box, season-ticket buyers pull out quickly, with no way for clubs to replace that kind of income. Baseball thrived originally, and through the Depression, milder recessions, and wartime, precisely because it was "everyman's game." If the affluence bubble ever bursts, a return to the old pattern may not be possible.

In theory, answers to all these problems are available and have been thoroughly discussed for many years. For example, adding two teams, to make a total of thirty-two, would solve all sorts of scheduling difficulties. Each sixteen-team league could have four four-team divisions, with only the division winners advancing to the playoffs, eliminating the need for the jury-rigged, wild-card system now used to provide the fourth team. But fewer viable locations remain thus far unoccupied. (Baseball has teams in twenty-four of the top twenty-five U.S. markets, missing only Portland, Oregon.) The present, weaker franchises want escape hatches left open, so they can use them as a threat, and as leverage in local bargaining, even if the team does not actually move to a new market. One can imagine, sooner or later, one way or another, a team in Mexico and one in Washington, and perhaps eventually in Havana.

But that's theory. Deciding what to do and how to achieve it depends on the desires of individual clubs, and the will of the majority to proceed. Since so many ownerships are new to one another, consensus is hard to reach. For example, the salary spiral can be checked in one of two ways. If all players were made free agents every year at the expiration of their existing contracts, market forces would go to work. Instead of several clubs competing for two or three top-grade free agents at a particular position, all players would be competing with all others for a job at any position. The supply-demand advantage would shift from players to clubs. The other way to check the salary spiral would be to negotiate some form of a salary cap, and that can only be done, even theoretically, by agreeing on a defined gross with a stipulated percentage of it earmarked for the players.

Yet, the first approach, universal free agency, has been rejected by the owners for nearly twenty-five years, and is abhorred by the players, who benefit from the artificial shortages the present restrictions create. If offered by the clubs, it could hardly be refused, but there's no indication that either side is considering it. The second way would be more practical—if definitions could be worked out. (Both the basketball and football salary-cap systems are geared to defined gross income, and fluctuate with it). Baseball's situation is far more complex and harder to deal with.

Take, for example, the Atlanta Braves. The team is owned by Turner television, which pioneered the "superstation" device of selling its programs to cable systems all over the country. The ballgames were the backbone attraction that made the package so successful. The television rights to Atlanta games cost Turner nothing; it was money going from one pocket to another.

In New York, Cablevision, an independent cable company that wanted Yankee games, had to outbid local stations and other cable companies for the rights. It did so by giving the Yankees a $500 million, twelve-year deal. Turner, on the other hand, could "pay" the Braves anything he wanted—say $3 million or whatever—according to what was best for the tax and other considerations of the parent company.

Under one set of definitions, all that $40 million or more per year collected by the Yankees would go into the "baseball-related income" calculation—while the Atlanta figure would be $3 million. Now, what is the true market value of those broadcasting rights? How would one determine it?

This is not an isolated problem, since other media conglomerates own teams—Chicago's Tribune Company has the Cubs and WGN, Time Warner has absorbed the Braves and Turner Broadcasting, Disney owns the Angels (and also ABC and ESPN), and Rupert Murdoch's News Corporation—which includes

Fox television—owns the Dodgers. And it's not the only problem, either. When Anheuser Busch owned the St. Louis Cardinals, it had exclusive advertising rights within Busch Stadium (and for the television pictures emanating from it). For this valuable asset, the Cardinals, as a subsidiary, got nothing. (When the Yankee contract began running out in 1999, Cablevision offered to buy the team for $600 million, instead of paying it that much for just another ten years of rights. And Cablevision was already a part owner of Madison Square Garden and its sports television network, as well as basketball's Knicks and hockey's Rangers).

Under such circumstances, how can you negotiate a "fair" or acceptable agreement with the union on what a salary cap would be? Not very easily. But hard does not mean impossible. The question is how long will it take, through how much turmoil, with what sort of compromises, to arrive at an agreement that assures the union of an "honest count" of true revenue.

Aside from the defined revenue question, ownership by media conglomerates raises large issues. Such companies use the baseball team as a pawn to benefit their more important television operations. The Cubs refused to shift into a more logical geographic division in the National League because it would upset their WGN schedule to have some West Coast games start later. (They went to court to make their refusal stick.) Whatever the situation, it's obvious that Fox, Disney-ABC, and Time Warner will make baseball decisions based on their larger corporate, not baseball, interests.

What's best for baseball—even in a strictly business sense—may not be what's best for such corporations. And what's best for a television network may be something harmful to baseball—such as World Series games at night, aired too late for children, who otherwise would be lured as lifelong fans.

When it costs hundreds of millions of dollars to buy a club, future owners will more likely be corporations than individuals. Even so, expansion from sixteen to thirty teams has made the smaller owners a larger majority. The biggest markets (New York, Chicago, Philadelphia, Detroit, Boston, and, after 1958, Los Angeles and the San Francisco-Oakland area) were always there. Each new team has joined the "small market" column. Even in theory, we don't know how to unify such diverse interests.

So what lies ahead for the new century's Baseball Dream? Above all, we must accept changes in the larger world. Baseball can't escape them any more than anything else can. Some aspects of the traditional baseball dream are gone forever. What today's mature fan grew up taking for granted no longer exists.

Among the things that have been lost is baseball's exclusivity. Baseball's mystique developed when no comparably intense sports experience existed. As other sports grew, adopting baseball's promotional techniques, offering their own virtues and claiming their share of the public's attention, baseball still had so great a head start that inroads into its special status were not visible for a long time.

A process that began in the 1960s was felt by baseball insiders only in the 1980s. The game that used to be the central sun of the spectator sports solar system is now only one of its planets—still the largest, but nevertheless only a planet.

In addition, baseball has lost its connection to the building of a national consensus. The "melting pot" idea, of changing immigrants into Americans, coincided with the era of baseball's exclusivity, enhancing both the idea and the activity. But since World War II, the melting pot image has been replaced by a focus on separatist "cultural identities" that stress each group's distinctiveness from the others while insisting on (properly) equal status and respect. The concept that baseball can somehow represent something uniquely "American" no longer holds, because now nothing is uniquely, unifyingly "American." In an age honoring diversity, baseball cannot be the cultural glue it once was, not because of any change in baseball, but because changes in the world around it have made any kind of glue weaker.

Along the same lines, an unquestioned and widespread devotion to "traditional values" and a "sense of history" do not have the force they had in midcentury culture. Baseball, of course, was wedded to exactly those frames of mind. As those attitudes have diminished, so have the elements of baseball connected to them. Tradition and history, so integral a part of baseball interest, are in themselves less powerful in society than they once were.

The pleasures of reading, for its own sake, are less common now, and the essence of baseball lore has always been (and must be) transmitted by what's written about it. Our taste for heroes has changed, as more effort is devoted to tearing down the mighty than to admiring them. The consequences for baseball are plain enough.

And above all, we live in a universe of greatly shortened attention spans. Television has done that in a variety of ways, and an older person need only notice how rapidly images change in quick-cut commercials, on MTV, and in the rapid succession of programs to realize how natural they seem to younger people, who have absorbed that pace from infancy. But baseball has always been (and must be) a long-attention-span activity, like reading and serious music, or paying attention to a lecture. Those craving action, action, action get more from basketball and hockey than from baseball's leisurely rhythm, which requires more of a cerebral engagement to be satisfying.

The baseball scene, having lost its exclusivity, has potent rivals for the follower's attention. There's television, in all its aspects—not just sports programs but the medium's general, nonstop presence. There's the computer, which has become even more obsessive because it's interactive. There are all the other sports to watch, read, and talk about, interesting in themselves in different ways. All these (and nonsports attractions) are being pitched at us by skilled professional promoters, advertisers, salespeople, persuaders.

Finally, there are the realms of "false interest" baseball: including fantasy baseball leagues and collecting baseball memorabilia for future profit. These seem to have a baseball content but actually they do not. Fantasy leagues are simply a form of mild gambling, like bingo games, in which the occurrences on the ball field merely determine which number comes up. The rotisserie player does not really care who wins or how, but rather only that "his" or "her" player's box score number shows what he or she hopes it will.

And the card collector who buys according to the card's market value (set by rarity and demand) does not really relate to the player on the card (as we used to when I was a child), but is simply acquiring something to hold or trade, such as a stock certificate. That their ostensible subject matter is "baseball" is incidental. Getting someone's autograph as a memento of a personal encounter, however brief, is one thing. Buying one primarily for its resale value (or to prove you can afford it) is something else. If Mark McGwire's seventieth home run ball was worth $3 million to the buyer, one must ask, "To whom? For what?" And wouldn't he trade it for a painting (of no intrinsic interest to him) worth $5 million?

But old dreams are replaced by new dreams. The woman who once dreamed of becoming a great stage actress had a daughter who dreamed no less of becoming a movie star, and eventually a granddaughter who dreamed of becoming the next Barbara Walters or Oprah Winfrey. A change in setting does not mean a change in desire.

Baseball fans—and writers, and readers—of the twenty-first century will love baseball no less, but not in the same ways its twentieth-century followers did. They will see it in their own terms, through eyes conditioned by a different upbringing, reading into it a different set of meanings.

On the technical level, they are already far ahead of previous generations, because the television camera gives us a far better look than we can ever have in the ballpark in person. It shows us how pitches behave, how fielding plays are made, how close plays were actually decided, how various batting and throwing techniques really work, how and when emotions play across participants' faces— all in slow motion, with repeated replays from different angles, accompanied by expert descriptions by former players who share their inside knowledge.

The new generation's ballpark experience will be different from ours, but no less enjoyable. To them, the extraneous promotional climate—loud music, scoreboard messages, public address announcers leading cheers, mountains of statistics on display—will seem like a natural environment, not a distraction (as it is to older fans). The poetry of green grass and crowd ambience will not be as strong, because their world has become less poetic.

Twenty-first-century baseball fans will not be as concerned, or as thrilled, by comparisons to the past because they relate very little to history at any level, in the emerging "me, now" cultural climate. But they will react even more viscerally to moments of climax. They will see stars as celebrities rather than as heroes, but they will be no less applauded for all that. They will have less patience with the quiet moments, and often switch channels to another game when the one they are watching bogs down. But to them, channel hopping will be natural and satisfying in its own way. They will feel less loyalty and involvement with any one particular team or players, but just as intense transient loyalty to whatever is currently exciting. "Root, root, root for the home team" will be a less prevalent attitude when so much from elsewhere is instantly and continuously available, but the broader canvas will let them choose what to enjoy among the varied, short-attention-span excitements offered.

In short, what future fans have never known they will not miss. Their writers of fiction and nonfiction will find just as much "meaning" to attach to the baseball they see, but it will be a different set of meanings and associations from the ones we have known. Baseball's place in American culture will not be diminished, but it will continue shifting. Day-to-day devotion may be less consistent, but peak moments, like McGwire's home runs, Ripkin's celebration of his 2,131st consecutive game, or a close pennant race, will command greater intensity (and availability) of interest than ever before.

It's the game itself, and its unique permutations, that made baseball popular in the first place, and that is not only unchanging but also enhanced by greater accessibility. We read into it whatever we want, and so will those who follow, but they will read into it their own interpretations while discarding many of ours—just as they will, and are doing now, about other aspects of life and culture.

As a business (of staging games in a league context) baseball enters the twenty-first century stronger than ever. In terms of artistry and competitiveness, it is having another Golden Age. Its best players are spread among thirty teams, but imagine how good teams would be if all these best players were concentrated on only sixteen. But, no matter. In terms of personal significance to those who care about baseball, new perceptions and new mental associations will be as powerful as ever and engage more people, worldwide, as it reaches them.

The American Dream came to encompass baseball over the past 100 years. For the foreseeable future, it will remain as deeply embedded as ever while it will be the dream that changes and evolves. The American Dream goes on, but it will be a different dream in a different America. And its baseball portion will be the part that changes the least.

PART III

Gendered Dreams: Women and Baseball

19

TO ELEVATE THE GAME
Women and Early Baseball

Darryl Brock and Robert Elias

AFTER THE CIVIL WAR, BASEBALL'S POPULARITY IN AMERICA BLOSSOMED DRAMATI-cally. Of course, most of those playing the game were men. But if we want to understand the baseball world of men in the second half of the nineteenth century, then we might well begin by turning to the women of the time. Women's relationship to baseball illustrates the kind of game those who most controlled baseball's future sought to achieve: an elevated, even purified sport that would make for better Americans.

Consider the following letter to the editors that appeared in the June 25, 1870 *Cincinnati Enquirer*:

> *A Wife's Protest* — To the Editors of the *Enquirer*: Are you in favor of base-ball? A plain question, and one that is easily propounded. Now will you give me a direct answer? My opinion is that you are an admirer and advocate (perhaps an occasional partaker) of the 'Great National Game,' so widely commented upon and so lavishly praised. This I judge from the extensive accounts we daily peruse in your paper. But be that as it may, just let me say that I am not in favor of base-ball; on the contrary, 'dreadfully' opposed to it.
>
> Now I am a woman, and a married one, too. That is the point. Perhaps it does well enough to single gentlemen to indulge to any extent; but when it comes to the married ones, dear me! it is certainly ridiculous. If I had no husband to look after, with shirts to keep in order, and base-ball paraphernalia to always regulate and put away when he comes home tired and weary after an afternoon's enjoyment, perhaps I wouldn't grumble.
>
> But as it is, I think I have a right to complain. I am not an advocate of 'women's rights,' yet I do think there are some rights I should have that I don't get, and a good many that I get that I ought not to have. I think if my husband is such a devotee to the great excitement that at present is turning the whole country upside down, as to go east, west, north and south, by river, rail and bus, to play other clubs, that I have a right to go along. When he married me, he took for good or ill, as it might be, and now that this is the ill side, and he desires enjoyment therefrom, I should be allowed to participate. If he chooses

to make a traveling menagerie of himself and his club, isn't it my privilege to accompany, as general showman, door-keeper, or ticket agent, whereby I might reap some of the benefits accruing from said enterprise? If not, is it my duty to stay at home at night, alone, until nearly (or quite) morning, waiting for him to come? I don't think so.

If the 'Fifteenth Amendment' is as good as a white man, am not I, my husband's better half, as good as he is? Haven't I a right to play base-ball, and wear blue pants, red shirts, or any like costume I please? If I am skillful enough (which I don't doubt), haven't I a right to be championess of the United States?

That is my opinion, and come, own up gentlemen, don't you coincide? Show your true colors—come out on my side. Do take pity on a wife, whose only rivals are a bat and a ball, and give some advice to those recreant husbands who to traveling 'round the country exhibiting their proficiency in pitching, batting, fielding, etc., instead of being at home trying to appreciate the little kindnesses and delicate attentions of a loving wife, which they will not realize until she is gone, and instead, they meet an altered woman, contending for her rights, both in the political field and the bases in a match game.

Ah! the day is not far distant, let us hope, when women will have an opportunity to avenge their own wrongs, and if ever I am presidentess, or even governess of this State, base-ballists, 'Red Stockings' and all, had better lay down their implements of friendly warfare, and resort to something else. I am treated unmercifully now, and can they expect mercy?

A Base Ballist's wife.[1]

The *Enquirer* editors responded:

Under the circumstances above narrated, we think the wife should use the bat as well on the husband. A few vigorous applications of that instrument to the husband's head would restore peace to at least one domestic circle.

But these are dissenting views. To the contrary, women were expected to defer to men's preoccupations, such as their growing interest in baseball. And newspapers would rarely encourage a woman to act in such an unladylike fashion as suggested above. Far more typical would be the following account of a game from the *Cincinnati Commercial* on July 16, 1867:

The crowd must have numbered between four and five thousand, among whom were a large and fashionable company of ladies, for whom raised seats were reserved. We are pleased to see that our fair beauties are beginning to take an interest in our national game, and are lending the charm of their presence to enhance the interest of the matches.[2]

Such accounts were particularly characteristic of Southern media coverage, a region to which baseball was rapidly expanding after the Civil War. Women were routinely characterized as "glittering assemblages," and by their "dewy skin," and by their fans, kerchiefs, and parasols. More daring were female supporters of the Cincinnati Reds, who raised their skirts a few scandalous inches while stepping onto the curb outside a Philadelphia hotel, to display ankles encased in red stockings that matched the ballplayers.'

Why was there this focus on women at baseball games, especially since it was not true for women at other sporting events? First, it provided an indicator of the sport's popularity and well-being. If women were attending, then it must be doing well, even though the game would soon be facing some daunting problems. It was important to have women help legitimize baseball as America's game. Women were encouraged to attend: special carriages were sometimes provided, or certain designated stands. Women were often admitted free, or free if they were accompanied by an escort.

Second, women's association with baseball was thought to "elevate" the game. It would help protect the sport, and provide it with a moral dimension. As suggested in the *New York Clipper*:

> Let our American ladies visit the ball grounds, and the most rough or rude among the spectators would acknowledge their magic sway, thus conferring a double favor upon the sports they countenance, because the members of our sporting organizations are usually gentlemen and always lovers of order, but they cannot any more control the bystanders than they can any other passengers along a public highway. When ladies are present, we are proud to be able to say that no class of our population can be found so debased as not to change their external behavior immediately, and that change is always for the better.[3]

This suggests that women were used to validate baseball while they also helped domesticate it and keep it from becoming brutish, as it might have otherwise become if left only in the hands of men. Thus, the presence of women in proximity to baseball games was always noted and urged, and almost always described in the most glowing terms.

But were these reports always true? And were women as routinely connected to the game as some have suggested? According to the Cincinnati newspapers, for example, some 300 women attended the Forest City game, "their vivid scarlets and plaids lighting up their stands picturesquely."[4] But another report, found in the private letter of a woman named Fannie, had this to say:

> At first Robert refused flatly to take me, declaring that but few gentlemen and no ladies would be seen at such affairs. I assured him that being so we would

not be known to anyone there, so he finally consented and I am sure he wanted to go quite as much as I. We drove to the Union Grounds and I shall not go again, for there were but few females present. And an awful creature near me was rouged and painted like a barber pole. [added:] Anyway, we rejoiced at the Red's winning by a score of 18 to 15.

So who knows the truth? No doubt the women out at games were not primarily drawn from the "opera crowd." But in any case, however high the female attendance, the value of having women at the games was almost universally agreed upon.

And let's not forget the excitement voiced by the "protesting wife" quoted above. What was going on in June 1870, both inside and outside baseball, which could have created such a stir? First, we have to remember that this was a vastly different America. Of its 40 million people, more than half still lived on farms. Rural life was far more the norm than urban existence. The nation had just experienced a terrible war—the Civil War—with the largest armies ever congregated. The wounds were still being deeply felt. The Radical Republicans in Congress now ruled the country. The South was under military rule, and the Ku Klux Klan was rapidly emerging. In Boston, preparations were being made for an enormous peace jubilee with choirs comprised of 15,000 singers. The Cincinnati Red Stockings—baseball's first openly all-professional team—had recently played in that city. Ulysses S. Grant had been president for only fifty-seven days: he'd be seen smoking many cigars but saying little. Victoria was the Queen of England, as she had been for thirty-two years. She would turn fifty soon, and rule another thirty-two years. Boss Tweed and his Tammany Hall political machine was running Manhattan, and the Red Stockings would soon face Tweed's own baseball darlings, the New York Mutuals.

Out West, Wild Bill Hickok, the sheriff of Hays City, Kansas, would shortly gun down several men. Like the Red Stockings' George Wright, Jesse James would turn twenty-two this year; he was already robbing banks but not yet famous for it. Colonel George Custer was patrolling the western plains, and would soon send a message back to Washington denying reports of his demise at the hands of the Pawnee. He's not yet a General, and he's seven years and one month away from his last stand, at the Little Big Horn. The transcontinental railroad was about to be completed, and a gold spike will be driven in to tie together the tracks from East to West.

On the sporting scene, there was a postwar boom in both participatory and spectator sports. Track events were popular. A velocipede craze was in full swing. Billiards and horse racing tournaments were held. Boxing was illegal but many matches nevertheless took place. Football was emerging in the college ranks.

But by far, baseball was king. By then, it had been played for only about twenty-three years, but it was already considered to be the National Game. The teams were formed around dozens of different groups: kids, clerks, juniors, "seconds," lawyers, reporters, teachers, blacks, Indians, and so forth. There were the "Fat Boys," "Sunny Jims," "Morning Glories," "Wildflowers," and the "Alerts." There were "muffin" teams comprised of the worst players. Women formed their own teams. The baseball craze faded a bit during the Civil War, with the exception of the military camps, where the game was widely played. Baseball was reignited in the broader society after the war not only by soldiers bringing it back home but also by the phenomenal popularity of the Cincinnati Red Stockings. Baseball diamonds were jammed by 1870, with more than 1,000 clubs in operation.

The Red Stockings would conduct a remarkable tour that year, beating one "champion" team after another. In New York, they beat the Mutuals twice, 4–2 and 17–8, with the latter game being played on November 6—which shows how late into fall the game was actively played. Cincinnati would also beat the Brooklyn Eckfords, 24–5 and 45–18, and twice beat the powerful Philadelphia Athletics. It beat the top amateur club in the nation, Rockford, Illinois' Forest City team, which was the "NorWes Champs" and featured a 6'1" kid pitcher, Al Spalding, whom Red Stockings manager Harry Wright would soon grab away. The Red Stockings beat the Maryland champs, 47–7; the Missouri champs, the St. Louis Empires, 31–14; the archrival Ohio Buckeyes, 103–8; and the Wisconsin champs, the Milwaukee Cream Citys, 85–7.

In San Francisco, the Eagles beat the Pacifics for the West Coast championship. The Red Stockings were among the first to ride the new transcontinental railroad, and arrived in Sacramento in September 1870 in time to beat the Eagles 35–4 and 58–4. The Pacifics fared even worse against the Cincinnati team, losing 66–4 in only six innings and also 54–5. A light earthquake occurred while the Red Stockings were in the Bay Area, and the players complained about the cold and wind during the games.

But the Red Stockings were not only successful, they were electrifying. The team was a true, national sensation. It was the glamour team of the nineteenth century. Its impact was felt everywhere. They were imitated by everyone. There was never anything like them before, and some old-timers insist that there never has been since. The Red Stockings were resplendent in their bright new uniforms. They were sensationalized by the media, glorified by women fans, and fiercely followed by men and children. Practically nothing could compete with the team for national attention.

If the Red Stockings helped turn baseball into a national sensation, then what role did the game's growing popularity play in America's development in the nineteenth century? For some, baseball inherently embodied certain ideals that Americans ought to live up to. For others, it was not so much what baseball could do naturally but rather the way baseball could be shaped, metaphorically, in the society to perform particular social functions.

Whether inherently or intentionally, what compelling values did baseball represent in these times? Most important, it was thought that playing the game of baseball correctly would or could make you into a better person. This would be accomplished because first, baseball would expose people to grass, sunshine, and fresh air. Similar to being in the Boy Scouts or Girl Scouts, it would expose youngsters to the outdoors and to all the benefits they were thought to hold. Accordingly, it would also keep kids and others out of "low dives," or disreputable establishments where one might develop unsavory companions. Second, baseball was valued for the cooperation and teamwork it would engender. Unlike other outdoor sports, such as hunting and fishing, baseball would require people to interact with each other and act like a team. Third, baseball was viewed as encouraging the "work ethic." Various terms of the day reinforced this notion: players were to be preoccupied with "work"outs, or team "work," or even head "work" (thinking about the game). According to the prevailing Protestant ethic, work was the key to success, not only in baseball but in all endeavors in society.

Last, it was thought that baseball would generate "better people" because the game promoted "manliness" in the sense of shaping gentlemen. This, of course, reflected the gender bias of the times, even though some women were also playing, and not merely watching, baseball. For men, baseball would promote discipline, deter cheating, and help regulate the baser instincts—assuming the game was played properly. It would ingrain in men a soldierly, almost courtly, stoicism. Unlike being a mere boy, one would learn to take defeat "like a man." And in victory, a real man would not exult or boast. Baseball would promote this behavior not only on the field but also off the field. As a reflection of the latter, the early amateur gentlemen's clubs, which sponsored many of the baseball teams, developed elaborate postgame banquets that, in part, tested these gentlemanly traits. Winners and losers were expected to sit around the same table, and share good cheer, along with drinks, dinners, and even boisterous singalongs.

Did baseball actually accomplish these objectives, and inculcate these values into players and observers? To a certain extent, yes. A kind of civility was often expected from players, both inside and outside the game. And yet, in other ways, these objectives might have fallen a bit short. Looking back, we can see some problems in baseball that are not dissimilar to current tensions.

Generally, players encountered an adoring media but the press would turn on those who violated certain values. Even in this early period, a star system was already developing among the players, which created some jealousies and dissension. Demands were frequent from players for more money. Disputes with umpires often occurred. Some players had problems with substance abuse. Accusations sprung up over allegedly juiced-up baseballs. And when reporters sometimes tried to hold players accountable for these problems, they were sometimes met with threats in response.

Aside from baseball's problems, this was a period notable for other developments. The first baseball scoresheets and symbols were devised. An elaborate nomenclature and idiom for the game began to emerge. Early versions of baseball trading cards were made available. The seventh inning stretch was invented, and spread from one team to another. Old-timers' games were even being played. And most significant, perhaps, was the sense of nostalgia around the game that was already developing. People talked about a "golden time" in the past when the game was better. Some things in baseball never change.

Besides a concern about the game's quality, people were also worried—as they are today—about the role of money in baseball. For example, the October 5, 1869 *Cincinnati Commercial* reported that:

> Base Ball in the East has sadly degenerated. It is under the control, in New York especially, of men who have no regard for the courtesies due visiting clubs, and who sustain their clubs for the money they produce.[5]

While various entrepreneurs sensed the great profitability baseball could generate, making money from baseball was still not widely accepted, and in some quarters was felt to violate the "gentleman's game." Even worse, people were concerned about the increasing evidence of gambling in the game, which threatened to corrupt the sport. Players were routinely "revolving" from one team to another, thus undermining the integrity of fixed teams in competition.

Ironically, as the first all-professional baseball team, where all players were paid salaries, the Red Stockings were viewed by some as a panacea for some of baseball's money concerns. While paid professionals undermined the amateur baseball mold, regular salaries could potentially undercut the role and lure of gambling in the sport. Even so, the resistance remained, as suggested, for example, in an October 30, 1869 report in the *San Francisco Golden Era*:

> Our Eagles and Pacifics . . . have been sacrificed to the cupidity of the proprietors of the Recreation Grounds. Our clubs are amateurs who devote little time to practice. The 'Red Stockings' are professionals, who do nothing else, and are paid for doing that.[6]

Obviously, some people resented the salaries professional ballplayers were earning. So, how high were the salaries? In the 1870s, skilled workers earned between $525 and $750 for twelve months of work. By comparison, the top four Red Stockings players were earning 15 to 70 percent more than the top craftsman's wage. This was not a huge difference but the potential for much higher earnings from baseball was clear enough.

By 1969—a hundred years later, earnings had increased, and yet were still relatively modest: according to Ken Burns, baseball players were making approximately seven times the average working person's wage. In 1976, a player made just eight times a worker's salary. But by 1994, the average major leaguer's salary was 50 times more than the ordinary worker's. As Roger Angell has suggested, this big jump in the salary differential has significantly distanced the players from the fans in recent years. Money has long been an issue in baseball; the difference now is in the magnitude.

But for the second half of the nineteenth century, baseball survived its various problems and challenges. For many players, being a professional gave them at least a small slice of the American dream; for a few others, fortunes were made from the sport. Baseball became the national game not necessarily because it achieved all its objectives in concrete terms. Moreso, baseball was a symbolic success. Thanks in part to the role played by women in "elevating the game," baseball came to embody some of the major images of American society—even if they are not all true. As we moved into the twentieth century, baseball took on still more facets of the American character, from patriotism to individualism to democracy. And why not? It had been, and still was, after all, the sport for creating "better Americans."

Notes

1. Letter to the Editor, *Cincinnati Enquirer* (June 25, 1870).
2. *Cincinnati Commercial* (July 16, 1867).
3. *New York Clipper* (August 8, 1867).
4. *Cincinnati Commercial* (July 16, 1867).
5. *Cincinnati Commercial* (October 5, 1869).
6. *San Francisco Golden Era* (October 30, 1869).

20

WOMEN, BASEBALL, AND THE AMERICAN DREAM

Gai Ingham Berlage

OFTEN I'M ASKED, "WHAT EVER MADE YOU DECIDE TO WRITE A BOOK ON WOMEN'S baseball?" Usually the intonation of the question implies two things: one, why would a woman be interested in baseball and two, how could anyone think that women even played a role in the history of baseball? Baseball, the American pastime, has been a male domain from which women largely have been excluded. Men wax eloquently about the importance of baseball in their lives and about father/son bonding. We can read quote after quote about baseball from famous men, from U.S. presidents to players. But the quote from the American poet, Robert Frost, stands out most in my mind. Frost said, "Nothing flatters me more than to have it assumed that I could write—unless it be to have assumed that I once pitched a baseball with distinction."

And it is that very loss—I never had the opportunity to pitch a baseball with distinction—that laid the seed for my writing *Women in Baseball: The Forgotten History*.[1] At age eight, my dreams of pitching a baseball were thwarted when I was told that only boys could play Little League baseball. Still, I falsely believed that I could run out onto the baseball fields with the boys at recess. I can still remember the teacher who grabbed me as I ran out to the field and admonished me: "Girls are supposed to stay on the blacktop."

Growing up a girl in the 1950s, my destiny was to play hopscotch and to jump rope. Still, throughout my early childhood my secret fantasy was that I would become a professional ballplayer. Socially conditioned to accept my role as female, I knew this was not possible and that baseball was a men's game. Consequently, it never occurred to me that there could exist a rich history of women players. It wasn't until the late 1980s, when I was doing some research on women's sports, that I came across a reference to girls having played baseball at Vassar College in 1866. It was a shocking revelation, but at the same time I felt elated. For I knew if they had played at Vassar, then they must have played at my alma mater, Smith College, as well. There had to be a forgotten history out there, just waiting to be discovered.

By historical rights, women should have a place alongside men as early pioneers in baseball. Women were playing baseball at Vassar College in 1866. This
was only a few years after the first intercollegiate baseball game was played
between Amherst and Williams College in 1859. In 1867, girls were playing
baseball at Miss Porter's boarding school in Farmington, Connecticut. The same
year, members of a Ladies Club in Pensacola, Florida, were playing in hooped
skirts, and there was a black professional women's team, the Dolly Vardens. At
the Baseball Hall of Fame Museum at Cooperstown, one can buy a postcard of
the Young Ladies Baseball Club #1 of 1890. The *Cincinnati Enquirer* in 1899
had numerous articles on the Chicago Bloomer Girls, a professional baseball
team that competed against men's teams throughout the Midwest. There were
also Bloomer Girls teams in Massachusetts, Texas, and other states.

At the turn of the century, there were women professional players, umpires,
and owners. Lizzie Arlington was a pitcher in 1898; Alta Weiss, a pitcher from
1907 to 1922. Lizzie Murphy, was a first basewoman from 1918 to 1935, Amanda
Clement, an umpire from 1905 to 1911, and Helene Britton was the owner of
the St. Louis Cardinals from 1908 to 1917. In the late 1800s, there were also
sportswriters such as Ella Black who wrote for *The Sporting Life,* and Sally Van
Pelt who was the baseball editor of the *Dubuque Times* in Iowa.

The press today treats issues of women ballplayers, women umpires, and
women sportswriters as creations of the Women's Liberation Movement of the
1960s. When the Colorado Silver Bullets, a professional women's baseball team,
was established in 1994 the press claimed this was the first time a women's
baseball team had played against men. Yet, in the 1890s, Bloomer Girls teams
regularly played men's teams. As recently as 1957, Arlington's All-Americans were
barnstorming throughout the United States and Canada taking on men's teams. In
1997, the St. Paul Saints of the Northern League signed pitcher Ila Borders and
proclaimed that she was the first woman to play in the minors. Although she may
be the first to be officially sanctioned by Major League Baseball, she is not the first
to play. In 1931 Joe Engel, owner and president of the Chattanooga Lookouts, a
class double-A minor league team, signed seventeen-year-old Jackie Mitchell as a
pitcher. She made baseball history when she struck out Babe Ruth and Lou Gehrig
in an exhibition game between the Lookouts and the New York Yankees on April 2,
1931. After the game, Baseball Commissioner Kenesaw Mountain Landis declared
her contract null and void. Are the baseball promoters and the press deliberately
misleading the public or are they unaware of the early history of women in baseball?

Let's give them the benefit of the doubt and assume they are ignorant. Why
is it that the history of women's baseball isn't better known? There are two
major reasons. One, baseball was defined culturally as a male domain, and two,
major league baseball was controlled by men, who barred women from playing.
Women, therefore, could only become marginal players not major leaguers.

On the professional level, women played on semipro teams rather than in the major leagues. In those rare instances in which a minor league owner did sign a woman player, the executives of major league baseball acted quickly and decisively to declare the woman's contract null and void. Newspaper coverage immediately called the signing a publicity gimmick to increase gate receipts. If the woman did get to play, it was usually in an exhibition game. All of this trivialized women's participation and made their skills suspect. It was almost impossible for a woman to be considered a serious player.

On college campuses, women were involved in play days and interclass competition rather than intercollegiate competition. On the playgrounds, they were separated from the boys and rules were often devised to make their games less strenuous.

Even as children, when young girls played as equals with the boys in the fields and streets, their play was seen as a passing fancy. By adolescence, girls were expected to give up their "tomboyish" ways and become "ladies." Boys, on the other hand, could aspire to become major leaguers. This marginalization of women was the result of cultural definitions of female and male social roles. Sport was defined as a male domain. The characteristics needed to succeed in sport were the personification of attributes that defined masculinity: aggressiveness, strength, competitiveness, and independence. Boys and men proved their manhood on the playing field. Cultural definitions of femininity stressed qualities such as passivity, submissiveness, and dependence. These qualities were the antithesis of those needed to excel in sports. Women proved their womanhood by finding a husband, marrying, and having children. There is a certain irony to the fact that men proved their masculinity by catching a ball and women their femininity by catching a man.

Traditional definitions of what were appropriate men's and women's sports discouraged women's participation in baseball and also served to obscure memories of that participation. Competitive team sports such as baseball, basketball, and football were considered masculine endeavors. Individual sports such as figure skating and gymnastics that require grace and agility were considered feminine. When women were allowed to play team sports such as baseball and basketball, the rules were often feminized to make the sport less physically taxing. In baseball, the basepaths and the distance from the pitching mound might be shortened or men might be added to the battery (pitcher and catcher). Another example of feminizing rules is seen in early women's basketball. To limit physical exertion, the court was divided into three equal sections and players were required to stay within the sections. To avoid physical contact, players were prohibited from batting or snatching the ball from opponent' s hands.

The final curtain that effectively obscured memory of the early history of women's baseball was drawn in 1933 when the Amateur Softball Association made the term "softball" official. This name then became substituted for the modified baseball games that girls had been playing.[2] Softball became the appropriate female sport. This demarcation of hardball for males and softball for the "weaker" sex was culturally accepted. In later years, if someone heard the words "women and baseball," his or her mind was culturally conditioned to substitute the word "softball." This substitution phenomenon became obvious when I was doing my research. Time after time when I told someone I was doing research on women's baseball, the reply was "It's nice that you are researching women's softball."

But even before softball became associated with women in the 1930s, baseball was considered a male domain. So how did some Victorian women come to play baseball? After the Civil War, baseball captured the hearts and souls of Americans. Women, just like men, were caught in the enthusiasm for the sport. By the late 1800s, baseball was the rage. It was the national sport and the major form of entertainment. Both men and women were avid fans. Every town had at least one ball field and a home team. It was only a matter of time before women would want to play. But first they had to be freed from the mystique of ill health and the belief that exercise was too taxing for their weak constitution.

Doctors believed that women were the weaker sex and had limited physical energy. They believed that if women overexerted they might fall victim to nervous exhaustion or have defective children. The "true woman" then was expected to conserve all her energy for childbearing. The "true woman," pale and frail, of the Victorian ideal, had to be transformed into the "new woman," robust and healthy, before women would have the opportunity to participate in physical exercise.

By the late 1800s, the belief in limited exercise for women was being questioned. First, there was concern that many immigrant women who worked in the factories were actually physically stronger and healthier than many upper-middle- and upper-class women. Second, doctors began to realize that exercise was healthy and that tightly laced corsets were responsible for fainting spells and misaligned organs. Third, women's colleges were formed with the philosophy that exercise was a necessary component for a healthy mind and body. Fourth, upper-class country clubs were established in which women could participate in tennis and other sports. But it was the establishment of the first women's colleges during the second half of the nineteenth century that was the major impetus for changing beliefs about the appropriate roles for women, changes in fashion, realizing the importance of exercise for health, the acceptance of sports for women, and for opportunities for women to play baseball. The image of the sporting woman came to replace the frail indoor type.

The elite Eastern women's colleges, sometimes referred to as the "Seven Sisters"—Smith, Wellesley, Mount Holyoke, Vassar, Radcliffe, Bryn Mawr, and

Barnard—had a tremendous impact on social perceptions of women's roles and sports. The "new woman," the educated, independent, athletic type, was a product of these schools. The early women's colleges were founded on the belief that women should receive an education equal to that of men, but in separate institutions so as to meet women's special needs and to preserve women's femininity. The founders believed that in order to have a healthy mind, it was necessary to have a healthy body. Exercise in the form of calisthenics or physical education was required of all students. These views were very progressive for the times and had many opponents.

Coincidentally, the founding of the first women's colleges occurred about the same time as professional baseball. In the 1880s, baseball was in its Golden Era and was the national sport. The "baseball fever" that affected the nation also caught the fancy of the women at these colleges. They began to play informal games of baseball. By the 1890s, sports for women, and especially baseball, had become part of college life. But these sporting activities were viewed as social events rather than as strenuous competitive sports that men played.

Vassar College had baseball eights in 1866 and nines in 1876. Smith College had teams in 1879, Mount Holyoke College in 1891, and Wellesley College in 1897. With rare exceptions, the games were intracollegiate and involved interclass, dormitory, or club competition. Baseball instruction also became part of the physical education program at most of these schools. For example, at Wellesley from 1911 to 1935, baseball was part of the official physical education program and credit was given for instruction in baseball.

The first women's college baseball nine team, the Vassar College Resolutes of 1876, was not seen as a threat to the masculine game. With their long dresses and unique style of sometimes stopping the ball with their skirts, their game was definitely a feminine version. However, once college women began playing sports and baseball, upper-class women soon followed. Country clubs and private athletic clubs became places for women's sports.

It wasn't long before a few opportunistic promoters capitalized on the novel idea of women's baseball teams. The first known team, in 1867, was the black women's team of Philadelphia called the Dolly Vardens. Promoters organized some early women's teams such as the Blondes and Brunettes of 1875 purely as publicity stunts. The Blondes and Brunettes played a modified game of baseball in which the distance between bases was fifty feet instead of ninety feet. The women were picked more for their attractiveness than their skills. Once the sensationalism of women playing subsided, promoters knew they had to recruit skilled women players if the public was to come out. By the late 1800s, there were girls who had grown up playing baseball with their brothers, and competitive women's teams could be formed. By the 1890s, Bloomer Girls teams had sprung up across the country and were regularly playing against men's teams.

One of the early women's teams that was highly successful was the Young Ladies Baseball Club #1, in 1890–91. Organized by promoter W.S. Franklin, the team of "bright and buxom ladies"[3] created a sensation when they played against men's teams across the country. They wore striped dresses belted at the waist, polka-dot scarves around their necks, dark stockings, and ankle-high laced leather shoes. On their heads were matching striped baseball caps. Although handicapped by their cumbersome uniforms, they still managed to annihilate the men's teams they played. Franklin was so thrilled with their ability that he talked about forming other teams. You can image the sensationalism of a woman's team beating a man's.

But when we look at the surviving picture of this team, we see that some of the women may have been men. In the early days, to make sure the women's teams were competitive against men's teams, some promoters strategically placed a few male ringers dressed as women in the lineup—often the pitcher, the catcher, or the shortstop. The male players sometimes wore wigs and were referred to as "toppers." Some of the names under the picture also suggest that some of the players may have been men. Effie Earl, May Howard, and Annie Grant may have been combinations of a female name with the first name of the male player.

Young boys were even known to run away from home to join Bloomer Girls teams much as youth ran away to join the circus. An article in a 1910 Nashville newspaper, for example, showed a desperate father asking if anyone knew the whereabouts of his son. Apparently, the boy had told his parents he was going to visit his grandmother, but instead joined a Bloomer Girls baseball team. The clue was a letter to his grandmother saying how much he enjoyed playing.[4] In later years, it was accepted that the women's team might contain a few men. The men no longer had to dress as women and wore regulation men's baseball uniforms.

One woman who played a major role in women's baseball was Maud Nelson. For forty years, from 1897 to 1935, Nelson was actively involved in women's baseball—first as a player then as a scout, manager, and owner. She started her career in 1897 as a pitcher for the Boston Bloomer Girls. Other teams she played for were the Cherokee Indian Base Ball Club in 1908 and the Star Bloomers. In 1911, she and her husband, John B. Olson, Jr., became owner-managers of the Western Bloomer Girls. After her husband died, she and her second husband, Costante Dellacqua, owned and managed the All-Star Ranger Girls.[5]

The Bloomer Girls teams were well respected. In fact, two major league Hall of Famers got their start playing Bloomer Girls baseball. In 1906, "Smokey" Joe Wood played for the National Bloomer Girls, a team out of Kansas City, Kansas. Wood is remembered as the Red Sox pitcher who pitched three winning World Series games against the Giants in 1912. Another Hall of Famer, Rogers Hornsby, had a similar start. He went on to become a second baseman for the St. Louis

Cardinals, and has the distinction of having the highest batting average in baseball history. In 1924, he hit .424. He was the National League batting champion seven times.

By the 1900s, the status of women ballplayers was changing. Now there were women who had grown up playing baseball and were knowledgeable about the game. Six women of this period managed to participate as full-fledged members in the world of men's professional baseball. Four were players: Lizzie Arlington, Alta Weiss, Lizzie Murphy, and Josie Caruso. One was an umpire, Amanda Clement; and one was an owner, Helene Britton. Promoters were well aware of the gate drawing power that came from the novelty of having a female ball player on a men's team. Professional baseball was considered to be a man's game. Even exceptional players such as Weiss and Murphy were regarded as promotional gimmicks.

Alta Weiss is another excellent example of the importance of male sponsorship. The middle child of three daughters, Alta was the apple of her father's eye. From early on, Dr. Weiss encouraged Alta to play baseball and to develop her talent. He even had a gym built onto his barn so she could practice in the winter. Her father worked hard to market his daughter's baseball image. He established a folklore around her extraordinary pitching ability. He swore that when she was less than two years old, she "hurled a corncob at the family cat with all the follow-through and wrist-snap of a big league pitcher."[6]

In 1907 at age seventeen, Weiss became the star pitcher for the Vermilion Independents, a men's semiprofessional team in Ohio. "Special trains were run from Cleveland and surrounding towns to accommodate the more than 13,000 fans who attended Vermilion's final seven games of the 1907 season." She was hailed as the "girl-wonder."[7] In 1908, Dr. Weiss bought an interest in the team and changed the name to the "Weiss All-Stars." To make her stand out from the men, he had the men wear white uniforms and Alta black. Alta continued to play until 1922. Alta was not just a pioneer on the diamond: she graduated from medical school in 1914, the only woman in the class.

Lizzie Murphy was a professional ballplayer from 1918 to 1935. Unlike Weiss, who came from an upper-middle-class background, Murphy was from the working class—her father was a millhand. Murphy supported herself on her earnings as first basewoman. At age fifteen, she began playing for a number of Warren, Rhode Island, men's amateur teams. When her skills improved, she played professional ball for the Providence Independents and then for Carr's All-Stars, a team composed of former major and minor league players that barnstormed throughout New England and Canada. She was billed as the "Queen of Baseball." In later years, Murphy liked to boast that she had played first base for the American All-Stars against the Red Sox in a charity game at Fenway Park in 1922. In 1928, she played for the National All-Stars against the Boston Braves.

She is probably the first woman to have played against major leaguers. Murphy attributed her ability to compete with men physically to the fact she did chores around the house as a young girl. She said, "I got in shape beating rugs and chopping wood. That kept me fit for running bases and driving the ball to the outfield."[8]

The first woman umpire was Amanda Clement. From approximately 1905 to 1911, she umpired in men's semipro games in the Dakotas, Nebraska, Minnesota, and Iowa. In the late 1800s and early 1900s, umpiring was a dangerous profession. Expressions such as "kill the umpire" were not just idle threats. Several minor league umpires actually lost their lives and many minor and major leaguers were brutally assaulted by fans.[9]

The strict division of the sexes, however, actually operated to Clement's advantage. No gentleman in the age of chivalry would insult a lady. So Clement never experienced the sexual harassment that afflicted later umpires such as Bernice Gera and Pam Postema. In a time when betting on games was rampant and umpires could be bought, Clement gained respect. She was known as an umpire who knew the rules and was impartial.

In 1911, Helene Britton became the first woman owner of a major league team when she inherited the ownership of the St. Louis Cardinals from her uncle. Other major league owners were not happy about having a woman in their midst. Although they came to respect her as a businesswoman, they never accepted her as a legitimate owner. To the bitter end the major league establishment maintained that ownership and management of a major league team was the proper domain of men only. From 1911 to 1916, she participated in all the league's annual meetings. She was not to be intimidated and sold her franchise when she wished and under her own terms in 1916.

The Great Depression of the 1930s meant that both major and minor league baseball teams had to search for ways to boost attendance. Innovation became a key factor. Joe Engel, owner, promoter, and president of the Chattanooga Lookouts, a class double-A minor league team, hit on the idea of having a seventeen-year-old woman, Jackie Mitchell, pitch an exhibition game against the New York Yankees. She was to pitch to the Yankee's murderer's row: Babe Ruth, Lou Gehrig, and Tony Lazzeri.

On April 2, 1931, when she accomplished the unbelievable feat of striking out both Babe Ruth and Lou Gehrig, Mitchell claimed it was her sinker pitch that did them in. Was it a publicity gimmick or did Mitchell legitimately strike out Ruth and Gehrig? Mitchell claimed to her dying day that it was for real, while skeptics claim it was rigged. Mitchell, however, was a good enough player to join the Greensboro, North Carolina, team of the Piedmont League for their road trips in 1932, and to play for the House of David, a men's barnstorming team, from 1933 to 1937.

But how did Mitchell play minor league ball if Landis had ruled her ineligible? First, the Piedmont League guides did not list her as a regular team member because she probably played off the books. Second, the Piedmont League was so low on the minor league circuit that no one paid much attention to it and her playing probably did not come to Landis' attention. This kept her playing unofficial and made it less likely to be remembered in later years.

In the 1930s and 1940s, there were other women who had short stints with minor league teams. Frances "Sonny" Dunlop played for the Fayetteville Bears against the Cassville Blues in a class D minor league game in the Arkansas-Missouri League on September 7, 1936. Since there was no advance publicity, baseball officials failed to stop her play. It was, however, the only game she played.

In 1948, Betty Evans, a top ranked softball pitcher, pitched an exhibition session in Portland Park, Oregon, for the class AAA Pacific Coast League. True to her nickname, "Bullet Evans," she struck out six of nine players. One writer stated, "Her feat of striking out six of nine near major leaguers still causes red faces in the American League. . . !"[10]

In 1934, major league promoters offered Babe Didrikson $500 a night to pitch in major league exhibition games. The promoters hoped to cash in on her popularity as a two gold medal winner in the 1932 Olympics. For the major league it was a good way to receive newspaper coverage and to attract fans. For Didrikson, who had few other opportunities available to her after the Olympics, it was a way to cash on her popularity. But Babe did not delude herself, she knew she was wanted for her name not her skills.

Hiring a woman ball player as a publicity stunt was not new. In 1898, during the Spanish American War, Edward Barrow, president of the Atlantic League, hired Elizabeth Stride to pitch in minor league exhibition games. As Barrow stated, "Talent was scarce and customers were scarcer. . . . I didn't want to see our Class A franchises fall. So I tried all kinds of stunts to keep the fans interested. . . . And when one of my scouts told me about a really good female pitcher from the mining area of Philadelphia, she was brought in for a trial. She knew all the fundamentals of the game, having been taught by . . . Jake Stivetts, who pitched many years [in the 1890s] in the National League."[11] She was billed as Lizzie Arlington, "the most famous lady pitcher in the world," and made her entrance on the field in a carriage drawn by two white horses. It was purely P.T. Barnum. When she failed to be a big attraction, she was released.

The events of World War II created a new type of opportunity for women to play baseball, this time in a league of their own. In 1943, P.K. Wrigley, chewing-gum magnate and owner of the Chicago Cubs, founded the All-American Girls' Softball League, the AAGSBL. He came up with the idea of a women's softball league as a way to fill the stadiums and to maintain public interest in baseball during the war. He feared that major league baseball would have to be suspended because of the number of men enlisting in the war effort. Patriotism rather than profit was the official reason Wrigley gave for establishing the AAGSBL. He wanted to provide wholesome entertainment to boost the morale of factory workers.[12]

Wrigley's idea for a women's softball league actually was not that novel. Softball was a well-established sport in the 1940s. In fact, women's games were better attended than men's. In 1939, it was estimated that 60 million people watched softball games. That was about 10 million more than watched baseball.[13] Softball was especially popular in the Midwest, and the first national softball tournament was held at the World's Fair in Chicago.[14]

But softball had an image problem. Women players were frequently pictured as being masculine, physical freaks, or lesbians. Teams also tended to have burlesque-type names such as Slapsie Maxie's Curvaceous Cuties.[15] This image of softball bothered Wrigley. He wanted to establish a professional high-class women's softball league that would be seen as good, clean, all-American family entertainment. He hoped to capitalize on the popularity of women's softball, but at the same time to create something new and better. In his new league, femininity would be stressed and the teams would have dignified, regular baseball names.

Wrigley's approach to setting his women's league apart from other softball leagues was two-pronged. First, he changed the game the women played from softball to a hybrid of fast-pitch softball and baseball. Second, he changed the image of the softball player from that of a physical anomaly to that of an attractive, feminine lady who just happened to possess masculine athletic skills. The image of femininity was accomplished by having the women wear uniforms with short skirts, by having them attend charm school, and by setting up strict rules for dress and demeanor.

The league began by playing with a twelve-inch ball that was slightly harder than a softball, a distance between bases of sixty-five feet, with forty feet from plate to mound, and with the pitcher using a windmill underarm delivery. Changes occurred over the years, so that by 1954 the women were playing by regulation major league baseball rules.

Early in the 1943 season, Wrigley realized the publicity advantages of referring to the women's game as baseball rather than softball. He asked the press to refer to the game as baseball. Although the press obliged, there may have been some debate over the name change by others. The game of hybrid baseball and softball was officially neither. Consequently, for some time the group was referred to as the All-American Girls' Ball League. It was not until 1945 that it was officially called the "Base Ball League" or the All-American Girls Baseball League (AAGBL). To attract fans and to make the women's game seem exciting, numerous publicity action shots were taken of the women playing baseball. Every attempt was made to highlight the women's baseball skills.

On July 1, 1941, the AAGBL made history by playing the first ever night game under the lights at Wrigley Field. The game was a benefit for the Women's Army Corp Recruiting Unit. It was a double header between the Racine Belles, Kenosha Comets, and the Rockford Peaches. In 1944, a second night game was played as a Red Cross fundraiser. The event became another historic first for women that either was deliberately ignored or totally forgotten by Wrigley Field publicists. On August 8, 1988, amid much publicity, Wrigley Field was officially illuminated for night games. The game under lights was billed as the first game ever to be played under lights on Wrigley Field. There was no mention of the AAGBL games.

The AAGBL was active in the Midwest from 1943 to 1954. Peak attendance was reached in 1948 with nearly 1 million fans attending games. Changing times in the 1950s brought a decline in AAGBL attendance, and in 1954 the league folded. After this, public knowledge of the league evaporated, and its history lay dormant. Although in 1989 the Baseball Hall of Fame at Cooperstown dedicated an exhibit to women in baseball, most of the public didn't become aware of the history until the release of the movie, *A League of Their Own* in 1992.

Also, few people are aware that Bill Allington, one of the most successful coaches of the AAGBL, continued the AAGBL's legacy by establishing a women's barnstorming team. From 1954 to 1957, Allington's All-Americans—composed of former AAGBL players—toured the country playing men's amateur and semi-professional teams. The team disbanded at the end of 1957 for financial reasons.

The 1950s marked the end of women's baseball and a return to the ideology that a woman's destiny was to be a full-time mother. Women may have done their patriotic duty by taking on men's jobs during the war, but once the crisis was over they were expected to return to domesticity. Both "Rosie the Riveter" (the character that represented women in wartime factories) and women ballplayers were a temporary phenomenon. Little League had replaced sandlot baseball and had a boys-only policy. The fact that women had played baseball during the war years was forgotten along with the rest of women's baseball history. It was to be another twenty-seven years before another professional women's baseball team was formed.

The Colorado Bullets, much like Allington's All-Americans, was formed as an all-women's team that would play against professional men's teams. The gimmick of the "battle of the sexes" unfortunately was outdated in the 1990s. After four seasons of play, 1994–97, they too folded for financial reasons.

Male promoters are still using women as publicity grabbers. In 1996, the management of the Colorado Silver Bullets arranged with the management of the AA Jackson minor league men's team for Pamela Davis to pitch in an exhibition game against the Australian Olympic team. This garnered great publicity for the Colorado Silver Bullets and the Southern League. *USA Today* labeled Davis's playing a "historic debut," and Doug Ferguson, an Associated Press sportswriter declared her the "Strikeout Queen." She made national news coverage and appeared on CNN, *Good Morning America*, and David Letterman.

Ila Borders has been promoted as the latest female phenomenon. Publicity credits her with a list of first milestones. The list is far from accurate, but being second or third doesn't sell newspapers or get you on television. For example, in 1994, it was reported that Borders was the first woman to pitch in a college baseball game. However, as recently as 1990, Jodi Haller pitched for NAIA St. Vincent's College in Latrobe, Pennsylvania. In 1997, Borders was credited with being the first woman to sign a contract with a men's professional baseball team. But she wasn't even close to being first. Some others before her were: Lizzie Stride in 1898, Jackie Mitchell in 1931, Babe Didrikson in 1934, Eleanor Engle in 1952, and Kendra Hanes in 1994. In 1998, Borders did score a legitimate first. She pitched for the Duluth Dukes against the Fargo Redhawks of the Northern Independent League and became the first woman officially credited with a win in a men's regular season minor league game.

But for Borders' pitching to be taken seriously, she must be judged by the same standards as other players. Publicity about her play should be accurate and based purely on her skills not her gender. Press comments such as the following undermine her achievements: "Her popularity was due not just to the fact that she is . . . 'button cute' (but) Ms. Borders can actually pitch."[16] Another article actually credited her success to her femininity. Jay Ward, coach of Thunder Bay, was quoted as saying, "It's the macho thing. They (male players) go out there terrified. They can't go back to the locker room and tell the guys that a girl struck them out. Some of them have gotten over that now, but others haven't. And they are the ones she gets out, every time."[17]

Ila Borders wants her pitching skills to be taken seriously. She has said, "I don't want to live my life as someone's idea of a stunt. I'm here on my road to the major leagues."[18] Her comments are reminiscent of Jackie Mitchell's in 1931. One worries that in future years her accomplishments will also be trivialized, and that she will be seen as another woman who was exploited for publicity purposes with the age-old gimmick of "the battle of the sexes."

Perhaps another woman will eventually play minor or even major league baseball. But for women to be judged purely on their own merits as athletes, they need their own leagues. Professional women's golf and tennis circuits have already demonstrated that the public will come to see women play and that women athletes can be accepted for their athleticism. The future success of the Women's National Basketball League Association formed in 1997 will indicate whether women's team sports have finally come of age.

Is there a future for women in baseball? Now and then another Ila Borders may come along, but such women will continue to be anomalies. The likelihood of a women's professional baseball team or league being formed in the near future is remote. The main reason is that most girls don't play baseball. The majority of little girls go out for Little League softball rather than baseball. At the high school, college, and Olympic level, softball is the established sport for girls and women. Softball is firmly entrenched as the female game and baseball as the male. Without a large pool of women who have played baseball throughout their lives, it will be impossible to form a competitive women's baseball league at the professional level.

Notes

1. For more information on the women ballplayers discussed in this essay, see Gai Ingham Berlage, *Women in Baseball: The Forgotten History* (Westport, CT: Praeger, 1994).

2. Morris Beale, *The Softball Story* (Washington, DC: Columbia, 1957), 29.

3. Announcement in *The National Police Gazette* (September 20, 1890).

4. "When Father Locates Earl the Bloomer Girls Will Need Another Player," *Nashville Banner* (September 9, 1910).

5. Barbara Gregorich, *Women at Play: The Story of Women in Baseball* (New York: Harcourt Brace, 1993), 6–11.

6. Sesquicentennial Historical Committee, *Ragersville, Auburn Township, Ohio, 1830–1980: The Sesquicentennial Story of a Community* (Berlin, OH: Berlin Printing, 1980), 193.

7. Debra Shattuck, "Eighty Years Ago in Vermilion: A 'Skirt' on the Mound Stuns Baseball Fans," *Vermilion Photojournal* (August 31, 1987), Sec. C, 5–8.

8. Berlage, 53–57; John Hanlon, "Queen of Baseball," *Yankee Magazine* (July 1985), 15–20.

9. John Thorn, *A Century of Baseball Lore* (New York: Hart, 1974), 18.

10. Beale, *The Softball Story*, 168.

11. Oscar Ruhl, "From the Ruhl Book: No Gal Players? Barrow Used One in '98," *The Sporting News* (July 9, 1952), 18.

12. Eric Zorn, "The Girls of Summer," *Chicago Tribune* (December 12, 1982).

13. Merrie Fidler, "The All-American Girls' Baseball League, 1943–1954," in *Her Story in Sport: A Historical Anthology of Women in Sports*, ed. Reet Howell (West Point, NY: Leisure Press, 1982), 591.

14. Felicia Halpert, "How the Game Was Invented," *Women's Sports and Fitness* (July 1987), 50.

15. "Ladies of Little Diamond" *Time* (July 14, 1943), 74.

16. Neal Karlen, "Diamonds Are a Girl's Best Friend," *New York Times* (September 6, 1998), 6(ST).

17. David Usbome, "American Times: Female Pitcher Strikes Out in a Man's World," *London Independent* (September 9, 1998), 13.

18. Karlen, "Diamonds," 6(ST).

A LEAGUE OF OUR OWN

Lois J. Youngen

A LEAGUE OF THEIR OWN, A COLUMBIA PICTURES FILM DIRECTED BY PENNY MARSHALL, was released in 1992 to coincide with the opening of the major league baseball season. The film chronicles the 1943 inaugural season of the All-American Girls Professional Baseball League, a women's professional baseball league, conceived by Philip K. Wrigley, the chewing-gum magnate and owner of the Chicago Cubs. Concerned that World War II might devastate major league baseball, Wrigley proposed to keep the entertainment value of baseball alive by financing women's teams in four small Midwestern cities: Kenosha and Racine, Wisconsin; Rockford, Illinois; and South Bend, Indiana.

During the twelve years of the league's existence, the women's game, which started as modified softball, changed dramatically. The size of the ball gradually decreased until the 1954 season when the official major league baseball was adopted. The smaller ball was also more lively, forcing an increase in the distances between bases and from the pitcher's mound to home plate. The pitcher's delivery was changed from underhand to sidearm to overhand to accommodate the smaller ball. To understand the women's game is to understand the central role given to base stealing; from the first league game until the last league game, base stealing; was not only allowed, but also encouraged, and most players had the "strawberries" to prove it.

The league became both popular and financially successful with teams playing six days a week, with double headers on Sunday, for more than 100 games a season. During the summer of 1948, ten teams attracted more than 1 million fans. Unable to survive in a changing postwar society, the All-American Girls Professional Baseball League was disbanded after the summer of 1954.[1]

The Film

Based on a documentary by Kelly Candaele—son of former All-American Helen Callaghan Candaele St. Aubin—and Kim Wilson, the screenplay for the film, *A League of Their Own*, was written by Lowell Ganz and Babaloo Mandel. The year is 1943, the country is at war, and, the All-American Girls Professional Baseball

League has just been formed. The film follows the progress of one of the four original teams—the Rockford Peaches—with humor, through their first baseball season. As the individual players come together as a team, we share in their excitement, their joys, and their disappointments.

The storyline explores the rivalry between sisters, pitcher Kit Keller played by Lori Petty, and catcher Dottie Keller Henson played by Geena Davis. Tom Hanks is cast as their manager: alcoholic, has-been, former major league Hall of Famer, Jimmy Dugan. Throughout most of the film, manager Dugan repeatedly asserts that a woman's place is at home—and not at home, first, second and third! At the end, a league champion is crowned—one sister wins and the other loses—sisterly love prevails as they embrace and say good-bye. Manager Dugan shaves off his whiskers and decides to return to manage the "Peaches" the next season, thereby admitting that maybe, just maybe, these women really could play ball after all! Written to appeal to a 1990s audience, the film was a critical as well as a financial success.

Truths and Half Truths

As someone who played in the All-American Girls Professional Baseball for several years, I'm in a good position to assess the film's accuracy. One major error dramatically affects the film: in 1943 teams would have been playing modified softball with underhand pitching—the game you see in the film would not have been played until 1948. Otherwise, the following threads woven through the film are accurate representations of the All-American Girls Professional Baseball League as it existed in 1943.

The short, one-piece, flared-skirted uniform worn throughout the film was a perfect replica of the original as were the baseball cap, shoes, and high socks. The wooden baseball bats, the small leather gloves, and the catcher's equipment were faithfully reproduced. The baseball park, including the grandstand, the playing field, the dugouts, and the locker rooms were representative of the era. The names of the teams were accurate: The Peaches, Belles, Comets, and Blue Sox. There were sisters who played in the league. I played with and against two sets of twins. Even Hollywood could not duplicate this feat. The portrayal of managers as older men with major league baseball experience was accurate. I was fortunate to have played for two baseball Hall of Famers, Max Carey and Jimmy Foxx.

Each team had a woman chaperone filling a variety of roles: surrogate mother, nurse, and secretary. In reality, in contrast to the film, she was never considered the enemy! Travel between cities was by bus driven by a male bus driver as shown in the film. However, to the best of my knowledge, a team was never stranded on purpose. Singing on the bus was a long-standing tradition and every player learned the All-American song. Actually, we sang quite often and quite well. Players were required to attend charm school in 1943 as indicated in the film. By the early 1950s, this practice was obsolete. Actually, I think they gave up on us!

Rules regulating dress and conduct as outlined in the film were well known and followed. We even wore hats on special occasions! And yes, there was a little boy who occasionally traveled with one of the teams. He was the son of a player and her husband who also managed the team. However, his name was not Stillwell Angel!

Penny Marshall should be congratulated. Through her movie magic, she was able to make actresses into convincing professional baseball players, if you don't look too closely at the technical skills. I didn't think it could be done! A few scenes at the beginning of the film as well as the end were filmed in Cooperstown at the Baseball Hall of Fame, which in 1988 opened the exhibit "Women in Baseball" dedicated to the women of the All-American Girls Professional Baseball League. The epilogue includes former All-Americans, on the baseball field, gray hair blowing, attempting to recapture their youth.

Pure Fiction

A number of scenes, with their accompanying dialogue, represent pure Hollywood fiction. But in all probability these are the very scenes most likely responsible for the film's financial success. For example, twelve years of the league's existence are compressed into the first year, 1943. Madonna, with her headfirst sliding, was way ahead of her time since there was very little of this in the league—feet first, ladies. Also, although the names were fictitious in the film, Walter Harvey was recognizable as owner Philip Wrigley, and manager Jimmy Dugan's character was a thinly veiled Jimmy Foxx. The roles of the players were composites of many former All-Americans.

There were some more serious discrepancies. For example, no male manager of a women's baseball team in 1943 would have presumed to enter a woman's locker room without permission. He would not have avoided active management on the field. He would not have been drinking in front of the players. He would not have used expletives or have made off-color remarks. And he would not have publicly yelled at a player that memorable phrase: "Are you crying? Are you crying? There's no crying in baseball."

In addition, no female baseball player in 1943 would have fought with another player on the field. She would not have thrown a temper tantrum or allowed her son to behave like the little boy Stillwell Angel. She would not have used expletives or made off-color remarks. And she would not have acted as unrestrained and free-spirited as "All the Way Mae," the character Madonna played in the film.

Observations

This film, besides its entertainment value, provides us with many cultural norms and beliefs about baseball, about women, and about women in baseball in 1943. We must remember the social context from which the league emerged. In the 1940s and 1950s, men were the breadwinners and the authority figures, women were housewives and mothers and just beginning to wear slacks. Children obeyed their parents and were expected to be seen but not heard. The family unit was strong and sex before marriage was not acceptable. The country was at war and men, women, and children were expected to aid in the war effort.

Young women were socialized into specific, sports-acceptable roles. Among the gender-appropriate sports of the day were the individual sports of golf, tennis, swimming, and ice skating. Team sports for women, including basketball and softball, were considered less desirable forms of competition. In 1965, Elizabeth Metheny, in her classic analysis of socially acceptable sports for college women, marginally approved of softball as an intramural sport but not acceptable for extramural competition.[2] College women of the day participated in intramurals, play days, and sports days which deemphasized excellence and winning while promoting the values of cooperation and participation.

Ageism, racism, sexism, and other "isms" were practiced during this era, but they existed only as unchallenged concepts not ready for public consumption. The fact that professional women's baseball was not a socially acceptable activity in 1943 is made eminently clear early in the film when we are treated to a social commentary on the radio by a middle-aged woman: "And now the most disgusting example of this sexual confusion, Mr. Walter Harvey of Harvey Bars is presenting us with women's baseball. Right here in Chicago, young girls, plucked from their families, are gathering at Harvey Field to see which one of them can be the most masculine. . . ."

In the real world of the All-American Girls Professional Baseball League, Wrigley was quick to counter this very real criticism with a variety of public relations techniques used to create the illusion that women baseball players were feminine, had sex appeal, behaved as ladies should, and possessed those household skills typical of young women of the era. The marketing of the All-American Girls Professional Baseball League had begun!

The first technique was to recruit and select as many young women as possible who combined the ability to play baseball with physical attractiveness. This theme is presented early in the film and repeated in the scene where the father tells the scout that he knows his daughter is "not as good looking as those other girls but she loves to play baseball."

The design of a short, one-piece, flared-skirt uniform was revolutionary! The most acceptable women's softball uniform of the day included matching shirt and pants that extended below the knees. The new uniform, impractical as it was for fielding ground balls, pitching underhand, and sliding into bases, succeeded in stressing the feminine qualities of the players. Never before had players shown so much bare leg! The players reaction was negative, as shown in the film, but the management made it clear, "If you can't play ball in this uniform, then you can't play ball in this league." In later years, using their female ingenuity, players removed the flare, straightened the skirt, and raised the hemline. Thus the miniskirt was born.

What could be considered more feminine than attending charm school especially if you had publicity photos to prove it? Under the watchful eye of Mrs. Wrigley, as well as other beauty consultants, the All-Americans were instructed in the finer points of female deportment: how to sit, stand, and walk, how to apply makeup, and how to style long hair. Philip Wrigley was serious in his desire to bring middle-class values to his baseball players. How much learning took place is another question.

In the league's promotional materials, in photos, and in feature articles—many with national distribution—the emphasis was most often placed on the feminine qualities and household skills of the players rather than on their exceptional baseball capabilities. Often the most attractive players, not the best ballplayers, were used for publicity purposes. The film treats us to one scene in which we see a player successfully pouring coffee, and in another scene we hear that Betty, another player, is very good at making spaghetti, and she also knits.

Wrigley's rules of conduct for players on and off of the baseball field were invaluable in presenting the image of a warm nurturing environment—just like home—in which chaperones were provided for safety, social life was monitored, curfews were observed, and dresses and skirts were to be worn at all times.

Even the naming of the teams, the Peaches and the Belles, and in later years, the Sallies, the Colleens, the Daisies, the Chicks, the Lassies, and the Redwings, appear to be attempts to feminize. It's unclear how the gender-neutral Blue Sox and Comets were named.

And so, in a web of quasi respectability, the sexually wholesome girl next door was created. But just ask any former All-American from the early league years and they will tell you in no uncertain terms: they were expected to look like Betty Grable and play like Joe DiMaggio.

Power and Control

Did men completely control the All-American Girls Professional Baseball League? Absolutely! The league was derived from an exclusively male sports institution—major league baseball. From 1943 through 1954, male owners, male managers, and male umpires held the decision-making power. This is not surprising since, with few exceptions, men of that era ran most institutions: business, politics, education, and religion.

Wrigley was the quintessential baseball owner. When the All-American Girls Professional Baseball League almost disbanded in the first year of operation due to lack of gate receipts, Wrigley's rhetoric quickly changed from, "It is your patriotic duty to play in the league and save major league baseball" to "Have we made a poor business decision?" As succinctly stated in the film, "No product, no profit."

We have already seen the power of the owners to dictate what the players would wear, how the players would look, and how the players would behave. But it was up to the manager to determine who would play, where they would play, and when they would play. True to the film, many managers were former major and minor league players, hired to be seen by the fans, and thereby increasing gate receipts. But these men were competitors, they had egos invested in winning, they were also teachers presented with gifted students, highly skilled athletes, who knew how to play softball and were eager to learn the complexities of baseball. Through the influence of the managers and the acceptance of the paying public, women's baseball changed from season to season. Former players, although well qualified to manage a team, most often found themselves in the role of chaperone.

Ultimately, the All-American Girls Professional League evolved into nearly a mirror image of our national pastime. All of the nuances of major league baseball playing techniques and strategies, innovations in equipment, and changes in the playing rules were assimilated by the women's game on an ongoing basis. The male model was all that existed: it worked, and it was adopted.

Players

What about the players? They came from all parts of the country, Canada, and Cuba, more than 500 of them in twelve years. They came from all socio-economic levels, but predominately from working-class families. They came because they simply loved to play baseball, they loved to win, they loved to make a great catch, they loved to feel the crack of the wooden bat on the ball and to know it would be a base hit. Not the rules and regulations, the uniform, nor charm school could keep them from playing baseball. Playing baseball was more important than the money (as long as you had enough to survive), more important than having to take directions from a man, and more important than letting a "strawberry" keep you out of the lineup.

If the film has a bias, it is in the direction of marriage and motherhood. In fact, the majority of women, when playing in the league, were single. Dating and dancing were part of the total experience, but remember, in those days you had to be asked! The feeling of camaraderie was strong—you were part of a team. As Stillwell, now a grown man, tells us at the end of the film, "Mom always said, it [playing baseball] was the best time in her life."

In one short scene in the film we are pointedly reminded that the ability to throw a baseball with power and accuracy is not the exclusive domain of white women. To my knowledge, no African American woman ever played in the league. As we know, it was not until 1947 that Jackie Robinson made his historical debut as the first of his race to play in the major leagues in the modern era.

Conclusion

The Hollywood depiction of the All-American Girls Professional Baseball League suffers from some historical inaccuracies, embellishments, and exaggerations. Nevertheless, the film introduced this very unique game of women's baseball to a very large audience, the American public. It has helped fill in a missing part of our history.

Also, for the baseball player, like myself, the doing of baseball is different from the watching of baseball and the writing about baseball. The doing of baseball is experiential, irrational, and emotional. As manager Hanks says to catcher Davis in the film, "Baseball is what gets inside of you and makes you light up." It is precisely these qualities that the film brings to life. Hollywood has captured the spirit of the league, the spirit of the game, and the spirit of the women who played. For these things, it ought to be applauded.

Notes

1. For a fuller history, see Barbara Gregorich, *Women at Play: The Story of Women in Baseball* (New York: Harcourt Brace, 1993).

2. Elizabeth Metheny, "Symbolic Forms of Movement: The Feminine Image in Sports," in *Connotations of Movement in Sport and Dance,* ed. Elizabeth Metheny (Dubuque, IA: William Brown, 1965), 43–56.

DREAM OR NIGHTMARE?
Baseball and the Gender Order

Anne R. Roschelle

SINCE ITS INCEPTION, BASEBALL HAS BEEN A MAN'S DOMAIN. DURING THE LATE NINE-teenth century, American society was undergoing tremendous social, political, and economic upheaval. As a result, white, middle-class men were experiencing a crisis of masculinity. Opportunities for women were increasing and nonwhite immigrants were entering into major industrial centers in droves. Workplace autonomy was declining under the burgeoning capitalist system. Many white, middle-class men recognized that their power within the social structure was eroding. According to Michael Kimmel, these powerful social structural shifts resulted in a crisis of gender identity. Fear over whether the traditional white, middle-class version of masculinity would prevail in the face of counterhegemonic forces was rampant. Subsequently, the emergence of the sport of baseball was one attempt to ameliorate this crisis.[1]

In the late nineteenth century, participation in sports by boys and men was considered to be an excellent way to build character. In addition to fostering good health, sports also inspired moral development. Most important, sports encouraged manliness and discouraged effeminate behavior. The values of man-hood became central in the popularization of baseball as the national pastime. Even Theodore Roosevelt extolled the virtues of baseball, arguing that it was one of "the true sports for the manly race."[2] Popular advice manuals and small-town newspapers throughout the United States lauded baseball as indispensable for suitable growth into "normal" manhood. Men who were insecure about their position in the capitalist order often turned to baseball to redeem their virility. The valorization of courage, strength, initiative, and competitive drive, endemic to baseball, were essential values of traditional masculinity.[3] The creation of organized sport constructed a male domain in which competition and violent physicality was valued while femininity was virulently devalued.[4] As a result, organized sport helped to sustain the dwindling ideology of white, middle-class male superiority and helped to reconfigure masculine hegemony.[5] Hence, the national pastime became a bastion of male dominance.

As Gai Berlage has discussed (see her essay in this volume), baseball evolved
as an almost exclusively male domain. Men controlled the national pastime, and
women were discouraged, and sometimes prohibited, from playing. In addition,
the characteristics of aggressiveness, strength, competitiveness, and independence—indispensable to baseball—were antithetical to definitions of womanhood. The cult of true womanhood pervading late-nineteenth-century
middle-class life demanded that women be physically and emotionally weak.
Lack of frailty and delicacy in a middle-class white woman was an indication of
sexual deviance and was often treated with painful surgery on reproductive organs.[6] Furthermore, the sexually aggressive verbal sparring that often accompa-
nies professional sports[7] was considered distasteful for proper women to hear.
Clearly, the national pastime was not an appropriate pastime for a "lady." As
Berlage suggests, however, women played professional baseball as early as the
1860s, but their participation was often trivialized. This trivialization kept baseball from becoming integrated and maintained the institution as a bastion of
male privilege and aggression.

A fundamental aspect of the culture of male athletes has been the phenomenon of sexually aggressive, discursive bantering. Through this process, boys are
socialized at an early age to talk about and treat females as dehumanized sexual
objects.[8] Shouts of "pussy," "girl," "faggot," and "act like a man" are commonly
heard on the baseball diamond. Coaches, players, and fans alike engage in this
verbal abuse. In baseball, the ultimate put-down of a pitcher is the familiar
refrain, "Hey, you throw like a girl." Underlying this aggressive boasting and
male bravado among young males is insecurity about their masculinity and their
sexuality. Individual insecurity combined with peer group displays of sexual
dominance too often translate into male athletes learning to treat women as
objects of sexual conquest. This can result in rape and other forms of violence
against women.[9] So while the national pastime is a mirror of the American dream
(as suggested by various essays in this volume), it also reflects a darker side of
American society. Cultural beliefs about the role of women both in relationship
to sport and in general can be found in baseball. In fact, baseball-induced displays of masculinity help maintain social hierarchies between men and women
throughout the social structure.[10]

An excellent example of how baseball maintains gender ideology and the ease
with which women become objectified as sexual objects can be found in the
discourse surrounding female spectators. Even during the relative sexual conservatism of the 1950s, players saw women as sex objects. Contempt among the
Brooklyn Dodgers, for example, toward women spectators was personified by
the phrase "Baseball Annies," the derogatory term for groupies. According to
Carl Prince, throughout the 1950s the Dodger organization, the press, and the
players all shared a contempt for Baseball Annies. On road trips, players drank

frequently and had sexual liaisons with as many women as possible. Players reveled in retelling stories of their sexual conquests to fellow players. One player, Dick Williams—who later became a big-league manager and who more recently was arrested for indecent exposure—proudly boasted that on a single road trip he had an assortment of black, Jewish, and Hispanic women to choose from.[11] Even the married men engaged in sexual relationships with women on the road. In fact, men justified cheating on their wives because they were at home and "barefoot and pregnant" anyway.

Baseball lore is filled with stories about players' sexual exploits. Throughout the 1950s, paternity suits were filed by women who bore the children of married baseball players.[12] Babe Ruth, Bo Belinsky, and Mickey Mantle are some of the more famous players from the past whose affairs with women were well known. A player such as Steve Garvey, who cultivated a squeaky clean, all-American image, was not the devoted family man he pretended to be. In fact, during his marriage to Cindy Garvey, Steve fathered children with other women. Baseball players have contributed to the sexual oppression of women. Most ballplayers who view women as sexual conquests have not necessarily perpetrated any physical abuse. Nevertheless, the culture of baseball, with its sexual objectification of women, may foster a climate for debasing and violating women. Recent accounts of spousal abuse and sexual assaults of women by professional ballplayers have become increasingly more common. Darryl Strawberry's struggle with drugs and his abusive relationship with his wife were forgiven by the fans as long as he kept winning. His recent bout with colon cancer has recast him in an even more sympathetic light.

It's fascinating to examine the discursive strategy male athletes use to depict their sexual conquests as nothing more than promiscuous whores. When I was in high school and then in college, I remember how women who had casual sexual relationships with players were denigrated and humiliated. It is not unusual to hear professional ballplayers refer to groupies in sexually derogatory ways. Nonetheless, these men are more than eager to engage in these sexual liaisons. In fact, for many men their masculine identity is integrally linked to these relationships. What does this say about these men? What is it about organized sport and the trivialization of women as sexual objects that contributes to this kind of behavior? How can one understand these male-identified attitudes and the concomitant behavior?

Theoretically, one must examine the gender order, which is a socially constructed hierarchy of power relations between men and women based on male privilege.[13] Notions of masculinity and femininity emerge in relation to the sociohistorical context in which they exist. The resulting patriarchal notions are constructed and reconstructed over time. Although patriarchy is an integral component of the social structure, all men do not share equal power over all women. Within the gender order there are competing masculinities (and femininities) at any given historical moment. Some of these masculinities have become an integral, seemingly natural part of the socially structured social order, and thus they are hegemonic. Other masculinities are marginalized and still others are stigmatized.[14] Although sport is a domain of contested national, class, and race relations, the hegemonic conception of masculinity in sport transcends those relations and unites men in their privilege over women.[15] Clearly, hegemonic masculinity is constructed in relation to various subordinated masculinities as well as in relation to femininities.

The gender order is thus a social system that is constantly being created, contested, and changed, both in the relationships and power struggles between men and women, and in the relationships and power struggles between men.[16] Essentially, male domination of women binds all men together but they do not share equally in this domination.[17] In addition, gender identity occurs in the process people experience when they interact with the social world. As a result, gender identity is a socially constructed, evolutionary process, not an inherent, immutable one.[18] Subsequently, people are not passive receptacles of culture. Rather, people have agency, which enables them to participate in and resist subordination to strict notions of appropriate gender identity.[19] Because gender identity is formed through a lifelong interaction between the internal self and the external social environment, not everyone reacts the same. Subsequently, there are many athletes who reject norms of male dominance and do not treat women as sexual objects. Nonetheless, given the pervasive attitudes of hypermasculinity traditionally associated with sport, and the tendency to utilize violent behavior to achieve one's goals in sport, it is not surprising that sexual violence is commonplace among professional athletes.[20]

At the risk of overgeneralization, it is nevertheless important to distinguish between baseball and other sports. Among professional male-dominated American sports, baseball is probably the least violent. Boxing, football, hockey, and even basketball are inherently more brutal as games. These sports require significant and repeated displays of violent aggression for athletes to be successful. As a result, violence is not only accepted but also encouraged by fans and coaches alike. Subsequently, the line between violence in the game and violence in everyday life may become blurred. News accounts, at least, of violence against women by professional athletes tend to be more common in these other sports than in baseball. But even if baseball seems more "civilized," its hypermasculinist culture still contributes to women's sexual objectification.

In fact, in recent years it has become widely accepted among feminist sport scholars that the institution of sport is a fundamentally male-dominated, sexist institution.[21] The masculinist orientation of sport has led to irresponsible sexual behavior among contemporary professional athletes. An increasing number of athletes publicly boast about their sexual promiscuity. Wilt Chamberlain and Jim Brown were among the most vociferous womanizers in professional sports. Fellow team members called Brown "Hawk" because he was so successful at "chasing women." Even at age fifty-three, Brown continued to view women as sexual conquests. In his book, he asserted, "My lady right now is nineteen. . . . When I eat a peach, I don't want it overripe. I want a peach when it's peaking."[22]

The public's exposure to athletes' sexual practices has popularized the term "groupie," a label applied to women who hang around athletes and often engage in sex with them. Clearly, there are women who pursue athletes solely for sexual purposes. However, according to Jeffrey Benedict, groupie behavior is atypical and only occurs among a small segment of women. Nonetheless, these women are common fixtures in the social life of professional athletes. Furthermore, their pursuit of sexual relationships with athletes reinforces the athletes' attitude of women as sexual objects. Unfortunately, the attitude athletes have toward groupies often extends to other women. Professional athletes begin to expect sex from all women. In fact, repeated sexual encounters with numerous partners narrows an athlete's view of women and convinces players they can act with impunity toward any woman who vies for their attention.[23]

Another problem is that, beginning with high school and into college, successful athletes are often buffered from nonsport related responsibilities. Coaches, teachers, scouts, and others often protect players from behavioral accountability off the field. Athletes' exemption from accountability is further facilitated by the teams' complicity in their players' participation in socially reprehensible conduct.[24] Even when college and professional players are associated with alleged sexual misconduct, the financial interests of the university or team take precedence over the allegation. One of the factors that encourage high levels of sexual assault among athletes is the consent that society gives men to engage in violent sexual behavior against women. Coaches, managers, and university officials generally regard sexual assault as nothing more than men giving in to their natural urges. After a rape has occurred, people often define it as consensual sex, and with the wink of an eye say, "Boys will be boys."[25] Athletes are relieved of their responsibility because so many people have a vested interest in seeing the charges dropped. According to Martin Schwartz and Walter DeKeseredy, journalists often report that police chiefs, college administrators, and others will brag about getting rape charges dropped. In those cases that do go to trial, the jurors themselves will often acquit athletes rather than see the upcoming season ruined.[26] Athletes are often treated as if the norms of society don't apply to them and as if they are above the law.[27]

When I was a graduate student at a Division I university, one of the basketball players was accused of raping a student. Allegedly, the basketball coach called the female student and tried to threaten her into dropping criminal charges.

The story around campus was that he was fired, given a several million-dollar severance package, and hired to coach at another university. The most interesting thing about the story was the response by male students, particularly athletes. Many at the university felt it was the coach's duty to dissuade this young woman from ruining the life of a potential NBA star. The lack of concern over the rape victim's life was astounding. As is often the case, she was defined as a groupie whore and was blamed for her rape.

Unfortunately, the athletic male peer group is often a setting in which discussing women as objects of sexual conquest is important for gaining status in the group. Although some people argue that athletes are not more violent against women but are simply more visible, research has illustrated that athletes learn that women are acceptable commodities and objects of their physical rage. In addition, athletes learn that they are indeed above the law and can get away with violence against women.[28] Given the hypermasculinized culture of sport, the ideology that all women are potential sexual conquests, and the duplicity among coaches, managers, and owners, it is not surprising to find numerous examples of sexual violence by players.

Although not all athletes approve of this behavior and reject the sexism endemic to sport, most go along with it for fear of being ostracized. However, some athletes are beginning to speak out against violence toward women. Many colleges throughout the United States have implemented date-rape workshops, and some professional teams are no longer protecting athletes from allegations of sexual assault. In addition, because baseball is not inherently as violent as other sports, there may be less sexual violence among professional baseball players in the first place. Perhaps baseball players could take the lead in speaking out against physical violence, especially off the field. When Robbie Alomar engaged in the relatively nonviolent act of spitting in an umpire's face, he was nevertheless ostracized by fans and most players, and was severely fined by organized baseball. Players could just as easily ostracize and speak out against their colleagues who engage in the far more violent practice of abusing and assaulting women. If baseball is to truly become a mirror of the American dream, and not a reflection of an American nightmare, then players, coaches, managers, and fans must commit themselves to treating women as equals and not merely as sexual conquests.

Notes

1. Michael S. Kimmel, "Baseball and the Reconstitution of American Masculinity, 1880–1920," in *Sport, Men, and the Gender Order: Critical Feminist Perspectives,* eds. Michael A. Messner and Donald F. Sabo. (Champaign, IL: Human Kinetics Books, 1990), 55–65.
2. Ibid.
3. Ibid.

4. Michael A. Messner, "Boyhood, Organized Sports, and the Construction of Masculinities," *Journal of Contemporary Ethnography* 4 (1990): 416–444.

5. Ibid.; N. Theberge, "A Critique of Critiques: Radical and Feminist Writings on Sport," *Social Forces* 60 (1981): 2; L. Bryson, "Sport and the Maintenance of Masculine Hegemony," *Women's Studies International Forum* 10 (1987): 349–360; M.A. Hall, "The Discourse on Gender and Sport: From Femininity to Feminism." *Sociology of Sport Journal* 5 (1988): 330–340.

6. Barbara Ehrenreich and Deirdre English, *Complaints and Disorders: The Sexual Politics of Sickness* (New York: The Feminist Press, 1973).

7. Michael A. Messner and Donald Sabo, *Sex, Violence & Power in Sports: Rethinking Masculinity* (Freedom, CA: The Crossing Press, 1994).

8. Ibid.

9. Ibid.

10. Kimmel, "Baseball and the Reconstitution."

11. Carl Prince, *Brooklyn's Dodgers: The Bums, the Borough and the Best of Baseball* (New York: Oxford University Press, 1996).

12. Ibid.

13. R.W. Connell, *Gender and Power* (Stanford: Stanford University Press, 1987).

14. Ibid.

15. Messner, "Boyhood, Organized Sports."

16. Connell, *Gender and Power.*

17. Messner and Sabo, *Sex, Violence and Power.*

18. Messner, "Boyhood, Organized Sports."

19. Ibid.

20. Ibid.

21. Theberge, "A Critique of Critiques."

22. James Brown, *Out of Bounds* (New York: Zebra Press, 1989), 105; Messner, "Boyhood, Organized Sports."

23. Jeffrey R. Benedict, *Athletes and Acquaintance Rape* (Thousand Oaks, CA: Sage, 1998).

24. Ibid.

25. Ibid.

26. Martin D. Schwartz and Walter S. DeKeseredy, *Sexual Assault on the College Campus: The Role of Male Peer Support.* (Thousand Oaks, CA: Sage, 1997).

27. Ibid.

28. Benedict, *Athletes and Acquaintance Rape.*

THE TUNE PLAYS THE SAME

Joan Ryan

MY CONNECTION TO BASEBALL CAME THROUGH MY FATHER, AND VICE VERSA. HE WAS born in the Bronx to a hard-drinking Irish cab driver and to a mother who, widowed young, stood in line for government-issue oatmeal to feed her eight children. There were no camps, no swimming holes. In my father's neighborhood, the afternoon Yankee game provided the background music to the summer. He never lost the habit.

Every summer weekend when I was growing up, he'd mow the grass and then sit in his lawn chair with a Pabst Blue Ribbon and watch his six children play Wiffle ball, the transistor radio on a folding table by his side. Joe DiMaggio had been his idol, but he fell hard for Mickey Mantle, as anyone who followed New York baseball in the 1950s and 1960s did. He figured God must be a Yankees fan or else how did Mantle happen to come along when DiMaggio was leaving, just as DiMaggio had come along after Gehrig?

"I remember when Mantle hit a ball off the facade of Yankee Stadium," my father would tell me. "It came within eighteen inches of going out of the park. It was like a bullet. I don't think he was even out of the batter's box when the ball hit the facade. He was such an awesome hitter he could have grabbed the bat by the barrel and hit the ball into the stands with the handle. And when he missed, there was nothing left in the batter's box."

When Mantle died a few years back, I called my father to ask if this meant the end of an era for baseball. No, he said. The era ended a long time ago, about the time when Mantle retired in '68. This was also the time when my father became increasingly irritated with the politics and music and clothing and attitudes of the generation coming up behind him. To my father, society at large and baseball were separate strands of the same knot, and as I get older, I am less inclined to disagree. The whole world was changing then, in the late '60s, and baseball was changing with it. Both had grown louder and more self-involved. As the "Me Generation" sought self-fulfillment, baseball players fought for and won free agency so they could choose where and with whom they would play.

The price of greater personal freedom, of course, is often the fracturing of community. Baseball rosters began to break up. Neighbors left and strangers arrived. The stability that gave my father so much comfort in his youth was crumbling. Even the press was changing and, to my father's way of thinking, making an irresponsible mess of things. It wasn't enough to bring down Nixon, who my father loved. Now reporters were exposing baseball's unseemliness as well: drug problems, marital difficulties, drinking binges, legal scrapes, salary haggling.

The nation was growing up, becoming less sentimental and more bottom line. Baseball was growing with it, leaving behind childhood crushes. We have our affairs today, but I'm not sure we commit ourselves to the ballplayers the way our parents did. We're not easily awed. When Mark McGwire hits a home run to the upper decks, we're impressed but inevitably some kid will say, "For the kind of money he's making, he OUGHT to be hitting them up there."

I understand why my father has no desire to go to ballgames. Most parks are huge bowls of noise now, with music and advertisements blaring between innings, a reflection of a culture in which movie theaters show ads and trivia quizzes before feature films, and stores and airplanes and elevators and telephone on-holds bombard us with music, as if we can't entertain ourselves for even a moment. The radio (thank goodness) still carries the games, but we're just as likely to find screaming sports talk shows when we flip on the dial.

Yet for all the changes, there is something absolutely unchangeable about baseball, something that survives generations no matter how loud the music and how business-oriented the players and owners. I feel at the ballpark the way other people say they feel on the golf course, which is to say, unburdened. There is no twinge in my brain that says I should be anywhere but where I am. Sometimes I'm lucky enough to sit next to Bill Rigney, the eighty-one-year-old former Giants manager. From him, I hear that Leo Durocher was the worst third base coach ever and that Ty Cobb solved his slumps (few though they were) by crowding the plate to shrink the strike zone, and that Ernie Lombardi kept his glove tucked tightly under his arm between innings because somebody had once stolen his glove and he wasn't about to let it happen again. Rig tells me how he'd rub his shoulder against Stan Musial when the Giants played in St. Louis, trying to grab a little magic, and Musial would smile and say, "Don't take too much, now."

The last time I went to Phoenix for spring training, the Rawlings sporting goods man was sitting outside the A's clubhouse behind a card table covered with the latest models in baseball gloves. They were for the players, but he agreed to sell me one for $100. I slipped one on my hand, then another. I found one that was perfect, a little stiff, of course, but the leather was creamy to the touch and smelled like ground balls and my father and clay infields. It was a work of art, black with deep brown accents and gold lettering along the pinky that said, "for the professional player."

I tried it out by playing catch with the A's team doctor and felt like the forty-five-year-old pitcher Rig remembered warming up many springs ago. "That ball doing anything?" the pitcher had asked hopefully. Rig hadn't been sure what to say. "Well," he finally replied, "it's reaching me."

It didn't matter. The ball smacked into my glove with the same thwack it always has. The motion of cocking my arm, shifting my body weight and releasing the ball—all the same, as if I were twelve and could hit home plate on a fly. It beats me why I love this glove so much. Maybe the reason is as banal as lost youth, I don't know. I feel no need to figure it out. Later, I sat down next to Rig, who was watching the batting drills from a golf cart behind the backstop. I asked him why he still loves baseball, in spite of the me-first attitude today and the players' seeming lack of interest in being well-rounded, and the musical-chairs rosters and the music, and the money.

He looked at the ninety feet from home to first, the sixty feet six inches from the mound to home, the green expanse of the outfield, and the young men in caps and knickers whipping the ball around the infield.

"The piano's a little different," he said, "but the tune plays the same."

But for my father, baseball will never be what it was. He'll always feel a little let down that it didn't hang in there with him, fending off the forces of change. He gets annoyed that the Marlins, the nearest major league team to him, play some games on Sunday night to accommodate ESPN. "Whoever heard of playing Sunday night?" he grumbles. He has no affinity for any of the players. "Nobody says Barry Bonds is a part of their lives," he says. "Mantle was probably the last one. The last of a breed."

I don't know that I agree. But I understand. He misses the quiet simplicity of another America, when gas cost twenty-five cents a gallon and your grandparents lived in the flat upstairs and the corner grocer was still there when you went off and got married. What's amazing to me, as someone who grew up in a time when baseball—like everything else, it seems—had become less personal, is that the depth and breadth of my father's sense of loss can be completely embodied in a single name, a ballplayer named Mantle.

BIBLIOGRAPHY

Adler, William M. *Land of Opportunity: One Family's Quest for the American Dream in the Age of Crack*. New York: Atlantic Monthly Press, 1995.

Aitken, Brian. "Baseball as Sacred Doorway in the Writing of W.P. Kinsella." *Aethlon* 8, no. 1 (1990): 69–70.

Albronda, Mildred. *Douglas Tilden*. Seattle: Emerald Point Press, 1994.

Alexander, Charles. *Our Game: An American Baseball History*. New York: Henry Holt, 1991.

Anastos, Philip, and Chris French. *Illegal: Seeking the American Dream*. New York: Rizzoli, 1991.

Ardolino, Frank. "Ceremonies of Innocence and Experience in *Bull Durham*, *Field of Dreams*, and *Eight Men Out*." *Journal of Popular Film and Television* 18 (1990): 46.

Asinof, Eliot. *Man on Spikes*. Carbondale: Southern Illinois University Press, 1998.

Barak, Greg, ed. *Crimes by the Capitalist State*. Albany: State University of New York Press, 1991.

Barber, Benjamin R. *Jihad vs. McWorld*. New York: Ballantine, 1996.

Barich, Bill. *Big Dreams*. New York: Vintage Books, 1994.

Barlett, Donald L., and James B. Steele. *America: What Went Wrong?* Kansas City, MO: Andrews and McMeel, 1992.

Beale, Morris. *The Softball Story*. Washington, DC: Columbia, 1957.

Beers, David. *Blue Sky Dream: A Memoir of America's Fall from Grace*. New York: Doubleday, 1996.

Bellah, Robert N., Richard Madsen, William Sullivan, Ann Swidler, and Stephen Tipton. *Habits of the Heart*. New York: Harper & Row, 1985.

Benedict, Jeffrey R. *Athletes and Acquaintance Rape*. Thousand Oaks, CA: Sage, 1998.

Berkman, Dave. "Long Before Arledge . . . Sports and TV. The Earliest Years, 1937–1947, as Seen by the Contemporary Press." *Journal of Popular Culture* 23, no. 3 (Fall 1988): 49–63.

Berlage, Gai Ingham. "Are Children's Competitive Team Sports Teaching Corporate Values?" In *Fractured Focus: Sport as a Reflection of Society*, ed. Richard E. Lapchick. Lexington, MA: Lexington Books, 1986.

———. *Women in Baseball: The Forgotten History*. Westport, CT: Praeger, 1994.

Bitker, Steve. *The Original San Francisco Giants: The Giants of '58*. Champaign, IL: Sports Publishing, 1998.

Boorstin, Daniel J. *The Image: Or What Happened to the American Dream?* Kingsport, TN: Kingsport Press, 1961.

Bormann, Ernest G. *The Force of Fantasy: Restoring the American Dream*. Carbondale: Southern Illinois University Press, 1985.

Boswell, Thomas. *Heart of the Order*. New York: Penguin, 1989.

Bouza, Tony. *The Decline and Fall of the American Empire: Corruption, Decadence and the American Dream*. New York: Plenum Press, 1996.

Bowman, Larry G. "Kansas City Monarchs and Night Baseball." *The National Pastime* 16 (1996): 80.

Boyle, T. Coraghessan. *The Tortilla Curtain*. New York: Harper, 1996.

Briley, Ron. "America, Baseball and Historical Memory in 1956: The Way We Never Were" (unpublished paper).

————. "Amity Is the Key to Success: Baseball and the Cold War." *Baseball History* 1, no. 3 (Fall 1986): 10.

————. "The Times Were A-Changin': Baseball as a Symbol of American Values in Transition, 1963–1964." *Baseball Research Journal* 18 (1994): 54–60.

Brooks, Kevin. "A Socialist Slider." *Minneapolis Review of Baseball* 11, no. 2 (1991): 39–41.

Brown, Bill. Book review of Springwood, *Cooperstown to Dyersville* in the *Journal of Sport History* 24, no. 3 (Fall 1997): 438–443.

Brown, James. *Out of Bounds*. New York: Zebra Books, 1989.

Bryson, L. "Sport and the Maintenance of Masculine Hegemony." *Women's Studies International Forum* 10 (1987): 349–360.

Butterworth, Dan. *Waiting for Rain: One Farmer's Struggle to Hold on to the American Dream*. Chapel Hill, NC: Algonquin Books, 1992.

Cagan, Joanna, and Neil deMause. "Bizbrawl." The *New York Times Magazine* (October 18, 1998), 66–67.

————. *Field of Schemes*. Monroe, ME: Common Courage Press, 1998.

Cahn, Susan K. *Coming on Strong: Gender and Sexuality in Twentieth-Century Women's Sport*. New York: Free Press, 1994.

Camarillo, Albert. *Chicanos in a Changing Society: From Mexican Pueblos to American Barrios in Santa Barbara and Southern California, 1846–1930*. Cambridge, MA: Harvard University Press, 1979.

Campbell, Joseph. *The Hero with a Thousand Faces*. Princeton, NJ: Princeton University Press, 1949.

————. *The Power of Myth*. New York: Doubleday, 1988.

Candaele, Kelly, and Peter Dreier. "Baseball Players Must Act Like a Labor Union." *Los Angeles Times*, Sunday Opinion section (May 19, 1996).

Carino, Peter. "American Dream, American Reality." *Elysian Fields Quarterly* 13, no. 2 (Summer 1994): 74–76.

Carlin, George. *Brain Droppings*. New York: Hyperion, 1997.

Catupusan, Benicio. *The Filipino Occupation and Recreational Activities in Los Angeles*. Saratoga, CA: R&E Research Associates, 1975.

Chasin, Barbara H. *Inequality and Violence in the United States: Casualties of Capitalism*. Atlantic Highlands, NJ: Humanities Press, 1997.

Chomsky, Noam. *The Common Good*. Monroe, ME: Odonian/Common Courage, 1998.

Clark, Dick, and Larry Lester, eds. *The Negro Leagues Book*. Cleveland: The Society of American Baseball Research, 1994.

Codrescu, Andrei. "A Kind of Love." In *The Muse Is Always Half Dressed in New Orleans*, ed. Andrei Codrescu. New York: St. Martin's Press, 1993, 141.

Cohen, David Stephen. *America: The Dream of My Life*. New Brunswick, NJ: Rutgers University Press, 1990.

Cohen, Michael Lee. *The Twenty-Something American Dream*. New York: Plume/Penguin Group, 1993.

Cohen, Stanley. *The Man in the Crowd*. New York: Random House, 1981.

Comer, James P. *Maggie's American Dream: The Life and Times of a Black Family*. New York: New American Library, 1988.

Coniff, Ruth. "The Joy of Women's Sports." *The Nation* (August 10/17, 1998), 26–30.

Connell, R.W. *Gender and Power*. Stanford: Stanford University Press, 1987.

Coontz; Stephanie. *The Way We Never Were: American Families and the Nostalgia Trap*. New York: Basic Books, 1992.

Cornuelle, Richard C. *Reclaiming the American Dream*. New Brunswick: Transaction, 1993.

Cramer, Richard Ben. "The America That Ruth Built." *Newsweek* (June 24, 1998), 28.

————. "The DiMaggio Nobody Knew." *Newsweek* (March 22, 1999), 53.

Crepeau, Richard C. *Baseball: America's Diamond Mind*. Orlando: University Presses of Florida, 1980.

Crimmins, James. *The American Promise*. San Francisco: KQED Books, 1995.

Danaher, Kevin. *Corporations Are Gonna Get Your Mama: Globalization and the Downsizing of the American Dream*. Monroe, ME: Common Courage, 1996.

Daniel, Dan M. "Television Opens Up Fantastic Avenues for Baseball Revenue." *Baseball Magazine* 80 (May 1948): 17–21.

————. "TV Must Go or Baseball Will." *Baseball Magazine* 84 (November 1952): 6–8.

Davis, Mike. *Prisoners of the American Dream*. New York: Verso, 1986.

Dawidoff, Nicholas. "Field of Kitsch: Is Nostalgia Wrecking Baseball?" *The New Republic* (August 17–24, 1992), 22–24.

Dawson, Robert, and Gray Brechin. *Farewell, Promised Land: Waking from the California Dream*. Berkeley: University of California Press, 1999.

Decker, Jeffrey Louis. *Made in America: Self-Styled Success from Horatio Alger to Oprah Winfrey*. Minneapolis: University of Minnesota Press, 1997.

DeLillo, Dom. *Underworld*. New York: Scribner's, 1997.

DeMott, Benjamin. *The Imperial Middle*. New York: William Morrow, 1990.

Derber, Charles. *Money, Murder and the American Dream: Wilding from Wall Street to Main Street*. Boston: Faber & Faber, 1992.

Deutschman, Alan. "Sly as Fox." *The New York Times Magazine* (October 18, 1998), 68–72.

"Diamonds in the Rough: Japanese Americans in Baseball." *Nikkei Heritage* (Spring 1997).

Domhoff, G. William, and Richard Zweigenhaft. *Diversity in the Power Elite: Have Women and Minorities Reached the Top?* New Haven, CT: Yale University Press, 1998.

Dorinson, Joseph, and Joram Warmund, eds., *Jackie Robinson: Race, Sports, and the American Dream*. Armonk, NY: M.E. Sharpe, 1998.

Dowd, Douglas F. *The Twisted Dream: Capitalist Development in the United States Since 1776*. Cambridge, MA: Winthrop, 1977.

Dowling, Colette. *The Frailty Myth: Women Approaching Physical Equality*. New York: Random House, 2000.

Drebinger, John. "Bobby Thomson, Scotland's Gift to Baseball." *Baseball Magazine* (October 1947), 379–381.

Dreier, Peter, and Kelly Candaele. "Pitchers and Pickets: Baseball's Labor Day Lessons." *Boston Sunday Globe* (September 4, 1994).

————. "Players Must Act Like A Labor Union." *Los Angeles Times* (May 19, 1996).

Driver, David. *Defending the Left.* Chicago: Noble Press, 1992.

Early, Gerald. "Performance and Reality: Race, Sports and the Modern World." *The Nation* (August 10/17, 1998), 11–20.

Editors. "What's Behind the Shrinking Number of African-American Players?" *Ebony* 47 (June 1992): 112–116.

Edwards, David. *Burning All Seasons.* Boston: South End Press, 1996.

Egerton, John. *Speak Now Against the Day: The Generation Before the Civil Rights Movement in the South.* Chapel Hill: University of North Carolina Press, 1994.

Ehrenreich, Barbara, and Deirdre English. *Complaints and Disorders: The Sexual Politics of Sickness.* New York: The Feminist Press, 1973.

Elias, Robert. "Baseball and Social Change." *Minneapolis Review of Baseball* 8, no.1 (1988): 24–27.

Ellwood, Wayne. "Inside the Disney Dream Machine." *The New Internationalist* 308 (December 1998): 20–37.

Engelhardt, Tom. *The End of Victory Culture: Cold War America and the Disillusioning of A Generation.* New York: Basic Books, 1995.

Eskenazi, Gerald. *The Lip.* New York: William Morrow, 1993.

Falkner, David. *Great Time Coming: The Life of Jackie Robinson from Baseball to Birmingham.* New York: Simon & Schuster, 1995.

Farhi, Paul, and Megan Rosenfeld. "Exporting America." *The Washington Post National Weekly Edition* (November 30, 1998), 6–7.

Feldman, Jay. "The Hidden Ball Trick, Nicaragua and Me." *The National Pastime: A Review of Baseball History*, 6, no.1 (Winter 1987): 2–5.

Fidler, Merrie. "The All-American Girls' Baseball League, 1943–1954." In *Her Story in Sport: A Historical Anthology of Women in Sports*, ed. Reet Howell. West Point, NY: Leisure Press, 1982, 591.

Fimrite, Ron. "Side by Side." *Sports Illustrated* (September 16, 1991), 66–77.

Fischer, William J. "The Conservative Curveball." *Minneapolis Review of Baseball*, 9, no. 4 (1990): 34–36.

Fishkin, Gerald Loren. *American Dream, American Burnout.* New York: Loren, 1994.

Flood, Curt with Richard Carter. *The Way It Is.* New York: Trident Press, 1970.

Folbre, Nancy. *The New Field Guide to the U.S. Economy.* New York: New Press, 1995.

Foucault, Michel. *The Birth of the Clinic.* New York: Pantheon, 1973.

Frank, Nancy K., and Michael J. Lynch. *Crimes Against Health and Safety.* New York: Harrow & Heston, 1992.

Frank, Robert, and Philip Cook. *The Winner Take All Society: Why the Few at the Top Get So Much More Than the Rest of Us.* New York: Penguin USA, 1996.

Frank, Stanley. "The Dodgers Won't Blow It Again." *Saturday Evening Post* (September 13, 1952).

Friedrich, Otto. *City of Net: A Portrait of Hollywood in the 1940s.* New York: Harper & Row, 1986.

Fromm, Erich. *To Have or To Be?* New York: Bantam Books, 1976.

Frommer, Harvey. *Rickey & Robinson: The Men Who Broke Baseball's Color Barrier.* New York: Macmillan, 1982.

———. *Shoeless Joe and Ragtime Baseball.* Dallas: Taylor, 1992.

Fry, August. "The Return of Joseph Jefferson Jackson, A Study in American Myth." In *A Centre of Excellence*, ed. Robert Druce. Amsterdam: Rodopi B.V., 1987, 90.

Gabler, Neil. *Life the Movie: How Entertainment Conquered Reality.* New York: Alfred Knopf, 1998.

Gallagher, Tom. "Lester Rodney, the *Daily Worker*, and the Integration of Baseball." *The National Pastime: A Review of Baseball History* 19 (1999): 58–64.

Gammons, Peter. "Foreign Markets Represent Baseball's Future." *Baseball America* (February 2–15, 1998), 6.

———. "1950 vs. 1960: A Tale of Two Eras." *Sports Illustrated* (April 16, 1990), 26–32.

Gargan, Edward A. "Field for Philosophizing and Other Dreams." *New York Times* (June 27, 1998).

Garman, Bryan K. "Myth Building and Cultural Politics in W.P. Kinsella's Shoeless Joe." *Canadian Review of American Studies* 24, no. 1 (1994): 46.

Gerlach, Larry R. "Babe Pinelli: Mr. Ump." *Society for American Baseball Research Annual* (1995), 43–45.

Giamatti, Bart. *Take Time for Paradise: Americans and Their Games.* New York: Summit, 1989.

Gillmor, Dan, and Stephen Doig, "Segregation Forever?" *American Demographics* 35 (January 1992): 35–41.

Gitlin, Todd. *The Twilight of Common Dreams.* New York: Metropolitan Books, 1995.

Goldstein, Tom. "The New Politics of Baseball." *Elysian Fields Quarterly* 15, no. 4 (1998): 2–4.

Goldstein, Tom, and Stephen Lehman. "Fighting Back: Baseball Fans of America in Revolt." *Elysian Fields Quarterly* 15, no. 2 (1998): 7–11

Gonzalez, Gilbert G. *Labor and Community: Mexican Citrus Worker Villages in a Southern California County, 1900–1950.* Urbana: University of Illinois Press, 1994.

Gorman, Tom. *Three and Two!* New York: Charles Scribner's Sons, 1979.

Gould, Stephen Jay. *The Flamingo's Smile.* New York: W.W. Norton, 1985.

Graham, Jr., Frank. *A Farewell to Heroes.* New York: Viking Press, 1981.

Grattan-Dominguez, Alejandro. *The Dark Side of the Dream.* Houston, TX: Arte Publico Press, 1995.

"Great Artists." *San Francisco Bulletin* (February 28, 1891).

Gregorich, Barbara. *Women at Play: The Story of Women in Baseball.* New York: Harcourt Brace, 1993.

Greider, William. *One World, Ready or Not: The Manic Logic of Capitalism.* New York: Simon & Schuster, 1997.

Grella, George. "Baseball and the American Dream." *Massachusetts Review* 16 (Summer 1975): 550–567.

Gropman, Daniel. *Say It Ain't So: The True Story of Shoeless Joe Jackson.* New York: Carol/Citadel, 1995.

Hacker, Andrew. *Two Nations: Black and White, Separate, Hostile, Unequal.* New York: Charles Scribners' Sons, 1992.

Hall, M.A. "The Discourse on Gender and Sport: From Femininity to Feminism." *Sociology of Sport Journal* 5 (1988): 330–340.

Halpert, Felicia. "How the Game Was Invented." *Women's Sports and Fitness* (July 1987), 50.

Hamper, Ben. *Rivethead: Tales from the Assembly Line.* New York: Warner, 1991.

Hanlon, John. "Queen of Baseball." *Yankee Magazine* (July 1985), 15–20.

Hanssen, Andrew. "The Cost of Discrimination: A Study of Major League Baseball." *Southern Economic Journal* 64, no. 3 (1998): 603–627.

Harper, Jim. "Gordon McLendon: Pioneer Baseball Broadcaster." *Baseball History* 1, no. 1 (Spring 1986): 42–51.

Harrington, Mona. *The Dream of Deliverance in American Politics*. New York: Alfred Knopf, 1986.

Hayden, Dolores. *Redesigning the American Dream*. New York: W.W. Norton, 1984.

Hayden, Tom. *The American Future*. Boston: South End Press, 1981.

Hedges, Burke. *Who Stole the American Dream?* Tampa, FL: INTI Press, 1992.

Heilman, Robert. "Field of Reality." *Elysian Fields Quarterly* 13, no. 2 (Summer 1994): 16–20.

Helyar, John. *Lords of the Realm*. New York: Villard, 1994.

Hochschild, Arlie Russell. *The Managed Heart: The Commercialization of Human Feeling*. Berkeley: University of California Press, 1983.

Hochschild, Jennifer L. *Facing Up to the American Dream*. Princeton, NJ: Princeton University Press, 1995.

Hoff, Joan. *Law, Gender and Injustice*. New York: New York University Press, 1991.

Hodges, Russell P., and Al Hirchberg, *My Giants*. Garden City, NY: Doubleday, 1963.

Horowitz, Ruth. *Honor and the American Dream: Culture and Identity in a Chicano Community*. New Brunswick, NJ: Rutgers University Press, 1986.

Howell, Reet, ed. *Her Story in Sport*. West Point, NY: Leisure Press, 1982.

Hudnet-Beumler, James David. *Looking for God in the Suburbs: The Religion of the American Dream and Its Critics, 1945–1965*. New Brunswick, NJ: Rutgers University Press, 1994.

Hudson, Michael, ed. *Merchants of Misery: How Corporate America Profits from Poverty*. Monroe, ME: Common Courage Press, 1996.

Hunt, George W. "Of Many Things." *America* (January 27, 1960).

Ichioka, Yuji. *The Issei: The World of First Generation Japanese Immigrants*. New York: Free Press, 1988.

Isenberg, Michael T. *John L. Sullivan and His America*. Urbana: University of Illinois Press, 1988.

Jacobson, Harold. "Shot in the Dark." *Film Comment* 25 (1989): 78.

Jally, Sut, and Justin Lewis. *Enlightened Racism: The Cosby Show, Audiences, and the Myth of the American Dream*. Boulder, CO: Westview Press, 1992.

Jargowsky, Paul. *Poverty and Place: Ghettos, Barrios, and the American City*. New York: Russell Sage Foundation, 1997.

Joffe, Linda S. "Praise Baseball. Amen. Religious Metaphor in *Shoeless Joe* and *Field of Dreams*." *Aethlon* 9, no. 2 (1992): 153–163.

Johnson, Berman E. *The Dream Deferred: Survey of Black America 1840–1996*. Dubuque, IA: Kendall/Hunt, 1996.

Jones, Gerald. *Honey, I'm Home! Sitcoms: Selling the American Dream*. New York: Grove Press, 1992.

Jones, Terry. "Racial Practices in Baseball Management." *The Black Scholar* 18 (May/June 1987): 16–24.

Kahn, Lawrence. "Discrimination in Professional Sports: A Survey of the Literature." *Industrial and Labor Relations Review* 44, no. 3 (April 1991): 28–36.

Kahn, Roger. "The Day Bobby Hit the Home Run." *Sports Illustrated* (October 10, 1960), 37–42

———. *The Era: When the Yankees, New York Giants, and the Brooklyn Dodgers Ruled the World*. New York: Tichnor & Fields, 1993.

———. "Still A Grand Old Game." In *The Complete Armchair Book of Baseball*, ed. John Thorn. New York: Galahad, 1997, 87.

Kammen, Michael. *Mystic Chords of Memory*. New York: Alfred Knopf, 1991.

Karlen, Neil. "Diamonds Are a Girl's Best Friend." *New York Times*, (September 6, 1998), 6ST.

Kaye, Harvey. "All That Is Solid Melts into Air . . . or Baseball and Capitalism, the View from Left Field." *Elysian Fields Quarterly* 12, no. 1 (1993): 26–28.

———. "From Bases to Superstructures: The Great Transformation of Baseball." In *Why Do Ruling Classes Fear History?* ed. Harvey Kaye. New York: St. Martin's Press, 1997, 87.

Kee, Lorraine. "Lions and Christians." *The Nation* (August 10/17, 1998), 37–38.

Kiernan, Thomas. *The Miracle at Coogan's Bluff*. New York: T.Y. Crowell, 1975.

Kimmel, Michael S. "Baseball and the Reconstitution of American Masculinity, 1880–1920." In *Sport, Men, and the Gender Order: Critical Feminist Perspectives*, eds. Michael A. Messner and Donald F. Sabo. Champaign, IL: Human Kinetics Books, 1990, 55–65.

King, Bill. "New Stadiums May Not Solve Old Problems." *Street & Smith's Sportsbusiness Journal* 14, no. 20 (December 1998): 13.

Kinsella, W.P. *Shoeless Joe*. New York: Ballantine, 1983.

Kitman, Jamie. "Way Out in Left-Center Field." *In These Times* (April 1–7, 1987), 12–13.

Kluger, Richard. *Simple Justice*. New York: Vintage Books, 1975.

Kohn, Alfie. *No Contest: The Case Against Competition*. Boston: Houghton Mifflin, 1986.

Koppett, Leonard. *Koppett's Concise History of Major League Baseball*. Philadelphia: Temple University Press, 1998.

———. *The New Thinking Fan's Guide to Baseball*. New York: Fireside, 1991.

Kozol, Jonathan. *Amazing Grace: The Lives of Children and the Conscience of a Nation*. New York: Crown, 1995.

———. *Illiterate America*. Garden City, NY: Anchor Press, 1985.

———. *Rachel and Her Children: Homeless Families in America*. New York: Crown, 1988.

———. *Savage Inequalities: Children in America's Schools*. New York: Crown, 1991.

LaBier, Douglas. *Modern Madness: The Emotional Fallout of Success*. Reading, MA: Addison-Wesley, 1986.

Labor Institute. *Corporate Power and the American Dream*. New York: Author, 1996.

"Ladies of Little Diamond." *Time* (July 14, 1943), 74.

Ladson, William. "Jackie Robinson Remembered." *Sport* 43, no. 1 (January 1990): 38–40.

Lamb, Chris and Glen Bleske. "Democracy on the Field: The Black Press Takes on White Baseball." *Journalism History* 9, no. 2 (Summer 1998): 27–35.

Lapchick, Richard, with David Stuckey. "Professional Sports: The Racial Report Card." In *Sport in Contemporary Society: An Anthology*, 4th ed., ed. D. Stanley Eitzen. New York: St. Martin's Press, 1993.

Lappe, Frances. *Rediscovering Americas Values*. New York: Ballantine Books, 1989.

Lasch, Christopher. *The Culture of Narcissism*. New York: W.W. Norton, 1979.

———. *The Minimal Self—Psychic Survival in Troubled Times*. New York: W.W. Norton, 1984.

Lehman, Stephen. "Intimations of Apocalypse." *Elysian Fields Quarterly* 18, no. 4 (Winter 1999): 2–5.

Lerner, Michael. *Surplus Powerlessness*. Oakland, CA: Institute for Labor & Mental Health, 1986.

Levin, Murray B. *Talk Radio and the American Dream*. Lexington, MA: D.C. Heath, 1987.

Levine, Peter. *A.G. Spalding and the Rise of Baseball*. New York: Oxford University Press, 1985.

Levine, Peter. *Ellis Island to Ebbets Field: Sport and the American Jewish Experience*. New York: Oxford University Press, 1992.

Levy, Frank. *The New Dollars and Dreams: American Incomes and Economic Change*. New York: Russell Sage Foundation, 1998.

Lind, Michael. *Up From Conservatism*. New York: Simon & Schuster, 1996.

Long, Elizabeth. *The American Dream and the Popular Novel*. Boston: Routledge & Kegan Paul, 1985.

Long, Patrick Du Phuoc with Laura Richard. *The Dream Shattered: Vietnamese Gangs in America*. Boston: Northeastern University Press, 1996.

Lord, Timothy C. "Hegel, Marx, and Shoeless Joe: Religious Ideology in Kinsella's Baseball Fantasy." *Aethlon* 10, no. 1 (1992): 46.

Lucas, John. "Sport—Mirror and Molder of American Society." In *Sport and the Humanities*, ed. William J. Morgan. Knoxville, TN: Bureau of Educational Research and Service, 1979.

Lupica, Mike. *Mad as Hell: How Sports Got Away from the Fans*. New York: G.P. Putnam's, 1996.

MacLeod, Celeste. *Horatio Alger, Farewell: The End of the American Dream*. New York: Seaview Books, 1980.

MacLeod, Jay. *Ain't No Makin' It*. Boulder, CO: Westview Press, 1987.

Mantle, Mickey with Phil Pepe. *My Favorite Summer, 1956*. New York: Doubleday, 1991.

Massey, Douglas, and Nancy Denton. *American Apartheid: Segregation and the Making of the Underclass*. Cambridge, MA: Harvard University Press, 1993.

Mayer, Andre. "Pirates of Pennants." *Boston Observer* (Spring 1986), 24–25.

Mayer, Margaret M. *The American Dream: American Popular Music*. Santa Barbara: University of California Press, 1994.

McGowen, Roscoe. "Branca, Boy Behemoth of the Brooks." *Baseball Magazine* (October 1947), 365–67.

Mander, Jerry. *In the Absence of the Sacred*. San Francisco: Sierra Club Books, 1991.

Marshall, William. *Baseball's Pivotal Era, 1945–1951*. Lexington: University Press of Kentucky, 1999.

Mate, Frederic. *A Reasonable Life*. New York: Albatross, 1993.

Mears, Elliot G. *Resident Orientals on the Pacific Coast*. Chicago: University of Chicago Press, 1928.

Meehan, Tom. "Ken Zenimura, Dean of Nisei Baseball in U.S., Recalls Colorful Past." *Fresno Bee* (May 20, 1962), 8.

Merelman, Richard M. *Making Something of Ourselves*. Berkeley: University of California Press, 1984.

Messner, Michael A. "Boyhood, Organized Sports, and the Construction of Masculinities." *Journal of Contemporary Ethnography* 4 (1990): 416–444.

Messner, Michael A., and Donald Sabo. *Sex, Violence & Power in Sports: Rethinking Masculinity*. Freedom, CA: The Crossing Press, 1994.

Messner, Steven F., and Richard Rosenfeld. *Crime and the American Dream*. Belmont, CA: Wadsworth, 1994.

Metheny, Elizabeth. 1965. "Symbolic Forms of Movement: The Feminine Image in

Sports." In *Connotations of Movement in Sport and Dance*, ed. Elizabeth Metheny. Dubuque, IA: William Brown, 43–56.

Miller, Frances Trevelyan. "Introduction." *Connie Mack, My 66 Years in Baseball*. New York: Winston, 1950.

Mills, Nicholas, ed. *Culture in an Age of Money*. Chicago: Elephant Paperbacks/Ivan R. Dee, 1990.

Misawa, Steven, ed. *Beginnings: Japanese Americans in San Jose*. San Jose: Japanese American Community Senior Services, 1981.

Mishel, Lawrence, Jared Bernstein, and John Schmitt. *The State of Working America 1998–1999*. Ithaca, NY: Cornell University Press, 1998.

Moffi, Larry, and Jonathan Kronstadt. *Crossing the Line: Black Major Leaguers, 1947–1959*. Iowa City: University of Iowa Press, 1994.

Mokhiber, Russell, and Robert Weissman. *Corporate Predators: The Hunt for Mega-Profits and the Attack on Democracy*. Monroe, ME: Common Courage Press, 1999.

Moore, Michael. *Downsize This! Random Threats from an Unarmed American*. New York: Random House, 1996.

Morrison, Roy. *Ecological Democracy*. Boston: South End Press, 1995.

Myrdal, Gunnar, Richard Sterner, and Arnold Rose. *An American Dilemma: The Negro Problem and Modern Democracy*. New York: Harper & Row, 1944.

Nackenoff, Carol. *The Fictional Republic: Horatio Alger and American Political Discourse*. New York: Oxford University Press, 1994.

Nader, Ralph. "Sports Reform Project: Fight to Advance the Nation's Sports (FANS)" (unpublished paper, 1998).

Nauen, Elinor ed. *Diamonds Are a Girl's Best Friend: Women Writer's on Baseball*. Boston: Faber, 1994.

Nelson, Eugene. *Pablo Cruz and the American Dream: The Experiences of an Undocumented Immigrant from Mexico*. Salt Lake City, UT: Peregrine Smith, 1975.

Newman, Katherine S. *Declining Fortunes*. New York: Basic Books, 1993.

———. *Falling from Grace*. New York: Free Press, 1988.

Noms, Frank. "San Diego Baseball: The Early Years." *Journal of San Diego History* 30 (Winter 1984): 5–15.

Noonkester, Barbara. "The American Sportswoman, 1900–1920." In *Her Story in Sport*, ed. Reet Howell. West Point, NY: Leisure Park, 1984), 186–194.

Novak, Michael. *The Joy of Sports*. Lanham, MD: Madison Books, 1994.

Oates, Bob. "Thomson's Homer Just a Single in L.A." *Baseball Digest* 18, no. 10 (October 1959): 59–61.

Oliver, Melvin, and Thomas Shapiro. *Black Wealth/White Wealth*. New York: Routledge, 1995.

Olney, Buster. "Baseball: Ten Reasons Why It's America's Pastime Again." *Athlon Sports: Baseball* (1999), 19.

Ownby, Ted. *American Dreams in Mississippi: Consumers, Poverty and Culture*. Chapel Hill: University of North Carolina Press, 1999.

Parenti, Michael. *Democracy for the Few*. New York: St. Martin's Press, 1995.

Patterson, Orlando. *The Ordeal of Integration*. Washington, DC: Civitas/Counterpoint, 1997.

Peale, Norman Vincent. *The Power of Positive Thinking*. New York: Prentice Hall, 1987.

Perrett, Geoffrey. *A Dream of Greatness: The American People, 1945–1963*. New York: Coward, McCann & Geoghegan, 1979.

Peterson, Harold. *The Man Who Invented Baseball*. New York: Charles Scribner's & Sons, 1963.

Peterson, Robert. *Only the Ball Was White*. Englewood Cliffs, NJ: Prentice Hall, 1970.

Peterson, Wallace D. *Silent Depression: The Fate of the American Dream*. New York: W.W. Norton, 1995.

Pierman, Carol J. "Cal Ripken and the Condition of Freedom: Theme and Variation on the American Work Ethic." *Nine: A Journal of Baseball History and Social Policy* 7, no. 1 (Fall 1998): 118–129.

Pinelli, Babe, with Joe King. *Mr. Ump*. Philadelphia: Westminster Press, 1953.

Pinelli, Ralph. "I Call Things as I See Them." In *This I Believe*, ed. Edward R. Murrow. New York: Simon & Schuster, 1952, 137–38.

Piven, Frances Fox, and Richard Cloward. *The Breakdown of the American Social Compact*. New York: New Press, 1997.

Postema, Pam with Gene Wojciechowski. *You've Got to Have Balls to Make It in This League*. New York: Simon & Schuster, 1992.

"Poverty in the United States: 1990." *Current Population Reports, Population Characteristics*, Series p-20, no. 450. Washington, DC: Bureau of the Census, 1991.

Powell, Cecil. "Of Willie Mays, Joe McCarthy, and Bobby Thomson." *Massachusetts Review* 32, no. 1 (Spring 1991): 106.

Prince, Carl. *Brooklyn's Dodgers: The Bums, the Borough and the Best of Baseball*. New York: Oxford University Press, 1996.

Rader, Benjamin G. *American Sports: From the Age of Folk Games to the Age of Spectators*. Englewood Cliffs, NJ: Prentice Hall, 1983.

Rader, Benjamin. *Baseball: A History of America's Game*. Urbana: University of Illinois Press, 1992.

Rampersad, Arnold. *Jackie Robinson: A Biography*. New York: Alfred A. Knopf, 1997.

Rees, Andrew. *The Pocket Green Book: The Environmental Crisis in a Nutshell*. London: Zed Books, 1991.

Regalado, Samuel O. *Viva Baseball: Latin Major Leaguers and Their Special Hunger*. Urbana: University of Illinois Press, 1998.

Reich, Charles A. *Opposing the System*. New York: Crown, 1995.

Reiman, Jeffrey. *The Rich Get Richer and the Poor Get Prison*. Boston: Allyn & Bacon, 1998.

Reporters of the New York Times. *The Downsizing of America*. New York: Times Books, 1996.

Rice, Damon. *Seasons Past*. New York : Praeger, 1976.

Rice, Grantland. "Is Baseball Afraid of Television?" *Sport* 4, no. 4 (April 1951): 12–13.

Richmond, Peter. "Joe Morgan's Cool Anger." *Gentleman's Quarterly* (October 1988), 105–111.

Rickey, Branch, and Robert Riger. *The American Diamond: A Documentary of the Game of Baseball*. New York: Simon & Schuster, 1965.

Riess, Stephen. *Touching Base: Professional Baseball in the Progressive Era*. Westport, CT: Greenwood, 1980.

Ritzer, George. *The McDonaldization of Society*. Thousand Oaks, CA: Pine Forge Press, 1993.

Rivlin, Alice M. *Reviving the American Dream*. Washington, DC: Brookings Institution, 1992.

Robertson, James Oliver. *American Myth, American Reality*. New York: Hill & Wang, 1980.

Robinson, Frank, and Berry Stainback. "Fighting the Baseball Blackout." *Sport* 79 (July 1988), 66–69.

Robinson, Jackie. *I Never Had It Made*. New York: G.P. Putnam, 1972.

Robinson, Rachel. *Jackie Robinson: An Intimate Portrait*. New York: Harry N. Abrams, 1996.

Robinson, Ray. *Home Run Heard 'Round the World*. New York: HarperCollins, 1991.

Robinson, Sharon. *Stealing Home: An Intimate Family Portrait by the Daughter of Jackie Robinson*. New York: HarperCollins, 1996.

Rodriquez, Angel. "Foul Play: Despite the Growing Number of Latino Players, Baseball Lacks Latino Managers and Executives." *Hispanic* (April 1999), 33–36.

Rogosin, Donn. *Invisible Men: Life in Baseball's Negro Leagues*. New York: Atheneum, 1983.

Ropers, Richard H. *Persistent Poverty: The American Dream Turned Nightmare*. New York: Plenum Press, 1991.

Rosenblatt, Aaron. "Negroes in Baseball: The Failure of Success." *Transaction* 3 (September 1967): 58–62.

Rosenfeld, Harvey. *The Great Chase: The Dodgers-Giants Pennant Race of 1951*. Jefferson, NC: McFarland, 1992.

Rosentraub, Mark S. *Major League Losers: The Real Cost of Sports and Who's Paying for It*. New York: Basic Books, 1997.

Ross, Murray. "Football Red and Baseball Green." *Chicago Review* 22, no. 2 (1971): 30–40.

Rounds, Kate. "Where Is Our Field of Dreams?" *Ms. Magazine* (September/October 1991), 44–45.

Rubin, Lillian B. *Families on the Fault Line: America's Working Class Speaks About the Family, the Economy, Race, and Ethnicity*. New York: HarperCollins, 1994.

Rudd, Irvin, and Stan Fischler. *The Sporting Life*. New York: St. Martin's Press, 1990.

Ruggiero, Greg, and Stuart Sahulka, eds. *The New American Crisis*. New York: New Press, 1995.

Ruhl, Oscar. "From the Ruhl Book: No Gal Players? Barrow Used One in '98." *The Sporting News* (July 9, 1952), 18.

Ryan, Joan. "Setting A Shining Example." *San Francisco Chronicle* (September 18, 1998), F1.

Sailer, Steve. "How Jackie Robinson Desegregated America," *The National Review* (April 8, 1996), 42–44.

Samuelson, Robert J. *The Good Life and Its Discontents: The American Dream in the Age of Entitlement, 1945–1995*. New York: Times Books, 1995.

Santoli, Michael. "King of Sports," *Barron's* (September 21, 1998), 31–35.

Schimmel, Kim, Alan Ingham, and Jeremy Howell, "Professional Team Sport and the American City: Urban Politics and Franchise Relocations." In *Sport in Social Development: Traditions, Transitions and Transformations*, eds. Alan Ingham and John W. Loy. Champaign, IL: Human Kinetics, 1993.

Schor, Juliet B. *The Overworked American: The Unexpected Decline of Leisure*. New York: Basic Books, 1991.

Schrag, Peter. *Paradise Lost: California's Experience, America's Future*. Berkeley: University of California Press, 1999.

Schwartz, Martin D., and Walter S. DeKeseredy. *Sexual Assault on the College Campus: The Role of Male Peer Support*. Thousand Oaks, CA: Sage, 1997.

Schwarz, John E. *Illusions of Opportunity: The American Dream in Question*. New York: W.W. Norton, 1997.

Schwarz, John E., and Thomas J. Volgy. *The Forgotten Americans.* New York: W.W. Norton, 1992.

Sennett, Richard. T*he Corrosion of Character: The Personal Consequences of Work in the New Capitalism.* New York: Norton, 1998.

Senzel, Howard. *Baseball and the Cold War.* New York: Harcourt Brace, 1977.

Sesquicentennial Historical Committee. *Ragersville, Auburn Township, Ohio, 1830–1980: The Sesquicentennial Story of a Community.* Berlin, OH: Berlin Printing, 1980, 193.

Seymour, Harold. "Baseball: Badge of Americanism." In *Cooperstown Symposium on Baseball and the American Culture,* ed. Alvin L. Hall. Westport, CT: Meckler, 1990, 1–22.

———. *Baseball: The Early Years.* New York: Oxford University Press, 1989.

———. *The People's Game.* New York: Oxford University Press, 1990.

Shattuck, Debra. "Eighty Years Ago in Vermilion: A 'Skirt' on the Mound Stuns Baseball Fans." *Vermilion Photojournal* (August 31, 1987), Sec. C, 5–8.

Sheed, Wilfred. *Baseball and Lesser Sports.* New York: HarperCollins, 1991.

Sidel, Ruth. *Women and Children Last.* New York: Penguin, 1986.

———. *On Her Own: Growing Up in the Shadow of the American Dream.* New York: Viking/Penguin, 1990.

Sitkoff, Harvard. *The Struggle for Black Equality: 1954–1992,* rev. ed. New York: Hill & Wang, 1993.

Sklar, Holly. *Chaos or Community?* Boston: South End Press, 1995.

Sklar, Holly, Chuck Collins, and Betsy Leondar-Wright. *Shifting Fortunes: The Perils of the Growing American Wealth Gap.* Boston: United for A Fair Economy, 1999.

Skolnick, Jerome H., and Elliott Currie. *Crisis in American Institutions.* Boston: Little, Brown, 1982.

Slater, Philip. *A Dream Deferred: America's Discontent and the Search for a New Democratic Ideal.* Boston: Beacon Press, 1991.

———. *The Pursuit of Loneliness: American Culture at the Breaking Point.* Boston: Beacon Press, 1970.

Smith, Curt. *Voices of the Game.* South Bend, IN: Diamond Communications, 1987.

Smith, Jr., Leverett T. *The American Dream and the National Game.* Bowling Green, OH: Bowling Green University Popular Press, 1975.

Smith, Red. "What It's Like on Color TV." *Baseball Digest* 10, no. 10 (October 1951): 23–25.

Smith, Ron A. "The Paul Robeson-Jackie Robinson Saga and a Political Collision." *Journal of Sport History* 6, no. 2 (Summer 1979): 27–35.

Schmookler, Aaron Bard. *The Illusion of Choice.* Albany: State University of New York Press, 1993.

Snider, Duke with Roger Kahn, "I Play Baseball for Money—Not Fun." *Collier's* (May 25, 1956), 44–46.

Sobran, Joseph. "The Republic of Baseball." *National Review* 42 (June 11, 1990): 36–39.

Spalding, Albert G. *America's National Pastime.* Lincoln: University of Nebraska Press, 1992.

Spalding, John E. *Always on Sunday: The California Baseball League, 1886–1915.* Manhattan, KS: Ag Press, 1992.

Spence, Gerry. *From Freedom to Slavery.* New York: St. Martin's Press, 1995.

———. *Give Me Liberty!* New York: St. Martin's Press, 1998.

————. *With Justice for None*. New York: Penguin, 1989.

Springwood, Charles Fruehling. *Cooperstown to Dyersville: A Geography of Baseball Nostalgia*. Boulder, CO: Westview, 1996.

Starr, Kevin. *Americans and the California Dream*. New York, Oxford University Press, 1973.

————. *Inventing the Dream*. New York: Oxford University Press, 1985.

————. *Material Dreams*. New York: Oxford University Press, 1990.

————. *Endangered Dream*. New York: Oxford University Press, 1996.

————. *The Dream Endures*. New York: Oxford University Press, 1997.

Suro, Robert. *Remembering the American Dream: Hispanic Immigration and National Policy*. New York: Twentieth Century Fund Press, 1994.

Szockyj, Elizabeth, and James G. Fox. *Corporate Victimization of Women*. Boston: Northeastern University Press, 1996.

Taylor, Betsy. "Enough." Tacoma Park, MD: Center for A New American Dream, 1998.

Taylor, Blaine. *The Success Ethic and the Shattered American Dream*. Washington, DC: Acropolis Books, 1976.

Terkel, Studs. *American Dreams: Lost and Found*. New York: Ballantine Books, 1980.

————. *The Great Divide: Second Thoughts on the American Dream*. New York: Pantheon Books, 1988.

Theberge, N. "A Critique of Critiques: Radical and Feminist Writings on Sport." *Social Forces* 60 (1981): 2.

Thernstrom, Stephan, and Abigail Thernstrom. *American in Black and White: One Nation, Indivisible*. New York: Simon & Schuster, 1997.

Thompson, Hunter S. *Songs of the Doomed: More Notes on the Death of the American Dream*. New York: Summit Books, 1990.

Thompson, William Irwin. *The American Replacement of Nature*. New York: Doubleday, 1991.

Thomson, Bobby, with Lee Heiman and Bill Gutman. *The Giants Win the Pennant, The Giants Win the Pennant*. New York: Zebra Books, 1991.

Thorn, John. *A Century of Baseball Lore*. New York: Hart, 1974, 18.

————. "Our Game." In *Total Baseball*, eds. John Thorn, Pete Palmer, Michael Gershman, and David Pietrusza. New York: Viking/Penguin, 1997.

————. "Why Baseball?" In *Baseball: An Illustrated History*, eds. Geoffrey C. Ward and Ken Burns. New York: Alfred Knopf, 1994.

Tilden, Douglas. "Art and What California Should Do About Her." *Overland Monthly* 5. no. 4 (May 1892): 509–515.

Tygiel, Jules. *Baseball's Great Experiment: Jackie Robinson and His Legacy*. New York: Oxford University Press, 1983.

————, ed. *The Jackie Robinson Reader*. New York: Dutton, 1997.

————. "The National Game." *Nine: A Journal of Baseball History and Social Policy*, 7, no. 2 (Spring 1999): 2–13.

Umphlett, Wiley Lee, ed. *American Sport Culture*. Lewisburg, PA: Bucknell University Press, 1990.

————. *Mythmakers of the American Dream: The Nostalgic Vision in Popular Culture*. Lewisburg, PA: Bucknell University Press, 1983.

Usbome, David, "American Times: Female Pitcher Strikes Out in a Man's World." *London Independent* (September 9, 1998), 13.

Veeck, Jr., William. "Don't Let TV Kill Baseball." *Sport* 6, no. 6 (June 1953): 10–14.

Verhoeven, W.M., ed. *Rewriting the Dream: Reflections on the Changing American Literary Canon.* Amsterdam: Rodopi, 1992.

Voigt, David Quentin. *America Through Baseball.* Chicago: Nelson Hall, 1976.

Wachtel, Paul L. *The Poverty of Affluence: A Psychological Portrait of the American Way of Life.* Philadelphia: New Society Publishers, 1989.

Walden, Daniel. "Where Have All Our Heroes Gone?" *USA Today* (January 1986), 20–25.

Wallace, Mike. *Mickey Mouse History, and Other Essays on American Memory.* Philadelphia: Temple University Press, 1996.

Wallis, Jim. *The Soul of Politics.* New York: New Press, 1994.

Ward, Geoffrey C., and Ken Burns, *Baseball: An Illustrated History.* New York: Alfred Knopf, 1994.

Weaver, Bill. "The Black Press and the Assault on Professional Baseball's Color Line, October 1945–April 1947." *Phylon* 5 (Winter 1979): 17–22.

Weiskopf, Don. *Baseball Play America.* El Dorado Hills, CA: Play America Press, 1999.

Weiss, Richard. *The American Myth of Success: From Horatio Alger to Norman Vincent Peale.* New York: Basic Books, 1969.

"When Father Locates Earl the Bloomer Girls Will Need Another Player." *Nashville Banner* (September 9, 1910).

White, G. Edward. *Creating the National Pastime: Baseball Transforms Itself, 1903–1953.* Princeton, NJ: Princeton University Press, 1996.

Whitson, David, and Donald Macintosh. "The Global Circus: International Sport, Tourism, and the Marketing of Cities." *Journal of Sport & Social Issues* 20, no. 3 (August 1996): 278–295.

Williams, Pete "Face Facts: Cashing in the American Way." *USA Today Baseball Weekly* (December 3–9, 1997), 5.

Winter, Robert. *Land of Opportunity: What's Really Happened to the American Dream.* Monrovia, CA: River Rock Press, 1994.

Wolff, Edwin N. *Top Heavy: A Study of the Increasing Inequality of Wealth in America.* New York: Twentieth Century Fund, 1995.

"World Series Stare." *Look* (October 1951), 29.

Wright, Esmond. *The American Dream: From Reconstruction to Reagan.* Cambridge, MA: Blackwell, 1996.

Wyllie, Irvin G. *The Self-Made Man in America.* New York: Free Press, 1954.

Zimbalist, Andrew. *Baseball and Billions.* New York: Basic Books, 1992.

Zingg, Paul J. *Harry Hooper: A Baseball Life.* Urbana: University of Illinois Press, 1993.

———. "The Phoenix at Fenway: The 1995 World Series and Collegiate Connections to the Major League." *Journal of Sport History* 17 (Spring 1990): 35–56.

Zingg, Paul J., and Mark D. Medeiros. *Runs, Hits and an Era: The Pacific Coast League, 1903–58.* Urbana: University of Illinois Press, 1994.

Zion, Sidney. "What About the Fans? Fuhgeddaboudit." *The Nation* (August 10–17, 1998), 31–35.

Zorn, Eric. "The Girls of Summer." *Chicago Tribune* (December 12, 1982).

About the Contributors

Dusty Baker was born in Riverside, California, and went to school in Carmichael and Sacramento, where he was a star in baseball, basketball, football, and track. He began playing professional baseball in 1967, and was a major league star for sixteen years, playing for the Braves, Dodgers, Giants, and Athletics. Baker was twice on the National League All-Star team, and appeared in four league championship series and three World Series. He was the National League Championship Series Most Valuable Player in 1977. He won a Gold Glove in 1981, was twice named to the Silver Slugger team, and was voted to the All-Time Dodger team in 1990. Baker is in both the Sacramento Sports Hall of Fame and the California Black Sports Hall of Fame. He has co-written the book *You Can Teach Hitting*, has produced videotapes on the art of hitting, and has conducted numerous baseball clinics. He's won the Sports Image Award and the Babe Ruth Baseball League Positive Image Award. After coaching for San Francisco for five years, Baker was named manager of the Giants in 1993. He was named Manager of the Year that year and again in 1997 and 2000.

Gai Ingham Berlage is a professor of sociology and chair of the Sociology Department at Iona College in New Rochelle, New York. She is the author of *Women in Baseball: The Forgotten History* and coauthor of *Understanding Social Issues: Critical Thinking and Analysis*. She has written numerous articles on women in sports, and is currently writing a book on the history of women's basketball, *Women's Hoops: From the Industrial Leagues to the WNBA*. Berlage is listed in *Who's Who in America* and in *Who's Who of American Women*.

Darryl Brock, a former teacher, is now a Berkeley, California, writer and historian, and an expert on nineteenth-century baseball and America. He's the author of the acclaimed book, *If I Never Get Back*, a novel about the 1869 Cincinnati Red Stockings and the inception of professional baseball. His most recent book, *Havana Heat*, is a historical novel about the pitcher Luther "Dummy" Taylor and his barnstorming adventures in Cuba with John McGraw and the New York Giants. Brock's articles on early baseball have appeared in numerous publications including *Sports Illustrated*.

Orlando Cepeda was born in Ponce, Puerto Rico, the son of Perucho Cepeda, a legendary Puerto Rican baseball player. Cepeda began playing in the major leagues in 1958, when he won the Rookie of the Year Award. He was a star for seventeen years, with the Giants, Cardinals, Braves, Athletics, Red Sox, and Royals. In 1966, he was the Comeback Player of the Year, in 1967 he won the Most Valuable Player Award, and in 1973 he won the Designated Hitter of the Year Award. He appeared in three World Series and was an eleven-time All-Star. Cepeda was elected to the Puerto Rican Sports Hall of Fame, was named an "Immortal of the Sport" by the Spanish language television network Univision, was selected by *Latinos in the Major Leagues* magazine as an all-time legendary player, and in 1999, was elected to the Baseball Hall of Fame in Cooperstown. Cepeda now works as a community representative for the San Francisco Giants.

Andrei Codrescu was born in Romania, has lived in the United States since 1966, and has been a citizen since 1981. He is a poet and teaches English at Louisiana State University in Baton Rouge, and lives in New Orleans. He has been an essayist and commentator for National Public Radio since 1983. Codrescu is the author of more than two dozen books. They include four poetry collections, three anthologies, two novels, and numerous essay collections such as *Zombification, The Disappearance of the Outside,* and *Raised By Puppets Only to Be Killed by Research.* His latest books are the novel, *Messiah,* and the nonfiction books, *Ay Cuba!* and *Hail Babylon.* He created and starred in the acclaimed documentary video, *Road Scholar,* and has authored five audiotape books, including *Fax Your Prayers, No Tacos for Saddam,* and *Plato Sucks.* Codrescu has appeared on *Nightline,* the *Tonight Show, David Letterman, Charlie Rose,* and numerous other media programs. He's won many awards, including the Peabody and the ACLU Freedom of Speech awards.

Peter Dreier is the E.P. Clapp Distinguished Professor of Politics and director of the Public Policy Program at Occidental College in Los Angeles. He received his B.A. from Syracuse University and his Ph.D. from the University of Chicago. He previously taught at Tufts University, and was director of housing at the Boston Redevelopment Authority and senior policy adviser to Boston's mayor, Ray Flynn. A leading national expert on housing policy, he drafted the Community Housing Partnership Act, now administered by the U.S. Department of Housing & Urban Development (HUD). He has written for dozens of magazines, newspapers, and scholarly journals. In addition to his previous books, his forthcoming books include, *Housing and the Devolution Revolution, Growing Together: Linking Regional and Community Development in a Changing Economy,* and *Place Matters: Rethinking Urban Policy.* Although a lifelong Democrat, Dreier allowed his parents to take him to a Richard Nixon rally in his New Jersey hometown in 1960 for the sole purpose of meeting Jackie Robinson. Dreier's interest in black ballplayers was also inspired by Joe Black, the former Dodgers pitcher who was his gym teacher and baseball coach in high school. Dreier treasures his autographed photo of his favorite New York Giants pitcher, circa 1954, which reads, "To Peter Dreier, a Future Major Leaguer, Your Friend, Johnny Antonelli." Dreier remains a Giants fan but regrets that Antonelli was a better pitcher than prophet.

William Edwards is a professor of sociology, faculty athletics representative, and former chair of the Sociology Department at the University of San Francisco. He also teaches in the Ethnic Studies and Legal Studies programs at USF. Edwards sits on the National Collegiate Athletic Association (NCAA) Strategic Planning Cabinet as a representative of the West Coast Conference. As a collegian, he ran track at Virginia Union University. His research interests have included Marcus Garvey and black nationalism, and more recently, globalization and the rise of world cities and informal labor markets. Edwards has been a long abiding fan of the Cleveland Indians.

Robert Elias is a professor of politics, chair of the Politics Department, and coordinator of the Legal Studies program at the University of San Francisco. He grew up in New York, was an outfielder for his high school's Suffolk County champion team, played baseball in college, and was invited to baseball tryouts by the Giants, Braves, and Orioles. He was educated at the University of Pennsylvania, the University of Strasbourg, and Penn State University. He's taught previously at Tufts University, the University of Maryland, Penn State, and the University of California, Berkeley. He's been a researcher at the Vera Institute of Justice, the Institute for Defense and Disarmament Studies, Oxfam-America, the International Institute of Human Rights, and the Geneva Institute of International Studies. Elias has published numerous articles, and his baseball essays have appeared in *Nine: A Journal of Baseball History & Social Policy Perspectives*, the *Minneapolis Review of Baseball*, the *Exquisite Corpse*, the *Berkeley Voice*, and the *Christian Science Monitor*. His books include *Victims Still*, *Victims of the System*, *The Politics of Victimization*, *The Peace Resource Book*, and *Rethinking Peace*. He has been the editor of *Peace Review* for ten years and recently co-edited a special issue of the journal on sports and globalization. He was a member of the Baseball for Peace tour of Nicaragua in 1987. In 1995, he won University of San Francisco's Distinguished Research Award. In 1998, Elias was the Davies Professor at the University of San Francisco, for which he ran a course and forum on "The National Pastime and the American Dream." He's now completing research on Curt Flood and on baseball and the Cold War.

Joel Franks is a native Californian, and teaches Asian American studies, Ethnic Studies and American Studies at San Jose State University, in addition to other Bay Area colleges and universities, including California State University, Hayward, Santa Clara University, De Anza College, and the University of California, Santa Cruz. He has published articles on baseball and other sports for publications such as *The Californians*, *California History*, *Southern California Quarterly*, *Chinese American History and Perspectives*, *Baseball History*, *Baseball Research Journal*, and *Nine: A Review of Baseball & Social Policy Perspectives*. His latest book is *California Baseball*, and he is working on another book on Asian Pacific Americans and sports.

Jeremy Howell received his Ph.D. from the University of Illinois, then spent two years as a Visiting Professor at University of California, Berkeley, before moving into the health and fitness industry for six years. Since 1997, he has been a professor in the graduate program in Sports and Fitness Management at the University of San Francisco, where he teaches contemporary culture and the promotion and consumption of sport and fitness practices and events. He remains involved in community projects, acting as an adviser on fitness strategies for the Western Athletic Clubs and for Netpulse Inc. He is also on the board of directors of Senior Assisted Living Inc. and is an adviser to San Francisco's RCH Inc. He has written widely on cultural topics, including stadium development, the new urbanism, healthcare, and the politics of lifestyle. His work has appeared in publications such as *Cultural Studies*, *Exercise and Sport Science Review*, *Sociology of Sport Journal*, and *Nurse Practitioner Forum*, as well as in edited books. He recently coedited a special issue of *Peace Review* on sports and globalization.

Roger Kahn was born and raised in Brooklyn, and now lives in the Hudson Valley, New York. He has been a sportswriter for the *New York Herald Tribune*, a sports editor at *Newsweek*, and a columnist and staff member at *Time*, *Esquire*, the *New York Times*, the *Saturday Evening Post*, and *Sports Illustrated*. He is the five-time winner of the E.P. Dutton Award for the best sports magazine article of the year. Kahn has written, edited, or collaborated on at least seventeen books, mostly, but not all, on baseball. His latest book is on the boxer, Jack Dempsey, and his many baseball books include *A Season in the Sun*, *The Era*, *Memories of Summer*, *The Seventh Game* (a baseball novel), and *My Story* (an autobiography of Pete Rose). For his book, *Good Enough to Dream*, about his year as an owner and president of the Class A Utica Blue Sox minor league team, Kahn won the 1985 Casey Award for the best baseball book of the year. His most recent baseball book is *The Head Game: Baseball Seen from the Pitcher's Mound*. He's probably best known for his best-selling book, *Boys of Summer*, about the 1950s Brooklyn Dodgers.

Leonard Koppett is one of the nation's most accomplished sportswriters. He was born in Moscow, shortly before the death of Lenin. At the age of five, he arrived in New York, attended high school in Brooklyn, and went to Columbia University. His earliest memories include seeing Babe Ruth hit and John McGraw manage. He's been writing about baseball since the 1940s, covering the Yankees, Dodgers, and Giants in New York through the 1950s, and then the Mets and Yankees through the 1970s, for the *New York Herald Tribune*, the *New York Post*, and most notably for the *New York Times* and the *Sporting News*. Koppett was the sports editor, then general editor, and now editor emeritus of the *Peninsula Times Tribune* in Palo Alto, where he's lived since the early 1970s, and remains a sportswriter and columnist for the *Oakland Tribune*. He has also taught at Stanford University and San Jose State University. He has written fifteen books, mostly about baseball, including *The New York Mets*, *All About Baseball*, *The New Thinking Fan's Guide to Baseball*, *The Man In the Dugout*, and his latest book, *Koppett's Concise History of Major League Baseball*. He is a member of the Veteran's Committee of the Baseball Hall of Fame. Koppett was awarded the J.G. Taylor Spink Award from the Baseball Writer's Association of America, and is the only sportswriter named to the writer's wing of both the baseball and the basketball Halls of Fame.

George McGlynn received his bachelor's and master's degrees from Syracuse University, and his Ph.D. in exercise physiology at the University of California at Berkeley. He's an emeritus professor at the University of San Francisco, and a former professor and chair of USF's Exercise and Sport Science Department. He's taught at the university level for forty years, and received USF's Distinguished Teaching Award. McGlynn is the author of more than fifty articles and eight textbooks, including *Cross-Training for Sports*; *Dynamics of Fitness: A Practical Approach*; *Dynamics of Strength Training and Conditioning*; and *Issues in Physical Education and Sport*. He's a member of the American College Sports Medicine Association, and he helped establish the Bay Area's first cardiac rehabilitation program. He was an infantry officer in the U.S. Marine Corps, and was stationed in the Far East. He's been a fitness consultant to college and professional teams, and for state and federal governments. McGlynn is also a professional artist, and has presented his work at three one-man shows. He was inducted into the New York State Athletic Hall of Fame in 1987. McGlynn was a former professional baseball player, who signed with the St. Louis Cardinals, and played for minor league teams in Rochester, NY, Decatur, IL, and Allentown, PA, in the United States and in Hamilton, Ontario, Canada.

Kerry Yo Nakagawa is the director of the Nisei Baseball History Project in Fresno, California. The project is dedicated to recognizing the sacrifices and pioneering efforts of the Issei and Nisei, and to preserve their baseball legacy for future generations. Nakagawa is a co-curator of the "Diamonds in the Rough" exhibit, on the history of Japanese American baseball, coproduced with the Japanese American Historical Society. This exhibit has been showing at museums around the nation, including the Cooperstown National Baseball Hall of Fame, where a permanent exhibit has been proposed. Nakagawa is also an actor, writer, historian, filmmaker, producer, and baseball player. His uncles, Johnny Nakagawa—the Japanese American "Babe Ruth"—Lefty Nishijima, and Mas Yano competed with baseball Hall of Famers Lou Gehrig, Babe Ruth, Jackie Robinson, Tony Lazzeri, and Lefty O'Doul, and they made goodwill baseball tours to Japan in 1924, 1927, and 1937.

John J. Pinelli grew up in San Francisco and is the grandson of the former major league player and umpire, Babe Pinelli. Aside from playing baseball, he was a figure skater and then a speed skater with the San Francisco Striders. He graduated from Archbishop Riordan College Prep High School, and then received a B.A. and an M.A. in biology from the University of San Francisco, with a specialization in lichenology. While he remains a biologist, he also began an administrative position in the College of Arts and Sciences at USF in 1977, and is now the executive director of Business Affairs. He follows professional baseball, football, and ice skating, raises golden retrievers, and is an active hiker, swimmer, and photographer.

Suzanne Griffith Prestien is completing her Ph.D. in American Studies at Case Western Reserve University in Cleveland, Ohio. She received her B.A. and M.A. degrees in English from Kent State University and the University of Toledo, respectively. After teaching English part time for several years, she is now a full-time instructor at Westminster College in New Wilmington, Pennsylvania, where she teaches public relations and English. She has presented various conference papers, most notably at the annual Colloquium on Literature and Film at West Virginia University and at the Seymour Medal Conference, sponsored by the Society for American Baseball Research, of which she is a member. Suzanne, her husband Mark, and daughter Emma, are diehard Cleveland Indians fans.

Samuel O. Regalado is a historian at California State University at Stanislaus, where he teaches U.S. history, sport and American society, ethnic and immigrant history, and Latin American and East Asian history. He was a Smithsonian Institution Faculty Fellow in 1994. His research on Latinos in baseball appears in the book, *Jackie Robinson: Race, Sports and the American Dream*. He's also the author of *Viva Baseball: Latin Major Leaguers and Their Special Hunger*. Regalado has also done research on Japanese-American baseball during the Nisei period, and he serves as a consultant to the Japanese American Historical Society's traveling exhibit, "Diamonds in the Rough." His uncle, Rudy Regalado, played in the major leagues with the Cleveland Indians from 1954–1956.

Anne R. Roschelle is a professor of sociology at the State University of New York College at New Paltz, and a former professor and director of Women's Studies at the University of San Francisco. She is the author of *No More Kin: Exploring Race, Class, and Gender in Family Networks*, which received *Choice* magazine's 1997 Outstanding Academic Book Award. She has been a research associate at the Center for Critical Global Homeless Studies at San Francisco State University, and is on the editorial board of *Race, Gender, & Class*. She's now finishing a book about homeless families in San Francisco.

Joan Ryan is an award-winning writer and journalist. She was a sports columnist for thirteen years with the *Orlando Sentinel*, the *San Francisco Examiner*, and the *San Francisco Chronicle*. She now writes a general column and features for the *Chronicle*, sometimes writing again about baseball. She has been awarded eleven Associated Press Editors Awards, the San Francisco Chapter of the National Organization of Women's Fabulous Feminist Award, the Women's Sports Foundation Award for Journalism, and the National Headliner Award. She was also named one of the San Francisco League of Women Voters' "Women Who Could Be President." Ryan is coauthor, with Stanford University basketball coach Tara VanDerveer, of the book, *Shooting From the Outside: How A Coach and Her Olympic Team Transformed Women's Basketball*. And she is the author of the book, *Little Girls in Pretty Boxes: The Making and Breaking of Elite Gymnasts and Figure Skaters*, which was made into a movie for the Lifetime television network.

Thomas J. Stillman has a B.S. in biochemistry and biomathematics, and an M.A. in Sports and Fitness Management from the University of San Francisco, where he's been an instructor of mathematics since 1982. He's been a programmer at Superior Business Services since 1981. Stillman scored baseball games for Jackson Research, Project Scoresheet, and STATS, Inc., and has been the official scorer for the Western League's Sonoma County Crushers since 1995. He's been the assistant sports information director at Dominican College, and Web master for the Recreational and Sports Facility site at the University of California, Berkeley. He currently serves as part of the "stats" crew for the San Francisco 49ers, and as the sports information director/assistant athletics director at Holy Names College in Oakland.

Randy M. Torrijos has a B.A. in politics and a certificate in Legal Studies from the University of San Francisco, where he worked as a teaching assistant and as an officer in the Pre-Law Society. He was a Davies Scholar at USF in 1998. He's been an intern at the San Francisco District Attorney's Office, has a J.D. from the University of San Francisco's Law School, and is now a practicing attorney. Torrijos is a lifelong San Francisco Giants fan and an avid follower of baseball movies.

Jules Tygiel was born in Brooklyn, New York, and for many years has been a professor of history at San Francisco State University. In 1998, he was honored with the National Endowment for the Humanities Chair at Albright College in Reading, Pennsylvania. Tygiel is an expert on American history and on American baseball. He has been the keynote speaker at numerous conferences on the national pastime and American culture, and he's the founder of the Pacific Ghost League. He's published many essays and articles on baseball and many other subjects. He's the author of *The Great Los Angeles Swindle: Oil, Stocks and Scandal During the Roaring Twenties*. He's also a highly acknowledged scholar on Jackie Robinson, and is the author of *Baseball's Great Experiment: Jackie Robinson and His Legacy*, and the editor of *The Jackie Robinson Reader: Perspectives on An American Hero*. His most recent book is *Past Time: Baseball As History*.

Laura Ward is a psychology and honors humanities student at the University of San Francisco, where she was also a Davies Scholar in 1998. She recently studied in Madrid, Spain, with St. Louis University's overseas program. She is the editorial assistant for the international journal, *Peace Review*. She has written for *Juxtapox* magazine, has been the assistant editor of *Slap*, and also edits *Baby Blue*, a small, irregular guerilla art publication. She's a lifelong Albuquerque Dukes fan, and is studying psychology with the hope of helping her father overcome the trauma he suffered when the New York Giants relocated to the West Coast.

Lois J. Youngen is an emeritus professor of physical education at the University of Oregon, where she taught from 1960 until 1996 and where she's been the director of Physical Activity and Recreation Services since 1991. At Oregon, she was also the head coach of women's track and field and women's tennis for many years. She also taught at Michigan State University, and received her Ph.D. from Ohio State University. For years in the early 1950s, Youngen played professional hardball with several teams in the All-American Girls Professional Baseball League (AAGPBL), which was popularized by the Hollywood film, *A League of Their Own*. In 1953, she caught the perfect game thrown by the AAGPBL star, Jean Faut, and in 1955, went on a national barnstorming tour with the Allington All-Stars. In 1988, she was made a part of the permanent exhibit at the Cooperstown Baseball Hall of Fame on "Women In Baseball."

Paul J. Zingg is the provost and vice president for Academic Affairs at the California Polytechnic State University in San Luis Obispo. He also served as the dean of Liberal Arts at Cal Poly, and from 1986–1993 was the dean of Liberal Arts at St. Mary's College in Moraga. He also served as assistant to the president, as an American Council on Education Fellow, and as a vice dean at the University of Pennsylvania in Philadelphia. He received his Ph.D. in history from the University of Georgia. Zingg has published several articles and books on American higher education, intercollegiate athletics, and sports history. He's just finished a book on golf, *A Good Round*, and is the author of two baseball books: *Harry Hooper: An American Baseball Life,* and *Runs, Hits & An Era: The Pacific Coast League, 1903–1958*. He was also a consultant to Ken Burns for his *Baseball* documentary series.

INDEX